Interpreting Christian History

For Alex and Sarah, again

Interpreting Christian History

The Challenge of the Churches' Past

Euan Cameron

Blackwell
Publishing

BLACKWELL PUBLISHING
350 Main Street, Malden, MA 02148-5020, USA
9600 Garsington Road, Oxford OX4 2DQ, UK
550 Swanston Street, Carlton, Victoria 3053, Australia

First published 2005 by Blackwell Publishing Ltd

1   2005

Library of Congress Cataloging-in-Publication Data

Cameron, Euan.
  Interpreting Christian history : the challenge of the churches' past / Euan Cameron.
    p. cm.
  Includes bibliographical references and index.
  ISBN-13: 978-0-631-21522-6 (hard cover : alk. paper)
  ISBN-13: 978-0-631-21523-3 (pbk. : alk. paper)
  ISBN-10: 0-631-21522-0 (hard cover : alk. paper)
  ISBN-10: 0-631-21523-9 (pbk. : alk. paper)
1. Church history. 2. History—Religious aspects—Christianity. I. Title.

  BR145.3.C36 2005
  270—dc22

                                                                2004029161

A catalogue record for this title is available from the British Library.

Set in 10.5/12.5pt Bembo
by SPI Publisher Services, Pondicherry, India
Printed and bound in India
by Replika Press Pvt Ltd, Kundli

The publisher's policy is to use permanent paper from mills that operate a sustainable forestry policy, and which has been manufactured from pulp processed using acid-free and elementary chlorine-free practices. Furthermore, the publisher ensures that the text paper and cover board used have met acceptable environmental accreditation standards.

For further information on
Blackwell Publishing, visit our website:
www.blackwellpublishing.com

Contents

Preface

This may seem an unusual book for a Church historian to have written. It is not quite Church history and not theology: rather, it is an attempt to reflect theologically upon Church history using historical approaches. It forced itself on to my attention some seven years ago and has demanded to be written ever since. Given its peculiarity, it may be useful to explain how its core ideas arose and why it felt necessary to write it.

My doctoral research focused on the Waldensian heresy, and led in due course to a controversial little book, *The Reformation of the Heretics* (Oxford University Press, 1984). Both the thesis and the book were based on extensive readings in the records of the trials of Waldensian heretics in the Alps of the Dauphiné and Savoy, between present-day France and Italy, in the late fifteenth century. According to traditional histories of heresy, the Waldenses rejected, uniformly and consistently, much of the apparatus of the late medieval Catholic Church for saving souls in this life and the next. In particular they renounced the prayers and masses for the dead so widely practiced at that time. Yet in the archival sources I read, many ordinary Waldenses seemed highly confused. Under interrogation they admitted to the standard "disbeliefs"; but they still paid for masses, said some sort of prayer for the departed, went on pilgrimages to shrines, and so forth. Some readers of my work suggested that these were merely ill-informed or duplicitous witnesses – "bad" representatives of the heresy, in effect (one critic referred to "low-grade evidence"). To me this seemed somewhat bizarre. Whose role was it to "define" what Waldensian heresy meant? Was the inquisitor who persecuted it, or the layperson who lived it, to say what Waldensianism required? If the definitions did not fit the evidence, then perhaps the definitions should be amended before the evidence was dismissed. An important point was emerging here: the identity and characteristics of a religion need not depend solely on the dictates or the constructs of the learned and powerful. When the learned and powerful are actually *hostile witnesses*, as in the case of a "heresy," they may lose the right to "speak for" ordinary people, in the way that they normally do for the majority.

My next work, *The European Reformation* (Oxford University Press, 1991) posed the issue of religious pluralism in a different form. It was vital to describe the religious climate of the sixteenth century so that *all* the various parties' views would make some sort of sense. One generation believed passionately that God had instituted a sacramental, purificatory piety through the Church for the good of the soul. Another group, inspired by Martin Luther's insights, argued that these "purifications" were illusory: they made false claims on God's response, and misunderstood what the "grace of God" really meant. The Reformation was not a conflict between an old, decayed, corrupted institution and the forces of spiritual revival, as some of the older histories had implied. In it two vibrant and sophisticated theologies clashed, then grew progressively further apart until they became quite incompatible systems, each fervently supported by sincere partisans.

Diversity did not stop there, however. Historians of the Reformation knew that for many of those who lived – and died – for the causes of Protestantism or Catholicism in the sixteenth century, the theological issues were hazy. It was not sufficient to say that the disputes were "defined" by their theological abstractions, because many people simply did not under-stand those abstractions. They understood perhaps only a few slogans, a partial picture or a second-order set of derivative conclusions. So what made a Protestant or a Catholic? Who "represented" the cause of one or the other?

It was becoming clear that the traditional picture, where Christianity was something integrated and uniform, defined by an elite theological profes-sion, guarded by a hierarchy of some kind, then disseminated and promoted by pastoral "troops on the ground" trained in a formal vocational education – an image derived essentially from Europe c.1550–c.1850 – did not describe much of Christian history at all accurately. When in 1996-7 I embarked on a study of the debate over "superstition" in the late Middle Ages and the early modern period, these doubts were reinforced to a shocking degree. Pastoral theologians wrote much in the fourteenth to seventeenth centuries about the "superstitious" beliefs of ordinary people. For many, perhaps most, medieval Christians the universe was full of spirits, sympathies, and forms of power that did not fit in with the theologians' systems: nymphs, dwarves, and other such creatures existed; formulae of unknown words or strange symbols could cure diseases; wounds could be healed by anointing, not the wound, but the weapon that caused it. Leading theologians like Jean Gerson lamented their failure, indeed their inability, to wean Europe's majority away from these modes of thought. They could not speak for all the higher clergy, let alone the laity. An educated Swiss canon lawyer in the mid-fifteenth century wrote a series of pamphlets in which he fervently defended healing spells and denounced theologians for narrow-mindedly criticizing such techniques.

Many of the studies of "Christian history" as carried out in the past have rested on a very rarefied definition of that history. Christian history was traditionally written as the history of doctrine. From the point when "doctrine" took shape, it was the preserve, not just of a social elite (the clergy) but increasingly of an intellectual interest group, the professional academics, who worked for much of Christian history at a distance from everyday experience. To some extent this narrowness of perspective was inevitable. Theologians generated the overwhelming bulk of the surviving literature and therefore of the historical evidence. However, they represented an astonishingly thin sliver of the actual Christian people of their age. Once one takes a broader view of what constitutes "Christian history" – as is now the norm for social historians of religion – the subject becomes terrifyingly more diverse. A metaphysician can align a late antique Church Father, a medieval scholastic, and a twentieth-century neo-orthodox theologian, and compare them without any sense of anachronism or incongruity. A social historian cannot imagine comparing ordinary Christians of these various periods without thinking very hard indeed about the historical and cultural differences that divide them.

So, who represents the different historic forms that Christianity has assumed? For me, it was increasingly clear that the professional rationalists, the intellectual elites, important as they were, did not constitute the whole story of what Christianity "was." Christian history, as lived and as experienced by the majority, was an enormously diverse thing. The cultural conditions – the ever-changing assumptions about life, the universe, the function of worship, the role of ritual, or the role of learning – played a huge part in defining what "the Christian life" constituted at any given moment. And therein lay a problem that was spiritual and psychological as well as intellectual. Was not my Christianity and that of my community just as conditioned by my environment and culture as those of the past? How could any modern Christian discern how far his or her religious priorities were "essentially" Christian, as distinct from (say) early twenty-first-century Western European?

As a result I began tentatively to explore the historical and theological responses to these questions that had gone before. Not surprisingly, it emerged that my first primitive reflections on this subject echoed those of nineteenth-century liberal theologians – although the process of thinking through the issues would not stop there. It also became evident that the subject was much less fashionable in the postmodern age than it had been a century earlier, and the developments in the writing of religious history as well as theology since the age of German Liberalism suggested that there was now much more to be said on the subject.

Simultaneously I explored the level of lay interest by offering, and delivering, a series of talks to my home parish of All Saints', Gosforth, in Newcastle upon Tyne, in the spring of 1997. Those talks (almost nothing of which survives in the present volume) offered a first sketch of some of the themes of what has become Chapter 2. The level of friendly interest generated by them encouraged me to prepare the idea for this book. In its final form the synopsis was entertained by Alex Wright, then at Blackwell Publishers, and entered its very long stage of pupation. In the intervening period I wrote another book and several articles, and was invited, "searched," and appointed to the Henry Luce III Chair in Reformation Church History in Union Theological Seminary, New York. Nevertheless, it should not be inferred that the decision to write this book derives from the choice to move from an arts faculty in a British secular university to a theological seminary in the USA. If anything the reverse may be partly the case, since the book was conceived before the career move.

What do I hope to achieve by the exploration of Christian history offered here? Despite the emphasis on historical diversity, I most certainly do not intend to depict Christianity as a formless and incoherent series of transient movements, sharing the name of Jesus, disputed and contentious texts, an often tormented political history, and a series of constantly reworked cultural artefacts. I do believe that there is an "essential" Christianity: though as will become clear, I also argue that this "essence" is inevitably hidden under transitory forms. In this book I have "talked up" the differences between different historic forms of Christianity to a slightly higher degree than I might believe them to merit on a perfectly balanced presentation. The reason for this is that interested nonacademic churchgoers will expect to find continuity, tradition, and permanence in the history of the Christian Church. Such stability and continuity would not surprise these readers: it would be just what they looked to find. In contrast, to find diversity, disagreement, discontinuity, loose ends, and wrong turnings may be downright alarming. There is already too much contradiction between different Christian churches. If to that is added the sudden discovery that the Christian churches had radically different priorities at various times in the past, believers may feel challenged, even shaken. How can this religion claim permanence, when so many of its defining characteristics in the past turn out to have been temporary, alien, sometimes even grotesque?

One important reason, then, for writing this book was to reassure general readers that historical awareness need not lead inevitably to the nihilism of the utter relativist, the despair of finding no certainty, nothing fixed to believe. The book suggests ways of thinking through Church history with clarity of vision and critical honesty as well as faith. A strong conviction, even just a strong and faithful curiosity, should be ready to confront the checkered history of Christianity and learn from it. (On the other hand, those who have not been so challenged or shaken need to be – there can be no real stability about a Christian faith that survives only by avoiding potentially unsettling information.)

A second practical reason is that churches are often disturbed by dissension over controversial disciplinary and ceremonial issues and (more rarely nowadays) over doctrines. In such disputes it is very common to hear one or even both parties in dispute cite the historic witness of the Church, the voice of tradition, the unanimous assent of those who have gone before, or similar phrases in their support. This sort of language often makes church historians wince. The "continuous witness" to which the disputants appeal may (in the issue under dispute) be entirely imaginary; or it may exist only in one tradition among many. Even if a belief or teaching really *is* unprecedented, it may be in good company for all that. Martin Luther was accused of contradicting exactly such "continuous witness" in advancing his Reformation theology.

The appeal to "history as authority" should always be seen as problematical. Many things have been done in the past history of the churches, from Pentecost onwards, which should certainly not be cited in support of anything. Church history, as the story of human beings and their activities, contains as many things to avoid as things to imitate. It does not matter whether some belief or practice is endorsed by the authority of a long-continuous institution, or is believed to date from a biblical or apostolic golden age: neither proves definitively that that thing is worth repeating. Members of the churches would do well to treat such partisan appeals to history with caution and even suspicion.

More positively, there are many advantages to an enriched historical perspective for the believing reader. Past "ages of faith" were not so rosy – nor so single-mindedly spiritual in their religious culture – that one should wish to abandon the more open and pluralistic present for the past, even if that were possible (it is not). Once one can cope with the many wanderings and contradictions in one's own tradition, one is all the better equipped for ecumenical dialogue. One is less prone to be naïvely confident in one's certainties, and more open to diversity.

Writing this book has led me deeper into serious issues, and led me in more directions than I ever imagined. It delves into areas of history and historiography that are almost pure research, but also contains, above all in chapter 1, some necessarily sketchy outlines to equip the interested nonspecialist reader. Inevitably, therefore, it is something of a hybrid. For nearly all the time I write as a historian, even when I am discussing theology: the format is that of a historical review or discussion rather than a theological discourse. Professional theologians will find many questions raised but not answered, or see potential arguments that I have not responded to explicitly (though it does not always follow that I am ignorant of them). It goes far beyond the ambit of this book to speculate about its implications for the main subject-matter of theology as such, and the book intends to offer no such speculations.

Theologians will also recognize some affinities — but also differences — between aspects of my approach and that of the liberal theologians of a century ago. Broadly speaking, I have adopted the historical-critical methods of the liberal theologians while discarding their optimistic anthropology and (it is hoped) other outmoded social and ethical assumptions of their age. I argue that theology, in the form that we received it, is devised by human beings and must be appraised as such, not as an unmediated revelation of the divine. I also argue that human beings suffer from a range of religious habits that have made the history of Christianity a continual struggle between fallenness and revelation.

I have incurred a range of debts of gratitude in the writing of this book. I must pay tribute to the encouragement, support, and fellowship of my then congregation at All Saints' Gosforth, for such a warm, creative, and thoughtful response to the first version of these thoughts seven years ago; and especially to Revd. Richard Hill, the Vicar, for allowing me to deliver those talks in the body of the church. Both the Revd. Richard Hill and the Rt. Revd. Alec Graham, then Bishop of Newcastle, gave welcome support at a critical time. More recently colleagues at Union Theological Seminary, especially Joseph C. Hough, John McGuckin, and Christopher Morse have offered invaluable pointers in many areas. The encouragement and astonishing patience of successive religion editors at Blackwell, most notably Alex Wright and Rebecca Harkin, deserves my thanks and my tribute. I am genuinely grateful to the variety of anonymous commentators on synopses and drafts who have believed that the book was worth writing, even as they gently chided me for my theological simplicity. The book would have been much worse without their interventions. Thanks also to my advisee at Union, Karen Byrne, and her husband Peter, two friends who spontaneously put at my disposal their home in Washington, DC with its theological library while I forged out the final version of the text. As always I am forever in debt to the patience and forbearance of my family for allowing this book to dominate two summers that could have been spent more agreeably otherwise.

E. K. C.
Capitol Hill, Washington DC
August 2004

Introduction

This book argues that knowledge of Christian history is essential to anyone
who wishes to understand the present-day Christian churches, or to assume
any position of leadership within them. Historical insight is not an optional
extra, a venture into the exotic, a distraction from more obviously urgent
present-day issues of Church polity or social ethics. The processes of
historical change and development are of the very essence of the diverse
and continuously unfolding Christian experience. Growing awareness of
such historical change has played a critical role in the rise of modern
theology, which cannot be understood without such awareness. In short,
one cannot understand faith working in society unless one sees it with the
help of a historical perspective.

Diversities of Belief, Practice, and Priorities

An outsider coming to Christianity unprepared might be astonished at the
scale and range of diversity that are now seen within even the most
mainstream Christian movements. Some of those differences, the most
obvious but also the most trivial, regard the externals of worship. These
may include the language, music, and visual adornment used; the relative
roles of worship leaders and congregation; the nature of worship (whether
predominantly eucharistic, expository, meditative, sung, or anything else);
the physical surroundings, which range from some of the oldest and largest
structures in human culture still used for their original purposes, to meetings
in small halls, private houses, or in the open air; and the quantity and type of
decoration and visual aids. When one goes beneath these superficial factors,
however, deeper and more compelling evidence of Christian diversity
appears. Christianity looks to Jesus Christ as its unique manifestation of

the divine. Yet the attempt to describe the nature and role of Jesus has led to multiple controversies and schisms, some of which still persist. Several widely accepted statements about who Jesus Christ is or was, and about his relationship to God, entail apparent contradictions or oxymoronic formulae which make a coherent and clear exposition almost impossible.

Christianity traditionally bases its faith on the Scriptures of the Old Testament (the Hebrew Bible) and the New Testament. Yet the role of the Scriptures has been and is read in radically different ways in different churches (and often within the same church). Some branches of Christianity entrust the interpretation of Scripture to a continuing hierarchical apostolic succession. Others regard it as the work of the Spirit on the individual reader. Some believe the Bible text to be divinely ordained and inerrant, while others point to the instabilities, uncertainties, and multiple versions of the texts. Some claim to follow the text literally, while others insist on the need for sensitive and discriminating interpretation in the light of its cultural context and the social conventions of the time when it was written. Some churches have included the "apocryphal" books (additional books of the Hebrew Bible preserved mostly via Greek translations) as equivalent to the other books, while others regard them as of secondary status and have resisted deriving doctrines from them. At various times some movements on the margins of Christianity have raised the direct inspiration of the individual to a level alongside or above Scripture, or have added new writings to the canon. What we know today as the "canon" of Scripture, the list of agreed books, is in any case the result of over three hundred years of writing, compilation, and selection.

Christianity often seems to suffer from a dizzying range of different preoccupations, some of which will be explored in the following chapters. Nearly all agree that it involves the worship of God: but that worship can be conceived as a sacrificial re-enactment of Christ's sacrifice on the cross, or as a proclamation of the divine promises re-enacting Christ's earthly ministry. The commonest Christian liturgical act is Holy Communion, although it goes by different titles: a sixteenth-century writer identified 16 different names given to this rite in the early Church alone. The Communion has been conceived as a congregational gathering embodying the unity of the community, or as a sacrificial ritual conferring spiritual benefits even on the dead. In some branches of the Christian tradition it is the focus of every major act of worship, while in others it performs no role whatever.

The ethical priorities of Christians diverge in many ways. Most modern churches have come to set a high value on the call of Christ to perform works of charity and mercy towards those in need (although experience suggests that political action leading to government legislation may be more socially transformative, if less morally uplifting, than individual or community-level efforts). However, even a slight acquaintance with the historical record will show that this priority has long coexisted with others. For much of the lifetime of the churches many of their members concentrated on performing the rites and keeping the rules that would ensure the eternal salvation of the individual soul. These might include acts of self-discipline or self-mortification. There has been, and continues to be, a minority of Christians whose life is dominated by membership of a disciplined ascetic community, or by mystical contemplation. Christian principles have been (and in some cases still are) invoked *for or against* warfare; liberation and revolution; democracy; equality of race, gender, and sexuality; or the emancipation of the unfree and the enslaved. Because of the way in which religious affairs are reported in modern culture, branches of Christianity can appear to be defined not by their most fundamental beliefs, but by the religio-political burning issues of the moment: in recent decades these have included family limitation and other issues in human reproduction, priestly celibacy, and the ministries of women and gay people.

There is a deeper level of difference which must also be kept in mind. Traditionally, when the question was asked, "what does the Christian faith say?" the answer was looked for in the official statements of the churches, in creeds, catechisms, decrees of councils, or pronouncements of theologians. It would have been taken for granted that Christianity was something dispensed from the top downwards. In recent historical work it has become much clearer that a religion may *function*, at local level, with a significantly different body of beliefs among its authorities and intelligentsia on one hand, and its ordinary members on the other. In the Middle Ages many of the lesser clergy and most laity (indeed nearly everyone who was not a theologian) tried to guarantee divine favor through particular supposedly foolproof rituals: such practices many "official" theologians called "superstitions" or at least "vain observances." In the modern West, ordinary congregations may often be more theologically conservative or traditional than many of their pastors. In each case different Christians in the same church actually think very differently. The same uncertainty can arise within an institutional church that operates within radically different cultures. The views held by (say) Roman Catholic clerics and religious people in parts of the Third World may differ greatly from those of their hierarchy in the Old World. Which of these is to be regarded as "representing" or embodying the Christianity of their community: the "official" or hegemonic minority, or the preponderant majority of the people?

History and Diversity

Diversity can readily be explained in the here and now in terms of geo-graphical distance, cultural difference, and differing paths to social and economic development. However, the historical perspective offers a particularly indispensable insight into all this variety. Where there is a modern disagreement over an issue of policy, the historical antecedents to the arguments advanced may shed light on *why* people think as they do. Some divisions in the Church are merely the legacy of fractures over what seemed in past ages to be absolutely key principles, but which no longer correspond to modern concerns in anything like the same way. If one perceives the distance between the present age and those in which the ruptures occurred, reconciliation may be easier to achieve. Conversely, the attitudes of past Christians on some issues, or even their total lack of interest in a question that now seems crucial, may appear so strange that present-day disagreements over "modern" issues will shrink into better proportion. An informed historical perspective turns cross-cultural aware-ness through 90 degrees. One learns to perceive one's own past as though it were an alien culture: yet it cannot be dismissed as merely "other," because it is both the source of the modern experience and yet alien from it. Historical scholarship can also guard against the abuse of textual evidence ripped out of its original context, a theological vice that has blighted the churches in the past.

However, looking at the history of the churches also poses a challenge to the observer. Even a secular outsider might wish to know, as a mere matter of analytical understanding, which of these multiple systems of belief rep-resents Christianity in its most typical and characteristic form. How is Christianity to be *defined*? For the believer, however, the question is much more pressing. How secure can the member of one fractional community in the wider Christian movement feel that he or she has absorbed the essence of what the promise of the gospel is about? How important is it to be a member of this or that continuous tradition, or indeed of any? If the divergences between different Christian traditions derive (as many of them do) from arguably obsolete theological or institutional disagreements, why assign priority to one tradition over another? Why keep so many separate traditions in existence at all?

Even a brief familiarity with the history of Christianity reveals disturbing things about the history of the Church. These things challenge us to think more deeply about the relationship between the transient and the essential in the Christian faith. Chapter 2 argues that much of Christian history consists of successive and sometimes concurrent leanings over towards one, then another, secondary priority in the life of the Church. The churches discerned particular *means* to fulfill their purposes, and then elevated those means into ends in themselves. There then ensued a furious pursuit of that secondary objective, in which all sorts of other obviously important ideals were forgotten.

Graphic instances of this phenomenon can be easily cited. Some Franciscan friars in the fourteenth century lapsed into heresy rather than accept the edict of the reigning pope that the order must own its own churches and houses, as opposed to vesting all their property in the papacy. Being utterly poor in the sense of owning *absolutely nothing* (a primary principle of Franciscan monasticism) was more important to these friars than being in communion with the Church hierarchy. In the nineteenth century a large part of the Church of Scotland went into an 86-year schism over fairly arcane issues of patronage over church posts. Here the absolute autonomy of the Church from secular interference, an ideal inherited from the Scottish Reformers, was deemed more important than unity. However, in this study it is contended that these radical manifestations of a single-issue fixation are just especially dramatic instances of a much more general trend. In every age the priorities and objectives of the Church are likely to be skewed towards one or another secondary means to lead the Christian life, this or that means to become holy in one's own eyes.

These differences in priorities mean that what appears absolutely vital to one age in the history of the Church may appear quite unimportant to another. Even worse, one age in the Church can regard some of its predecessors' most typical beliefs as repugnant to vital Christian principles. Now apply that insight to the present predicament. How can we be sure that what we perceive as "Christianity" is not yet another skewed or deviant reading, which will appear as off-center to future observers as many Christianities of the past now appear to us? Is there (either on an intellectual or a spiritual level) anything that one could call "essential" or "core" Christianity, that can be discerned apart from the multiple manifestations of the religion in so many and varied historical contexts?

Steering Between Two Extremes

There are two simple, straightforward, and – I would argue – both mistaken answers to the problem of diversity and "essence." One answer is the positivist, absolute dogmatic position, though it exists in more and in less sophisticated forms. In its simplest forms, this view argues that, in truth, only one "correct" Christianity has been handed down, and that all others are erroneous and deviant. This approach underlies all sorts of fundamentalisms as well as the conservative postures of some in the traditional churches, although it has been difficult to sustain in the West since around 1700. To an outsider it must seem absurd to accord to only one of the many Christian traditions the name of "Christianity" and deny that name to others from which it differs in important ways. The ways for a Christianity to flourish are too numerous and too diverse, for any one manifestation to be exclusively "correct." Even to most Christians it will be theologically implausible that a transcendent God should be confined and defined by the terms of human theological controversies. To see true Christianity only in oneself and not in one's neighbor sounds far more human than divine. A more sophisticated view of tradition exists in the Eastern Churches; though one might argue that here the different perspective – where the diversities of the Christian West seem so much less important – enables a sophisticated version of tradition theory to subsist more easily.

The other extreme answer is that of unrestrained relativism. It claims that no manifestation of Christianity enjoys any logical or theological priority over any other, the smallest sect as much as the longest-lived or widely dispersed world church. Since Christianities are so different, they are all equally right and equally wrong. (The same argument can of course be made of all *religions* in general.) Historical theologians have been aware of the problem of relativism at some level since at least the later nineteenth century. Postmodern thought has given further impetus to the relativistic approach (though paradoxically, it has also given birth to some highly ingenious theological approaches that justify dogmatic orthodoxy in much more subtle ways than those summarized above). To the radical relativist, anything that happens to be called or calls itself Christian is as entitled to the name as anything else. This extreme relativist position would more usually be taken by those quite uncommitted to any version of religious belief. Applied to Christianity, it certainly cannot be acceptable to the believer or theologian, and is arguably inadequate in intellectual terms as well.

A particular point of view will be proposed here, that excludes both the most simplistically dogmatic and nihilist-relativist approaches. This view is that all historically visible Christianities are partial manifestations of an essence that is never seen in an unmixed form, and can never be seen in its wholeness and entirety on earth. The "God's eye" view of the eternal Christian Church is just that. Every manifestation of Christianity is partial because it is always a composite. The churches never escape their social context and the values of their host society. So the Christian message and the Christian life always combine elements drawn from the ethos and assumptions of the age (which of course Christianity may, in turn, help to shape). In Medieval Europe Christians assumed that patron–client relations between saints and their devotees were part of the natural order on earth and heaven. Today we tend to refer to that system of patronage as favoritism (if not corruption) and would have difficulty imagining such a system in eternity. Secondly, the Church at any given moment suffers from human limitations, jealousies, partisan spirit, self-referential spiritual pride, and a host of other religious bad habits. At best, human limitations and sublime messages interact and develop across the centuries as human culture develops and interacts with itself.

Although the time-bound quality of human religious experience is a problem and a challenge, it is also an inescapable and constant fact of life. Human religion is a vitally important constituent part of human culture as well as (it is thought) a glimpse of the beyond. Theological statements that claim a "timeless" quality for this or that specific encapsulation of Christianity (say one of the sixteenth- or seventeenth-century confessions of faith) overlook the inescapably transient quality of human language and culture. Even if a church remains collectively committed to its traditional documents or passionately devoted to its old liturgies, sooner or later historical changes of perspective will make those inherited texts or rituals mean something significantly different from what they meant in the past. The tunic and cloak of late antiquity become the sacramental vestments of alb and chasuble. A truly timeless definition of Christianity, shorn of all improper additions or errors, and capable of being expressed in the same language and symbols forever, cannot be devised as long as human culture constantly devises new world-views, new philosophies, new languages and idioms. No creed, no institution, no interpretation of a text will be so perfect that it will not need to be rethought over and over again.

The Compass and Structure of the Book

This book divides into four quite distinct main chapters. The first attempts to set out a basic narrative sketch or outline of those aspects of general Christian history that are most relevant to the rest of the book. This is offered in the expectation that not all readers of this book will be familiar with the entire spread of the two Christian millennia. A discussion as brief as this must of course be selective to the highest imaginable degree. No attempt is made to do proper justice to the Eastern churches or to modern Christianity outside Europe and North America. The sketch is intended to demonstrate the principal interactions between the main themes of evolving European and North American culture and Christian thought, practice, and polity. This chapter is not supplied with fully detailed references.

Neither in the narrative nor in the interpretative sections will this book focus on the debates over the search for the "historical Jesus." The controversies generated from that search likewise fall outside the book's compass. So much has been written on the "Jesus of history," and so complex are the issues raised, that it would not be feasible to discuss this topic here. This book is essentially concerned with the post-Pentecost experience of the Christian churches: that is, of the human beings who have tried to interpret the *meaning and message* of Jesus Christ within the cultural and traditional terms that they inherited from their predecessors. In one sense, of course, Jesus is by definition never absent from any discussion of Christian history. However, the focus on the *person and image* of Jesus has generated a distinct subset of Christian thought and literature, and falls outside the themes discussed here. For those who wish to see how the Christian churches' images of Jesus have changed and evolved over time, one can recommend Jaroslav Pelikan's enormously stimulating *Jesus Through the Centuries*, though Professor Pelikan's view of doctrine is more traditionalist than the one proposed here.[1]

The second chapter contains the core of the book's observations about the collective behavior of the churches down the centuries. It argues that both the interaction between Church and environment, and the churches' inner dialectic, contributed to a series of oscillations between one stretched or extreme manifestation of a particular style of religious behavior and another. These extremes do not eliminate the possibility of continuity between one age of Christianity and another, but they form an inseparable attribute of the Church in their particular period. It makes no sense to imagine an early Church without asceticism or the miraculous, or an early modern Church without the project of mass catechetical instruction.

The wanderings and changes visible in the history of the Church raise the question of how far Christian scholars perceived these processes at the time. That is addressed in Chapter 3, which discusses attitudes to change in the Church in a selected range of Christian historians up to the modern era. The overall thesis here is that through the Middle Ages one sees a gradually greater readiness to admit that people, even within the Church hierarchy, might err; but that the common teaching of the Church was believed to be perfect and timeless. Then, in the Reformation, the unanimity of medieval Europe disintegrated. Various leading reformers conceived of a dynamic relationship between doctrine and error in the Church. Their conception of that relationship was, in many respects, highly historical. However, dogmatic certainty overwhelmed the historical perspective for much of

the seventeenth century. By the nineteenth century, the growing specialization and secularization of the profession of Church history left historians
less and less interested in the theological implications of their work.

In the fourth chapter the book turns to explore some theological analyses
of the issue of the churches and their history. Nearly every major trend in
theological scholarship in the reformed traditions in the past 150 years has
responded, in some way or other, to the challenge of the historical perspective. However, responses have been varied and inconsistent. Here again the
selection makes no claims to be comprehensive. Protestant theologians
figure much more than those from the Roman Catholic tradition: in the
latter, responses to the problem were more complex and ambivalent, not
least because of the hierarchy's reaction against "modernism." The summary
discussions offered here suggest how central this book's theme has been to
theological concerns in the past century or so. There is no intention to offer
a definitive judgment on the different theological perspectives described;
nor do I argue that all these views are worthy of the attention of theological
thinkers at the present day. The review of theologians in Chapter 4 is as
much a historical exercise as the review of historians in Chapter 3.

History and Theory

Many theologians, and most historians, are aware that the historical perspective has suffered a range of critiques from critical theorists in recent
years. While the vogue for radical postmodern assaults on history has
probably passed its peak, the debate has left some interesting and in many
ways helpful lessons for this book. Critical theorists' axioms regarding
history include the claims that no historical representation denotes "reality"
in a complete or absolute sense, and that historical perspectives often reflect
the political location and power-play of the writer. To these one must
add the postulate that writer and reader(s) are never thinking exactly the
same thing when they have the same text in front of them. Taken too
seriously, these theories can have a paralyzing effect on historical writing.
Taken with a grain of salt, however, they can also help in elucidating the
ideas of this book. Historians who take critical theory seriously have agreed
that no single historical perspective is satisfactory or all-sufficient: indeed
historians knew this long before critical theorists pointed it out. Nevertheless, they argue that by triangulating from several different perspectives, by
exploring a multiplicity of diverse and even conflicting accounts of the same
historical process found in different sources, one can still infer something
useful about the past. This book will suggest something similar for the

analysis of the history of Christianity. Christian history cannot be adequately perceived if it is studied through the eyes of only one period, one movement, or (I might argue) one class or category of Christian believers. This "triangulation" based on different perspectives is a crucial technique for anyone who does not accept that only a single one-dimensional view of Christianity is the correct one.

This book is offered in the conviction that only a discriminating and highly sensitive approach to the Christian experience, well-grounded in an appreciation of the diversity of the past, can equip Christians, including Christian scholars, to face the future with integrity and honesty. Historical change is not an option, a political or theological choice for the churches and for individual Christians. It is their inescapable predicament.

Chapter 1

The Unfolding of Christian History: a Sketch

Christianity today demonstrates a bewildering range of diversity. Most of this present-day diversity results from historical processes of change, development, disagreement, and diversification. Yet the present state of affairs, confusing as it is, does not exhaust the diversity of the Christian experience. The Christian Church has taken on many other forms (especially in the preindustrial West) that no longer exist. History starts to explain the present level of diversity; but it also introduces us to new levels of difference and variety that the modern observer barely sees.

A brief thumbnail survey and exploration of the history of the Christian Church up to the present is here offered, in the expectation that most nonspecialist readers may not have a clear idea of the overall history of the Church over the past 20 centuries. It is (obviously) the very opposite of comprehensive. It is open to challenge on nearly every point. This brief and very selective sketch serves only two specific functions. It aims to give a framework for the phenomena of diversity described in the Introduction, and to explain how some of them arose. It also opens up the field for the remainder of this discussion, since analysis of the theological implications of the diversity of Church history cannot proceed without some skeleton of the most basic data.

Christianity: a Jewish Heresy Spreads Across the Eastern Empire

The movement of the followers of Jesus, as described in the Epistles and the Acts of the Apostles, began as a dissenting tendency within the Jewish communities of the Eastern Mediterranean. As Paul put it, "according to the Way which they call a sect [Greek *hairesis*, root of our word "heresy"] I worship the God of our ancestors."[1] Rapidly, but not without controversy, it spread to attract interest among non-Jewish sympathizers with Judaism, and then among entirely non-Jewish "Hellenized" peoples (that is, those who embraced the Greek culture of the dominant educated classes) in the region. One of the first and clearest symbols of this spread is the language of the New Testament itself. It was mostly written in the second half of the first century CE in a form of classical Greek, in which sentence structures were simplified and complex constructions reduced. In this way those from diverse linguistic backgrounds could easily understand "common" Greek as a second language.

The New Testament texts describe a movement still coming to terms with issues of its basic organization and discipline. For the first few decades after Pentecost many people in the proto-Christian communities probably lived in the expectation of a return of Christ in glory and the end of history within a generation or so.[2] Christians took seriously the need to create "churches," to collect their correspondence, and to write down their stories, traditions, and procedures as it gradually became clear that the apocalypse was not, after all, going to occur any day soon. Neither at this early stage, nor for long after, was there a defined body of Christian texts called "the New Testament." There was a range of writings, prepared in different places and written from different perspectives, some surviving in fragmentary or edited forms. These were progressively added to as time went by, creating what are now called the New Testament "apocrypha." Only later would those texts be definitively filtered out of the list of "authentic" Scriptures, and the survivors recognized as a more or less agreed "canon" of early Christian writings. While the majority view is now that the "apocryphal" New Testament texts are indeed nearly all later in date than the received Scriptures, scholars continue to use some of them as collusive evidence for the climate of debate and discussion in the first two or three centuries CE.

Early Christianity was not, however, allowed to develop merely in terms of its own inner revelations and instincts. As soon as it came into contact with people who did not share the background of the first followers of Jesus, it had to negotiate its own identity with intellectuals from a wide variety of backgrounds and traditions. The Eastern Empire was awash with philosophies, cults, mysteries for initiates, and many other ways of responding to the elemental puzzles of the human predicament. The message preached by the first followers of Jesus and their successors interacted with these beliefs. Those beliefs almost immediately modified the message. One of the earliest examples of this process is seen in the complex interaction between the message of Jesus and the "Logos" doctrine of the eternal principle as "Word" seen in John 1.

However, movements of so-called "Gnosis" had possibly the greatest and (with hindsight) the most distorting impact on the reception of the early

Christian message. So-called "Gnostics" claimed that a secret knowledge, available uniquely to followers of a particular brotherhood, could enable adepts to rise to a higher spiritual plane and attain a form of release from the material world. It remains slightly controversial whether these movements anticipated Christianity and then interacted with it, or developed from Christianity in the second century CE through a process of diversification, though modern opinions favor the former. One interesting case in point here is the "Gospel of Thomas." This is generally agreed to be an early writing, which presents Jesus's teachings as a sequence of sayings rather than a story. In a somewhat shadowy way, it appears to reflect the notion that these sayings are "secret truth" to be revealed to initiates.[3] Whatever the truth of the origins of Gnosticism, what we now think of as "orthodox" New Testament Christianity was, almost from birth, struggling to preserve its identity amidst an array of rival movements that also claimed to embody the "true" Christian message. The greater the intellectual sophistication with which Christianity was embraced, the more likely it was to generate free thought and divergence.

According to a tradition in some Western Christian thought, the first centuries are sometimes depicted as a progressive fall from the grace of simplicity. Was it still appropriate to conserve and express the teachings and traditions of a traveling rabbi from Judea, who was also identified as the visible incarnation of God, in the simplest possible forms of language? Or should one try to understand and express the meaning of those beliefs with the aid of all the intellectual and cultural equipment available in its host culture? Many of the early Christian writers of the post-Apostolic age chose to add greater philosophical and literary sophistication. The result was the introduction into Christian writing of language and concepts that were not familiar to the first disciples. That development need not of itself have meant corruption. Intellectual analysis is not always destructive, distorting, or unfaithful to the material that it analyzes. Moreover, Christianity did not borrow uncritically from its classical exemplars: neoplatonic Christianity was very different from and hostile to pagan neoplatonism, for example. It did mean, however, that the emerging Christian traditions progressively took on more and more of the cultural garb peculiar to the cultural, linguistic, and educational worlds of the late antique Roman Empire.

Greek and Latin, East and West

One of the most momentous distinctions between the different Christian traditions has its roots in the structure of the Roman Empire itself. In this great sprawling system there were, broadly speaking, two main language areas. In the Western Empire, including much of North Africa as well as modern-day Western Europe south and west of the Rhine and the Danube, Latin was used as the language of administration and communication. In the Eastern Mediterranean, from the Balkans eastwards, the most widely used common language was Greek. It was natural for the leaders and writers of the early Christian churches to use the language of their part of the Empire. As a consequence, distinct Greek and Latin traditions of Christian literature grew up over the first four centuries CE. Greek had been the first, and long remained the dominant language of Christian literature; but from the North-African writer Tertullian (c. 160–225) onwards a parallel Latin tradition grew up alongside it.

One should not, of course, assume that the two traditions were distinct, let alone antithetical from the start, though they became both of these things in the course of centuries. Ultimately the churches would divide into two distinct traditions over issues of theology and (somewhat later) issues of jurisdictional supremacy. However, some differences appeared early on, rooted in the diverse geography of the Mediterranean world. First of all, Greek did not retain the status of sole official language of the Eastern Church in the way that Latin did in the West. The Semitic languages, especially Syriac, served as important vehicles for religious thought and literature from the first. Syriac Bibles, theology, and poetry all survive, as well as Syriac translations of Greek Fathers.

As it spread into northeastern Africa and the Middle East, Eastern Christianity generated literatures in the other local languages. In the patriarchate of Alexandria in Egypt, alongside Greek there grew up a parallel literature in Coptic, an ancient Egyptian language heavily laden with Greek words and written in an alphabet similar to the Greek. The Coptic Church contributed to the formation of churches in the Sudan and in Ethiopia. The Ethiopian Church, established in the fourth-sixth centuries though tracing its origins to the encounter between Philip and the Ethiopian eunuch in Acts 8: 26–39, generated its own literature of translations and elaborations in Ethiopic or Ge'ez. Far to the east of Palestine, the Church in Armenia was one of the earliest to become a national state church in the early fourth century. The Armenians developed their own alphabet, language, and liturgy, and entertained complex and tortuous relations with the Greek and later with the Roman Churches.

The churches of the East, in short, were born in diversity and grew in contest and conflict, especially (as we shall shortly see) over issues of doctrine. A particularly potent surviving emblem of these rivalries is the Church of the Holy Sepulchre in Jerusalem. Ironically, the present building originates with the Latin Crusader kingdom in the twelfth century, though heavily restored in the nineteenth century. Different parts of the building are under the control of Greek Orthodox, Roman Catholic, and Armenian Orthodox groups of clergy. Representatives of the Ethiopian, Coptic, and Syrian churches are also established in the building. Following the fall of the Crusaders' rule in Jerusalem to Saladin in 1187–8, in 1246 Sultan Ajub (supposedly despairing of achieving agreement between the quarreling Christian sects seeking a presence at the site) assigned stewardship of the keys to two Muslim families, whose descendants still act as doorkeepers of the main door.[4]

In early centuries the Western churches were not nearly so uniform nor so obedient to their one patriarchate, that of Rome, as some later historians were to claim. Nevertheless, the Latin language gained a degree of ascendancy in the West more absolute and unrivaled than the ascendancy of Greek. In the East, Greek had to compete with other language groups with different scripts. The Christian communities of different language groups tended to form distinct "orthodox" churches. In the West the Latin language spread over nearly all of Imperial Roman Europe and gradually dissolved into a range of local dialects. By infinitesimal stages these became separate "Romance" languages in their own right. Some, mostly for political reasons, became major national languages (French, Spanish, Tuscan Italian) while others remained as minority languages (e.g., Catalan, Provençal, and some regional Italian dialects). While this diversification was taking place, rulers such as Charlemagne (in his *General Admonition* of 789) established the principle that only "good," that is, quasi-classical, not "low" Latin should be used in worship.[5] Around the same time, missionaries were evangelizing the pagan Germanic peoples who lived outside the frontiers of the old Empire. Their language was much more remote from Latin than the Romance vernaculars: so right from the start the language of Christianity was entirely incomprehensible to untrained laypeople. Latin thus enjoyed a cultural and spiritual ascendancy over the vernacular languages of Europe that Greek did not enjoy in the East. Pure Christian learning, in the West, had to be expressed in the scholarly and priestly language of Latin.

This centralization of Christian culture on the Latin language tended to homogenize the culture of the learned, and to centralize and unify the priestly classes in the Church. This unity facilitated the later attempts to centralize the Western Church around the Roman papacy. Secondly, as the literary language of educated Christians diverged from the language of the people, gulfs opened up between the clergy class and the rest of the population. Ordinary people could no longer understand the language of liturgy and doctrine, even if they had been able to do so in the past.

Persecution, Legal Establishment, Empowerment, and Retreat

Early church historians (such as Eusebius of Caesarea, of whom more later) wrote the history of the early Church around two types of event. First, there were the challenges of "heresies" (meaning those versions of Christianity that historians disapproved of, or that failed to gain ultimate acceptance as the shared belief). Secondly, there were the persecutions of Christians by pagans. In each case the rhetorical image in the story was similar: true Christians were assailed and persecuted by adversaries, suffered for their defense of the truth, but ultimately prevailed. This view of Church history reflected a biblical typology: the history of the Church reflected the history of the people of God in Scripture.

It is, however, now generally agreed that there was no organized, general, centrally directed persecution of Christians in the Roman Empire before the edict of Emperor Decius in 249 (which remained in effect only until 251). However, there seems to have been a widespread popular suspicion of Christians, as a class of people who challenged the ancient pieties and refused to take part in traditional religious rituals for the common civic welfare. They did not even confine themselves within the behavioral rules laid down for the Jewish people, whose resistance to paganism was largely tolerated by Rome. If natural disasters threatened the community, or if reports of cannibalistic or promiscuous practices inflamed popular feeling, Christians could be threatened by mob violence and executed by provincial officials to keep the peace. None of this appears to have been laid down in legal texts: the mere fact of "being a Christian" and refusing to recant could justify a capital sentence.[6] In the second half of the third century CE the attitude of the governing elite in the Empire changed, just as (it seems) popular hostility to Christians was abating from its earlier levels. In 250-1 and 257–60 Christians were subjected to harsh edicts emanating from the emperors themselves, though neither of the ensuing bouts of persecution lasted very long. The only prolonged and very widespread "great persecution" of Christians was that initiated by Diocletian (puzzlingly, long into his reign) in 303. It lasted until 305 in the West but continued until 311 in the East (with some sporadic episodes thereafter).

Relatively suddenly, the fourth century CE saw the legal status of the Christian churches change from persecuted minority to an official, and potentially persecuting, elite. The Emperor Constantine (306–37), in the Edict of Milan in 313, offered freedom, toleration, and encouragement to Christians. Later in the same century Theodosius I (379–95) initiated a policy whereby Christianity gradually assumed a commanding position. The social changes this development imposed on the churches must have been considerable. If persecution had been erratic and occasional for most of the first three centuries, the *idea* of being the persecuted spiritual minority had played a major part in Christian self-perceptions and writings. With threats from a pagan state and a pagan majority culture now removed, the challenge was to address threats as it were from within, especially from dissenting factions within Christianity itself.

One alarming aspect of this transformation was the rise of violent dissent and division over theological issues between c. 325 and c. 450. Disagreements over belief were as old as Christianity itself. However, with the rise of a public, official, legally sanctioned structure of "churches," issues of doctrine could now become issues of allegiance and political power to an unprecedented degree. Believers in this or that contested doctrine could form separate obediences, even separate churches. In other words, it now mattered much more who was right. The precise questions under dispute were chiefly, though by no means exclusively, the precise and correct description of God as Trinity, and the precise and correct description of Christ as God and Man. At the heart of the fourth-century controversy between Arius and Athansius was Arius's denial that the Son was coeternal and consubstantial in the Trinity with God the Father. The Nicene Creed of 325 and the Constantinopolitan Creed of 381 insisted on the Son's coeternity. The Creed in use in the Western churches today (which is not exactly the creed of either Nicea or Constantinople, but a later recension of both) is therefore a relic of this controversy.

The manner in which Christ partook of the divine substance, and the way in which the divine and human coexisted in his nature, was fecund with bitter controversies. In 431 the Council of Ephesus debated this issue in the light of the statements of Nestorius, Patriarch of Constantinople. Nestorius argued for a sophisticated description of the distinctions between the divine and human natures in Christ; therefore he challenged the formula by which his opponents referred to the Virgin Mary as *theotokos* "bearer (or mother) of God." Following further controversial statements by Eutyches, the Council of Chalcedon in 451 "settled" the issue, at least in the eyes of the West, by a complex and somewhat paradoxical formula. However, not all the Eastern churches accepted this formulation. At various times and in various parts of the Empire disputes flared up over (for instance) the proper response to Christians who had lapsed under persecution. Manichaeanism, a late third-century development of dualist themes named after Mani

(c. 216–76), a Persian exponent of Gnostic Christianity, virtually became a new religion. It emphasized a radical disjunction between an evil world of matter and a good world of spirit, and attracted many adherents, especially in North Africa. At around the same time the canon of the "New Testament" crystallized, and became more or less settled as the collection of books that we know today.

It is important, from a modern perspective, not to indulge in facile moralizing over the changes brought about by the rise of an established public hierarchy. It is not always the case that persecuted minority status is "good" for the church and that established, civil status is necessarily "bad." In the late fourth century, bishops like Ambrose in Milan and Augustine in North Africa clearly felt an overwhelming duty to protect their people. Protection from error, error that could endanger the soul, was now more urgent than protection from violence and persecution. Indeed, threats to the soul were and had always been more serious than threats to bodily existence. The need to defend against such dangers, however, allowed St Augustine to indulge in the (to modern eyes) dangerous sophistry of arguing that when the official church persecuted heretics for the good of their souls, it was doing so out of love.[7]

It is interesting that the emergence of Christianity as a public religion was accompanied by a growing contrary shift away from the public sphere. The fourth century saw a significant increase in organized movements of ascetic withdrawal from the world, and the growth of what would become known as monasticism. The term *monachos*, source of the Latin and English words meaning "monk," refers to someone who lives as a solitary, away from society, in the wilderness or *erémos* (source of the word "hermit"). The first "Desert Fathers" who developed the characteristic form of the ascetic life were truly hermits in the desert. However, as time went on, the need for discipline, for organized communities, for rules of behavior, ensured that monasticism developed principally as a community activity, as a *coenobium* or "common life." Indeed, the complete submission of one's individuality and one's property to the community rapidly became one of the defining features of the ascetic life.

It would of course be facile to suggest that the only reason for the development of ascetic lifestyles was a reaction against the rise of a potentially rich, privileged hierarchy. There were many reasons behind the trend, some of which reached back to the Gospel stories of Christ's temptations in the desert. Ascetic attitudes will be discussed more fully later. For the time being it is interesting that ascetics often described their lifestyle in terms of conflict: conflict with demons, conflict with temptations, conflict with human fleshliness. Spiritual purity was something to be defended with spiritual weapons, whether one was a bishop or a hermit.

The Eastern Church, the Spread of Islam, and Expansion Northwards

Most of the examples used for this discussion will, after the fall of the Western Roman Empire, be drawn from the Western Church. That selection is chiefly determined by my own personal specialization. However, there are deeper reasons why the history of the "Orthodox" churches of the East becomes somewhat inaccessible to most Western scholars after the first half of the first millennium. Just as Christianity was establishing itself as the dominant faith and cultural system in the West, it began to lose that status in the East. After the death of Muhammad (570–632 CE) the armies of Islam embarked on a process of expansion, which wholly overshadowed the much more gradual spread of Christianity. Within less than a century Muslim Arab power expanded into Syria, Egypt, Persia, and North Africa. At the same time Arabs overwhelmed the Visigothic kingdom in the Iberian peninsula. In the eighth century, their expansion northwards into what is now France was only arrested at the battle of Poitiers in 732. "East Rome," the surviving part of the Empire around Constantinople, shrank to most of Asia Minor, the Greek peninsula, parts of Italy, and the southern Balkans. Between the eighth and the early sixteenth centuries it gradually shrank further under the pressure of Muslims from the East and hostile inroads by Latin Christians from the West. After the battle of Mohacs in 1526, the frontiers of Muslim imperial power more or less reached the southeastern boundaries of Latin, Western Christendom. Vienna remained a frontier town in a precarious position, several times besieged from the east, until the eighteenth century.

Over the centuries a series of hegemonic monarchies would be established in the Muslim world, under Caliphs in Damascus and later Baghdad, and most durably under the Empire of the Ottomans, based in Istanbul after that city, formerly Constantinople and Byzantium, was conquered in the last great phase of expansion in the middle fifteenth century CE. Most, though not quite all, of the churches of the East were one by one subsumed within this wave of expansion. Some of the remainder, to the south and east, were cut off from the rest. They were not obliterated; indeed, churches were tolerated under Islam on payment of a regular tax known as the *jizya*. Islam's record in tolerating the presence of nonbelievers within its spheres of control was often more creditable than that of Christianity. It showed a measure of respect to Jews and Christians because they possessed a body of sacred scripture and a prophetic tradition: they were "people of the book" and in this respect like Muslims. Key passages in the Qur'an pour scorn on the idea that God could have had a son; but that renders Christians foolish rather than abominable.[8] Like medieval Christianity, however, Islam could be ferocious towards those who embraced it and then deserted it for another faith.

After the rise of Islam the Eastern Orthodox Churches did not usually enjoy the political power, or the automatic alliance with such power, which they gained in the West. As a result their traditions of church government were confirmed in their traditionally more collegial attitudes. Obedience became more a matter of voluntary respect than of enforced submission. These circumstances also allowed unrestrained and continuous bitter theological debate between the various factions left over from the theological controversies of the fourth and fifth centuries. In late medieval Greece, for example, possession of episcopal sees could become a battleground, with rival candidates deposing each other and being deposed in their turn. In comparison with the Roman papacy in the West, the synodal structures of the East diffused authority more widely. From the ninth century onwards Orthodox Christianity expanded northwards into the Balkans and towards Russia. Initially these were missionary churches of Constantinople. However, over time they acquired independent characteristics, a distinct liturgical language now known as Old Church Slavonic, and a separate set of national hierarchies.

The Western Church of Late Antiquity and the Early Middle Ages

By about 400 one is justified, probably for the first time, in regarding the Western, Latin Church as having attained a level of intellectual and spiritual distinction to compare with the Greek Church. It owed this status above all to three very different theologians and writers: Ambrose, Bishop of Milan (c. 339–97); Jerome (c. 345–420) monk, biblical scholar, and translator of the Bible; and Augustine of Hippo (354–430), bishop, controversialist, theologian, and spiritual writer. These writers formed a constellation of authorities whose reputation would dominate much of the later history of the Church. All believed in a prestigious Church that could demand the support and the obedience of the politically powerful. All were convinced of the truth of "Catholic" Christianity and the utter wrongness of heresies. All were ascetics, who taught that Christian virtue required the subjugation of human physical nature. Within those broad limits their careers and their priorities were quite different. Ambrose was more of a practical churchman, while Augustine and Jerome were more scholarly. Ambrose and Augustine largely confined their activities to the West, while Jerome traveled in the East and founded a monastery at Bethlehem.

All three of these "Catholic Fathers" were products of the declining decades of the Roman Empire in the West. During their lifetimes the hold of the Roman imperial system on Western Europe was gradually slackening. The traditional image of the Roman Empire assailed by and finally falling to hordes of Gothic invaders has long since been shown to be seriously misleading. It was rather that the imperial system gradually crumbled into obsolescence. It relied more and more on Gothic warlords to sustain it on its frontiers. It welcomed them into peripheral and then more central regions of the Empire, and exchanged cultures with them. Ironically, some of the "barbarians" who arrived in Western Europe were Visigoths, Vandals, and Ostrogoths from the lands around the Danube whose forbears had already been converted to "Arian" Christianity (regarded as heretical by Catholics) in the mid-fourth century. Despite this, Catholic Rome perceived the siege and sack of the city by the Visigoth king Alaric in 410 as an unparalled disaster. Some who had only reluctantly embraced Christianity in the previous century blamed the city's sack on the desertion of the pagan gods. To answer these Augustine wrote his colossal work, *The City of God Against the Pagans*, a monumental defense of Catholic Christianity against all comers.[9]

In the course of the fifth century the institutions of the Western Roman Empire gradually unraveled. Roman people and Roman-style communities remained, but they had to subsist alongside a militarily powerful minority of Gothic arrivals who assimilated themselves gradually and selectively into the surrounding environment. In this climate certain types of center preserved the "Romanness" of imperial, Christian culture more successfully than others. Probably the most important were those cities that had become the centers of a Christian bishop. Bishops in the fifth and sixth centuries became the embodiment of civic pride, community identity, and political cohesion. They might address barbarian warlords on behalf of their communities, or use their churches' wealth to ransom captives. That did not preclude their showing holiness or asceticism, as the case of the celebrated and saintly Martin, Bishop of Tours in the fourth century, had proved. It added greatly to their public visibility and importance.

The other centers for the conservation and protection of Catholic Christian culture were the monasteries. Soon after monasticism had developed in the West, it acquired a role as a locus for education and learning. Not all monastic leaders approved of undue concentration on literature, especially the surviving secular literature of ancient paganism: Pope Gregory I (pope 590–604) was particularly wary. However, under the influence of Cassiodorus (490–583) and others, monasteries conserved ancient culture like no other institutions between the demise of the Empire and the multiple "Renaissances" of the Middle Ages. Their libraries, far more than any material mythically rescued from Byzantium before the Turkish advance, would ultimately feed the classicizing Renaissance of the fifteenth century in Europe.

The early Middle Ages was also an era of conversion. Conversion meant different things to different missionaries and their varied audiences. Where Christianity had not been obliterated by the barbarian arrivals, it was a question of exporting Christian belief from its centers in cities and monasteries out to the countryside, which had never been fully Christianized. In such places the missionary priest strove to persuade country people to abandon their animist beliefs in the forces of nature, and to use the mechanisms of the Christian Church for their protection and benefit. Caesarius (Bishop of Arles 504–42) wrote definitive and much-copied descriptions of the popular beliefs, supposedly derived from paganism, which Christian teaching had to eradicate.[10] However, there were other kinds of European peoples whom missionaries sought to convert in the early Middle Ages. In the east and center of much of Britain, Germanic invaders displaced the Romano-British Christian elites (and possibly other peoples too, though the subject is controversial) in the course of the fifth and sixth centuries. To the north and east of the Rhine and Danube, the Germanic lands had never been either Roman or Christian. From the end of the sixth century onwards the Anglo-Saxon peoples were evangelized by Irish Christians from the west (themselves a fairly recent development) and by Roman Christians from the south. From about 700 onwards representatives of these forms of British Christianity began the huge task of converting the peoples of central and northern Germany. With the arrivals of successive waves of Viking invaders from the north, new conversions were required across northern Europe in the ninth and tenth centuries.

What did this process of cultural conservation and promotion do to the Christian Church in the West? As everywhere, generalizations are dangerous. However, the encounter with the folk-religions of the Germanic invaders and the new challenges to the Christian way of thinking could not fail to have a particular impact on Christian thought. Spiritual authority was demonstrated, among other things, by spectacular displays of supernatural power. Saints, and their relics, worked miracles. Heroic performances of ascetic holiness would be rewarded and authenticated by astonishing displays of quasi-magical power in life or after death. These were not entirely new phenomena: but they achieved a degree of prominence they had not had for several centuries.

Early medieval Christianity did not become in some crude sense "barbarianized" or surrender to barbarian modes of thought. It remained as imbued with Latin culture and its theological heritage as before. An Anglo-Saxon monk like Bede (d. 735) could acquire in northeast England a level of literary and theological learning to compare with nearly any of his predecessors. After Bede, the court of the Frankish king Charlemagne (768–814) nurtured one of the first great revivals of classical culture that punctuated medieval Europe. But alongside that level of culture, there subsisted a powerful sense that Christianity was a form of spiritual power, an impressive "countermagic" to the dark forces of paganism and demonic spirits. To win over country people whose need for magical and supernatural reassurance was basic to their lives, the Church presented itself, and was perceived as, purveying a better, more powerful class of magic than its rivals.

Disputes over Control, and the Rise of a Continental Church

Missionaries intent on converting barbarian warlords had used many strategies, but one of the most effective was the appeal to the powerful. If the king were convinced, his servants would follow. As the early medieval kingdoms matured and developed, it was therefore natural for close patron–client relations to become established between devout secular rulers and their bishops and clergy. A king like Charlemagne saw himself as not only a patron of learning, but also as a patron of good religious practice. Unfortunately, patronage is an ambiguous tool. Seen from a different perspective it can look like manipulation or even exploitation. From the year 1000 onwards one key issue dominated many of the most important events in the life of the Catholic Church in the West: the effort to secure more self-government, autonomy, and legal immunity for the clergy.

This issue demonstrates better than most the way in which spiritual and political issues had become intermingled. For devout Catholics the independence and immunity of the priesthood was a moral issue: to allow the Church to remain "in the power of laymen"[11] was a sin. For political observers, especially in Germany where the worst conflict occurred, it seemed that Italian clerics were interfering in issues of domestic political relationships. On the surface, the issues in dispute included the obligation on priests to be unmarried and celibate, the alleged illegality of paying money for appointment to church posts, and the practice whereby lay rulers ceremonially "invested" a new bishop with the ring and staff of office. Underneath, something more fundamental was at work. Zealous "reformers" in Rome and elsewhere saw it as a necessary part of their program to bring the clergy of the peoples of Europe under more direct and continuous obedience to the Roman papacy than had ever been the case in the past.

The dispute raged particularly severely, and involved most acute conflicts of loyalty, within Germany. This was because of the complex constitutional structure of what had become known as the "Holy Roman Empire." This vast and nearly ungovernable territory included all of Italy save the Byzantine lands in the south, a wide swathe of land stretching (according to present-day political boundaries) from southeast France across to Slovenia, and including much of central and western Germany, Switzerland, Austria, and the Czech Republic. The elective emperors of this territory were German; but the Catholic Church, and the Roman papacy, enjoyed a special status here. Prince-bishops ruled much land personally, as princes of the Empire. The status of leading clergy as spiritual leaders had become hopelessly entangled with their status as prominent subjects of the Emperor. This is not a blow-by-blow narrative, and not the place to review the "Investiture Contest" in detail. In the late eleventh century the confrontation between Pope Gregory VII (pope 1073–85) and King (later Emperor) Henry IV of Germany (1050–1106) turned first acrimonious and then violent. Ultimately a compromise was worked out, whereby the spiritual superiority of the papacy over the clergy was recognized, but their political duty to their secular rulers as princes was also accommodated. This compromise remained in force not just in Germany, but everywhere in Europe that bishops held landed estates, until the end of the Middle Ages and beyond. How well it worked depended, as a rule, on the personalities of individual popes and individual monarchs. An overbearing king or an ambitious pope could easily overbalance what had become a fragile equilibrium.

In the meantime there gradually grew across Western Europe the concept that the Church was a special kind of supranational institution. Various legal entities transcended political frontiers and established Europe-wide rules. Monasteries had in the past generally been self-sufficient communities obeying their chosen rule; now they acquired international overarching structures as "orders." The reforms based on the monasteries at Cluny (mid-tenth century) and Cîteaux (early twelfth century) developed familial relations between one house of the order and another across political borders, and held regular chapters-general to maintain discipline. Over several centuries there was gradually collected and codified a body of "canon law," the basis for the proper conduct of church affairs both in internal administration and in relations with the laity. The process reached a peak with the production by Gratian of Bologna of the "Concordance of Discordant Canons," generally known as the *Decretum*, in the 1140s. This personal collection of texts became *de facto*, with the addition of subsequent "decretals" from later popes, the standard dossier or digest of the law of the Western Church. Its study also became an academic discipline, which (along with the study of Roman civil law) became the most important route to career progress for ambitious medieval churchmen.

By the High Middle Ages a principle had won general acceptance, which is almost impossible for the modern mind to grasp. The principle was that only by being in a legally correct relationship with the administrative hierarchy of the Catholic Church in the West could one's soul achieve eternal salvation. It was at best deeply dangerous, at worst fatal, to be in schism, that is, to be in a state of broken relations with the Church; to be excommunicate, that is, personally excluded from the sacraments, services, and prayers of the Church; or, worst of all, to be a heretic, that is, knowingly and stubbornly to hold a form of Christian belief that had been denounced as wrong by the Universal Church. None of these forms of wrong relationship were newly invented by c. 1100–1200. Some of them can be traced back quite easily to the writings of Augustine (extracts from whose works had been incorporated into Gratian's *Decretum*) and even earlier. However, what was new, and grew to be of increasing importance in the West, was the erection of an efficient system of administrative and spiritual control based on those beliefs. It was at this time, also, that the arrangement of Christian society into parishes with their parish churches and priests, began to be standardized and applied across the continent.

A second ruling principle came to flowering in this period, largely as a consequence of the elaboration of canon law. This was the principle that Christian society was divided into two irreducibly separate classes, the clergy and the laity; and that the clergy were spiritually the superior of the two. The clergy were engaged in spiritual activities, granted access to the sacred things of the Christian religion, and were in some senses above national loyalties. They were subject to a higher level of disciplinary requirements than most laypeople; therefore they were subject to church courts and not to lay courts. Laypeople were engaged in the mundane business of this world, were allowed to marry, and were bound to support the Church with their offerings and their protection. They were not allowed to sit in judgment on the clergy in any shape or form. Even kings, it was argued in the High Middle Ages, were mere laymen, as subject to the clergy as anyone else.[12]

The High Medieval Synthesis

Presented merely as a system of government and law, the medieval system can look oppressive, possibly arrogant, and little else. That does an injustice to a body of belief that was articulated with great theological sophistication. Between the twelfth and the thirteenth centuries Western European theology developed a strikingly cohesive theory of God's grace and how to distribute it to needy souls. In part, this system depended on the rise of what we know as "medieval scholasticism." Scholasticism was not a single or coherent philosophy so much as a range of techniques and habits of thought. This intellectual technique displayed sufficient confidence in human reason to allow theologians to deduce from known and agreed texts (above all, Scripture) the unknown answers to metaphysical questions. If the available authorities appeared to lead to contradictory answers, then truth, which was one and indivisible, could be attained by disputation and the establishing of fine distinctions. In this system, dialectical rigor and "subtlety," the ability to make the distinctions necessary in pursuit of truth, were highly valued qualities.

An added impulse to the scholastic enterprise was the renewed availability of classical texts, especially the texts of ancient Greek philosophy, from the twelfth century onwards. The logic and metaphysics of Aristotle became available, initially through Latin retranslations of Arabic translations of the Greek originals. Knowledge of Greek was by this time extremely rare in the Latin West; fresh translations of Aristotle from Greek originals began to be made from the later Middle Ages. One crude misconception must be avoided here. Christian theology was not in any sense "sold out" to ancient pagan philosophy. Carefully selected elements of that philosophy were appropriated in the belief that they offered a rational means to demonstrate, discover, and articulate the truths of Christian revelation.

From the early thirteenth century, Western, Latin Christianity became a system of faith and ritual conduct of unprecedented clarity and rigor. Believers were, it was agreed, unable to save themselves by their own efforts. However, the merits of Christ, won by the sacrifice of the Cross, were available to save souls through the ministries of the Church. To receive the "grace" offered through those ministries, believers had to be obedient sons and daughters of the Church. They were required to present themselves at least once a year, normally in Lent, to their parish priest and make formal confession of all their sins, express sorrow for them, and receive priestly absolution. At all other appropriate times in life they were to seek the services of the Church as appropriate. Seven special rites, the "seven sacraments," were deemed to be of special significance, though it was not normal for everyone to receive all of them. Baptism as soon as possible after birth, confirmation at the age of discretion, and extreme unction at the point of death, marked milestones in life. The sacrament of penitence (or penance) comprised the regular confession described above; it was normally required before taking communion in the Eucharist, the most important of the repeatable sacraments. Ordination to priesthood was a once-only and irreversible sacrament; marriage was for the rest of society (those described in one source as the "unperfect") and could only be repeated if the bond was broken by death.

One further aspect of the medieval Western system deserves notice. In this form of Christianity the Eucharist played a special role, or series of roles. First, it was a sacrifice, albeit of a special kind. The offering made by the priest consecrating the Eucharist on the altar dispensed a finite "quantum" of the merit won by the sacrifice of Christ on the cross. The benefit of this offering could be assigned to individual souls, living and dead. Secondly, the Eucharist offered, quite literally, the tangible and visible presence of the risen Christ. The words of Christ at the Last Supper, "this is my body" were taken to mean that when they were repeated at every Eucharist, there the physical risen body of Christ was literally present. Again, this was not a new doctrine at the start of the thirteenth century. What was new was the dogmatic certainty and philosophical elaboration with which it was set forth.

Two ironies about the medieval Eucharist deserve notice. Although the eucharistic service lay at the very heart of medieval Christian practice, the lay people as a whole actually took communion very rarely. In the vast majority of Eucharists or "masses" either there was no communion, or only the priest partook of the elements. The Eucharist was something watched rather than consumed, except at Easter and (for the devout) some other great festivals. It embodied the presence of Christ in the mysterious work accessible through his Church, not the sense of community of the Christian congregation. Secondly, when laypeople did receive, their second-rank status was emphasized. Only the consecrated bread (or wafer) was given to laypeople; the consecrated chalice of wine was reserved for the clergy. This was not through economy, or fear of disorder, since lay people were in some countries given unconsecrated wine to help them swallow the wafer.

It was simply a matter of marking the spiritual distinctions between different orders in society.

There was nothing cynical or deliberately oppressive about this system. From reading the correspondence of its most powerful and eloquent exponent, Pope Innocent III, one does not form the impression of an unscrupulous manipulator of people. Rather, conviction had been built upon conviction, to the point where the medieval system was really thought to be the one legally binding route to salvation. Anyone who wandered from the path, or led away others, committed a terrible crime. In part, some of the absoluteness of the medieval papacy arose because it faced challenges from a range of heresies. These movements denied, in different ways and for different reasons, the claim of the Church to mediate the power of Christ to believers. Their traveling "good men" or poor preachers seemed a reproach to the wealth and institutional, sedentary character of the established Church. They claimed a different kind of holiness for themselves, a holiness based in the simplicity of their lives as opposed to the grandeur of the Church.

In response to this challenge, the practice of organized, legally structured inquisition took shape in the 1230s. Not "the Inquisition," an office with a bureaucracy; that came later. What arose at this point was a procedure, a legal mechanism whereby a traveling, specialized church lawyer acted as investigator, prosecutor, judge, and jury over those who erred from the faith. The procedure resembled that applied to ordinary penitents. Those thought to be in sin were called to repentance and subjected to a detailed interrogation. If they confessed and showed contrition, they were pardoned with a penance. If they were stubborn, or offended a second time, they were to be handed over to the secular power (since churchmen did not shed blood) and put to death. This system was, in the eyes of its proponents, a pastoral one: only by bringing, and if need be forcing, lost sheep back to the fold could souls be protected and saved.

At the same time, the Church took care to supply in itself the kind of service that had made the leaders of the heretics attractive. The thirteenth century saw the rise of the "mendicant" or begging friars. These religious orders abandoned the traditional monastic accumulation of lands and other communal property. Their most famous leaders were Francis (1181/2–1226) and Dominic (c. 1172–1221), after whom the two major orders were named. Their communities lived hand-to-mouth from the gifts of the faithful; they tended to gather in towns and cities and engaged in pastoral work. As with other monastic orders, they comprised both male and female communities. However, the male friars were both more numerous and, in that culture, inevitably more influential. They also served in the front line of the defense of orthodox doctrine. Friars supplied the bulk of the preachers and theologians, as well as nearly all the inquisitors, in later medieval Europe.

Later Middle Ages: the Era of Fragmentation

A professional disease of the historian is the desire to characterize whole periods. The late thirteenth, fourteenth, and fifteenth centuries have traditionally been depicted as the "later Middle Ages," the era when the high medieval synthesis started to go wrong, when everything became exhausted and overblown. People at the time experienced no such perception. There were certainly crises: this was an age of devastating wars and (from the end of the 1340s) even more devastating visitations of plague. However, the idea that the Middle Ages were naturally declining to their end is a constructive modern fiction.

There were, however, signs of fragmentation, as all the previous centuries' work matured. The most ambitious project of medieval scholasticism was the work of the Dominican friar and theologian Thomas Aquinas (1224/5–74). Up to his death he was working on an immense synthesis of classical logic and Christian theology. Although he received great veneration and was soon recognized as a saint, his intellectual effort was controversial almost at once. Some of his successors argued that it was not possible to demonstrate that the current divine dispensation was the one logically necessary way for things to be, as Aquinas had argued. Disagreement arose over whether the divine rule of the cosmos was governed by logical necessity, or was merely conventional, the product of divine decisions and choices that could have gone otherwise. Such disagreement helped to foment what became known as the "strife of the ways" in late medieval theology, between the "ancient way" of Aquinas and the "modern way" of some of his successors. This strife did not, of itself, cause political ruptures and ructions outside the universities. No definitive judgment was ever delivered on many of the issues in dispute, at least before the mid-sixteenth century. The "strife of the ways" did, however, tend to make theological disputes somewhat arcane, though even this trend can be overstated.

There were serious and severe political rifts within Christendom apart from the intellectual ones. A particularly bitter row between the King of France and Pope Boniface VIII (pope 1294–1303) at the start of the fourteenth century culminated in the death of the pope from stress and shock. His successors for several decades were Frenchmen under French influence, who settled in an enclave of papal territory at Avignon. The popes at Avignon developed the administrative claims of the papacy over the offices of the Church to their utmost, "providing" (i.e., appointing by remote control) clerics to a huge range of church benefices. Predictably, this generated a reaction from secular rulers. Increasingly the component parts of the Western Church became organized on national lines. The popes' often partisan intervention in the politics of the crowned heads of Europe did little for the spiritual esteem of their office. When the papacy returned to Rome in 1377/8 and the then pope died almost immediately, the Roman mob exerted pressure on the cardinals of the Church to elect an Italian pope, Urban VI (pope 1378–89) who proved to be a brutal and cruel despot. A group of cardinals escaped and elected one of their number as a rival pope, "Clement VII," at Avignon. Soon the allegiances of Christendom were divided between the two popes, mostly along national lines. The English, for instance, sided with the Roman pope, while their traditional enemies the French and the Scots chose the Avignonese. The "Great Schism of the West" lasted until 1417, when the three rival contenders then vying for the see of St Peter were persuaded to resign or were deposed, and a new election was held. During the tortuous process of trying to heal the schism serious and influential people aired hitherto barely thinkable ideas: that the papacy might be a constitutional or limited monarchy, or that ultimate authority might rest in the representatives of the body of the whole Church. These ideas did not in the first instance lead anywhere: the papacy rebuilt much of its prestige in the later fifteenth century.

Neither councils of the Church nor popes were very effective in dealing with the schism of the Church of Bohemia. In 1415 the Council of Constance, called to heal the Schism, had bungled the trial of the Czech academic and popular preacher Jan Hus. Hus had written some very bold, but not obviously heretical, things about the sins of the clergy and the flaws of the visible Church. Faced with a demand that he recant and withdraw statements that he insisted he had never made, Hus refused and was burned as a heretic, a martyr to his own conscience. The outrage caused by his execution was fanned into a flame of rebellion in his native Bohemia by a series of stresses: ethnic, intellectual, and sociopolitical. By the 1420s Bohemia was in a religious ferment. The authority of the bishops and the Roman hierarchy had collapsed. Eventually the most conservative and more peaceful elements in Bohemia won out, and an anomalous special area grew up within the Western Church, to last until the seventeenth century.

That is the traditional image of the history of the late medieval Church as seen from the perspective of "great events" and high politics. For most people, things were much more peaceful. In the late Middle Ages, the voluntary choices of the faithful played an increasingly large part in the shape of the Church's life. The sacrificial mass was, as explained earlier, thought to help souls alive and dead. In the later Middle Ages it became increasingly common to focus devotional effort on the departed, and on one's own preparation for the hereafter. It was expected that most of the souls of the faithful would spend some time after death in a state of purgation, which corresponded to the penances owed for sins in life but not completed while on earth. Dante Alighieri articulated this system with great theological precision in his three-part Italian verse epic, *The Divine Comedy*. To assist the faithful departed to their eventual destiny in heaven, there were not only memorial masses in ever-increasing numbers; there were also various ritual fasts to protect against dying suddenly and unprepared, and there was a panoply of saints who could pray for and support their devotees. On earth, it became popular to belong to lay brotherhoods and sisterhoods, where a communal devotional life was lived alongside, and overflowing from, the parish community. These confraternities supported their members in need and prayed for them after death.

One emblem of late medieval devotion, which encapsulates many of these trends, is the fashion for field-shrines in Germany. These were new devotional sites, which grew up more or less spontaneously in rural areas away from the centers of power. They were often centered on a miracle, typically the appearance of a miraculously formed image or of a bleeding or indestructible eucharistic host. They operated somewhat independent of the hierarchy, though they could be enormously profitable to the local community. Church leaders did not positively encourage such places, and some theologians actively disapproved of them. Yet they flourished and proliferated up to the Reformation era.

Challenges and Ruptures: Renaissance and Reformation

By telescoping history a little, it was possible, in church history of an earlier generation, to argue that the fragmentation of the fourteenth and early fifteenth centuries led inevitably and successively to the more profound and lasting ruptures of the sixteenth. That view no longer commands general acceptance. Indeed, the way that the Renaissance and Reformation unfolded requires the exact opposite to have been the case. By 1500 the hierarchy had overcome its earlier challenges and become dangerously secure, even complacent. The complex and subtle relationship between high theology, pastoral control, and popular devotion had become routine. Because things had become routine, no-one was sufficiently prepared to respond to the extraordinary events that took place, and that shaped the churches in the West for the next five centuries up to the present.

The European Renaissance was a challenge to medieval orthodoxy that chose not to mount a direct attack on it. Classical scholarship had been cultivated throughout the Middle Ages, but in certain specialized forms. Because of the vogue for Latin rhetoric in the civic life of late medieval Italy, around 1400 a need came to be felt for whole, entire texts of classical authors. The result was a surge of interest in ancient literature, studied for its form and style as well as for its content. From this enterprise there arose philological criticism, an appreciation of the evolution and distinctive characteristics of language. These techniques were applied to the texts first of Latin, and then of Greek, literature. However, the same techniques could be used on the texts of Christian history and Christian revelation. The Dutch scholar Erasmus of Rotterdam (1467–1536) duly applied those techniques to the New Testament, most publicly in his successive editions of the Greek and Latin New Testament from 1516 onwards.

This rise in textual and literary scholarship had two important effects. First, the grammarians and the literary scholars staked a claim to verify the text of Scripture *before* the theologians could affirm anything. Secondly, they showed that the text of Scripture had a history. These insights had potentially devastating effects on theology as then practiced. It had been assumed that the Latin Vulgate text, largely but not entirely the work of Jerome, was authoritative, inerrant, and timeless, and that all that was needed was to explain its meaning by applying formal logic. Now it was pointed out that the Vulgate was a seriously corrupt text, and that the nuances conveyed by a Latin word might be quite absent from the Greek or Hebrew originals. Suddenly doctrines deduced by scholastic exposition of the Latin Vulgate were cast into doubt.

A second challenge came from the Renaissance scholars, or "Renaissance humanists" as they are somewhat misleadingly known. These were Christians of refined ethical and spiritual sensibilities. They were repelled by the materialistic, mechanical quality of much of the popular piety that they saw around them. They could not believe that God could respond with predictable, guaranteed favor to the saying of this or that psalm or prayer, the observance of the feast of this or that saint, irrespective of whether the devotion was well-founded or well-intentioned. Erasmus expressed his disapproval of this crass piety in his *Handbook of the Christian Knight*, a piece first published in 1503 but only a success in the Reformation era. Most humanists, however, kept their doubts to themselves and within their elite coteries of like-minded people. This was a challenge that did not confront the Church. Indeed, it assumed that the received pieties and procedures were indestructible, and that the handful of elite souls who bypassed them in favor of a more interior, more spiritual, more ethically focused religion would have no impact on the system as a whole.

In one sense they were right, but in another they proved to be catastrophically wrong. Barely had the ideas of the Renaissance had time to filter through to the intellectuals of northern Europe, when a quite different kind of challenge came bursting out from the theological culture of northern Germany. Martin Luther (1483–1546) was a product of an expansion in the universities of Germany at the end of the Middle Ages. He served as professor of theology in the new Saxon university of Wittenberg, and as a leading light in the reformed Augustinian monastery there. He managed to combine in one person much of the Renaissance humanists' literary awareness and skepticism about vulgar piety, with a scholastic's passionate desire to uncover the absolute truths of theology. He also had a gift for written and spoken Latin and German expression, an unshakeable conscience, and a formidable mind, apt to discover and defend ideas of terrifying originality.

Luther began by doubting the reassurances offered by the pastoral theology of his day. Conventional pastoral teaching told people to bring their best spiritual efforts into the forum of sacramental confession, where their sorrow for sin would be enhanced by the sacrament and they would live purer lives. This teaching envisaged a sort of cycle, in which believers sinned, were sorry for sin, confessed their sins, and were absolved in a (usually) yearly rotation. Luther could not believe that a sufficient level of moral and spiritual purity could be attained by such methods. Initially these doubts led him to morbid self-discipline; then he turned to scathing skepticism (expressed in his *95 Theses Against Indulgences* of 1517) about techniques that seemed to offer cheap grace *without* requiring inner purity. However, by 1518–19, when he was already becoming notorious, Martin Luther reached the end of his personal theological journey. He arrived at a radically new ruling principle about the whole business of saving souls from their sinful nature.

In Luther's new conception, divine grace played a trick (so to speak) on divine judgment. In the "justifying" of sinners, a garment of Christ's righteousness was as it were "draped over" the still putrescent mass of sin. Sinners were forgiven for Christ's sake, and that gift made them acceptable to God. Underneath this covering cloak of "alien" righteousness the sinner was gradually, imperfectly, haltingly improved. However, this "regeneration" was not the reason for being declared righteous: it was only the after-effect and the consequence of it. As Luther put it in one of his most precise statements on the subject: "If you remove mercy from the godly, they are sinners and really have sin, but it is not imputed to them because they believe and live under the reign of mercy, and because sin is condemned and continually put to death in them."[13]

This radical new definition of righteousness inherently, *necessarily*, entailed an equally radical transformation of the worship life and the administrative structures of the Church in the West. By 1500, nearly every liturgical act served as a conduit for the divine grace that, infused into the soul, purified it from sin. That very process of purification, Luther had now argued, rested on a fundamental misconception of how God worked. The churches were not there to channel sacramental grace. Rather, their task was to *proclaim* a grace freely accessible, directly and without intermediaries, set forth in the gospel. They had to teach in the vernacular, not administer mysteries in incomprehensible Latin. Churches that served as teachers of the gospel, rather than devices for the transmission of negotiable grace, did not need to be structured as a single, international organism. Their personnel need not be ritually or legally separate from the rest of the community. The visible Church became nothing more than each ordinary community, living out its spiritual role.

When the quest for personal purification – or, as Luther would have put it, the search for "justification through works" – was abandoned, the ideal of the Christian life necessarily changed. The exceptional, sensational holiness of the monks, nuns, friars, or hermits, who overcame their lower nature by ascetic devotions and the power of a holy vow, now appeared as nothing more than a dangerous and arrogant self-delusion. A good, ordinary neighborly life, even that of a domestic servant, was more holy than the devotions of a monk or nun.[14] Secondly, everyone, not just the clerical elite, now had to know and understand the contents of Scripture and the promises of the gospel, through catechizing and basic education. Luther himself admitted in 1520, as he argued against the belief that the mass was a sacrifice conferring grace on souls living and dead:

> I am attacking…an abuse perhaps impossible to uproot, since through century-long custom and the common consent of men it has become so firmly entrenched that it would be necessary to abolish most of the books now in vogue, and to alter almost the entire external form of the churches and introduce, or rather reintroduce, a totally different kind of ceremonies. But my Christ lives, and we must be careful to give more heed to the Word of God than to all the thoughts of men and of angels. I will perform the duties of my office and bring to light the facts in the case. As I have received the truth freely [Matt. 10: 8], I will impart it without malice. For the rest let every man look to his own salvation; I will do my part faithfully…[15]

At the Imperial assembly in the city of Worms in 1521, Martin Luther made his famous declaration that he would not recant his beliefs, even when pressed to do so by the Emperor and the papal representatives. That act of defiance unleashed a process of radical change, in liturgy as well as in ideas. Within relatively few years the very process of abolition, alteration, and revision of buildings and ceremonies that he envisaged in 1520 had in fact taken place. In many places, it had occurred sooner and more dramatically than Luther wished.

The Reformation unleashed by Luther's key insight became a political and social as well as a religious process. The reasons why it succeeded where it did, especially in northern Europe, and failed where it did, especially in the south, are complex and still not fully understood. In the short term, the ideal was that each community, whether a city-state, a principality, or a kingdom, would make a collective decision (though often, in reality, it was the rulers who decided, sometimes under pressure from below) to adopt the Reformation. It would then invite experts in reformed theology to reorder its worship, teachings, and church structures. That is more or less what happened in areas where a reform close to the ideals of Luther took hold, above all in northern Germany and Scandinavia, the heart of the "Lutheran" churches.

Elsewhere matters were more complex. The worst experiences afflicted those countries where enough people gathered together to urge Reformation-type changes, but not quite enough to convert the whole nation or principality. This occurred in the Netherlands and France. Protestants in both these countries embraced the second-generation model of reform inspired by, among others, John Calvin (1509–64), a French émigré settled at Geneva. Calvin, unlike Luther, was willing to sanction the establishment of minority churches to agitate for reform, if it was not possible to convince the majority at one stroke. Although Calvin's Geneva was a wholly reformed free city-state under the loose overlordship of the Swiss canton of Berne, many "Calvinist" churches in continental Europe were associated with the struggles of minorities to gain establishment and security. Even where the whole nation was reformed (as in England and Scotland) zealots for godly Reformation, mindful of their past experiences as persecuted minorities, would cling to their ideals with a tenacity that their rulers often found disturbing, even subversive of good order.

So great is the upheaval created in European religious history, and the subsequent experience of the churches, that it is easy to forget that it only affected rather less than half the people of Europe in any positive way at all. Nearly all of Mediterranean Western Europe, and significant parts of France, Germany and Eastern Europe either remained Catholic or reverted to

Catholicism after brief tentative experiments with Protestantism. However, both absolutely and in relative terms, the Catholic Church in the West was changed by the experience of the Reformation. It became for the first time, in much of Europe, one form of Christianity among several. It had to engage in intellectual and spiritual self-defense against other churches as never before. It had to renew and revitalize its ongoing and long-established efforts to discipline, regulate, and purge its practices and personnel.

There is some disagreement as to how far the ideals of the Roman Catholic Church after the Reformation departed from those of the Catholic Church of the later Middle Ages. In many respects there were no great differences. The heritage of the Catholic Church in the form of the creeds, decrees of councils, and writings of the Fathers of the Church was conserved and revered. In many parts of Europe, especially in the south, there were probably only limited changes to the appearance and activities of the churches. However, the new circumstances, and the new methods for furthering the old ideals, changed the character and "feel" of the Church. There was a greater quest for uniformity in practice and in the Church's teachings than at any time in the past. The decrees of the Council of Trent (1545–63) laid down Catholic Western teaching with unprecedented precision and, in many cases, programmatic militancy. The Roman Catechism (1566) made them accessible to preachers in handy form, while the Council of Trent's Profession of Faith allowed believers to know in a nutshell what they subscribed to. In place of the regional variations in liturgical practice, a new uniform order for worship was laid down. Instead of the unwieldy and complex mosaic of jurisdictions in the old Church, diocesan bishops were given relatively unimpeded pastoral authority over the clergy in their dioceses. In many parts of Europe they were able to impose discipline regularly, through diocesan and provincial synods, in ways that had been at best experimental under their predecessors.

There was an important change in the spiritual ideals of Catholic life, intended or not. In the past the practice of confession and communion had tended to bring the community together in shared experiences of seasonal fast and feast. In the new dispensation, spiritual discipline tended to become more individual. Christians were encouraged to confess not just in Lent, but whenever they felt the need. Ethical advice, dispensed in private in the newly invented confessional box, focused on individual morality more than on collective relationships. Those who sought an active apostolate were encouraged to undertake missionary activity either in Protestant Europe or in the (newly enlarged) wider world. Typically, male religious orders at this period served the community through welfare work rather than retreating from it into ascetic solitude. Female religious orders displayed many of the same aspirations but tended to be herded into ever more strict enclosure by the hierarchy.

The greatest cultural change that ensued from the Reformation crisis affected the relationship between clergy and people. In the past, the clergy had been ritually and legally set apart from the rest. However, this separateness had faced a credibility problem when priests proved no better educated, no better off, and not always more moral than their flocks. In the Reformation era both Catholic and reformed churches set about ensuring that the clergy were more educated, more professional, more fully removed from the cultural levels of their people. Colleges and seminaries were founded to offer, for the first time in the West, focused professional training for ministry. To the extent that this project achieved its aims, it was not an unmixed blessing. To some extent it meant a return to the relationship of the age of Caesarius of Arles in the sixth century, when learned urban intellectuals tried to dissuade mostly illiterate country people from superstitious and magical rites. Cultural and intellectual formation increased the mental and moral distance from the ordinary parishioner.

The Age of Competing Orthodoxies

Popular history sometimes depicts the Reformation crisis as a campaign for freedom of thought and belief. There is a half-truth in this claim. Those churches that sought the status of tolerated minorities often argued that persecution was an evil, that belief could not be coerced, and so forth. Among "Anabaptist" churches, which eschewed legal establishment, such statements were common. However, this was also an age in which people still believed in absolute truth. Therefore, if one believed that one had reached such absolute truth within the heart of one's church, there was no justification for allowing error simply for the sake of it. English Puritans who migrated to Massachusetts Bay in the 1630s did so to escape the unfriendly attentions of a Church of England whose leaders had turned against strict Calvinism. Once they arrived and set up their communities, they constructed a discipline much more rigid and unforgiving than the one they had left behind, but on their own terms.

Between c. 1560 and c. 1720, and in some areas for much longer, the churches in Europe and the West were gripped by the certainty of the absolute rightness of their own confessional documents. Each denomination, whether Catholic, Lutheran, or reformed, and even minority groups like the Eastern European Unitarians, produced official texts which laid down their teachings, and to which their people were required implicitly or (more often) explicitly to subscribe. These texts included confessions of faith, articles of belief, and catechisms. In an age that had suddenly faced insecurity about the way to salvation, documents such as these provided stability and the illusion of certainty. They enforced uniformity within a given church, and formed a banner around which people could defend their church against its external enemies. This era is variously known as the "era of orthodoxy" or "the confessional age." It was characterized by some of the bitterest fighting over religious creeds in the history of Western Europe. In France the last 40 years of the sixteenth century were blighted by intermittent civil warfare, made more savage by the religious hatred that inflamed many of the combatants. The people of the Netherlands fought an 80-year struggle to free themselves from the rule of the Spanish Habsburg dynasty; only the northern provinces succeeded, partly through the support of networks of reformed supporters and sympathizers. In Germany from 1618 onwards 30 years of destructive warfare were sparked off when the Protestant Elector Palatine of the Rhine accepted the offer of the Crown of Bohemia from rebels against the Catholic Habsburgs of Austria. In none of these conflicts were religious motives unmixed, or even always uppermost in people's minds. However, as recent experience across the world has shown, the desire to serve one's image of God can inspire to far worse acts of violence than the desire merely to please oneself.

The hardening of political lines of allegiance was matched by a parallel hardening of the theological arteries. The rhetoric of the Renaissance had been intended to open up debate; that of the age of orthodoxy tried to shut it down. Finding ordinary language too imprecise for the fine detail of theological controversy, theologians resorted to a revived scholasticism. Theology became once again technical and inaccessible to all but specialists. Unlike the scholasticism of the Middle Ages, however, early modern neoscholasticism did not explore and discuss possible alternative explanations. It forced and bullied the reader to recognize the inevitable truth of one single dogmatic line. All the mainstream churches in the West were equally responsible for this state of affairs, and all joined in the mutual recriminations and polemics.

Despite the striving for uniformity within individual confessions, internal splits did occur, and led to some of the most acrimonious struggles. Lutheranism experienced some of the earliest of such strife from just after Luther's death until c. 1580. In Catholicism, struggles over the heritage of Augustine, especially in the area of the theology of justification, opened up divisions in France between the Jansenists, who tended to an ascetic, puritanical lifestyle, and their adversaries. Strife over the doctrine of predestination divided the reformed churches of the Netherlands into the followers of Gomar and

Arminius: this particular dispute mapped itself on to political fault lines in the Dutch Republic and caused intermittent civil strife. Disputes over liturgy and Church polity blew into a major storm in England and Scotland in the 1630s. While such disputes did not solely and of themselves cause the mid-century convulsion of the British civil wars, they played a far from insignificant role. Confessional politics remained a dominant issue in the British political systems until at least 1690.

There was an intellectual response to the excesses of orthodoxy, which will be discussed in the next section. However, there was also a religious response. From the middle of the seventeenth century, a few individuals considered the possibility that the truths of faith were known in a more intimate, more affective, and less cast-iron dogmatic fashion than most of the orthodox believed. The reaction against orthodoxy tended to be mystical rather than doctrinaire. It described the emotive experiences of the soul possessed by Jesus Christ, rather than the forensic, formal justification of sinners. It even showed some signs of cross-confessional sympathy. The Lutheran Pietist Gottfried Arnold (1666–1714) translated works by the Roman Catholic Quietists Miguel de Molinos and Madame Guyon. The founder of the Moravian Church, Nikolaus Ludwig, Count von Zinzendorf (1700–60) was inspired to begin his career as a religious innovator by receiving Bohemian Brethren as exiles on to his estates.

Challenges to Orthodoxy: Reason, Enlightenment, and Revolution

For much of the period since the conversion of pagan Western Europe Christianity had been a compulsory religion, into which nearly everyone was born. There were (mostly) relatively small pockets of Western European Judaism, which subsisted in some areas and were persecuted or exiled in others. The once very substantial Muslim population of the Iberian peninsula suffered gradual attrition through the Middle Ages and was either exiled or subjected to forced conversion in the early modern period. For the overwhelming majority, to be Christian was a matter of inheritance and obligation rather than choice. From the start of the eighteenth century, however, possibly the most important challenge arose to the status of Christianity since antiquity, although the scale of this challenge only became apparent much later. By slow degrees, it became socially and politically respectable to avoid religious duties or religious profession; to disavow or ridicule religious belief; and to affirm, even to print, statements of explicit atheism, skepticism, or unbelief. This is not to say that the eighteenth century was an age of unbelief, a claim that has long since been disproved. Rather, it was an age in which radical skepticism about religious dogma, which at its most extreme could lead to sheer unbelief, became open for public discussion. Skepticism became thinkable and writable rather than normal.

The relationship between reason and revelation had been unstable for centuries. The scholastics had explored, and disagreed over, how far the divine plan was accessible to logical reasoning. In the Reformation era, it was agreed by all sides that Scripture was authoritative, and that reason (aided, in the Catholic viewpoint, by the traditions of the Church) could at best help one to reach truths within limits set by divine revelation. In all of this, it was assumed that divine authority, set forth in Scripture, must be superior either to human reasoning ability (which was fallible) or to human experience (which could be deceived).

The erosion of this almost limitless trust in the divine status of authoritative texts is one of the most important aspects of the transition to the modern era. It took a very long time indeed. Martin Luther, confronted with the fact that the four rivers of Eden (traditionally identified as the Tigris, Euphrates, Nile, and Ganges) manifestly did not flow from the same source as the book of Genesis claimed, argued that this must be because the physical geography of the world had been disrupted after the Fall of humankind, not (heaven forbid) because Moses got something wrong.[16] It was one thing to discover, as the geographers and astronomers did in the sixteenth and seventeenth centuries, that one knew things unknown to the ancient pagan writers. It was quite another to think that one could second-guess the Bible. However, very gradually, confidence grew in intellectual methods based on pure human reasoning and synthesis built up from sense-impressions. Much of the history of Western philosophy in this era is concerned with method and the philosophy of how we know things.

The intellectual response to orthodox dogma that we know as "the Enlightenment" tended, at least initially, to attack not religion as such but the deplorable consequences that militant dogmatism led to. "Superstition" was the result of unreasoning faith in arbitrary manifestations of the divine. "Enthusiasm" occurred when supporters of a given creed allowed their partisan loyalties to overwhelm basic ethical norms. At worst, it led to fanaticism, and fanaticism produced conflict, suffering, and misery. The French Protestant writer Pierre Bayle initiated this line of argument in 1686, in a scathing critique of Augustine's justifications for the persecution of heretics in his *Philosophical Commentary*.[17] However, the abhorrence of fanaticism and its consequences became a commonplace of writers of the fully fledged Enlightenment of the mid-eighteenth century, including

Voltaire, David Hume, and Diderot and the other editors of the *Encyclopédie ou Dictionnaire raisonné des sciences, des arts et des métiers*. Any instances of hardline confessional cruelty, such as the expulsion of Protestants from the Archbishopric of Salzburg in 1731, were held up to the ridicule of the intelligentsia.

If persecution was such a manifest evil, where did that leave the issue of the intellectual claims of religion? Here the writers of the Enlightenment came up with a great variety of possible answers. Some were themselves involved in church ministries of various kinds and found no moral or intellectual difficulty in continuing to minister, even though they might not have endorsed all the statements in their churches' creeds. Many appear to have dreamed of a purified, simplified, natural religion shorn of all supernatural, miraculous, or arbitrary elements. This was the spirit in which Thomas Jefferson notoriously reworked the New Testament into a philosophical and ethical discourse drawing on the words of Jesus, excluding all the miracle stories and mythic elements. In this era some rationalist outgrowths from the Reformation, like Socinianism, which had been marginal since their foundation, became more mainstream. Some Enlightenment thinkers became Deists: they were willing to believe in a God who constructed the cosmos along flawlessly rational lines, but who then left it to work in its own perfect fashion, not interfering in any arbitrary, let alone miraculous, fashion. Some embarked on the study of religions as a historical or proto-anthropological exercise, steadfastly refusing to privilege Christianity over any other ancient and outmoded cult. Citizen Dupuis published his *Origine de tous les cultes, ou religion universelle* (Origin of all cults, or universal religion) in year 3 of the French republic, better known as 1795 CE.[18]

This intellectual vogue had only limited effect on the polity and workings of the churches themselves. Most people worshiped as they had done since the Reformation, unaware of the intellectual ferments among the elites. In most of Europe there was still an established church, which the subjects of any given state were expected to attend. In a few areas there were explicitly biconfessional arrangements where uniformity had proved elusive. However, it was only in the United States of America that absolute freedom of conscience was overtly embodied in an act of state. That case did not reflect any decline of religious sentiment (though some of the founding fathers were influenced by the Enlightenment). Rather, so many different émigré creeds and religious communities made up the new union that no single standard could be agreed, let alone imposed. In the era of the French Revolution the ideal of confessional uniformity began to enter its terminal decline. The French revolutionaries, after overthrowing absolute monarchy, declared it to be a basic right of the citizen to enjoy religious toleration. The

National Assembly then decreed the solution to the state's financial woes by confiscating vast tracts of the landed property of the Catholic Church on November 2, 1789. Initially, the revolutionaries intended the Catholic Church in France to be an obedient servant of the state, like a Lutheran Church with a different theology. Within a few years the revolution had progressed to the point of forcible "dechristianization," when it was recognized that the old Church was acting as a focus for discontent. The anti-religious fervor of the French Revolutionaries would, however, be short-lived.

However, the idea that religious minorities must by absolute justice be second-class citizens had suffered a fatal blow. Anticipating a little, in country after country legal and civil discriminations rooted in post-Reformation religious divisions fell into disuse in the early nineteenth century. In 1817 Friedrich Wilhelm III marked the 300th anniversary of the Reformation by decreeing the mutual absorption of the Lutheran and Calvinist congregations in Prussia into a single Evangelical Church, within which each congregation would maintain its own traditions. (Prussia did, however, remain anti-Catholic, most notably in the 1870s under Bismarck.) In England the most important civil disabilities on Roman Catholics dating from the sixteenth and seventeenth centuries were withdrawn in the Roman Catholic Relief Act of 1829. Most striking of all, the severe restrictions on the few thousand Protestant subjects of the Kingdom of Sardinia in Piedmont-Savoy, in northwestern Italy, were removed when they were given full civil rights in 1848.

The Era of Romanticism and its Implications

The Enlightenment, with its at times arrogant confidence in the sufficiency and sophistication of well-informed human reason, did not endure in that form as a dominant cultural trend. It tended to efface the differences between cultures, postulating a general, cosmopolitan humanity. It appeared to be too much of the head and too little of the heart. Predictably, it generated a reaction against itself. Already Jean-Jacques Rousseau had argued that the key entity in political and social development was neither the individual nor universal humanity, but "a people," an ethnic group with its distinctive collective memory and culture. Rousseau was a little ahead of his time. However, by the early nineteenth century the movement known as Romanticism had embraced and articulated an appreciation of the cultural, emotive, sentimental things that made a people special. Romanticism had a spectacularly diverse effect on Western Christian modes of thought.

The reaction against the overbearing rationalism of the Enlightenment could, in certain hands, become a reaction in favor of the Christian religion. Enlightened refinement had led to a sort of anemic, cosmopolitan rationalism, and had been unable successfully to engage the spiritual side of humanity. Attempts to generate a purely natural and reasoned veneration of an abstract Supreme Being failed to attract more than a handful of thinkers. The actual religious traditions of Western Europe, on the other hand, were bound up with the collective memories, the folk tales, the cultural inheritance of Europe's peoples. One of the most interesting aspects of Romanticism is its fascination with traditional popular culture. The Romantics viewed it, not as horrendous ignorance and superstition to be escaped from, but as a fragile relic to be collected and conserved. Folklorists like the Grimm brothers and Ludwig Bechstein systematically collected stories and folk tales for the first time. Many of these tales incorporated the memory of the medieval past, with its priests and monks and (in Protestant Europe) half-forgotten rituals. Even in Catholicism there was a similar sense that religious traditions were bound up with the medieval past. François Réné, vicomte de Chateaubriand (1768–1848), in his enormously successful *Génie du Christianisme, ou Beautés de la religion chrétienne* (The Spirit of Christianity, or the Beauties of the Christian Religion) of 1802 evoked medieval Catholicism as an emblem of the historical cultural past of the French people: a modern church building could never stir up the same sensations as an ancient Gothic cathedral.[19]

Romanticism produced a new style in theology as well. F. D. E. Schleiermacher (1768–1834), a reformed minister in Prussia, produced the prodigiously influential *On Religion: Speeches to its Cultured Despisers* in 1799. Under the influence of contemporary philosophical trends but also drawing on his background with Zinzendorf's Moravian Unity of Brethren, he defined religion as an intuitive sense of union with the infinite, distinguishing it strictly from metaphysics and ethics, with which it had in the past been combined:

> Religion's essence is neither thinking nor acting, but intuition and feeling. It wishes to intuit the universe, wishes devoutly to overhear the universe's own manifestations and actions . . . Praxis is an art, speculation is a science, religion is the sensibility and taste for the infinite . . . To accept everything individual as a part of the whole and everything limited as a representation of the infinite is religion.[20]

Dogmatic or rationalistic attempts to pin it down, to define the miraculous against the ordinary, simply showed a lack of inner awareness of what religion was about. In his mature work Schleiermacher defined religion as a sense of dependence on the infinite, which might take different forms among different peoples (hence the diversity of religions) but of which Christianity was the highest form.

In other hands the Romantic spirit could lead to a more hard-core revival of medievalism. In England during the 1830s and 1840s there arose a reaction against the relatively relaxed latitudinarian Anglicanism that had dominated the eighteenth century. A group of religious writers and thinkers centered on Oxford sought to revive a more elevated style of liturgy, a greater sense of the mystery of worship and the status of the priesthood, and a sense of the continuity between the Church of England and its medieval origins. Ultimately many of the leading figures in this movement were received into the Roman Catholic Church around 1845, most famously the future cardinals John Henry Newman and Henry Manning. The "Oxford Movement" entailed some constructive reinterpretation of history, as when Newman notoriously attempted to demonstrate the Catholic character of the 39 Articles of the Church of England, originally devised under the Protestant Elizabeth I. It also accompanied the phenomenally successful revival of the Gothic style in architecture and the decorative arts, especially in the hands of its short-lived inspirational genius A. W. N. Pugin (1812–52). The Oxford Movement, somewhat inevitably, generated a reaction against itself from those in the Anglican tradition who were more consciously Protestant. The rift between "Evangelical" and "High Church" Anglicanism that it produced persists to this day.

Medievalism was also revived in certain sections of the Roman Catholic Church proper. Confronted with what it saw as the dangerous trends of modern philosophical and Protestant theological thought, the Catholic hierarchy responded by evoking the achievements of medieval Christian philosophy. In 1879 Pope Leo XIII issued a decree calling on the faithful to rediscover their medieval theological heritage as a defense against modern trends. This approach (perhaps surprisingly) was highly effective. A scholarly industry of neoscholastic theology grew up, focused above all on rediscovering and discussing the work of Thomas Aquinas. Medievalism in Catholic thought was not in all circumstances irreconcilable with critical spirit. Indeed, the scholarly standards aspired to and often attained by Catholic medievalists made critical scholarly awareness indispensable. However, towards the end of the twentieth century the opinion of the hierarchy turned against the sort of critical thought that had in the meantime developed in the reformed churches. This reaction culminated in a definitive condemnation of so-called "Modernism" in 1907.

The prevailing nineteenth-century intellectual challenge to orthodox Christianity came from what one could loosely call scientific thought. By this is meant the attitude that human society, its religious aspects included, is a behavioral system susceptible of analytical study: that religion is something one scrutinizes, rather than something in which one is immersed. Ludwig Feuerbach (1804–72), a trained theologian turned philosopher, argued under the influence of G. W. F. Hegel (1770–1831) that all religions, including Christianity, were reflections of the self-perceptions of different peoples. The Christian God, for Feuerbach, was the self-projection of idealized humanity: the things human beings recognized in themselves in an imperfect form were located in an imaginary deity and an idealized savior.[21] Feuerbach's approach was probably most influential through Karl Marx, who reduced all ideology to top-dressing applied over the brutal realities of class struggle and economic motivation. Marx's notorious claim, that religion was used as a sedative by the elites to keep the proletariat in awe and subjection, has had a momentous effect on modern historical readings of religious history, even among those who do not fully embrace Marxist economic determinism. His insight, for instance in his *Contribution to a Critique of Hegel's Philosophy of Right*, that a critique of religion was funda-mental to an understanding of society, in due course affected theologians as well as nontheistic social philosophers. Marx's perception (not shared by some of those who looked to him for inspiration) that religion would naturally wither of itself in the modern world, has contributed to the prevailing "secularization thesis" that informs much modern sociology of religion.

Just as important for the changing perception of Christianity were the evolutionary theories of early anthropologists and sociologists. Enlighten-ment thinkers had developed theories of natural evolution before Charles Darwin proposed a biological model for the process. In the latter half of the nineteenth century writers like F. Max Müller (1823–1900), Edward Bur-nett Tylor (1832–1917), and Emile Durkheim (1858–1917) speculated about the origins of all religions, which they assumed to lie in something resembling the religions of "primitive" peoples in the world. Such thought suggested that there was a cultural and religious ascent from primitive religious forms to more sophisticated ones, ultimately producing the so-phisticated monotheisms of the great world religions. Thought of this kind had the potential to break religion decisively from its supposed supernatural roots. Religion would become a human construct. The spiritual or intel-lectual quality of a religion could become nothing more than a barometer of the level of cultural sophistication attained by its adherents.

Documents of the Christian heritage were not exempt from these ex-plorations and speculations. For the first time, the events of biblical history were exposed to detached historical investigation; the texts of the Bible were exposed to various forms of critical analysis. New texts were brought into play, especially the Codex Sinaiticus (discovered for the world of scholarship in 1844–59) the earliest known volume to contain a complete New Testament as well as parts of the Old. Others long since kept in Europe, such as the Codices Alexandrinus and Vaticanus, were incorporated into textual scholarship. In 1881 a major new edition of the Greek New Testament, that of Westcott and Hort, superseded the "received text" that had been canonized since the early seventeenth century, to the scandal of many conservative churchmen.

In response to these trends theologians, predominantly in the Protestant world, began to reshape the intellectual content of Christian teaching in the most radical way since the Reformation. If the Enlightenment had been an assault on Christianity from outside, this was a challenge from within. A somewhat premature attempt to apply this approach to early Christianity was the work of the Tübingen school under F. C. Baur (1792–1860) in the 1840s and 1850s. This applied the dialectical theories of G. W. F. Hegel to the rise of early Christianity. It postulated radical splits between followers of Peter and Paul, and claimed these were resolved only in the mid-second century, when (Baur argued) much of the New Testament was written. D. F. Strauss (1808–74), a pupil of Baur, argued as early as the 1830s that the supernatural stories in the Gospels were the product of mythic elaboration of the story of Jesus in the hundred years or so after his ministry. The detailed evolution of historico-theological criticism of Christianity will be explored later. The overall point is that by the mid-nineteenth century theologians regarded the whole source-material of Christian revelation as open to critical analysis. Dates, authorship, the underlying intellectual thought-patterns, were all exposed to the judgment of the detached critic.

This line of thought argued that Christianity needed to be stripped of the material that had accrued around it in the early centuries of metaphysical and philosophical elaboration. This instinct was similar to that felt by the sixteenth-century reformers. However, it tended to be antidogmatic where the reformers were dogmatic. Whereas the reformers "pruned away" material from the Middle Ages, the liberal theologians went much earlier and were much more drastic in their purges. Albrecht Ritschl (1822–89) argued for the priority of sense of community and ethical norms over metaphysical speculations. Adolf von Harnack (1851–1930) depicted the metaphysics that invaded Christian teaching in the early centuries as a "Hellenization" of an essentially pure message of divine love, Christian brotherhood, and ethical goodness. Possibly the fullest elaboration of this trend in Protestant liberalism was manifested in the work of Ernst Troeltsch (1865–1923), a theologian who was also a distinguished and scholarly church historian. Troeltsch's historical arguments will be considered in full later. His significance lay in a readiness to apply the lessons of history, and especially the historical study of religion, to dogmatic theology in an unblinkingly frank way. He proceeded about as far one could go from the idea of Christianity as "timeless" truths, while still remaining a Christian theologian.

It is as dangerous to characterize the Christianity of the nineteenth century by the work of its most radical theologians as it is to characterize the eighteenth by the thinkers of the Enlightenment. For most of the century the churches worshiped and worked with a vigor uncomplicated by philosophy. The popular awareness of intellectual developments was probably restricted to the most public innovations. In the English-speaking world the revision of the text of the Bible ultimately issued in the "Revised Version" of the King James Version of the Bible in 1885, the first "official" revision since 1611. Churches began to keep track of their active membership, which proved to be very significant. Proliferating denominations and sects, now no longer at a legal disadvantage, channeled the energy and the money of the faithful into an unprecedented number of new church building projects.

The important challenges were those produced by industrialization and urbanization and their accompanying social problems, about which German liberal theologians had on the whole surprisingly little to say. In North America, however, concern for the conditions of the poor, and liberal emphasis on Christianity as ethics, produced the "Social Gospel" movement. This was conspicuous in the main Protestant denominations in the United States and Canada. It urged greater concern for the conditions of the working people and for some restraint on the economic power of capital. "Christian Socialism" had a checkered experience in the churches elsewhere: some clerics espoused it vigorously; some (especially in the hierarchies) perceived it as a threat to order. On this even the Vatican sent out mixed messages at different times.

The Multiple Crises of the Twentieth Century

There was a problem with liberalism, which became brutally obvious in the course of the twentieth century and contributed (perhaps excessively) to its discredit for much of that century. Typically of its age, it manifested a belief in the steady improvability of people and society. If people were correctly taught and influenced, their religious lives and their lives as a whole would become purer and better. This has been a repeated instinctive feeling at various stages since the Renaissance: it can be seen in the work of Erasmus as well as in some thinkers of the Enlightenment. Its chief weakness is a tendency not to take seriously enough the defects of human nature and the extent of human social problems.

The crisis of liberalism began with the experiences of World War I, which brought much of nineteenth-century thought and attitudes, especially its melioristic tendencies, up against harsh reality. The figure most associated with the reversal of many late nineteenth-century positions was the Swiss theologian Karl Barth (1886–1968). Barth's reaction against liberalism was twofold. On one hand, in reading Paul and the theologians of the Reformation, he found that the liberals' belief in the improvability of human nature was radically contradicted by the testimony of earlier theologians. On the other, the experiences of World War I seemed to discredit liberal views once and for all. His response, though ostensibly an exercise in pure exegesis, was to return to many of the theological positions regarding human sin and the need for grace that were most characteristic of the mainstream Reformation. Barth's ideas were developed (somewhat against his intentions, he claimed) through the advocacy of a sympathizer, Adolf Keller, into a theological school known as "theology of crisis" or "dialectical theology."

The theological details of the dialectical approach are discussed below.[22] For this historical overview, Barth's approach matters because it discredited one of the premises of liberal historicism, that the Church must (and should) adapt its forms of expression to the changing circumstances of its time. Barth and his followers could thus conceive of a Christianity that was fundamentally at odds with the prevailing culture, and a Church that might be called to witness against that culture. The advent of Nazism in Germany placed Barth, then teaching at Bonn, in a position to inspire and guide the "Confessional Church" that separated from and resisted the "German Christians," those German Protestants who threw in their lot with the prevailing regime. Barth's manner of writing and thinking was manifested in the "Barmen declaration" of May 29–31, 1934. This document united "confessing" members of the Lutheran and reformed (Calvinist) denominations in a declaration against the claims of the state to control the Church, and to act as a second source of moral and spiritual authority alongside Christ and the gospel. One of Barmen's anathemas attacked what could be regarded as a principle of liberal theology: "We reject the false doctrine, as though the Church were permitted to abandon the form of its message and order to its own pleasure or to changes in prevailing ideological and political convictions." Another attacked, in language redolent of Luther, the "confusing of the two kingdoms" of state and Church: "We reject the false doctrine, as though the State, over and beyond its special commission, should and could become the single and totalitarian order of human life, thus fulfilling the Church's vocation as well."[23] The position of the Confessing Church was to cost Barth his German academic post; but it cost the life of Dietrich Bonhoeffer, in some respects Barth's (critical) follower, along with that of numerous other members of the Confessing Church.

In a keynote of twentieth-century Church history, the churches in much of the world have found themselves called to witness against their own governments, or even to be estranged from and hostile to the objectives of their governments. Unlike Church–state conflicts of the Middle Ages, which were largely jurisdictional rivalries, these estrangements have tended to be ideological and ethical first, and legal only as a consequence. They were not confined to regimes with totalitarian methods or aspirations, though they were naturally most severe where the state claimed the right to be the sole controlling force in every aspect of its subjects' lives and thought. In France, the Catholic Church came to be perceived as dangerously anti-Semitic in the wake of the Dreyfus scandal. A series of harshly anti-Catholic measures were passed in 1903, though most of these were revoked after a few years.

The worst and longest case of persecution of the Christian Church in the twentieth century occurred in the Soviet Union, though even this varied in intensity. The Russian Orthodox Church had long been far closer to the state than many of its Western European counterparts. In 1918 Lenin proclaimed the subjugation of the Church to the state; the ideology of communism stated that religion must wither away in time, but the state could not wait. All Russian monasteries were closed by 1939, many churches were demolished, and the priesthood winnowed by persecutions. In 1941 Stalin temporarily changed course and reached an accommodation with the Church, which still served as an embodiment of national sentiment for many Russians. After the end of the war persecution resumed during Stalin's lifetime and only gradually abated. Under communism the challenge to many churches was similar to that faced in 1930s Germany: whether to purchase bare survival at the cost of allowing a great deal of intervention and oppressive supervision by the state, or to enter into a clandestine existence as a secretive resistance movement. In several countries the end of communist rule c. 1989 revealed churches, both Catholic and Orthodox, badly split by the consequences of these choices.

In Latin America the rifts caused by this dilemma have been and remain acute. In most of central and southern America, Marxist ideologies have rarely succeeded in establishing any sort of hold on government for any length of time. Marxism therefore continues to be perceived in its nineteenth-century sense, that of a sociological analysis of the reasons for the oppression of the poor majority, and of the means for their liberation. This has often made it highly difficult for members of the European Catholic hierarchy, who perceived Marxism as the ideology of an atheistic totalitarian superstate, to empathize with their Latin American subordinates, who saw Marxism as offering relief to the poor. The "liberation theologians," including such leading figures as Gustavo Gutiérrez and Leonardo Boff, perceive the people as needing political and economic help and empowerment as a key part of spiritual uplift. They denounce economic and religious systems that impose alien models of economic development (usually of a highly unregulated capitalist form) and alien models of highly conformist, top-down pastoral theology. This movement has led to acute tensions in Catholicism between Rome and Latin America, and between conservative and liberationist elements in the Latin American Church. By a cruel irony its most famous martyr, Archbishop Oscar Romero of San Salvador, was murdered in 1980 less than five years after being converted from a highly hierarchical antiliberation stance to the liberationist position.

For many centuries the churches had accepted that social differentiation, by class, by gender, by race, by free or unfree civil status, was a fact of life. An exception to this, in the nineteenth century, was the vigorous campaign for the abolition of slavery in the English-speaking world (though that saw professed Christians taking positions on both sides of the argument). In the latter half of the twentieth century, most of the churches reversed the traditional argument for social differentiation, and asserted that spiritual equality and ethical standards dictate that all human beings receive equal treatment in both civil and religious issues regardless of gender, creed, or race. In the developed world many churches (though not all) are gradually extending that argument to include equality regardless of sexual orientation. On the whole, though, many of the churches appear in this respect to lag rather behind secular ethics in this respect. In the increasingly important and numerous churches of the developing world, the pursuit of liberation from the last vestiges of colonialism has not meant echoing the other liberations of the West and North. On the contrary, it has freed the churches, in parts of Africa especially, to be resolutely conservative on some social and ethical issues.

In the United States, there grew up from the late eighteenth and early nineteenth century a structure of largely self-governing African-American Protestant churches. These developed and nurtured their own liturgical and homiletic traditions and styles. The external forces of enslavement followed by enforced segregation, together with internal autonomous theological developments, created separate trends in worship, often more charismatic and revivalist than in other Protestant churches. They were liturgically innovative, if sometimes also very conservative in theology. From the 1960s onwards a distinctive black theology has been developed, having affinities with liberation theology in general. This identifies the Jesus of the oppressed underclass of Roman Judea with the oppressed underclasses of modern society. In this theology "blackness" becomes a symbol of the spiritual condition of those to whom Jesus specially directed his ministry.

For centuries the status of women in the Church had reflected that of women in society. Fairly rigid gendering of society was regarded as normal in all premodern societies, including those of the New Testament era. The scriptural prohibitions on women assuming public leadership roles in the Church were regarded as universally binding, as were the patriarchal ideals of family and household structure found in the Pastoral Epistles. When women assumed heroic status in the early stages of the ascetic movement, their asceticism was sometimes described as turning them, in effect, into honorary males. In the early Reformation, however, the sudden release of women from monasteries prompted some to venture into print with their ideas, in an atmosphere where all religious and social hierarchies were temporarily shaken. Again, in England in the 1650s the breakdown of the state church left many women free to write and publicize their religious views. In the seventeenth to nineteenth centuries a sort of permissive niche for female religious expression existed: women could write and publish devotional works and hymns, serve as lay educators, and as philanthropic leaders in the churches.

However, the progressive campaign for the civil emancipation of women since the late nineteenth century has had quite different effects on the status of women in the churches. Women who could vote, graduate from universities, and serve in the professions could see no reason to be denied leadership roles in every aspect of the church's work. In those reformed churches that conceived of ordained ministry in terms of a specialized teaching role rather than a sacramental priesthood, it was easier to overcome traditional objections to female ministry. These churches generally ordained women earliest. A handful of women were ordained in the late nineteenth and early twentieth centuries, but after many years of accepting the theological possibility, most churches only began significant female ordinations in the 1960s. The Anglican Communion inherited from the nineteenth century a strange ambiguity about the ministry: different members conceive of it in either a Catholic or a reformed sense, according to belief and preference. Nevertheless, the weight of opinion swung in favor of ordaining women to ministry in most provinces by the 1990s. The Roman Catholic

Church and the Eastern Churches continue to reject female priesthood on theological and/or institutional grounds.

The intellectual correlative to the rise of women in reformed ministries is the rise of feminist (or among some African Americans and Latinas respectively, "womanist" or *mujerista*) theology. This approach claims that, by sensitive reading of the written heritage of the churches, the work and role of women in the past can be retrieved from the obscurity into which centuries of male-centered theological and historical writing consigned it. Some of the implications of this movement will be discussed later. Feminist theology makes the uncontroversial and fundamentally orthodox point that God transcends gender. However, it draws from this the implication that all liturgical and theological language that casually equates maleness with the divinity, or subsumes the female under male linguistic forms, must be abandoned or reversed. That demand is, somewhat piecemeal, becoming accepted in many churches. Feminist theology continues to evolve along with the context of secular feminist and postmodern thought within which it develops and operates. The precise relationship between bodily difference and cultural gender differentiation remains debatable.

There is a risk in all of these developments that the greatest challenge of all to the churches will be overlooked. To observers from outside, the dominant trend in the Christian churches, in the developed world, is not their sometimes-anguished attempts to justify keeping abreast of the social, cultural, and ethical changes going on around them. It is the possibility that these churches will be simply overwhelmed by the flood of modern popular culture and become irrelevant and obsolete. In its era of greatest influence, the Christian Church had made universal claims to the spiritual allegiance of its people. It had been the arbiter of ethics. It was the structure within which most or even all education, welfare work, and high art were carried out. It had secured its material future by vast endowments and compulsory taxation. It had provided a large and compelling amount of popular entertainment.

None of these activities were necessarily intrinsic to the Church's work. In the nineteenth to twentieth centuries, in the developed world at least, most of these activities have been stripped away. State sponsorship has turned into indifference or sometimes active hostility. Church membership among the traditional denominations has declined in much of Western Europe, catastrophically so in some countries. In the United States overall Christian participation has grown roughly in step with the population, but the influence and relative size of the traditional Protestant denominations has declined relative to that of independent, often charismatic, urban "megachurches" and, to some extent, of Roman Catholicism. Churches have generally lost access to tax revenues, and their endowments have dwindled. Mainstream churches often struggle to maintain even a modest level of ministry, at the expense of constant pleas to their members for material support. Some sociologists detect a tendency for fairly consistent adherence to one denominational church to decline, and foresee its replacement by a more eclectic, pick-and-mix approach to spirituality. Religion in such circumstances risks becoming a consumer commodity like anything else, or a subset of the vast and constantly growing industries in mass media, mass entertainment, and consumer goods.

It remains to be seen how far the predictions of the churches' decline will be realized, and how far the trends will continue. The twentieth-century decline has to be set against the abnormal surge in voluntary membership in the nineteenth century, and the longer-standing inheritance of cultural hegemony derived from the Middle Ages. An important and as yet incalculable influence may come to be wielded by growing conservative churches in the Third World. As in every era since the apostles, the Christian churches are negotiating their position in a changing society.

Reflecting on the Process of Historical Development

The process of historical change in the Christian churches is immensely complex, and poses both intellectual and spiritual challenges to its members. The remainder of this chapter will offer some suggestions as to how these processes of change may be analyzed and explained at a certain level of generalization. One can begin by considering briefly the unhistorical, positivist position. Such a stance might argue that the Christian churches have a timeless body of inherited teachings and practices. They have the Scriptures, the ancient creeds, baptism, and the Eucharist. As long as these are preserved in their timeless purity, the churches need not be concerned about historical change. The only kind of change that could afflict these core documents would be error and deviation. Christian history is the history of the transmission, well or badly, of this core heritage. The core is what matters; the time-limited dressing is peripheral and ultimately insignificant. Many religious thinkers, from many different branches of the Christian Church, have held a version of this view for much of Christian history. In a muted form it is probably held by many laypeople today: one sometimes hears it argued that the churches only suffer and decline because they lapse from their fundamentals, their heritage documents, their pristine ethical and doctrinal standards. A recent publishers' catalogue exhorted its customers to read a work whose author "identifies more than 15 timeless truths . . . and encourages Christians to build on that rock-solid foundation."[24]

As an explanation for the historical diversity and evolution of the churches, however, the simple positivist or absolutist explanation rapidly reveals itself to be inadequate. First, the supposedly "timeless" elements in the Christian heritage are nothing of the kind. Each document bears the imprint of the age and circumstances in which it was produced. The doctrinal statements of Christianity, even the most ancient, were nearly all written because divergence and controversy had led to a contest, in which the majority, or the ultimate victors, decided what statements would become canonical. The New Testament writings are just as diverse, just as full of controversy, and just as specific to their cultural context as any later documents from the Christian heritage. The history of even the most central Christian practices of worship is one of continuous development and diversification around a basic theme. The notion of a pristine, timeless, ideal Christianity does not bear the light of day.

Second, there are simply too many different ways for a *successful* Christian church to exist. Indeed, difference often stimulates a vigorous definition of one's identity rather than impeding such definition. Unless one takes an extraordinarily narrow view of what constitutes "Christianity," one must accept that large, long-lived Christian communities have formed around mutually incompatible principles. Very often the most potent and effective emblems of Christian "identity" are precisely those things *not* shared with the broadest possible range of other believers, whether it is loyalty to the pope or the cult of the Virgin Mary in Roman Catholicism, or the extreme simplicity of silent worship found among Quakers. For much of the past five centuries in the West especially, the documents of the faith most able to generate loyalty have been creedal statements born out of the disputes of the sixteenth and seventeenth centuries. In a broader sense still, Christian communities have a historical tendency to define their identity in a sectional way. Ever since the followers of Apollos and Cephas disputed with those of Paul at Corinth in the 50s CE, religious orders, denominations, and sects have defined their closeness to Christ largely, even chiefly, in terms of their difference from their rivals. Erasmus of Rotterdam said caustically of the orders of monks and friars of his own time that "they are not interested in being like Christ, but in being unlike each other."[25]

If one is not to take an ahistorical or antihistorical view of the rise and subsistence of the Christian Church, one must take a historical view. That is, one must analyze the churches' development in relation to their contexts, and explore their evolution and change within the many and diverse human societies in which they have nestled. In the abstract, the process may be described in something like the following way. A religious movement is founded when an idea of powerful originality or arresting insight arises within a given human culture. Whether one believes in the divine origin of that insight does not, to the historian, matter too much. Anything that arises in human culture will inevitably be expressed in the language, the symbolism, and the conventions of its environment. The interaction between the idea and its context will produce a secretion, a bundle of memories, practices, and a living community that embodies these things. That secretion will nearly always crystallize into a corpus of written materials, as it certainly did in early Christianity. The writings, however, will not subsist independently of their host community and its memory. Rather, the writings will receive authentication and validity from the collective memory. Reciprocally, the memory and the community will reinforce, authenticate, and validate themselves, more and more as time progresses, by reference to the writings.

Unless a religious movement is to remain fixed and confined to one time and one culture, it must sooner or later find itself among a group of people whose language and outlook are not those of its first founders. So the distillation of the movement, including its sacred writings, its body of traditions, its customary rituals, will somehow have to accommodate itself within a different body of people with different presuppositions. A faith nourished in Palestine found itself transplanted to the sophisticated and polyvalent "tiring superculture"[26] of the Hellenistic Eastern Mediterranean. The synthesis thus created was imported in turn to late antique Rome, thence to barbarian Gaul and to other areas where the Roman Empire had disintegrated. With the transition from the early Middle Ages to the much more sophisticated, urbanized culture of high medieval Europe, another layer of thought, language, imagery, and expression was added to the Christian experience. Medieval Europe then gave way to early modernity both within Europe and beyond, in a suddenly more interconnected world. And so it has continued, and continues. Each generation, each phase in the cultural evolution of the Christian world, assimilates and incorporates the synthesis of beliefs, literature, liturgy, and structures inherited from its forbears (who in turn have done the same with *their* antecedents). By that process of assimilation, each generation in turn creates a new layer of documents, practices, and memories that become part of the Christian heritage for the generations that follow.

There are two further points to note about the transmission process. First, religion is not a merely passive recipient of influences from its host culture. On the contrary, it forms an important constituent part of that culture: it plays a major role in shaping it. Religion should be regarded as one of many participating forces, alongside kin and family structures, secular legal systems, political structures and conventions, art, literature, folk belief, and any other factors that make up the complex of referents by which human beings lead their lives. It partakes of influences from all these other factors, and in turn feeds into the forms that all these other aspects assume. When one explores the life and literature of, say, Chaucer's or Shakespeare's England, this complex of interactions is so glaringly obvious as to be a truism. However, it is all too easy to forget such complexities in trying to theorize about Church history in the abstract.

The second point to remember is that Church history is full of divergences and (more rarely) of convergences between traditions. After a breach between two branches of the Christian tradition (say between Trinitarians and Arians, East and West, Catholic and Protestant, or even between rival branches of a Protestant denomination) the reaction *against* the opposing side becomes a part of the heritage of each fragment, to be passed down as part of the collective memory and allegiance. To use the Nicene Creed is to bear witness to the rejection of Arius. To use the Heidelberg Catechism or Westminster Confession is to share in a culture that rejected medieval Catholicism (and also turned aside from strict Lutheranism). To adopt the Catechism of the Council of Trent is to inherit the rejection of all the Lutheran and reformed teachings anathematized by that Council. Anglicans who turned Foxe's *Actes and Monuments* into a quasi-official Church document were embedding in the English folk memory the sufferings of their Protestant predecessors and their allies at the hands of a persecuting Catholicism. The negative factors can become as important as the positive shared items in establishing an unfolding and dynamic tradition.

An outsider to Christianity might expect that modern-day followers of a given Christian denomination would feel some sense of embarrassment at this loading of their heritage with the material left over from old controversies. How could a faith derive support and satisfaction from the testimony to its past and (in many cases) continuing divisions? In practice, this embarrassment is more rarely expressed than might be expected. In the initial stages of a religious controversy, each side is convinced of its own rightness. To those whom hindsight declares to have taught the "correct" faith, controversy brings the vindication of truth. If the victory is complete, the movement stigmatized as "heresy" may literally die out and disappear. The teacher or confessor is thus vindicated on grounds of doctrine as well as charisma (as, for example, Augustine was viewed for most of the succeeding centuries). In a more ecumenical or at least broad-minded atmosphere, traditions tend to celebrate what is best in their leaders according to generally shared ethical standards. A theologian who may have been a ferocious, even at times vindictive, controversialist may still earn broader approval for selfless dedication, for Christian learning, for zeal for the honor of God. It is relatively easy to make figureheads even of the leaders of divided churches, if one's standards of what makes a prophetic Christian are sufficiently elastic. The Church of England does not formally "canonize" its great members from the past, but does record the "commemorations" of distinguished Christian men and women in its calendar. This has the ironic effect that the same church commemorates Thomas More (July 6), martyred in 1535 for his defense of the papal primacy over the whole Catholic Church against the claims of Henry VIII, and also William Tyndale (October 6), martyred the following year for his defense of the principles of the Lutheran Reformation and his work in translating the Bible into English.[27] The two men wrote immense and often vitriolic controversies against each other, and each would almost certainly not have regarded the other as a member of the one true Church.

Christian history must, then, be regarded as a continuously productive ferment of beliefs, ideas, and often of sincere but fervent controversies. All these have left, and will continue to leave, their substrate of residue to form part of the foundation of future ages in the life of the Church. Ordinary Christians, even unconsciously, will communicate with the primordial witness of Christianity through the filters of these past experiences, since those experiences will shape the liturgical life and the traditions of biblical interpretation and preaching in their Church. However, there is much more to be said. Christian history is not just the story of the formation and continuing evolution of traditions. It is also the story of the shifting, unstable priorities of different epochs in the Church. As the cultural forces of contemporary societies pressed on the Christian tradition, the churches responded by developing now this, now that, aspect of their witness to become the predominant aspect, the defining Christian priority. Those who study Christian history must confront this instability, which forms the theme of the next chapter.

Chapter 2

Constantly Shifting Emphases in Christian History

Means to Holiness Become Ultimate Goals

This chapter will explore how shifting sets of priorities about how to lead the Christian life have reshaped the churches over time. Beliefs about how to be a good Christian are not uniform or static. At one era, Christianity will seem to be predominantly a quest for spectacular displays of personal holiness and charisma. At another, it will urge on its people the correct performance of especially important ceremonial rites, assuming that the institutional Church binds the here and the hereafter in a great system of patronage and protection. At yet another, the Christian religion may appear as an intellectual and pedagogical exercise of immense and forbidding sophistication. Evolving patterns of Christian thought and experience always reflect the fluidity and diversity of human culture and human priorities. Each epoch in Christian history has identified a different bundle of themes and objectives as ultimately important. The chosen themes and objectives of a given epoch will somehow both reflect, but also help to shape, the cultural milieu and intellectual development of their host society.

In many cases the chosen themes first gain in importance because they are seen as especially valuable *means to an end*, as paths *towards* the ideal Christian life as it is then envisaged. The process is something like the following. If self-denial is a means to Christian perfection, if learning is a means to greater faith, if self-sacrifice represents the ultimate imitation of Christ, then let self-denial, or Christian learning, or even martyrdom be the primary target of the Christian's existence. In order to achieve Christian perfection, one raises the *means* to such perfection, those "secondary objectives" to the level of fundamental ideals.[1] If one of these putative "secondary" goals is widely accepted and single-mindedly pursued, the whole center of gravity of the Christian culture of a given age can be thrown (as it were) "off balance." One priority may grow so much in importance that other Christian imperatives – and perhaps especially the commandment to unconditional love – are relegated to insignificance or entirely forgotten. This "off-balance" quality will, in all probability, be invisible to people living through that time. They, or at least the majority, will regard their era's priorities as equivalent to "essential" Christianity: they will take their own historically bounded perspective for granted. It is only with a long and broad historical (and sometimes also geographical) angle of view that these swings in priorities can be seen at all.

One possible misunderstanding must be guarded against. This chapter does not argue that asceticism, sacramental religion, or catechesis are in any sense "bad things" or that the Church would be better off without them. All have been at various times inspirational or creative. The point is not to make a case for some bland, featureless religion that contains none of these things. It is rather that, from the historian's viewpoint, different emphases have, at various times, crowded each other out; and secondly, that when one emphasis or one attribute of Christianity is pursued to an excessive degree, the results can be extreme or sometimes even grotesque. Some observers may find this description of certain priorities as "off-balance" to be judgmental and *a priori*, as though there were a centered, "balanced" perspective from which one could pass judgment on all the "deviant" or "extravagant" manifestations of the Christian life. That is not the meaning here. The point is relativistic rather than absolute. From one perspective, another era's preferences will appear "off-balance," and vice versa. The problem is the same wherever one stands in Christian history. This chapter does not aspire to hold up to the historically informed observer a sequence of "distorted" or "unbalanced" Christianities, and then to suggest triumphantly at the end that an essential, context-free, timeless Christianity can be discerned, if only one abandon the quest for secondary aims. Rather, one should recognize that some degree of distortion, some temptation to excessive pursuit of this or that secondary objective, is an inescapable part of the Church's historical predicament. It constitutes one of the flawed, limited features of Christianity, a religion practiced by flawed, limited human beings.

It would not be difficult to turn this review of shifting priorities into a freak show of successive extravagant deviations by eccentric sects and individuals within Christian history. Since the Enlightenment, secular critics of early Christianity have pointed to St Simeon Stylites praying on his column, the Circumcelliones pursuing their violent and dangerous form of Christian extremism, or radical sects that rejected civil government, monogamy, or the wearing of clothing.[2] To enumerate the most bizarre extremes (even if those involved did not think themselves bizarre) would serve little purpose and would miss the point at issue. It must be appreciated that at various times the majority of Christian leaders and peoples, those who regarded themselves as being in the very center of gravity of substantial mass movements within the Christian Church, have leaned over in various directions towards one or another secondary objective and pursued certain selected aims as though they were, at least, the pre-eminent means to Christian living; at most, as though they were ends in themselves.

This chapter will consist of a series of thematic exploration of the shifts in emphasis and in priorities that form part of the historic Christian experience. There is no attempt here to introduce a rigid scheme of Christian chronology: one trend does not give place to another in a steady or neat sequence. Some trends belong more naturally to the early period (the ascetic ideal and the expectation of the miraculous) but remain visible in some parts of Christianity today. Others belong more naturally to the early modern or modern eras, such as the drive for mass Christian education and the building up of voluntary membership, but may be seen in a minor key at other times. These shifts in emphases and priorities will not, of course, follow the same pattern across all the churches at the same time. Moreover, at those moments in Christian history when the majority view in a given Church tends most dramatically to drift towards one extreme or one emphasis, one frequently observes a minority trend, a small contrary drift, which rebels against the majority view and tends in some respect in the other direction. The interplay between these major and minor trends forms a second theme of this analysis, which will be developed at the end of the chapter.

Asceticism: Giving Things Up for God

One of the defining notes of the preaching of Jesus was a capacity for withering sarcasm: "John [the Baptist] came neither eating nor drinking, and they say, "He has a demon"; the Son of Man came eating and drinking, and they say, "Look, a glutton and a drunkard, a friend of tax-collectors and sinners!"[3] Jesus here pointed out the inconsistency of critics who could simultaneously deride John as insane for his abstinence and denounce Jesus as wicked for his lack of abstinence. He also observed that his own lifestyle was focused on building links with other people, not on conspicuous heroic feats of self-denial.[4] And yet various passages in the New Testament could be, and have been, used to justify a lifestyle of systematic abstinence. Jesus reportedly urged his followers to abandon their possessions, family, and former lives in order to follow him in an urgent and itinerant ministry of proclamation.[5] Paul's utterances on the subject of abstinence are complex and can be interpreted in several directions. On one hand he suggested that an unmarried life of hard work and self-denial was a good thing; on the other he did not criticize those leading apostles who were married and who received material support as a reward for their preaching.[6]

For those who wished so to read the sources, there was support within the scriptural texts for the idea that a more holy life consisted in divesting oneself of goods, of wealth, of the pleasures of food and drink, of sexual relationships, and life in a stable, settled household. There might be various plausible reasons why one would undertake a life of abstinence. If one expected an imminent Second Coming and saw the need to preach the gospel as a literal emergency, then the traveling preacher must be unencumbered with everyday preoccupations. If one expected early martyrdom, it was futile and cruel to involve others in one's loss. If the Christian life was a life in the spirit, then one should rise above material and fleshly concerns. If Christ suffered for humanity, then a life of penitence and suffering might be the appropriate response. By all of these means it was possible to argue that a simple, abstemious life was more holy than one filled with the pleasures, anxieties, distractions, and commitments of ordinary people.

From these reasons and concerns there arose the instinct towards "asceticism." The term derives from a Greek word meaning "training" or "discipline," but has in the Christian tradition nearly always been understood to involve the renunciation of comforts for the sake of the religious life. The degree of renunciation, and the range of things renounced, can vary considerably. However, since those who renounce marriage (for example) commonly renounce some other things as well, it is not practical to analyze all the different forms of ascetic self-denial systematically. This section will therefore simply explore and sample some of the forms that the ascetic impulse has assumed.

There is no doubt that the instinct to renounce marriage and sexual fulfillment began to play a role in Christianity fairly early on in its history. A host of not always consistent forces contributed to this instinct. Some of the Gnostic movements of the second century took over from Greek philosophy the idea that matter and spirit were irreconcilably opposed. The spirit realm was divine, the material realm crass and even demonic. (Those who held such views generally disbelieved the incarnation, contending that Jesus merely *seemed* to have a body).[7] From that perspective anything that trapped the soul in the material and this-worldly realm had to be evil. From the Gnostics onwards one can argue, very broadly, that extreme dualist "heretics" in early Christianity denounced matter, and therefore also sex, as unquestionably evil. Marcion believed that an evil God, the God of the Old Testament, had created matter and imposed the humiliating and repulsive method of procreation on human beings, something his followers avoided at all costs.[8] Orthodox Christians – or those whom later ages deemed orthodox – would argue that the created order and everything about it was created by God and was good, and that there was nothing intrinsically evil about marriage. Nevertheless, a growing movement of Christian authors argued that while the married life might not be a positive evil, the celibate life was nevertheless more convenient, more appropriate to the spiritual person, in a word more holy.

The boundaries between the heretical and orthodox standpoints were, moreover, much less clear than that schematization suggests. To take one example, some relatively early evidence for praise of celibacy is found in the apocryphal New Testament text known as the "Acts of Paul and Thecla," which was part of a larger corpus of post-Pauline literature known to the early Fathers from the third and possibly as early as the second century. Thecla was reputedly a young girl converted by Paul's preaching, who renounced her engagement to a future husband and was sentenced to be burned. She escaped burning by a miracle and went off to follow Paul in a life of mission. At Paul's first appearance he made his priorities clear:

> After Paul had gone into the house of Onesiphorus where was great joy and bowing of knees and breaking of bread and the word of God about abstinence and the resurrection. Paul said, "Blessed are the pure in heart, for they shall see God; blessed are those who have kept the flesh chaste, for they shall become a temple of God; blessed are the continent, for God shall speak with them; blessed are those who have kept aloof from the world, for they shall be pleasing to God; blessed are those who have wives as not having them, for they shall experience God."[9]

The text skillfully weaves in passages from the Gospels and Paul's letters, but shifts the emphasis decisively towards the idea that sexual abstinence is the supreme spiritual ambition and achievement for the Christian. The pre-eminent mark of the Christian is virginity, and conversion is symbolized by, even synonymous with, the choice to renounce marriage. In other apocryphal Acts also, miraculous stories are woven around the importance of chastity. A gruesome and almost pornographic legend in the Acts of John about the Christian woman Drusiana only made moral sense if the paramount virtue, in the author's eyes, was chastity. In various other texts saints were led to martyrdom for their refusal to consent to sexual activity even with their legitimate spouses after conversion to Christianity.[10] Some of these apocryphal texts tinged with Gnostic ideas have been represented as treating women with rather greater respect than the canonical New Testament. If that is so, the price for a higher vision of the female was a much lower estimate of human sexuality.[11]

In the early fourth century the movement that became known as monasticism began to take shape. This would in due course institutionalize ascetic patterns of life and establish a number of "classic models" for life apart from the world. Since not all Christians could become ascetics, it also institutionalized the distinction between higher and lower levels of Christians, between the more perfect ascetics and the less perfect laypeople.[12] However, at the very beginning of the process the ascetic impulse was anything but institutional. In the third century, or possibly even earlier, individual Christians (often women) resolved to live as virgins, *parthenoi*, renouncing marriage and some of their dignities as members of the social elite, devoting themselves to humility, prayer, and manual work. Some of these virgins lived as the celibate companion-housekeepers of celibate priests, a state of life that carried obvious dangers of scandal and was quite widely criticized (though also widely practiced).[13]

By around 300, however, there also developed a more heroic model of the ascetic life, according to which men (and some women) left society altogether to lead solitary lives in the desert places of Egypt and Palestine. They retreated to a life of prayer, fearsome physical hardship, and (theoretical) isolation from the rest of the community. Their lifestyle was often described in terms of an almost physical struggle with demons, who would harass them and tempt them by every means possible to abandon their striving for greater perfection. In the traditional histories of asceticism, the monastic ideal is traced back to a number of heroic founder-figures: Antony of Egypt, the hermit (d. 356); Pachomius (d. 346), the founder of community or "coenobitic" monasticism, who also worked in Upper Egypt; and Shenoute (d. c. 466), the organizer of Coptic monasticism. In the middle of the fourth century a parallel movement arose in the more gentle climates of Asia Minor, through the inspiration and guidance especially of a sister and brother, Macrina (c. 327–80) and Basil of Caesarea (c. 330–79).[14] It now appears that several of these leader-figures were actually not so much the first founders as organizers and harmonizers of a much broader and more inchoate pre-existent movement of ascetic discipline. In some (though not all) cases, they introduced relative moderation into what had begun as heroic but unsustainable feats of self-mortification.[15] By the late fourth and early fifth century the ascetic movement spread to the Western Church as well. Martin of Tours (d. 397) inspired and led an ascetic movement in Gaul on the Loire valley outside the city where he became bishop. His biography, written by Sulpicius Severus, became widely known across the Christian world within a few years of its completion.[16] Melania the Elder (342–411) imported monastic practices from the Palestinian desert into Campania, outside Rome. In 415 John Cassian (360–435) arrived at Marseilles, and through his writings, the *Institutions* and the *Conferences*, made the traditions, achievements and miracles of the desert fathers known in the West.[17]

The purposes of this ascetic retreat were multiple. In a strictly religious sense, withdrawal from the world made prayer easier, and offered an approach to mystical union with the divine. It provided a context for the struggle for mastery over one's body and its "lower" physical needs and instincts. Interestingly, the Greek word *enkrateia*, often used to describe the state of mind to which ascetics aspired, meant "mastery over the body" achieved by self-discipline; but it also gave its name to a heretical movement, the "Encratite" heresy, that regarded the body as inherently evil and sinful.[18] However, non- or pre-Christian impulses also played their part in the origins of the ascetic movement. Curiously, the term *anachoresis*, meaning retreat into the wilderness, and the source of the term "anchorite" used to describe a hermit, was already used before the monastic movement arose, to describe the practice where poor farmers left their land and fled to the desert to escape the tax collectors.[19] More strikingly, in some of the accounts of the early ascetics the life of abstinence was described as "philosophical," the life removed from material cares and distractions to which the Hellenistic wise man or woman aspired. Gregory of Nyssa's life of his sister Macrina described her lifestyle as the embodiment of the "philosophical life."[20] Eustathius of Sebaste, a founder of monastic life in Asia Minor, apparently affected the wearing of the philosopher's cloak, the *peribolaion*, which his father, a bishop, thought unfitting.[21] The idea of the philosopher as ascetic dated back (for example) to Philostratus's life of the philosopher-hero Apollonius of Tyana, whom Philostratus described as unshaven, unshod, wearing simple clothing, and taking neither meat nor wine.[22]

By around 400 Augustine had more or less entrenched in Western Christianity the principle that the ideal life must entail complete sexual abstinence and self-control. It is often pointed out that Augustine did not condemn marriage comprehensively (as did the Manichaeans, whom Augustine followed in his early life but later renounced and opposed). Nevertheless, from his *Confessions* it seems clear that Augustine interpreted the passages where Paul condemned disorderly sexuality to mean that, for the Christian idealist, the perfect life must be a continent one, without physical temptations of any kind.[23] This approach was by no means unique to Augustine. Nevertheless, his and Jerome's attacks against "heretics" such as Julian of Eclanum and Jovinian helped to establish the principle that the continent and the abstinent were a clearly higher order of Christians than those who lived the lives of ordinary laypeople.[24]

In the wake of the collapse of the Roman imperial system in the West, monasteries became one of the key reservoirs in which Christian culture was preserved in early medieval Europe. Gradually the Western models associated with the rule attributed to Augustine, and the rule of Benedict (d. c. 547) who founded the model monastery at Monte Cassino, took precedence over other models and examples. The monastery of men or women was a disciplined community where Christian devotees led lives of strict abstinence but also of sustainable moderation. They ate adequate and regular but poor food, had sufficient but coarse clothing, and practiced regular prayer and physical work in rotation with sufficient (but interrupted) hours of sleep.[25] The key to the astonishing prevalence of the ascetic ideal in the medieval West was this very moderation and sustainability. Closely regulated customs and routines limited the possibilities of excess and (to some degree) the risks of laxity as well. The life of the ascetic could be enormously attractive in times where secular society was violent and brutal and the fear of judgment was constant. Inspirational founders and reformers – Odo of Cluny, Bruno, Bernard of Clairvaux, Francis, Dominic – would in wave after wave reinvigorate and subtly modify the ascetic patterns of previous generations.

The presence of an elite order of Christian ascetics helped to embody in Christian teaching the principle that some Christians are more holy than others, and that some can be trusted to be holier *on behalf of* those who were not so holy. In the Middle Ages in the West a curious tradition interpreted part of the parable of the sower (Mt. 13: 3–23; Mk. 4: 3–20; [cf. Lk. 8: 5–15]) where, in two Gospel versions, the good seed is said to bear fruit "thirtyfold, sixtyfold, and a hundredfold." According to medieval exegetical tradition, the "hundredfold" yield referred to those who lived without sin in complete virginity; "sixtyfold" referred to those who lived chastely and gave material support to the highest order of ascetics; "thirtyfold" referred to those who married to avoid fornication, kept themselves from serious sin, lived by faith and prayer, and gave as much as they could to the spiritual elite.[26] So high a value was attached to sexual abstinence that a rhetorical passage in Scripture with no obvious reference to the subject could be interpreted in such a way as to justify it.

One should not infer that sexual abstinence was always and everywhere the primary objective of Christian self-denial. At other times the focus fell on different aspects of the ascetic life. One of the most notorious disagreements in the medieval West arose between different branches of the Order of Franciscan friars over the issue of collective poverty. In the lives of Francis it was clear that Francis viewed the absolute renunciation of all possessions as the mainspring and beginning of his apostolate.[27] However, once the movement became established with conventual buildings, churches, and so forth, it became increasingly difficult to maintain the founding principle that the Order should collectively, as well as individually, own nothing whatsoever. The stricter branch, the "Spiritual" Franciscans, overcame the difficulty by vesting their property in the pope: evidently the Vicar of Christ could suffer the spiritual disadvantage of owning property which a friar could not! However, in the early fourteenth century Pope John XXII refused to continue the arrangement. A section of the Franciscans reacted to the pope's change of policy by denouncing him as the Antichrist and lapsing into what became known as the heresy of the Fraticelli.[28] Eventually the order divided into two wings, a strictly observant wing and a more moderate wing, recognized as two separate orders between 1517 and 1897.[29]

At other times different aspects of asceticism came to the fore. While the traditional lifestyle of the anchorite or hermit was not fashionable in the West (the dangers of unsupervised asceticism were too obvious), self-denial through solitude and silence retained its allure. In Carthusian monasticism, founded by St Bruno in 1084, the hermit lifestyle was given an institutional framework. In Charterhouses each monk lived in a small cell-like building with its own entirely private dwelling and miniature garden, was vowed to strict silence, devoted long hours to prayer, and met the other members of the community only for worship and for certain festival meals.[30]

So, for much of the early Church and the Middle Ages a life of self-denial was accepted almost unquestioningly as the higher and nobler form of the Christian life. According to some commentators, ascetic discipline allowed people to aspire to the angelic state, or the state of souls after the general resurrection. It allowed women to transcend their gender and become (according to the standards of the age) as spiritually exalted as their male counterparts.[31] Yet in the churches sprung from the Reformation, the ideal of a life vowed to self-denial has been largely discredited. Puritans fasted as an act of "humiliation"; some Puritans displayed anxiety about sexual activity, at least at specially holy or significant times; but despite those exceptions, the ascetic impulse was radically downgraded in the main reformed churches.[32] Partly at least, this was for theological reasons. Asceticism was (potentially) self-referential and works-righteous. It encouraged the adept (as Luther, and those who followed him, would argue) to think that he or she could acquire some surplus "merit," or deserve something special from God, by the act of heroic self-denial, especially if reinforced by a binding vow.[33] Rather than encouraging help of one's neighbor, it might lead to neglect of one's spiritually inferior neighbor in pursuit of ever-greater spiritual exaltation for oneself.

In modern centuries the monastic lifestyle has survived, and clerical celibacy continues (at least for the time being) in those churches that still insist on it.[34] However, one could not easily argue that whole communities still suppose themselves to depend on the superhuman efforts of their holy men and women to make up for their collective spiritual deficiencies. Ascetic or monastic lifestyles are matters of conscious choice for those who feel called to them and can prove their vocation. Asceticism may perhaps suit the ascetic; it is not the single highest ideal, nor the salvation of the community as a whole.[35] In the Enlightenment, moreover, secular critics deemed it "unnatural" and therefore perverse to deny human nature the gratification of needs and comforts which a provident creator had (presumably for good reason) instilled in humanity when the species arose.[36] Insofar as there is now any coherent "modern" vision of human nature, it is probably one informed by the thinking of physicians and social scientists. Human behavior is best when its instincts are "healthy" and correspond to some perceived norms. The messiness of this sort of descriptive-cum-normative thinking need not concern us here.[37] The significant point is that Christian society largely embraced an ethic of self-denial as the highest style of life for many centuries. Much of Christian society then largely ceased to be ascetic *before* it largely ceased to be Christian.

Expecting Miracles

The spectacular holiness of the ascetic has long been linked, in Christian culture, with the charisma of the miracle worker. On this issue the evidence of the New Testament was clearer and less ambiguous than in the case of asceticism. Christ worked miracles; his apostles performed them with greater or lesser degrees of success. Miracle working continued in the post-Pentecost church through the healing work of the apostles and the miraculous deliverances of Paul. It is too glib to say, as some commentators do, that in the ancient world miracles were "expected" or "normal."[38] The whole point of a miracle is (and was) that it is *abnormal*: that it defeats contemporary norms about the way that nature operates, and therefore proves the divine mission and status of the miracle worker. Even in the time of Jesus there was debate (which continued afterwards) as to whether the healing miracles were really magical illusions produced by dealing with demons: that was why Jesus was accused of exorcising demons by the power of Beelzebub (Lk. 11: 15–20). One may look for a miracle and hope that one will occur; but that expectation must be based on a belief that direct divine action is always hovering beneath the surface of routinely observed reality.

The question for the growing Church was this: how far should individuals who were not Christ, and were not the first apostles, continue to expect that they or their colleagues should work deeds of power to show their divine favor? Across the history of the early Church and the Middle Ages there was an *increasing* expectation of ever more spectacular and even bizarre miracles. Rather than gently fading away, more and more dramatic (not to say fanciful) miraculous feats were attributed to Christian saints and heroic figures. Eventually there was a collapse of confidence in such things; but not before the expectations they generated had had a major impact on Christian culture.

In the New Testament the miracle stories of Jesus, very broadly speaking, served two purposes. Some (such as his birth, the transfiguration, or the resurrection) demonstrated Jesus's unique divine status. The majority of the remainder were miracles of healing or of exorcism. In other words, miracles illustrated the compassion, the generosity, the patience of Jesus. Coincidentally they might make dogmatic points: that the love of God took priority over the ceremonial demands of the law, over the Jewish code of ritual purity, or over the distinction between the chosen people and the Gentiles. They might have an apocalyptic function: miracle working was a sign of the approaching end-times (especially in some of the sources of the Gospels). They might (especially in the Pauline corpus) serve to "build up the community" for the future rather than the end.[39] In the apocryphal New Testament writings the contrast between the canonical and the later miracle stories is very marked: it has even been suggested that these stories may have been influenced by late antique romance literature.[40] In the *Protevangelium of James*, an account of the birth of Mary and of Christ probably written in the second half of the second century, the retelling of the marvelous has already become more extravagant. The birth of the Virgin Mary was itself attended by angelic prophecies. She was presented to the temple and "received food from the hand of an angel." Joseph was chosen to be her husband by the appearance of a dove over his head. Later, when Joseph had left Mary in a cave about to give birth, he witnessed time standing still, the birds and animals frozen in mid-movement, at what is presumed to be the birth of Jesus. When a woman accompanying the midwife examined Mary internally to test her virginity, miraculously preserved after Mary gave birth, the woman's hand was consumed by fire until she touched the infant Jesus and was healed.[41]

The *Infancy Gospel of Thomas*, another apocryphal writing from the early Christian centuries, filled the childhood years of Jesus with a series of miraculous feats whose moral or theological significance was at best unclear. Aged five, Jesus created 12 sparrows out of mud on the Sabbath and made them fly away. He withered up a child who disturbed a pool he had made. A child who bumped into his shoulder promptly fell down dead. Those who accused him of being a public menace were struck blind. When at the age of six he broke a water-pot, he was able instead to carry water in his clothing. Jesus's words and wishes were so powerful that everything he said was immediately translated into fact.[42] In other writings of this period miracles could become contests for spiritual authority (as between the apostles and Simon Magus) or be used as punishment (to a far greater degree than those already seen in the canonical book of Acts).[43]

One of the most influential pieces of early Western religious biography was the *Life of St Martin of Tours*, written by his friend and follower Sulpicius Severus (c. 363–420). Martin was a formidable ascetic and charismatic bishop of the city of Tours in Gaul. His *Life* presents a series of highly dramatic miracle stories to emphasize the work of divine grace within him. Early on in his mission, he ate hellebore by accident, but recovered from the poisoning by prayer. He restored to life a catechumen who had died before baptism; he likewise resuscitated a slave who had hanged himself.[44] He temporarily paralyzed an entire funeral procession when thinking, mistakenly, that they were carrying a pagan idol. When he demanded that a tree consecrated to a pagan god be cut down, the pagans insisted on tying him down in the path of the tree as it fell. He agreed, and by making the sign of the cross caused the tree to fall away from himself and almost to crush the pagans who had felled it.[45] Pagans who tried to attack him found that they either collapsed or their weapons disappeared. More conventionally, he performed cures and exorcisms. He could always recognize the devil, even when disguised as Jesus, and even preached to him on one occasion.[46]

There was an increasing tendency to derive the miraculous power from the personal charisma of the ascetic religious leader. Moreover, miracles tended to become linked to conversion: the missionary performed a miracle to win over pagans and unbelievers. As the Roman Empire dissolved in the West, missionaries more frequently became involved in contests over supernatural power with adversaries from indigenous Germanic folk-religions. Christianity made headway as a superior form of magic.[47] One of the most interesting manifestations of the twilight of Roman Imperial culture in the West comes from the late sixth-century pope Gregory I "the Great" (born c. 540, pope 590–604). In his *Pastoral Rule* this pope displayed a highly sophisticated and urbane analysis of the mode of conduct proper to a bishop.

Yet in his *Dialogues* he displayed a credulous reception of miracle stories so naïve that some analysts have doubted whether he truly wrote the work.[48] In the second book of the *Dialogues* Gregory related the life of the founder of Western "Benedictine" monasticism, Benedict of Nursia. As a child Benedict repaired, by the power of prayer alone, a sieve which his nurse had allowed to be broken (and which was thereafter hung up as a relic at the door of the local church).[49] When he was abbot of a monastery, some disobedient monks wished to poison his wine: he made the sign of the cross towards the glass and made it break.[50] When a Goth lost the head of a farming implement in a deep pond, Benedict placed the shaft in the water and caused the metal head to rise up and join itself to the handle.[51] Benedict removed by his prayers a stone which had been blocking the enlargement of the monastery by driving away the devil who was sitting on it.[52] When a wall collapsed during building work and crushed a young monk, Benedict was able to restore him to life and health even though many bones had been broken.[53] He was gifted with prophetic insight, identifying impostors posing as Gothic kings, knowing the deeds of his monks done secretly, and generally foretelling the future. He could see the souls of the departed (including his own sister, the nun Scholastica) ascending to heaven.

One should not assume, however, that all early Church writers displayed the same intense taste for the miraculous as Sulpicius Severus or Gregory I. John Cassian provided in his *Conferences* a full and varied insight into the monastic culture of the Eastern deserts. Although aware of charismatic gifts of healing, he argued that miracle working was *not* the pre-eminent sign of holiness. "The height of perfection and blessedness does not consist in the performance of those wonderful works but in the purity of love. . . . For all those things are to pass away and be destroyed, but love is to abide for ever." Cassian advised against judging holy people by their miracles: how they conquered their own vices was a far better guide.[54] Nevertheless, even Cassian could not resist retelling a few miracle stories. Abba Macarius challenged a heretic named Eunomius to go to the tombs above the Nile and revive a corpse to show his spiritual power. When the heretic fled, Macarius briefly revived a long-dead Egyptian to prove his own authority.[55] Abba Abraham, on the other hand, achieved more commonplace miracles of restoring lactation to a mother unable to give suck, and curing a man who was lame.[56]

In the high and later Middle Ages the collecting of miracle stories became a recognized and standard activity within the Church. The classic collection of such tales was the *Dialogue of Visions and Miracles* collected by the Cistercian monk Caesarius of Heisterbach (c. 1170–1240).[57] It was most successful in its time: at least 50 manuscripts survive, and it remains an important guide to thirteenth-century culture and attitudes. Even more successful was the *Golden Legend*, compiled by Jacopo de Voragine (c.1230–c.1298). This work, which was published in over 70 editions in the first 50 years of printing alone, served as an encyclopedia for the hagiography and the associated stories of visions and miracles that had accumulated up to the time of its compilation in the West.[58] Nor did the tradition die down as the Middle Ages came to their end. The Dominican friar Johannes Nider (1380–1438) gathered in his "Formicarius" or "Book of the Ants" a sequence of stories about the manifestations of holiness found in the marvelous workings of supernatural providence.[59] In England, John Mirk or Myrc (fl. c. 1403) produced in the *Festival* or *Festial* a collection of specimen sermons for the feast days of the Church's calendar year, including the anniversary celebrations of many saints. It was issued in multiple Latin and English editions on the eve of the Reformation. Mirk included in his account one of the most fantastic of miracle stories, even (one would imagine) to medieval ears. A devout virgin named Winifred was assaulted by a Welsh prince named Caradoc who, when she would not consent to sex with him, beheaded her. St Beuno, who was close by, picked up the body and the head and took them into church, where he said mass and preached. He then prayed for Winifred to recover: the head and body rejoined and she revived. She then led a long career as a nun.[60]

It will be clear by now that for the first 15 centuries or so the Church lived with the regular expectation that outstanding holiness would be manifested, more or less often, in spectacular displays of supernatural power. The most extreme and graphic displays of this credulity are less important than the general expectation of the miraculous that suffused Christian culture as a whole. Then, in the Reformation era, there was a fairly abrupt change of gear. In the early years of the Reformation movement, groups of people in the relatively sophisticated culture of Swiss and German cities began to draw sharp distinctions between the gospel on onehand, and the "fables" of human invention regularly used by the older style of preachers on the other. It was precisely the indiscriminate credulity of the older sermon literature that discredited it in their eyes.[61] The taste for the supernatural did not disappear immediately, by any means. Indeed, some modern scholars have taken great pains to demonstrate that images of Martin Luther, or Protestant Bibles, might be ascribed the same miraculous preservation from destruction as medieval eucharistic wafers or holy relics.[62]

Notwithstanding these signs of continuity, the expectation of the miraculous fell sharply out of favor among the shapers of opinion in the reformed churches. Catholic propagandists urged that the possession of miraculous gifts (such as exorcism, or the cure of possessed people) proved that Catholicism was the authentic form of Christianity. Protestant apologists replied that such "spiritual gifts" were just another form of demonic magic, and proved the wrongness, not the rightness, of the Catholic Church. According to the great Puritan pastoral theologian William Perkins, among others, the power to exorcise had been an exceptional, miraculous gift. It was given by God directly to buttress the faith in the early days of the Church, and was not based on the use of any specific forms of words. When "Popery that mystery of iniquitie beginning to spring up, and to dilate itself in the Churches of Europe, the true gift of working miracles then ceased; and instead thereof came in delusions, and lying wonders, by the effectual working of Satan... Of which sort were and are all those miracles of the Romish Church."[63]

As a result of this historic divergence, the churches in the West now live, in theory, with two contradictory notions of the workings of the cosmos. In the mainstream reformed tradition it is conventional to regard the laws of nature as, for all practical purposes, firmly set. Indeed, Christian thinkers in the seventeenth and eighteenth centuries played a significant part in discouraging expectation of the miraculous. They argued that the very perfection and balance of those natural laws demonstrated the supreme skill of the divine architect and engineer who had devised them, better than any arbitrary subversion of those laws.[64] Opinions about the biblical miracles diverge: modern exegetical and scholarly interest will explore them as part of their wider cultural context. Many commentators are less concerned with whether they "really" happened or can be "explained" in some allegedly rational manner. The resurrection of Jesus may (or in some cases may not) be privileged as a unique and incommensurable occurrence. What matters is that day-to-day miracles are no longer expected to confront ordinary people. On the other hand, the official view of the Roman Catholic hierarchy is that miracles do continue to occur within the Catholic tradition. Vatican officials investigate and, as appropriate, either authenticate or disprove miraculous cures, visions, and other supernatural manifestations. The canonization process has long required the careful inspection of alleged miracles as part of the means to prove sainthood.[65]

In practice the state of affairs is much more confused. On the margins of the Protestant churches, and sometimes at their hearts, one finds those who believe that charismatic miracles of healing can and should be performed. In some forms of Pentecostalism such healing may appear a relatively routine matter. Most notoriously, from the early 1990s the evangelist Morris Cerullo has claimed to perform healing miracles in prodigious numbers within mass meetings.[66] A book and series of videotapes entitled *A Course in Miracles*, distributed from the "Miracles Communication Center" in Lake

Delton, WI, USA, has achieved phenomenal success. Its publications include a "Miracle Healers Handbook": this conveys the impression that miraculous healing is not a particular gift reserved to special individuals, but a technique accessible to all (though it also blurs the lines between objective "healing" and psychological readjustment to one's predicament).[67] On the other side, many in the Roman Catholic hierarchy and intelligentsia are vastly more skeptical and rationalistic than their medieval forbears, and some of their modern congregations. The greater religious freedom – not to say chaos – of the modern era has made it possible for localized cults of miraculous statues, miraculous visions, as well as healing at sacred shrines to burst the confines set by the hierarchy of the Church.[68] Whereas in the early Church miraculous charisma was the preserve of the specially exalted holy man or woman, it has (somewhat like asceticism) become a more marginal but also more diffuse phenomenon, a matter of personal belief and personal choice.

Martyrdom

Jesus continued his healing and teaching ministry even when threatened, and confronted rival teachers at the cost of his own life. The accounts of the Passion show Jesus consciously heading towards his fate, renouncing all opportunities to escape it. Relatively early in Church history, his death was seen as sacrificial, as expiatory, as profoundly meaningful in cosmic history. The Christian churches have generally abstained from trying to impose one interpretation of the mystery of the Cross, one theology of the atonement, upon believers. However, one byproduct of focus on the Cross is that Christian discipleship, the imitation of Christ, can potentially be seen as involving, even requiring, the sacrifice of one's own life. References in the Gospels to "taking up one's cross" to follow Jesus can be read literally as well as metaphorically. At various stages in the history of the Church, the willingness to court death for the faith has assumed far greater prominence than at others. One point must be clarified here. In many epochs – even the present – Christian believers might be ready to *risk* death when challenged to renounce values they held dear, or to betray fellow-believers. The "cult of martyrdom" in its more radical form, however, means more than this. It means that martyrdom is seen as the *normal, even the necessary* path towards salvation for the Christian. A committed believer will go out of his or her way to encounter martyrdom, even to seek it as a conscious choice. That attitude, that cult, can be discerned claiming a dominant place at some specific points in Christian history.

Contrary to popular tradition, the first three centuries of Christianity were not times of steady or consistent persecution. Persecution was sporadic, intermittent, and mostly local. It usually attacked those who refused to participate in the officially sponsored cult of the emperor's divinity. Those Christians (including some Gnostics) who consented to participate merely formally in the cult of the emperor could escape punishment.[69] The majority of those who would later be deemed "orthodox" Christians, as well as some heretics, however, would insist on affirming their faith and accepting the consequences. There were disturbing potentialities to this attitude. Ignatius of Antioch, martyred some time around 110 CE, affords a complex example. Although he did not in any sense "offer" himself for martyrdom, his surviving letters refer to a "lust for death" and enumerate in gruesome detail the physical tortures which he expected to suffer. He apparently asked the Christians in Rome, where he was to be executed, to do nothing to save him.[70] It has been suggested that these early Christians were inspired by the stories in the Four Books of Maccabees (part of the "apocryphal" or "deuterocanonical" text of the Old Testament), in which the defenders of the Jewish inheritance offer themselves up to suffer appalling torments and death rather than renounce their beliefs.[71]

According to Tertullian, who embraced the rigorist and apocalyptic movement known as "Montanism" late in his life, its founder, a Phrygian called Montanus, positively encouraged his followers to seek martyrdom.[72] There is a fine line here between the reckless and obstinate admission of one's Christian faith under questioning, and something approaching voluntary suicide in time of persecution. In his work *Ad Scapulam* Tertullian described how, around 185 CE, all the Christians of a town in Asia presented themselves to the Proconsul Arrius Antoninus and demanded the privilege of martyrdom. The Roman official told most of them that if they wished to die, they could hang themselves or throw themselves from precipices.[73] According to the Church historian Eusebius, the young Origen (c. 185–c. 254) was so passionately determined to become a martyr that he was only prevented from offering himself to the persecutors when his mother hid all his clothes and so forced him to remain indoors.[74] In the story of Alban, traditionally believed martyred in Britain c. 305 (but possibly a century or so earlier), Alban voluntarily takes the place of a priest whom he has been concealing at his house, and is sentenced to death. On his way to execution he comes to a stream, and prays that it will dry up to allow him to reach the place of execution more quickly, which it does. His appointed executioner there and then also declares himself a convert and suffers the same fate.[75] During the Great Persecution of the 300s, more and more Christian people, including the young, voluntarily presented themselves to the authorities to affirm their

Christianity in the desire and expectation that they would be martyred.[76] Often the Fathers and bishops of the Church warned against the rash courting or soliciting of martyrdom, and even suggested that people who behaved thus should not be included in the martyrologies. Nevertheless, the fierceness of their protests, and the evidence of some of the accounts of the martyrs themselves, argues that many people (especially the Montanists) did in fact behave in such a way.[77]

For much of the Western Middle Ages after Constantine martyrdom was simply not an issue. However, Christian minorities found themselves facing martyrdom at the hands of other Christians, occasionally in the medieval period and much more frequently thereafter. Those who obstinately or repeatedly confessed to holding heretical opinions could find themselves sentenced to death under inquisitional tribunals from the 1230s onwards. Before that date a combination of lynch law and crusade had cut swathes through the Albigensian or "Cathar" population of the Languedoc.[78] In the main, those who belonged to durable and persistent heretical movements, especially those known as Waldenses, did not court martyrdom at all. Their traveling friar-like teachers and confessors avoided capture at all costs, and ordinary believers would routinely renounce their heresy and admit its wrongness at ecclesiastical tribunals.[79] By this means the numbers executed for heresy in the medieval period were, in most periods and circumstances, relatively low. The somewhat frantic persecution of Christian converts who had allegedly relapsed to Jewish or Muslim practices, carried out under the structured Office of the Inquisition established in Spain in the late 1470s and early 1480s, was horrendous to many observers, even at the time; but it was by no means typical of the Middle Ages as a whole.[80]

With the Reformation, martyrdom once again became a possibility, though not in all places equally. Generally speaking, Lutheran states reformed in a body, and only small numbers of ordinary Protestants faced legal penalties, usually isolated individuals like William Tyndale or Patrick Hamilton. The leaders of the Lutheran churches, especially Philipp Melanchthon, worked hard to achieve compromise with Catholic powers and the Empire, specifically to save the lives of their ordinary congregations. Those who embraced reformed "Calvinist" Protestantism later in the sixteenth century, however, and Anabaptists of all periods, were often minority communities in the midst of persecution. A chance encounter with a persecutor, a change of route or a change of regime, might and often did bring book-peddlers or traveling preachers into court. Followers of the reformed faith considered that their Christianity consisted so fundamentally in affirmations of belief and doctrine, that to renounce those beliefs was unthinkable. So the inquisitors and ecclesiastical judges, whose forbears had been called into existence to extort confessions from the reluctant, were now confronted with large numbers of defiant and obstinate dissenters.

Did a martyr-cult develop among such people? The evidence is mixed. There was, especially in Italy and France, much discussion of the alternatives to potentially suicidal public witness. Another option was to wait out the time of persecution while hiding one's beliefs and conforming to the officially enforced cult. It is impossible to know how many people took this attitude. Such an approach, known as "Nicodemism," elicited some scathing criticisms from John Calvin; but his favored alternative was exile to another country rather than self-immolating martyrdom.[81] On the other hand, the reformed churches (and Catholicism where it was a persecuted minority, as in England) rapidly took up the custom of commemorating and celebrating those who bravely faced death for their beliefs. The reformed churches produced their "martyrologies": Crespin for the French martyrs, van Haemstede for those of the Netherlands, and above all John Foxe's *Actes and Monuments* for those of England and Scotland. Each branch of the reformed Church to some degree celebrated the martyrs of the others, so a common consciousness and a sense of common cause grew up between these geographically scattered movements. The scale and quantity of these testimonies have led some recent scholars to suggest that every reformed Protestant, and every Anabaptist, was a potential martyr; that martyrdom was an intrinsic part of the career of an adherent to these movements.[82]

However, one should beware of insisting that martyrdom became *the supreme* mark of Christianity for such people. It was faith, not the suffering, that made the martyr; and in any case, salvation was sought from divine grace, not through acts of self-immolation. Even so, there are disturbing moments recounted even in the mainstream Protestant martyrologies. Take the following story from the very end of the persecution of English Protestants under Mary I Tudor:

> At what time the seven last burnt at Smithfield...were condemned and brought to the stake to suffer, came down in the name of the King and Queen a proclamation...commanding that no man should either pray for them, or speak to them, or once say, God help them. It was appointed before, of the godly there standing together, which was a great multitude, that so soon as the prisoners should be brought, they should go to them to embrace and comfort them; and so they did. For as the said martyrs were coming towards the place in the people's sight, being brought with bills and glaves as the custom is, the godly multitude and congregation with a general sway made towards the prisoners, in such manner that the billmen and the other officers, being all thrust back, could nothing do, nor any thing come nigh. So the godly people meeting and embracing, and kissing them, *brought them in*

their arms (which might as easily have conveyed them clean away) to the place where they should suffer.... Master [Thomas] Bentham, the minister then of the congregation, ... as zeal and Christian charity moved him, and seeing the fire set to them, turning his eyes to the people, cried and said, "We know they are the people of God, and therefore we cannot but wish well to them, and say, God strengthen them!" With that all the people with a whole consent and one voice followed and said "Amen, Amen!" The noise whereof was so great, and the cries thereof so many, that the officers could not tell what to say, or whom to accuse.[83]

John Foxe here appears unaware of the extraordinary effect that this scene produces. The supporters of the martyrs mob the officers carrying out the execution. The martyrs could easily have escaped, but instead they are brought to the stake to be burned and (presumably) accept their fate in the exalted atmosphere of the moment. The whole congregation then deliberately frustrates the resolve of officialdom to prevent a public declaration of support for the victims.

For clear evidence of a general, conscious, and consistent courting of martyrdom, one can turn to the records of the Anabaptist movement in the sixteenth century. Since these people disavowed all public office holding and envisaged the church as a gathering of elect believers, they were always a minority, nearly always in danger. Yet the interrogations of several such people from 1529, as recorded in the *Hutterite Chronicle*, show a suicidal boldness in admitting their beliefs and facing the consequences, among very ordinary men and women of no particular education or spiritual authority in the movement. One typical captured Anabaptist "said that the priests practice idolatry in the morning and commit fornication in the afternoon. What he confessed with his mouth he wanted to witness to with his blood; he would not renounce his faith but remain true to it until the end."[84] A man by the name of Georg Baumann was imprisoned at Bauschlet in Württemberg and tortured until he made a recantation. Asked to repeat his recantation a third time in public,

He told the priests and their assistants, "You scoundrels! You got the upper hand: you tortured and plagued me until I agreed to give up my faith and follow you. But now I am sorry I did it, and I repudiate it all." ... They immediately seized him again and sentenced him to death. He sang joyfully as they led him to the place of execution. It was very muddy in the village. His shoes got stuck in the mud but he walked straight ahead, leaving them behind, and hurried to the execution place, singing for joy that God had again given him such courage. And so he was beheaded.[85]

It seems clear, even allowing for the hagiographic gloss peculiar to martyrologies, that among these Anabaptists martyrdom had become an integral part of their witness. Two Anabaptists, Hans Denck and Hans Hut, argued that there were three crucial conversion experiences in a Christian's life: inner conversion, external baptism, and the final testimony in blood, by martyrdom.[86]

Since the early modern period there have been occasional instances where missionaries in far-flung parts of the world have risked and sometimes lost their lives in seeking to introduce Christianity to very different cultures. On the whole these episodes are more likely to be lamented as unfortunate miscalculations and misunderstandings than lauded as a means to salvation for the victims. Occasionally missionaries would display a lack of calculation which appears to suggest excessive risk-taking, even an expectation of self-sacrifice. For instance, the traditional narrative of the so-called five Jesuit martyrs killed at the village of Cuncolim near Goa, in India, on July 25, 1583, contains such elements. Of the Portuguese Antonio Francisco, it was said "that whenever he said Mass, he prayed, at the Elevation, for the grace of martyrdom; and that on the day before his death, when he was saying Mass at the church of Orlim, a miracle prefigured the granting of this prayer." The five missionaries went to try to bring about the destruction of a Hindu temple, and were massacred by the crowd. Their bodies were thrown into a well, which thereafter acquired healing powers; when the bodies were recovered a few days later they had not decomposed.[87]

In the modern era the rise of totalitarianisms of the right and the left, and the arrogant claims of secular movements to total domination over the minds and bodies of their subjects, have greatly increased the numbers of those who have suffered because of their principled resistance to arbitrary and godless authority. However, the numbers of simple innocent victims, rather than deliberate martyrs to conscience, immolated in the Holocaust and in modern mechanized warfare, vastly eclipse them. Interfaith conversations make the death of one believer at the hands of another a subject for grief rather than glory. So the modern parallels to the past cults of martyrs are really not very close. Dietrich Bonhoeffer, Martin Luther King, Jerzy Popieluszko, and Oscar Romero are rightly commemorated for their principled resistance to moral evils – as are other such people of many faiths. They will not, however, generate or form part of a "martyr cult" in the traditional sense. They and their contemporaries would have agreed that there were many forms of Christian witness, not all as ultimately costly. Most Christians would not draw conclusions about their eternal destiny from the particular manner of their deaths, seek their intercession with God, or try to imitate their particular paths. The assumptions fundamental to the old martyr-cults, including absolute certainty of the truth of one embattled creed over all its adversaries, have passed away.

Sacrament and Sacrifice: the Eucharistic Church

Asceticism, miracle working, and martyrdom belong to a style of Christian discipleship that one might call heroic. These manifestations of Christian idealism are typically the achievements of exceptional individuals and charismatic figures. Such things were prominent especially, though not exclusively, in the early centuries of Christianity. By the high Middle Ages in the West, the concept of the Church as a coherent entity, indeed as an institution, had grown vastly. The power of God naturally seemed inherent in things rather than people. In these conditions one observes a different kind of charism arising in the Church. Rituals, consecrated objects, places, and institutions, become vested with particularly high proportions of the power and presence of an omnipotent and omnipresent God. This kind of holiness does not depend on the strength or weakness of individuals. While saints may – and do – continue to appear, it is not necessary to depend on their appearance. The holiness of the Church can manifest itself in things purer, cleaner, and simpler than a fallible person. This transference of holiness from persons to things was, incidentally, reflected in important changes in the way that Church history was written, as will be seen later.[88]

The strongest evidence for this trend lies in the place occupied by the Eucharist in the life of the Church. It may seem grotesque at this point to suggest that the Eucharist could ever be a "distortion" of the Christian message. The Eucharist is, after all, the supreme Christian ritual, the re-enactment of both the Last Supper and Calvary, the embodiment of the Christian community in a collective action of great symbolic power. It is important therefore to be clear about the purpose of this section. At certain critical stages in the history of the Church the Eucharist has become, as it were, a holy thing to be venerated and cultivated in itself and for itself. The means of access to God has become something divine. By dwelling on such a potent and essential symbol, the Church fostered a confusion or mingling of the attributes of the sign and the thing that it represented. This suggestion (though hardly new in Christian theology) will not win general assent. It may, however, be illustrated by what follows.

The earliest Christian gatherings included literal meals. In I Corinthians, Paul describes scandals caused in Corinth when different groups of believers brought their own food to feasts and reserved it to small cliques, leaving others to go hungry. In the context of denouncing this abuse, Paul wrote the earliest written description of the Last Supper as a shared communion.[89] However, within fairly few decades the eating part of the Eucharist became vestigial, and the ritual assumed priority. Thereafter the first five or six centuries of Christian worship were characterized by the progressive elaboration of the eucharistic ritual. This is not a point of contention between Protestants and Catholics: the fact that the ritual grew over time is agreed.[90] The only dispute has been over whether that growth was a good thing or not.

By the Middle Ages, certain elements had established themselves in the rite, and continue to this day in the Roman Catholic and Anglican/Episcopalian traditions. These elements coalesced into a bewildering variety of local and provincial customs, which were not standardized until the drives towards liturgical uniformity in the second half of the sixteenth century. Broadly speaking, the first part of a Eucharist consisted of a greeting, general confession and absolution (normally using the Greek formula *Kyrie eleison, Christe eleison, Kyrie eleison*), and/or the hymn *Gloria in excelsis*, a "collect" seasonal prayer, then readings from the Epistles and Gospels, followed by a homily or sermon. In the second part of the liturgy, the Niceno-Constantinopolitan creed was said (though the form used in the West does not follow exactly the text laid down by either of these Church Councils). Then a "secret" prayer began the consecration, followed by the canticle "Sanctus" and the "canon" or prayer of consecration and oblation. Prayers were offered for the departed, the canticle "Agnus Dei" was said or sung, and the communion was distributed. Before or after distribution the Lord's Prayer was said and the peace was passed around (in the Middle Ages, in the form of a "pax" board to be kissed). After ritual ablutions the congregation was dismissed.[91] These were the main elements. Frequently there was some variation in their order. Other materials would be added or deleted according to the seasons.

Because of the perceived holiness of communion, there has been a historic tendency to restrict, rather than to make universal, lay sharing in the elements of bread and (especially) wine. In the high Middle Ages, only those who had made a prior full private confession of their sins, received absolution and done penance were normally allowed to receive the Eucharist (though the relationship between absolution and communion could be more complicated). Those who were in feud with their neighbors sometimes refused to communicate with them.[92] Full communion in some of the reformed congregations required full "membership" of the church, only attainable after formidable catechetical tests.[93] In the Middle Ages, the difficulty of communicating meant that the vast majority of ordinary laypeople took communion only at the Easter season. A minority might communicate also at Christmas, and members of exceptionally devout confraternities perhaps four times in the year in total. However, this did not mean that other noneucharistic services were held at other times. The regular and usual Church worship attended by most Christians was the Eucharist (or the mass, as it became increasingly known in the West). Simply, most people came only to watch and pray (at best): they did not receive the bread and wine. The rite originally devised as an embodiment of communion through shared eating and drinking had become a sacred spectacle merely to be observed.

Yet the power of medieval Christianity rested overwhelmingly on the vast strength of popular devotion to the Eucharist. That devotion continued even though (perhaps because) this supremely holy thing was removed from regular participation by the congregants. The holiness of the Eucharist at its height consisted in two things: the belief in the real physical presence of the body of the resurrected Christ in the consecrated bread and wine, and the belief that the Eucharist was a "sacrifice" from which flowed specific, even measurable, benefits for souls living and dead. By means of these two beliefs the Eucharist rose to quasi-divine status. In a certain sense it "was" God; its performance remedied the consequences of sin and restored the souls of sinners.

The eucharistic presence derived from a literal reading of the words of Christ at the institution: "this is my body." The medieval and early modern West was peculiar in Christian history for the persistence with which it pursued the meaning of this phrase. Paschasius Radbertus of Corbie (c. 790–860) wrote the first theological monograph on the Eucharist, *On the Body and Blood of the Lord*, in the 830s. He insisted that the body of Christ in the Eucharist was absolutely and literally the same body with which Christ lived, died, and rose again. This implied that at every consecration a miracle took place, in which the finite body of Jesus was multiplied and proliferated *ad infinitum*. The "emphatic literalism" of Paschasius provoked a speedy response from Ratramnus (also of Corbie) and Rabanus Maurus, who both urged a more spiritual and more symbolic understanding of Christ's words.[94] The debate flared up once again in the eleventh century, when Berengar of Tours (c. 1010–88) argued that it was not necessary to invoke a material change in the eucharistic bread and wine to explain the presence of Christ. He in turn provoked hostile verdicts from three Church councils under three popes, and rebuttals from a range of theologians, most famously Lanfranc of Bec (c. 1010–89). The tide had by now turned in favor of a literal understanding of eucharistic presence.[95]

By the late twelfth century Aristotelian philosophy tried to explain how the "miracle" happened. In consecration the "substances," the essential material, of bread and wine, were physically transformed into, or (in some accounts) annihilated and replaced by the "substance" of the body and blood of Jesus. However, the "accidents" or "species," the attributes of bread and wine accessible to the senses such as taste, color, texture, and so forth, remained unaltered. This, put simply, is the meaning of the term "transubstantiation" (literally the transformation of substances). It was decreed to be Catholic doctrine in the Fourth Lateran Council in 1215 and articulated in Thomas Aquinas's *Summa Theologica* some 50 years later.[96] It did not go entirely unchallenged in the Middle Ages. The Oxford theologian John Wyclif (d. 1384) argued that the idea of accidents or species existing separated from their essences was logically absurd.[97] Nevertheless, the real presence had a quite dramatic effect on popular piety. When the priest, after consecration, raised the eucharistic wafer above his head to be seen by the entire congregation, laypeople could look at God – literally. Someone who saw the Eucharist was safe from dying suddenly, that is, without absolution, for the rest of the day. In effect, seeing mass every day could save one from ultimate damnation. One need not necessarily attend the full mass. The eucharistic wafer was displayed in a monstrance, a stand topped by a glass container shaped to include the Eucharist, and usually surrounded by a sunburst of rays issuing forth from it in gold or silver. The bread of the Last Supper was thus turned into a talisman, the mere seeing of which conferred physical and spiritual benefits.

The folk-tales and specimen sermons of high medieval Europe abounded in stories to illustrate the miraculous and mysterious holiness inherent in the eucharistic wafer or "host" (from Latin *hostia*, meaning sacrificial victim). A demon who possessed a young nun explained why an older woman had been assaulted by demons for many years: she had taken a eucharistic host and crumbled it over her vegetables to make them grow.[98] When a bee-keeper placed a eucharistic host in his beehive to make the hives more productive, the bees instead built a little church in the hive out of honeycomb and venerated the host there.[99] The most common tales, however, had to do with personal appearances by Jesus during mass. In the most common later medieval version, a priest questioned the real presence before celebrating mass with Pope Gregory I. Gregory prayed for a divine demonstration, and Jesus appeared on the altar surrounded by all the attributes of the Passion at the moment of consecration.[100] When in 1383 the field-chapel at Wilsnack, in Saxony, burned down, three eucharistic hosts were discovered intact among the ruins. These wafers were venerated as relics, and when exhibited in the rebuilt chapel they occasionally shed drops of blood. Wilsnack attracted vast hordes of pilgrims in the fifteenth century (and a small number of imitator shrines elsewhere).[101]

In the middle of the thirteenth century the Eucharist actually acquired its own festival. In 1246 a bishop of Liege instituted a special devotion to the *Corpus Christi*, or Body of Christ. After some false starts, the festival became general in the West from the early fourteenth century, and settled on the Thursday after Trinity Sunday. Lay guilds or brotherhoods grew up to maintain the cult and to hold religious dramas. Typically the festival was marked by a parade in which the consecrated wafer was carried in procession through the community, displayed in a monstrance and covered by a pillared canopy like that of a sovereign on a progress.[102] Some of the pressure to further Corpus Christi festivals arose because bishops were keen to "domesticate" eucharistic devotion, and provide an alternative to laypeople traveling the countryside in vast numbers to visit shrines like Wilsnack.[103]

The belief in Christ's physical presence was, however, only a part of the significance of the Eucharist to the Church. The Supper was understood to commemorate and embody not only the meal of Maundy Thursday, but also the sacrifice of Christ on Good Friday. Over the course of time theologians began to use the language of "sacrifice," more and more precisely and constructively, to describe what happened in the Eucharist. In the early centuries, the Eucharist was just one of many "sacrifices" or offerings, including prayer and almsgiving, that a Christian might offer.[104] Cyprian of Carthage (d. 258) argued more closely: "that priest truly discharges the office of Christ who imitates that which Christ did; and then he offers a true and full sacrifice in the church to God the Father when he proceeds to offer it."[105] Some 150 years later, Augustine could write, in language that would be echoed centuries later in Western Church councils: "Thus He [Jesus Christ] is both the Priest who offers and the Sacrifice offered. And He designed that there should be a daily sign of this in the sacrifice of the church, which, being His body, learns to offer herself through Him."[106] Subtly and by gradual degrees, the belief grew that in celebrating the Eucharist, the priest and the Church were so to speak offering Christ symbolically to God the Father, and therefore making the benefits of the Passion available to humanity. Gregory the Great reported seeing in a vision that by celebrating 30 masses for the soul of a departed brother he had helped the brother to fare better in the hereafter.[107]

However, nothing in the Fathers or the early Church prepared Christendom for the veritable explosion in sacrificial Eucharists that occurred in the later Middle Ages in Western Europe. Although the belief was not officially decreed for the whole Church, it was generally agreed that since more masses meant more devotion and more love, then the more masses said, the better for the soul for whom they were celebrated.[108] So the numbers of masses said, of the priests saying them, and of the altars where they were celebrated, all increased enormously in the fourteenth and fifteenth centuries. The story from Gregory I about the virtue of 30 masses inspired the celebration of the "trental," a cycle of 30 masses said on particular days of the year with special prayers.[109] For the very wealthiest, it became the ultimate status symbol to endow a "perpetual chantry," where the endowment was supposedly sufficient to fund the saying of masses for the soul for the rest of time. Some schools and colleges owed their foundation to this bloated display of postmortem piety.[110] Not only was the mass applied as a general spiritual preservative; it was also used as a specific cure for social ills. Mass-books might include masses dedicated to particular saints to guard against particular evils. An English example included the following rubric:

> A Mass to turn away pestilence, which our Lord the Pope Clement [VI, pope 1342–52] composed, and ordained in college with all the cardinals . . . All who hear the following mass ought to carry a single burning candle in their hand through the five days following, and to hold it in their hand throughout the whole of the mass, themselves kneeling, and sudden death shall not be able to hurt them. This is certain, and has been proved at Avignon and in the surrounding neighboring parts.[111]

This elaboration of sacrificial Eucharistic piety was blown away in the early years of the Reformation. The reformers attacked what they called "private masses" and the idea that such "good works" earned merit at God's hand on theological as well as ethical grounds.[112] More subtly and with less noise, Roman Catholicism refocused its attention on the moral disposition of the penitent rather than the sheer quantity of ritual celebrated to help the soul. As a result, much of the mystique and (one might say) the accumulated magic of the Eucharist has been stripped away. As the preparatory rituals have simplified, congregational Eucharistic communion services now occupy center stage in the Anglican tradition and in much of Roman Catholicism. It would be easy to assume that, because the words and structure of the Eucharistic liturgy are ancient and traditional, the modern congregational Eucharist, celebrated weekly in the common tongue to a self-selecting, unscrutinized, and voluntary group of communicants, has ever been thus. Even those of us who find that form of worship highly congenial and appropriate dare not allow ourselves to be so mistaken. It is truly a most recent phenomenon.

The Company of Heaven: the Communion of Saints

While the life, the message, and the meaning of Jesus were in truth always at the heart of the ministry of the Christian Church, the power of Jesus could

be discerned and routed through a diverse variety of channels and manifestations. It has already been seen that the followers and imitators of Jesus
could perform feats of self-denial to compare with (or exceed) Jesus's 40
days' fasting in the desert, and supposedly perform miracles to compare with
(or exceed) Jesus's miracles of healing. The logical extension of this belief
was the rise of the communion of saints and the veneration of those
esteemed as saints. Christianity is not polytheistic (although some secular
commentators have from time to time so described it). There is a clear
difference in all mainstream Christian thought between the power of God
incarnate in Jesus Christ and the grace of God manifested in the work and
witness of human beings.[113] Nevertheless, the communion of saints established for early and medieval Christianity a body of invisible patrons,
protectors, intercessors, and fellow-worshipers that was sublimely immune
from fault or discredit. It allowed the holiness that would otherwise have
focused solely on one figure and one story to become dispersed and
multiplied into many stories, around which the cultural identity of different
peoples and congregations could grow.

The first people perceived as "saints" in the Church were the early
martyrs. Heroic self-sacrifice for the name of Christ implied that one was
one of the elect, and inspired commemoration and imitation. The contemporary account of the martyrdom of Polycarp of Smyrna, who was burned
to death at a pagan festival in Asia Minor around the middle of the second
century, already contains many themes that would become standard in the
later devotion to saints:

> And so we afterwards gathered up his bones, which were more valuable than
> precious stones and more to be esteemed than gold, and laid them in a
> suitable place. There the Lord will permit us to come together as we are
> able, in gladness and joy to celebrate the birthday of his martyrdom, for the
> commemoration of those who have already fought and for the training and
> preparation of those who shall hereafter do the same.[114]

The gathering and conservation of relics, the commemoration of the
anniversary, and the stimulus to imitation would all in later years become
elements in saint-cults. This cult entailed some important and dramatic
changes of emphasis from previous classical practice. In pagan antiquity
and in pagan philosophy the dead body was of little significance: what
mattered was that the soul be emancipated from its material prison. Rest-
ing-places for the dead were kept separate from the habitations of the living.
In contrast, the Christian cult of saints would derive continuing powerful
holiness from the physical, material remains. The shrines, which were also

graves, would in consequence foster and encourage the building of places of worship for the living among, over, and around the bodies of the dead.[115]

The cult of the relics of the martyrs posed, initially, a challenge to the authority of bishops in the early Church. The physical remains of the martyrs were the property of their families and descendants. However, as wealthy and devout individuals came to collect larger numbers of relics of saints, there was a risk that the shrines of martyrs would become alternate foci of worship and miracle-working outside the control and authority of the bishops. During the fourth and fifth centuries in the West bishops such as Augustine, and above all Ambrose of Milan, who discovered and translated the remains of Gervasius and Protasius, succeeded in vindicating episcopal control over the cult of saints.[116] They did this by, quite literally, seizing and translating their relics, then enshrining those relics with glorious spectacle in richly ornamented churches. They established the identity of the episcopal see with its saintly patron. Rome, of course, became supremely identified with Peter and Paul. Tours became identified with St Martin, Milan with Gervasius and Protasius, then later with Ambrose himself. As will be seen later, the monks of Bury St Edmunds regarded themselves as the literal embodiment of their Saxon martyr-king Edmund.[117] Saints became the localized and specific expressions of the divine. To participate in their holiness one had either to move the relics, or travel on pilgrimage to the shrine. Both things happened, very often. The Renaissance Pope Pius II, whose attitude to churchmen of his own time was thoroughly cynical, could still receive a relic of St Andrew to Rome with unalloyed enthusiasm and sumptuous ceremonial.[118]

So, what were saints for? They became infinitely more than just examples of heroic virtue to be imitated. First of all, they became patrons, more individual and less universal than Jesus. The ascetic Paulinus of Nola venerated his patron St Felix as a powerful but invisible friend, a tutelary spirit or *daimōn* who had also been a human being. St Macrina the Younger was overshadowed by the prototypical holy virgin Thecla, to whom she was dedicated at birth.[119] In the medieval West the notion of patronage would grow and become universal. Baptismal names were usually the names of saints. In late medieval Germany lay Christians were expected to choose an "apostle" to act as a personal patron and focus of devotion.[120] Saints served as patrons of individuals, but also of whole communities. Venice, for example, was the city of St Mark; its emblem was the lion of the apocalypse, associated with Mark the evangelist. If the community possessed a relic of its patron, the relic might be deployed to invoke the patron's help in danger. When early sixteenth-century Genoa was threatened by Mediterranean storms, the relics of John the Baptist were carried in procession to protect the town.[121] In late sixteenth-century Spain a census discovered that large numbers of towns and villages had chosen to adopt a particular patron for their community and to vow collectively to keep that patron's feast with special devotion. Sometimes communities chose their patron by a process of trial and error. If they asked one saint for rain after drought, or relief from pests on their crops, and no response followed, they would pray to a series of other saints until a satisfactory response was obtained.[122]

The role of patron was closely linked with the role of intercessor. The argument was that saints who abounded in love for their fellow people in life must undoubtedly feel the same love in the hereafter, and must have access to God to ask for mercy and forgiveness for their devotees.[123] It has been suggested that greater anxiety about one's own holiness – even among the most dedicated ascetics – made some of them willing to invoke the assistance and support of those who had already finished the race.[124] The idea of intercession developed quite early. In Eusebius's church history the virgin Potamiaena reportedly appeared after her martyrdom in Alexandria to Basilides, the soldier who escorted her to her fate, promising to pray to God for him and encouraging him to convert.[125] The fourth-century anchorite Onufrius is reported to have told Paphnutius, who later wrote the story of his life, that he would intercede for those who made even the least of offerings for love of his name.[126] Both these stories were handed on by the fifteenth-century Dominican Johannes Nider, to prove to his own age not only the validity, but the sure and certain benefits, of the intercession of saints.[127]

One saint emerged in the Middle Ages as rather more than just an intercessor. The cult of the Virgin Mary had its vicissitudes in the early Church. Debates over the nature of Christ caused the title *Theotokos*, or "Mother of God," to become highly controversial in the East until it was eventually endorsed.[128] By the medieval period in the West, however, all doubts were silenced. All save the most hardened heretics regarded prayer addressed to the Blessed Virgin as nearly as fundamental a part of Christianity as prayer to God. Mary, especially if one believed her to have been born without original sin, represented a midpoint between the human and the divine more accessible and closer to humanity even than Jesus.[129] Liturgical and paraliturgical writings encouraged the faithful to approach her as the supreme mediator – at the very least. An example of such an invocation is the following: "If the sinner flees to her with trust and good intention, in repentance and sorrow and horror for his sins, with firm and strong faith, *she* receives him mercifully and covers him under her mantle of grace and mercy."[130] The image of the Virgin covering the faithful with her mantle of mercy was physically represented in many carvings of the period. In some cases Jesus was not present, even as an infant.[131] Here the saint had become more than an intercessor. As was remarked of the sermons preached about her in late medieval Germany, she had become the "coredeemer" of humankind.[132] So universal was the cult of the Virgin that her devotion ended up by being localized according to particular shrines, each endowed with particular properties and benefits different from the other.[133]

Intercession for the faithful before God was welcome, but did not exhaust the potentialities of the saints. They were believed to heal people and to cleanse them from evil spirits in their own right, even (sometimes especially) after death. These miracles were extensions of the miracles worked by the saint in life. There was no real difference between the miraculous power exerted by the living and that exerted by the departed: it was the same person displaying the same divine graces and the same charitable purpose. Postmortem cures manifested a curious appropriateness. Saints would acquire after their deaths the power to heal illnesses that in some way corresponded to the manner of their martyrdoms. For instance, Gregory of Tours reported that he was cured of a headache by washing his head in the fountain where the head of the martyr St Julian of Brioude had been washed after it was cut from his body.[134] In the Middle Ages these correspondences between the manner of martyrdom and the benefit asked for in intercession developed into a sort of saintly pharmacopoeia. Not just the uneducated devout, but learned theologians would support and reinforce the identification of saints as specialists. Antony cured a disease known as St Antony's fire, Rupert cured rabies, Agatha protected against fire, and so on.[135] A group of relatively minor saints were assembled and entitled the "Fourteen Holy Helpers," specifically delegated to deal with the material dangers and necessities of the faithful.[136]

Healing might also happen through accidental contact with things or places associated with the saints. Gregory the Great described how a mad woman, wandering at random, happened to stray unknowingly into the cave once occupied by Benedict of Nursia. After sleeping the night there she was completely and permanently cured.[137] Martin of Tours dressed himself in sackcloth as a sign of humility; but when people extracted threads from the sackcloth and tied them round the fingers of the sick they were healed.[138] Many centuries later, an imitation of this practice was reported of the (then still living) St Francis. When a woman suffering a painful and dangerous labor missed meeting Francis, but was met by one of his followers leading the horse he had ridden, the woman's family took the reins and bridle which Francis had used when riding, applied them to her womb, and promptly ensured a safe delivery.[139] Such experiences prompted and encouraged the collecting of relics. Not only the bones and body parts of the saints, but physical objects, pieces of clothing, pieces of furniture, anything that participated in their numinous aura, would be collected. Where the remains did not survive, they would be invented. By the end of the Middle Ages some of the most celebrated saints would have several complete and some incomplete bodies: four complete bodies and two fragmentary heads of Sebastian were exhibited in various places. Much of the clothing and furniture of the holy household (besides the house itself, at Loreto) was exhibited in Christendom somewhere or other.[140] Healing was routinely attributed to things such as Peter's staff, the girdle and shroud of Paul, the staff and shroud of St James, wool and straw from the bed of St Martin, St Jerome's bag, St Agatha's dress, and Jesus's letter to King Abgar of Edessa.[141]

Finally, the saints of the Christian West lived on not only in their physical remains and their attributes, real or spurious, but also in their images. Saints were venerated as icons in the East (save for the chaotic period of the iconoclastic controversy in the eighth and ninth centuries) and increasingly as images and statues in the West. An image of a saint's life and ministry would routinely form part of an altarpiece. When the altar was dedicated to the saint, this necessarily entailed that prayer was made in the name of the saint and before the image of the saint. The image of a saint might manifest patronage in a symbolic way, as when donor-patrons of great altarpieces were shown being presented to Christ or the Virgin by their tutelary or patron saints.[142] Images might also partake of the miraculous. Where no relic existed, an image might be discovered supposedly created by a miracle, like the "Beautiful Virgin" of Regensburg c. 1520. Alternatively, a particularly ancient statue or painting might attract a cult because of its very antiquity and associations, such as the Black Madonna of Le Puy.

In the Reformation the veneration of saints would suffer a frontal attack. Even before Protestant theology was articulated, Renaissance humanists like Erasmus had likened the pantheon of Christian helper-saints to the pagan gods of antiquity: The Virgin Mary had become the protector of sailors and voyagers by sea, replacing the patronage of Aphrodite/Venus (and also Isis) for people in the same circumstances.[143] The Zurich reformer Heinrich Bullinger picked up on the resemblances, and demonstrated a series of parallels between the two: Catherine succeeded Minerva, Gregory succeeded Mercury, and so on.[144] Reformers could argue that the cult of saints represented heaven as like earth, but in its corrupt aspects. To reach God one needed to approach the divine with the help and support of a favored courtier.[145] In the Enlightenment it was assumed, not quite accurately, that the cult of saints arose as a direct transfer from paganism, and that it was made necessary by the alleged influx of converted pagans in the fourth century, overwhelming the reserve of earlier Christian intellectuals.[146]

In reformed Catholicism, the concept of sainthood was subtly revised, in such a way that the best of the tradition was seen to continue. There was a hiatus in canonizations between 1523 and 1588, after which only six saints were proclaimed in the rest of the sixteenth century. There were 24 new saints in the seventeenth and 29 in the eighteenth centuries, though after 1767 there was another hiatus for 40 years.[147] The calendar of saints was simplified and purged of many spurious or obscure names. Saints were ideals to follow and intercessors for spiritual needs. The saints, now canonized according to a process more selective and more judicial than in the Middle Ages, tended to be those who displayed outstanding missionary zeal, discipline, or pastoral care and energies.[148] Over time theologians, controversialists, and even some popes would be elevated. In this context, the sudden rush to canonize under Pope John Paul II represents something of an aberration from the past four centuries of Roman Catholic practice. John Paul II has so far presided at 145 beatification ceremonies (1,330 *beati* proclaimed) and 51 canonization ceremonies (declaring 482 new saints) during his pontificate. For comparison, only 302 saints were proclaimed in the entire period between 1592 and 1968.[149] This process has not, however, restored the medieval assumption that a vast corporation of heavenly specialists was at work caring for the every needs of the devout faithful. Sanctity has become what perhaps it had been at the beginning, an act of commemoration.

Purity of Doctrine and Instruction: the School of Faith

All ages and all forms of Christianity are equally at risk from the exaggerated pursuit of secondary aims – not just the Christianities of the early or medieval periods. In this section we shall consider catechesis, the formal instruction of the people in an organized and stereotyped form of Christian doctrine. This trait is, if anything, most prominent in the early history of the reformed denominations. Right or wrong, it clearly manifests a deviation from the average towards an extreme, and a different kind of extreme from those discussed so far.

Defining correct doctrine was a concern of the Christian churches almost from the very beginning. The clarification of orthodoxy was narrated, from Eusebius onwards, as the defense of "orthodoxy" against "heresy." Given the tormented history of debates over the Trinity, it is perhaps better to speak of multiple interpretations of the meaning of Christian beliefs, of which one or two became definitive in the leading branches of Christianity. However, in all of this there was only a limited opportunity to take theological controversies to the people as a whole. Tertullian acknowledged that some doctrinal issues were incomprehensible to those who had not received some specialist training.[150] Even some monks, never mind lay-people, lagged behind the theologians and bishops in grasping the points at issue. After the fall of the Roman Empire, and the linguistic isolation of the clergy from the majority, this trend intensified. Medieval people were divided into the literate and the illiterate, the "clerks" (which carried the dual connotations of literate and ecclesiastical) and the rest.[151] In the wake of later heretical developments, theological authority went even further. Not only was it practically difficult to instruct the laity in the intricacies of theology: it was actually undesirable. "In the affairs of the faith, skilled spiritual men are said to understand: the rest of the people only simply to believe," wrote Thomas Netter of Walden (c. 1375–1430), a Carmelite friar struggling to deal with the damaging effects of the Lollard heresy on the English faithful around 1400.[152] The faithful were told to believe "implicitly," by the mere fact of being obedient sons and daughters of the Church.

Medieval historians will rightly object if anyone suggests that there was no "catechesis" in the late medieval Church. Things were certainly taught. A collection of short descriptions and mnemonics known (with unintended irony) as *Ignorantia Sacerdotum* (The ignorance of priests), contained in a decree of Archbishop John Pecham of Canterbury (d. 1292) in 1281, set out the basic standards and content of instruction in the 14 articles of faith, seven sacraments, seven virtues, and seven deadly sins for clergy in England. The repeated use of the auspicious number seven was deliberate.[153] A curious folk-tale related how a plowman was tricked into learning the Lord's Prayer, one clause at a time, so as to be able eventually to repeat all of it *in Latin*.[154] Guides to the Lord's Prayer and its interpretation abounded and survive in numerous manuscripts.[155] If only a minority of priests used the sermon-guides and manuals available to them, and only some faithful attended Corpus Christi festivals and plays or scrutinized the paintings on the church walls, the faithful would have had a grasp of basic religious knowledge that might have compared favorably with the levels of knowledge of many modern-day Christian congregations.[156] However, that is not quite the point. Before the Refor-mation, it was not thought necessary or proper for laypeople to know the "why" of their belief and practice, or how beliefs directed the forms of worship. After the Reformation, to be ignorant of such things was seen as deplorable. In the era of "orthodoxy," dogmas were pinned down with an almost fanatical specificity, which in due course provoked a reaction against itself.

In the Reformation, knowledge suddenly mattered much more, because of how Martin Luther reconceived the means and effects of salvation. God did not, as in the medieval Church, institute a set of procedures which believers must obediently follow to purify themselves from sin and acquire grace to salvation. Rather, God offered forgiveness, undeserved and undeservable, and implanted saving faith in the believer. Salvation was experienced rather than earned. The appropriate response for the Christian was utter trust in the divine goodness, profound gratitude, and an overflowing desire to do whatever one could in love of God and neighbor. This Christian life could not be lived by proxy; it could not be appreciated without understanding. Intellectual knowledge was not nearly sufficient; but it was an indispensable basic starting-point.[157] Luther did not control the entire Reformation: but his vision of justification, in its intellectual and rational characteristics, was definitive. The theologian in the Reformation mainstream who departed furthest from Luther, Huldrych Zwingli of Zürich, was even more of a rationalist and an intellectualist than Luther.

In his early preaching, Luther seems to have been almost naïvely confident that the people would willingly embrace and learn the theological content of his message. The phenomenal success of his pamphlets, sold in their thousands around 1518–24, and the enthusiastic participation of laypeople in sermons and disputations, must have seemed to confirm this belief. When Luther returned to his base at Wittenberg in March 1522 after a period of protective custody, he told his hearers to wait until the whole congregation shared the same understanding of reform *before* making any changes to public worship.[158] Then, in the autumn of 1528, he and his colleagues went on a pastoral visitation in the villages of Saxony, authorized by Elector John the Steadfast. Luther had the rudest of rude shocks:

> The deplorable conditions which I recently encountered when I was a visitor constrained me to prepare this brief and simple catechism or statement of Christian teaching. Good God, what wretchedness I beheld! The common people, especially those who live in the country, have no knowledge whatever of Christian teaching, and unfortunately many pastors are quite incompetent and unfitted for teaching. Although the people are supposed to be Christian, are baptized, and receive the holy sacrament, they do not know the Lord's Prayer, the Creed, or the Ten Commandments, they live as if they were pigs and irrational beasts, and now that the Gospel has been restored they have mastered the fine art of abusing liberty.
>
> How will you bishops answer for it before Christ that you have so shamefully neglected the people and paid no attention at all to the duties of your office?

May you escape punishment for this! You withhold the cup in the Lord's Supper and insist on the observance of human laws, yet you do not take the slightest interest in teaching the people the Lord's Prayer, the Creed, the Ten Commandments, or a single part of the Word of God. Woe to you forever![159]

In 1529 Luther produced two catechisms: the shorter, a modest piece able to be learned by heart (source of the above extract) and a longer catechism for the instruction of preachers, which contained full explanation of the main points. Luther was not the first to perceive the need for mass theological education in the Reformation movement. Already many other reformers had already begun to issue their own specimen treatments of reformed theology for mass education.[160] By the 1530s and 1540s there was an exuberant growth in the market for texts of organized theological instruction, from all the major branches of the reformed churches. These mostly followed a similar pattern. They were often formal question-and-answer texts, in which a teacher, pastor, or parent asked questions and the student or pupil responded. They established knowledge of the Ten Commandments, the Apostles' Creed, and the Lord's Prayer. Usually they also explored the two sacraments, baptism and the Eucharist, that Protestant churches retained. There might then be paragraphs of instruction in the moral duties of Christian people within their household and community structures and hierarchies. The simplest of these texts might be accompanied by a basic alphabet or primer; at the opposite extreme, some of the longest and fullest were manuals of theological instruction running to several hundreds of pages.

The rise of catechizing was potentially subject to the same degree of inflation and exaggeration as any other secondary religious objective. While many catechisms were short and straightforward, there was also a contrary tendency, whereby the more one tried to clarify, the more one had to develop. This in turn led to the implication – though it would never be an explicit statement – that the best Christian was the one who was able to define his or her faith with the greatest intellectual sophistication. At times the levels of expected understanding and knowledge apparently (one must stress the "apparently") bordered on the bizarre. The mid-sixteenth-century English Protestant Thomas Becon (1512–67) dedicated his *New Catechism*, written in the early 1560s, to his sons Theodore and Basil and to his daughter Rachel.[161] It took the form of a dialogue between a father and his young son, where the son gave the answers. In the initial conversation, the son protested his relative youth and inexperience to his father, who answered:

This thing is not unknown to me. Thy age is young, thy years are few, thy continuance in study is small, for as yet thou are not six years old. Therefore my mind is only at this present to talk with thee, not of things which far exceed thy age and capacity, but of such matters as be meet for children to know.[162]

There followed a detailed exposition, with copious scriptural and patristic references in support, of all the elements of the catechism described above. No punches were pulled: for example, the discussion of the Eucharist embraced the classic Protestant critiques of the doctrine of eucharistic sacrifice and transubstantiated presence, as well as the Catholic practice of giving the laity only the bread.[163] After over 500 pages in the original folio edition, the five-year-old son told his father that he has done his best: but "if I have not in all points satisfied your expectation, I shall desire you to consider my young and tender age, and my small exercise as yet in matters of Christian religion." He hoped that he would learn more as he grows older.[164] This need was taken seriously. At the end of Bunyan's *Pilgrim's Progress*, the figure of "Ignorance" was cast into the pit after earlier displaying a (to Bunyan) deplorable ignorance of the finer points of the reformed theology of justification.[165]

A second risk was that, the more one tried to clarify, the more one drew attention to contentious or problematical issues. Catechisms, together with confessions of faith, played a crucial role in the process known as "confessionalization." They allowed ordinary people not only to know what they *did* believe, but why they did *not* believe what other kinds of Christians did. Each denomination defined its identity through its official (and many unofficial) catechisms. Luther's catechisms became normative for the Lutheran churches. But followers of Luther who held views slightly different from each other, such as Philipp Melanchthon, David Chytraeus, and Martin Chemnitz also wrote their own versions.[166] The Heidelberg Catechism of 1563 became the official text for those churches in Germany that embraced reformed ("Calvinist") Protestantism. In Scotland the so-called "Negative Confession" of 1581 set out in aggressive detail all the aspects of Roman Catholicism which its people were called on to reject.[167] Catechisms could and did generate volumes of commentary and interpretation, which themselves would identify further areas of potential controversy.[168]

One should not overstate the effect here. Some catechisms consciously avoided discussing the most controversial issues, where such thorny topics would cause confusion and distress to the less expert.[169] The three texts at the heart of the Catechism, the Ten Commandments, Lord's Prayer, and Creed were after all the shared heritage of Christianity. Nevertheless, the sheer abundance and diversity of reformed catechisms, including potentially "shocking" documents such as the Unitarian Racovian Catechism of 1605, threw doctrinal disagreement into the forefront of public attention and religious identity as never before.[170]

A contrary effect could also occur. Catechesis could in certain conditions support a drive for uniformity and subordination among the people, in both social and theological terms. The ethical advice given in the early modern catechisms tended to be, to modern eyes, socially very conservative. In that respect it simply echoed a moral commonplace of the era, which was that differentiation between people by status according to rank in society, profession, age, gender, and marital status was not only natural but right and essential.[171] Since the greater emphasis on universal rights derived from the Enlightenment, such identification of the gospel with a highly struc-tured and hierarchical social order has appeared ever more alien.

In Protestantism, despite the stated intention, the drive for absolute theological uniformity was doomed from the start, since the sheer abun-dance of catechetical material and the weakness of censorship allowed people to read documents from many traditions if they wished. In England alone some 678 editions of different catechisms were published between 1530 and 1740.[172] In the Roman Catholic tradition, however, the drive for uniformity was much more successful. The 1566 *Roman Catechism* suc-ceeded in eclipsing nearly all its rivals, with the possible exception of the three exemplary orthodox catechisms of the Jesuit Peter Canisius.[173] If a church becomes too certain that it has pinned the sublime and eternal down to a perfect form of words, it may come to regard that product as timeless. Some commentators on the Roman Catechism have literally called it "a book in which to find catholic truth in all certainty" and a "timeless exposition of a timeless faith."[174] There has, of course, been a substantial recasting of the Roman Catholic Catechism, issued in 1994.[175] However, it is tempting to ask, as many contemporary Catholics have done, whether such a stately and comprehensive official exposition of doctrinal certainties is even appropriate in the current climate of ideas.[176]

In the reformed more than in the Catholic world, the arid and argumen-tative intellectualism of the early modern period generated a response against itself. Pietists in Germany and Methodists in Britain argued that Christianity must not be reduced to an intellectual game, and stressed its emotive and experiential aspects. There was a resurgence of interest in mysticism around 1700, which sometimes transcended the divides between denominations.[177] John Locke said in 1695 that he had asked dissenters whether they even understood the theological controversies at issue in their churches: they admitted they did not.[178] Nicolas Ludwig von Zinzendorf put it in a salutary if unsettling way in *Der deutsche Sokrates* in 1732: "Religion can be grasped without the conclusions of reason; otherwise no one could have religion except a person of intelligence. As a result the best theologians would be those who have the greatest reason. This cannot be believed and is contradicted by experience."[179] In nineteenth-century liberalism (as will be seen later) the elaboration of doctrine came to be regarded as one of the sins of the early church. Theological hypertrophy had drawn the early Christian movement away from the simple ethical principles with which it had been born. The twentieth century saw something of a contrary drift, but only a partial one. The greatest theologian to revive dogmatic sophistication was Karl Barth. However, his fascination with precise dogmatic formulae left him by the end of his life relatively isolated from most of his contemporaries.[180] As the "postliberal" theologian George A. Lindbeck has remarked, the present age finds dogmatic precision profoundly uncongenial. It suggests exclusiveness and lack of respect for the other: "the very words "doctrine" and "dogma" have the smell of the ghetto about them."[181]

The Christian Community and its Membership

It is much harder, the closer one comes to the present age, to identify the exaggerations and/or distortions that characterize the churches of the present. Since those distortions will inevitably reflect their contemporary host culture, it takes some effort of imagination to think oneself outside a context which is also one's own context. This chapter will therefore conclude with a briefly stated suggestion. The suggestion is that from the nineteenth century onwards, especially since participation in organized religion has largely ceased to be a marker of civil participation or civic respectability, the churches have become preoccupied to an unprecedented degree with defining, charting, sustaining, and (where possible) increasing their lay membership.

For much of Christian history the churches have not regarded their "membership" as much of an issue, because for most of the time the Church has been, in its areas of greatest influence, effectively synonymous with the entire community. This was not so in the centuries before Constantine, nor in the regions outside the Roman Empire where conversions had to be made. Christian belief was introduced from scratch, for good or ill, to many parts of the non-European world from the sixteenth century onwards. But there is a difference between conversion, which will often be seen in apocalyptic, elemental terms, and the modern concern to keep membership close and cohesive in an atmosphere that is not so much hostile as potentially indifferent.

In the medieval West the "Christian community" was so nearly all-embracing that to have been concerned with "membership" would have been almost redundant. There was a significant non-Christian Muslim and Jewish population in the Iberian peninsula, and Jewish communities subsisted elsewhere, especially in France, Italy, and Eastern Europe. But these minorities were too small or too localized to give "Christendom" much sense of itself as a community defined against an "other." The best evidence of this point is that in most of Europe Christians identified themselves not simply as Christians, but by their membership in lesser, particular communities. One might be a member of a parish guild or confraternity.[182] If one was a cleric, it was of the greatest importance whether one was a regular or secular cleric, and if regular, to which order (or branch of an order) one belonged. In other words, a sense of identity and belonging inhered more in one's subdivision of Christianity, less in the Church as a whole.[183]

In the Reformation, one's choice of confessional allegiance might sometimes be a matter of life and death. However, in most of Europe it was only for a brief period, if ever, that membership involved a conscious choice by the individual layperson. The norm was for whole communities to convert (or be told to convert) and thereafter to stand by their decision. While occasional brave souls defied the choice of their government and faced exile, persecution, or death by standing out, the conforming majority did not form a conscious "membership" of a church in any way distinct from their geographical community or neighborhood. The germ of the modern concept of a "gathered church" can be seen in only a few instances at this time. The Anabaptist churches were, as noted earlier, resolutely voluntary, and at a fateful risk to themselves. They believed, or at least lived as if they believed, that the godly could recognize each other and form a people apart. For most of the reformers and all Catholics this represented a sectarian error.[184] Within the majority or mainstream churches, however, there did from time to time arise "inner rings" or "core members" of churches that were otherwise supposed to be comprehensive. In Strasbourg in the 1540s, the reformer Martin Bucer despaired of instituting an effective Christian discipline in a city whose rulers firmly distrusted their clergy. So for a few years he instituted voluntary societies or "Christian communities," which had a listed and defined membership. They met much more often than weekly, and received instruction apart from the rest of the parish.[185] In England under the reign of Elizabeth I, many Protestant leaders found the lack of official discipline and reformed instruction similarly unsatisfactory. Since they could not have a compulsory discipline, they instituted voluntary ones: self-selecting members of the national church gathered together for sermons, rolling seminars or "exercises," and the mutual reinforcement of rigorous moral standards.[186]

The tendency among English "puritans" to define themselves as the "saints" or the "elect people" generated a good deal of resentment and a great deal more mockery.[187] The voluntary associations *within* an established church did not last long in that precise form. The established English church dissolved in the chaos of the post-Civil War years of the 1650s; after its re-establishment in 1660–2 it was strong enough to expel the refractory altogether. However, the "puritan" model was enormously significant in the New World. Most of those who took part in the "Great Migration" to Massachusetts Bay in the 1630s and thereafter were fairly typical of committed Protestant members of the Church of England. They were unhappy with the hostility shown towards their theology and their values by the Anglican hierarchy of the time.[188] However, by translating their communities across the ocean, the context and therefore the function of the voluntary community changed. Instead of existing in spite of the authorities in church and state, the voluntary congregations *became* the embodiment of the civil community. To be a full, that is, catechized and examined communicant member of the "godly church," became a condition of holding civil rights as a leading citizen of the colony. Those who resented or objected on theological grounds to the Massachusetts approach soon left or were expelled to found new, equally voluntary colonies elsewhere in New England.[189] Relatively quickly, this form of "membership" became so demanding and daunting to secure that the "half-way covenants" had to be devised to cater for the otherwise unchurched and disenfranchised.[190]

The relationship between voluntary church membership and civil rights that became characteristic of colonial New England did not, however, set a standard for the rest of the Old World. During the eighteenth century the European powers gradually became less resolute over religious uniformity. The last great expulsion of minority Protestants from a Catholic territory took place in the prince-bishopric of Salzburg in 1731. It was seen, especially by "Enlightened" observers, as a somewhat grotesque anachronism, the predictable result of clerical narrow-mindedness.[191] Napoleonic France emancipated its religious minorities in the early 1800s. By 1850 many great and small states had done the same.[192] They thus established a separation between civil citizenship and religious affiliation. In these circumstances, for the first time, it made sense for the churches to start to count and to keep records of their "members."

The results of this new preoccupation with statistics were interesting. It is estimated that in England around 1800 something like 18 percent of adults could be regarded as church "members" in the sense of being consistently active within a church community. After several decades of theological and cultural warfare within the Church and energetic evangelism in new urban areas, the proportion rose to some 26–7 percent in the second half of the nineteenth century. A peak in attendance in the Church of England was reached around 1866. From around that period membership and participation began a long slow decline, reflected in most of the countries of Europe, to around 14 percent or less in 1990.[193] It should be noted that some of the surge in overall church membership in the middle of the nineteenth century was generated by the exotic diversity of new Protestant sects and denominations (and in Scotland, fractured branches of the national church) that flourished in the new climate of freedom from civil disabilities. Students of religion, and perhaps especially religious journalists, have taken a fascinated interest in exploring the significance of these figures. Part of the fascination seems to derive from a most peculiar form of empiricism: if the membership of the churches continues its decline, does that prove that religion is after all a human construct of merely passing significance, destined to obsolescence in a new world of mass communication, mass entertainment, and supposedly all-conquering scientific and technological worldviews? "The churches trusted in God: let us see if their God will deliver them from irrelevance?"

The maintenance of large congregations can also become a "performance indicator" for the leaders of the churches and the clergy in particular. This attitude reflects the final revenge of secular culture on the religious mind. Religion is turned into a consumer good and a commodity. The most successful (therefore true?) religion must be that which generates the greatest sense of need for itself and the most enthusiastic support among its following. Numbers can be kept up by stick or by carrot, depending in part on the target audience. One can drum up support by instilling intense fear of hell-fire, or purgatorial fire; one can generate enthusiasm by theatrical displays of charismatic preaching or evangelism. One can arouse a sense of guilt, or a feeling of hope, comfort, and reassurance, or a more nebulous sense of "belonging." Those who are less cynical or manipulative may still try to discern what are the religious and spiritual "needs" of contemporary society, then tell the churches what they need to do to meet those needs.[194] God is, in effect, to be turned to fit the shape of the spiritual "hole" putatively remaining in the lives of those who are materially fairly secure, and no longer need religion as a substitute for medicine, technology, a reliable food supply, or indeed a focus for sociability. It can be argued that the concepts of the intercession of saints, and Anselm's doctrine of substitutionary atonement, testified to the influence of the high medieval feudal culture of substitution and vicariousness on the twelfth-century Church. If that is so, then the commodification of religion testifies in exactly the same way to the influence of twentieth- and twenty-first-century consumer culture on the churches of the industrialized West. This picture is of course a gross caricature. Most churches are not so consciously consumer-oriented as all that. But the theological question needs to be asked: why should it now be thought so important to maximize membership? After all, for centuries the churches regarded their people as having a duty to follow, rather than a choice to make. The choice to be religious or not reflected on the individual, not the Church.

Reflections on Shifting Priorities

The arguments so far advanced do not amount to a suggestion that *everything* about the Christian religion is quite different and entirely incommensurable at one time from every other. There are of course elements of continuity. However, the elements of continuity and change are always intertwined. One cannot focus on the threads of continuity without also acknowledging that they operate in a constantly changing context. What, if anything, drives the shifts in priorities that have been proposed here? At a very broad level, there are some major movements in culture and civilization which one can deploy to try to explain these shifts: many historians and commentators have done so since the Enlightenment. It makes sense that in the early Middle Ages, where institutions were relatively inchoate, holiness focused on heroic figures rather than institutions. With the rise of a more sophisticated political and cultural structure after the year 1000, holiness began to inhere more and more in things and in procedures rather than in people.[195] In modern industrial society, the shift away from an inclusive religion towards a gathered community of choice reflected the voluntarism, the consumerism, and the separations of church and state that characterized that period.

However, these rough-and-ready comparisons between cultural changes and their religious manifestations are too crude to be entirely satisfactory. In particular, they do not help very well to explain the largest and most dramatic shift of the past thousand years, the Reformation and Catholic Reformation. In the early sixteenth century the medieval system based on the allegedly reliable link between earthly ritual and heavenly grace had reached its peak. It then toppled over as though by its own weight, and a new emphasis on the intellectual and spiritual internalization of the gospel by the individual quite suddenly arose to replace it. Historians down the years have tried to link this to the Renaissance, the rise of new economic or political structures, or "modernity" *tout court*. More recently scholars have tended to discard these big theories as though in despair. There is simply no sufficiently crucial cultural, economic, or social shift (and certainly not in Eastern Saxony where Luther studied and taught) to "explain away" the religious changes that occurred.

It probably makes as much sense to conceive, at least some of the time, of a kind of dialectical progression within Christianity itself. Sometimes agiven movement develops and extends itself in a more or less linear fashion towards an extreme. More and more people become ascetics, or Cistercian monks, or missionaries. A secondary ideal is pursued to its logical end-point. The traffic in indulgences that sparked off Luther's protest in 1517 was arguably just the extension *ad absurdum* of what had seemed at the time a perfectly rational principle, that is, that the Church could "transfer" its collective and negotiable holiness as a reward to faithful people who performed some meritorious act. After many decades of linear progression, that development can suddenly appear so extreme as to forfeit credibility, and the bubble bursts. So medieval ceremonialism gives way to early modern intellectualism, which in turn gives way to Pietistic mysticism and emotionalism. Enlightenment superrationalism calls forth the diversity and counterrationalism of the Romantics as a reaction against itself. This phe-nomenon can happen on a smaller as well as a larger scale. The studied simplicity of Cistercian monasteries, and their carefully balanced regime of work, study, and worship, reflected a critique of the elaborate liturgy and vast buildings of the order of Cluny.[196] Baroque liturgical music in Eastern European Catholicism developed towards ever-greater musical elaboration until the 1770s; there was then a quite sudden reaction among the "Reform Catholics" in favor of a much simpler style of worship, quieter and more congregational.[197] However, it is unlikely that any one philosophy of history will address sufficiently the infinite complexity of the religious life of the Christian world. The temptation to try to restore some form of Hegelian dialectic is there, but should be resisted. All plausible models will work with some examples but fail with others.

It is perfectly consistent with the model of successive "exaggerations" of this or that aspect of the Christian life for there to coexist at the same time "minor" as well as "major" trends. In other words, even when the majority culture favors one of the major trends explored above, one should expect to find some dissenters. The cult of asceticism provoked a contrary response from Jovinian. The cult of saints provoked a reaction from Vigilantius.[198] Neither of these expressions of dissent was sufficient to resist the prestige and authority of Augustine and Jerome; but the alternate view could exist. The late fourteenth and fifteenth centuries, the age *par excellence* of sacramentalism and ritualism, were also the age of the English and Rhenish mystics, the Brethren of the Common Life, the English Lollards, and the high-profile preachers of the towns of France and Germany. In the midst of innumerable sacrificial masses, processions of relics, and dedications of new shrines, there were some who also wished to contemplate in tranquility or to listen to the exposition of Scripture. Later on, amidst the wave of dogmatic rationalism that dominated the post-Reformation, some people hankered after a more emotive, more sensory religious experience, or sought more supernatural and miraculous evidence of the divine. The era of Protestant Orthodoxy was also the age of the movement in England known as "Laudianism" that emphasized the sacraments and the liturgy, the proto-Pietism of the Lutheran Johann Arndt, and the popular collections of "providences."[199] It does not, by any means, follow that one century's minor trend will blossom into the major movement of the next, although historians may sometimes try to conclude that such was the case.

So, can the churches ever get things right? Will it ever be possible to escape from a cycle of repeated lurches into one extreme after another? If the reason for these lurches, theologically speaking, is an innate human tendency to pursue secondary objectives in the religious life, a religious manifestation of original sin, then the answer may be no. However, an ever deeper and broader understanding of the past may, in itself, enable the churches to look at their choices more calmly and with more discrimination. It would at least be unreasonable to exclude a priori the possibility that one might forearm the churches against some of the more excessive deviations in the future. This issue may even be explored empirically, by looking at how Christian historiography has itself developed. Have historians over time shown a greater willingness or ability to confront the issues of diversity, indeed of error, within the Church as a whole and their own traditions in particular? That forms the theme of the next chapter.

Chapter 3

Church Historians' Responses to Change and Diversity

The previous chapter argued that Christian history is, in large part, the history of shifting emphases, of a constant tendency to stress one feature of the Christian message over another, and to veer to extremes of some sort or other. This suggestion may offend those whose perception of Christianity is that of a timeless faith, the same yesterday, today, and forever. It may be objected that mine is a relatively recent approach, informed by a theological standpoint little more than a century old. This is therefore a good moment to change the perspective slightly. Since the writing of the Book of Acts, the Church has kept written records and told stories of its experiences and activities. The Christian heritage includes a rich and very diverse array of historical writings. The approach that these writings take to Church history is constantly evolving. It develops, as one would expect, under the influence of unfolding cultural and intellectual trends in the society around it.

The shifting nature of Church historiography itself gives important insights; but it also sheds light on issues discussed in the previous chapter. For much of the modern era, two broad perspectives on church history have been contending for influence. One view, generally speaking, looks for continuity and stability in the Church's witness. Another sees the history of the Church as unstable: at times it is perfectly possible for the majority church to lose sight of something important, and to cease to be the "true" Church. The question of continuity and identity in the history of the Christian Church is a complex and a very open one. This chapter will therefore sketch out a little of the evolution of Christian historical writing. It will not present an exhaustive survey, which would make hard reading and would require far more than the space available. It will rather discuss a number of examples chosen from key epochs. The point is to show that the churches have not always perceived their past in the same way. Gradually and over time, the perception has grown that the Church is not a timeless crystalline entity. It has been seen to be a shifting, variable thing peopled by fallible human beings and subject to the ebb and flow of politics. For the past 400–500 years it has been perfectly possible to argue, in certain contexts, that a large section of the Church "went wrong" in some way or other in the past.

The Early Church: Eusebius of Caesarea

Eusebius (c. 260–339), bishop of Caesarea in Palestine from about 313 until his death, is generally regarded as the first historian of the Christian Church. He lived nearly all his life in Caesarea, a city where pagan, Jewish, Samaritan, and Christian elements mingled. He had access to a vast library and wrote prolifically, though some of his works are lost, and others survive intact only in Armenian or Syriac translations. His most famous work, *The History of the Church*, narrates the rise and development of Christianity from Jesus to the time of Constantine. He wrote a chronicle of world history, an account of the Christian martyrs of Palestine, and lives of both his own teacher Pamphilus and the Emperor Constantine (the first of these is lost). He also wrote works of theological controversy and biblical scholarship. He had, and still has, the reputation of enormous erudition but not of profound intellectual insight. He was hampered as a theologian by his own past. He arrived at the Council of Nicea in 325 as a passionate follower of Origen, and even an alleged sympathizer with Arian doctrines on the noneternal nature of the Son, to be condemned at that council. He left the council as a supporter of Trinitarian doctrine and subscribed to the condemnation of Arius. Many of his writings, both before and after Nicea, had to do with the bitter theological controversies of the time. He also wrote in response to the intellectual attacks mounted by pagan philosophers on Christianity.

Eusebius wrote in a late antique world that had produced some of the most eloquent and literary works of history ever written. Both Greek and Latin classical historians had laid down principles and set examples for writing annalistic narrative political and military history. However, there were no exact precedents for the kind of Church history that Eusebius set himself to write: he had to invent the genre largely by himself. Like an ancient annalist, Tacitus for example, he arranged the books of his *History* according to the reigns of the emperors of his age. (This had the unintended effect of representing all persecutions as initiated by the emperors, which is now known not to have been the case before 249 CE.)

Unlike classical literary historians, Eusebius had no taste for inventing speeches and inserting them into the mouths of his characters. If he quoted anyone, he quoted the authentic words of the source. He included many original documents, some of which would not otherwise have survived. He cited some, though not all, of the sources that he used. He included many quite extended quotations from documents written for other purposes: a lengthy quotation from Josephus in Book 3, a long letter about the persecutions of Christians from Asia Minor at Vienne and Lyons in Gaul in Book 5; and substantial extracts from the writings of Dionysius of Alexandria in Book 7. At times the work appears to contain chunks of material written for other purposes, such as Eusebius's Palestinian martyrology or a short biography of Origen, whom he greatly revered.

The immediate and somewhat disjointed quality of the book is revealed by some radical stylistic differences. The first seven books are an assemblage of materials around a chronological framework. Subjects succeed each other without any apparent design, and there is no flowing narrative. It has even been suggested that these first books may have been written much earlier than the remainder, possibly before 303, though this remains controversial.[1] Books 8–10 of *The History of the Church* comprise a history of the Great Persecution of 303–13 and its aftermath in the accession of Constantine and the restoration of the churches. These books are written in a much more eloquent, fluid style. The rhetoric is much more exalted, and there are far fewer interruptions save for the most important of documents. Near the end Eusebius inserts a long speech of his own, written as an address to Bishop Paulinus on the occasion of the rededication of a church in Tyre.[2] This speech may once have been intended to mark the end of the entire work; but in the present form of the text some more material has been added afterwards.

Whether the author was conscious of his intent or not, certain themes and attitudes are sometimes announced, sometimes betrayed by Eusebius in this first of Church histories. First of all, he believed that Christianity was not a 300-year-old religion, but the "first, most ancient, and most primitive of all religions,"[3] the worship of the one true God, known to the earliest patriarchs and restored by Jesus Christ. For Eusebius, as for many in antiquity, ancient meant good; modern meant novelty, instability, and error. Those who denounced the Christians as innovators usually appealed to the antiquity of the worship of the pagan gods. It was therefore natural for Eusebius to turn the weapon back against them.

Truth, Eusebius argued, was unique and indivisible. He did not write anything remotely resembling a "history of the development of Christian doctrine." He implied, rather than saying explicitly, that the true Church taught only the same things from the apostles to his own time. There is an elliptical quality to this argument, since those who taught something that the Church ultimately decided was *not* true doctrine would be listed in Eusebius's copious catalogue of heretics. There are many ironies in this. Eusebius's own position on the Trinity was somewhat unstable. He wrote in an age when the precise content of "orthodox" Christianity on the Trinity was still waiting to be agreed, and wrote much controversial material himself.

In his concern for the uniqueness of truth, Eusebius spent some time reconciling apparent disagreements or inconsistencies in his sources. He explained at length why the different genealogies of Christ in Matthew and Luke were both correct.[4] He likewise sought to reconcile apparent, and more significant, differences between the Synoptic Gospels and John over the location and chronology of Jesus's ministry.[5] Like many a historian after him, he also tried to bring sources from different accounts into harmony. So he used the (now controversial) passages about John the Baptist, Jesus, and James from Josephus's *Jewish Antiquities* to reinforce and compare with the Gospel accounts.[6]

Eusebius's concept of the Church, though probably instinctive rather than consciously formulated, shows through clearly. The Church, he implied, is the continuous succession of those who have ministered in it and followed its teachings since the time of the apostles. He listed important writers and thinkers in the history of the Church; but quoted their writings, if at all, somewhat haphazardly. Even among Christian writers it was the continuity of persons that guaranteed the continuity of teaching, not the other way around.[7] In particular the Church subsisted, for Eusebius, in the "apostolic succession" of bishops.[8] Without any sense of anachronism, he traced back the institution of one leading priest in each major city as far back as he could. To prove this he from time to time presented lists of people, some of whom were no more than mere names.[9] Writers as early as the Reformation, and subsequently, have argued that the institution of a leading presbyter or "bishop" emerged only gradually in the early Church, and that many city churches were at first collegial rather than hierarchical. Eusebius showed no awareness that such a development was happening. He likewise fell into an anachronism when he quoted Philo writing about the Jewish monastic sect of the "Therapeutae." He insisted that they must have been Christian monks. Christian monasticism was only taking shape in Eusebius's own lifetime, yet he projected it back into the relatively distant past.[10]

Personal continuity was essential to the Church, because the textual heritage of the early Church was still unstable. At the time that Eusebius wrote, there was no universally agreed "canon" of the approved books of the New Testament. At several points he discussed, or quoted others discussing, the authenticity of particular biblical books. His queries regarding authenticity and authorship have generally been endorsed by later biblical scholarship: Hebrews was not written by Paul (as Origen correctly surmised); some of the later Epistles are pseudonymous; Revelation is by general consent a highly problematic text.[11] He was aware of the numerous "apocryphal Gospels" and, perhaps a little hastily, condemned many as not spurious or doubtful, but entirely heretical.

Eusebius for the most part defined the Church in terms of the challenges and sufferings that it faced and experienced. He continually depicted heresies as cropping up, assaulting this or that part of the Church, and dying out or being defeated by the energy of orthodox Christian controversialists. Like the Church, the anti-Church of heresy consisted in people more than ideas. While he discussed some early heretics' ideas (often drawing on Irenaeus) he showed more interest in the moral failings and bad ends of the leaders. He referred briefly to Manichaeanism, which grew up in his lifetime, outlived him, and presented the fourth-century Church with a major threat. Yet Eusebius spent more time playing on the punning relationship between "Mani" and "maniac" than discussing the content of Mani's ideas. The inadequacy of Eusebius's critique is apparent when it is compared with the massive theological assaults written by Augustine (a former dabbler in Manichaeanism) some 80 years later.[12]

Eusebius came into his own in the narrative of the Great Persecution, which forms Books 8–10 of the presently surviving text of the *History*. The version in the *History* is more broadly based, and has more political narrative, than his *Martyrs of Palestine*: the latter work consists simply of sections narrating the life and death of each martyr or group of martyrs in turn. Books 8–10 of the *History* makes the best claim to be a genuine classical historical text. Ironically however, it works better as a scathing, mordant narrative of the misdeeds of the persecuting Emperors, rather in the manner of Tacitus, than as a history of the acts of the Church. Eusebius as a Church historian was therefore in something of a bind. History demands actors and events; but his concept of the Church was a largely static one. As a result, the Church that he depicted was more often passive, suffering things done to it by persecutors and heretics, than achieving positive things for itself.

Early Medieval Church History: Bede

The writing of Church history in late antiquity began with Eusebius and continued after him. Eusebius's work received continuations by Socrates "Scholasticus" (c. 380–c. 450), Sozomen, Theodoret, and in the West by Rufinus of Aquileia, who also translated Eusebius into Latin, and Cassiodorus

(c. 490–c. 580). Paulus Orosius (fl. c. 400), a native of the Iberian peninsula who traveled in the East, wrote a work entitled *Histories Against the Pagans* in the early fifth century. This work, in parallel with Augustine's contemporary *City of God*, defended Christianity against the charge of weakening the empire. In the late sixth century a Gallo-Roman aristocrat, Gregory, bishop of Tours (538/9–94) wrote the *History of the Franks*, a crucial source for early barbarian Francia, as well as books of martyrology and collections of miracles: but in Gregory's case the political history and the martyrology were not really integrated.

After the dissolution of ancient Roman culture in Western Europe, there was a long interval before a Church historian of real stature appeared in the "barbarian" West. When one did appear, however, he proved to be a scholar of towering significance. Bede (672/3–735) lived his entire adult life as a monk in the double monastery of Wearmouth-Jarrow, in the Anglo-Saxon kingdom of Northumbria. He was ordained deacon and priest, but seems to have held no positions of high authority in his church. Although he was a scholar of prodigious learning and a writer of great eloquence in the ecclesiastical Latin of his era, and enjoyed connections at Rome and personal links to the most senior bishops of his church, he remained a library-bound scholar all his life. However, thanks to his connections with career clerics who traveled to Rome regularly, his monastery amassed one of the great book collections of Christendom. Bede had access to many of the most important works of Christian scholarship without having to leave north-east England.

Although Bede is now best known for his *Ecclesiastical History of the English People*, completed in 731, he would probably not have regarded himself merely or even principally as a historian. The greater bulk of his work consisted of compilations of commentaries on Scripture. He wrote lives of the saints (especially local saints), and lives of the abbots of his monastery. His passion, as far as we can tell, appears to have been the accurate reckoning of time, and the art of assigning accurate dates to events. He popularized, though he did not invent, the custom of using the continuous sequence of years of the Incarnation as a means of dating reigns, lives, and major occurrences (the modern Common Era). He also computed the years of the history of the world since creation, and used his version of that framework in the *Greater Chronicle* that he inserted into his work *On the Computation of Time*.

Bede is now famous as a historian of the Church because, while many scholars before and since have written on the Gospels, and our knowledge of chronology has advanced considerably, he remains a uniquely detailed source for the religious history of early Anglo-Saxon England. He is not the only authority, but he is the most copious and the richest source. Moreover, he wrote what was consciously described and designed as ecclesiastical history: that is, the history of the establishment, nurture, and experiences of the Christian churches within the lands and society of the Anglo-Saxon peoples up to his own time. His history is concerned with the arrival of Christianity, first in Roman Britain, then among the Angles, Saxons, and Jutes who appeared in the island of Britain in the middle of the fifth century. These peoples had established kingdoms across all but the western extremities of what is now England and southern Scotland. He took an interest in the political structures and the vicissitudes of rulers that made the implantation of Christianity possible, and charted the rise of monasteries and bishoprics, those two fundamental units of Dark Age Christianity. In the case of England these two usually overlapped: often bishops were monks, and ran their churches from monastic centers. He described the gradual triumph of Roman Christianity over Celtic Christianity in Northumbria. He wrote into his history the lives of leading saints, and the accounts of the miracles and visions that their holiness made possible.

Bede was a highly intelligent, immensely learned, and critical scholar, who was also utterly and absolutely a man of his own age. His critical acuity was shown in his use of sources. Like Eusebius, he preferred to insert copies of original documents where possible. Through contacts with clerics traveling to and from Rome, Bede secured copies of many original letters written by, among others, Pope Gregory the Great.[13] He inserted the synodal decrees of Archbishop Theodore from 673 as evidence for growing pastoral control by the archbishop.[14] When reporting miracles and visions, he often took care to identify the person who told him the story, and to clarify how many degrees of separation stood between himself and the events. He was clearly aware that hagiography encouraged the growth of legends, and was concerned to prove that his accounts were authentic.

So, what was Bede's view of the Christian Church? As with Eusebius, a certain amount has to be inferred from what his statements, and his silences, imply. Bede was a Catholic Christian, devoted to the Roman way of doing things. He charted with approval the arrival of a Roman hierarchy, Roman liturgy, Roman chant, and, above all, Roman ways of arriving at the ecclesiastical calendar. This preference for things Roman was by no means axiomatic. In the middle 630s Bede's Northumbria had been evangelized by Celtic monks based in Ireland and what is now western Scotland. In western Britain other forms of pre-Anglo-Saxon Christianity still lingered. Bede regarded all such non-Roman Christians as "heretics," and saw their misfortunes as just punishment.[15] However, he was more than willing to admire the dedication and the asceticism of many Irish monks, and to applaud their zeal as missionaries.[16] Most dreadful of all in Bede's eyes, it seems, was the Irish Christians' stubborn refusal to accept the Catholic means of computing the date of Easter. This was clearly an important crux, since the credibility of Christianity was diminished if different groups of its adherents held their chief festival on different days. However, Bede returned so many times to this issue in the *Ecclesiastical History* that it is difficult not to see it as something of a personal obsession.[17] In general, Bede seems to have found numbers and computation fascinating. He equated the five languages of the British Isles (including Latin) with the five books of Moses; he adopted the custom of listing the persecutions of the early Church as 10 distinct phases, like the plagues of Egypt.

So meticulous an observer of the passing of time might have been expected to show a sense of the temporal quality of Christian teaching. However, Bede did not, any more than Eusebius, subscribe to that kind of Christianity. He shows only limited awareness, if any, that doctrine in the Church was an evolving thing. For instance, several of the visions described in the *Ecclesiastical History* cast a fascinating light on beliefs about the relationship between penance and the hereafter. Prayers and masses said for the dead – or even those just thought to be dead – had miraculous effects.[18] A man who received a vision of departed souls saw some being tormented to purge them of sins for which they had not done penance; but he also saw some saved souls being given a partial, incomplete vision of heavenly bliss before the Last Judgment. This latter "half-way house" would not form part of the doctrine of purgatory as it later developed.[19] Bede referred briefly to the struggle to ensure that people did not use magical or pagan ceremonies and amulets to protect themselves in time of illness; but he was much less interested in this phenomenon than many modern historians now are.[20]

On the other hand, Bede showed a fascination with the intricate and (for the Church) crucial details of Anglo-Saxon royal and aristocratic politics. Northumbria consisted of two kingdoms, Bernicia and Deira, at risk of breaking apart in the absence of a strong king. Rival dynasties vied for control; neighboring rulers intervened in the struggles to secure their borders or to take advantage of any weaknesses. Bede has been accused of having a Northumbrian perspective on all this politics. He arguably saw Northumbria as the center of the Anglo-Saxon world and as the natural leader of its peoples. It is perhaps fairer to say that he was a Roman Christian first and a Northumbrian second. When the aristocrats of midland Mercia rebelled against Oswiu of Northumbria and set up Wulfhere as their king, Bede described Wulfhere quite positively, because he upheld Christianity.[21] His prevailing attitude, perhaps, was providentialist: God would ensure that whatever the fratricidal chaos of barbarian politics, eventually justice and Christianity would be served.[22] Bede did show, with total clarity, that the conversion of a people depended on convincing those in power, the king above all. He narrated the conversion of Edwin of Northumbria in a deliberately long-drawn-out way, emphasizing all the king's hesitations and repeated seeking of advice.[23] When Edwin lost his throne and his life in battle in 633, another member of the royal line, Oswald, who had been brought up in Ireland, imported Irish Christianity rather than the Roman Christianity of Edwin's missionary Paulinus.[24]

Did Bede have a sense that the Church itself had a political life? It seems that he did, although the language of the *History* is measured and even guarded at times, and much has to be made of Bede's omissions and silences. When Augustine of Canterbury was about to meet some British (what would now be called Welsh) churchmen from Bangor Iscoed, the British clerics were told to see if Augustine would stand up, out of respect and humility, when they arrived. When Augustine remained seated, the British priests decided he was proud and overbearing, and their discussions soon broke down.[25] The Catholic proto-evangelist of England hardly comes well out of the story. Bede described, but did not draw attention to, the slow process whereby Theodore, Archbishop of Canterbury, gradually acquired some sort of administrative control over the rest of the Anglo-Saxon clergy in the 670s. This must have entailed some complex political discussion, since previously individual kings had regarded bishops as their personal protégés.[26] Most interesting of all is his attitude to the aristocratic and influential Anglo-Saxon bishop Wilfrid of Hexham. Bede seems not to have liked him very much. It is reported that some followers of Wilfrid accused Bede of heresy in the bishop's presence because of his theories about the ages of the world.[27] Bede reports in copious detail how Wilfrid, after temporary expulsion from his see, was on two occasions accused of monothelite heresy in the presence of successive popes, though acquitted both times.[28] At times it is more by implication and comparison that the clergy are differentiated: John of Beverley worked many miracles, but Wilfrid did not.

In comparison with some of his other work, the *Ecclesiastical History* shows a somewhat formal, reticent quality. In the *History* Bede on the whole depicted what was best in the Church, its bishops, monks, and nuns. His narrative of how the monastery of Coldingham was burned down as a punishment for the evil lives led by the nuns there, in Book IV, was quite exceptional, and was written to illustrate a point about the visions of Adamnan.[29] Yet in Bede's last work, his pastoral letter to the aristocratic Archbishop Egbert of York, he denounced much more freely the lives of some bishops who lived in luxury, wasted time in frivolous conversation, ate much rich food, or demonstrated excessive greed and avarice.[30] He claimed that many of the nobility were acquiring land and founding monasteries in order to set up leisured, endowed communities with no thought for discipline or moral standards. They thus became nominal abbots while simultaneously remaining royal councilors and living as laymen.[31] There is nothing whatever of this sort of comment in the *History*.

Bede clearly felt that it was the best in the Church that deserved commemoration, so much of the *Ecclesiastical History* consists of the lives of great holy men and women. The particular qualities that he found admirable do much to define his age. First of all, the great Christians were ascetics like Aidan, Hild of Whitby, Aethelthryth (Etheldreda) of Ely, Cuthbert of Lindisfarne, or John of Beverley. They lived simply, took limited food, did not acquire property, treated their bodies harshly, and were of course inviolably celibate. They had great personal charisma, achieving conversions and spiritual improvement in those who heard them. They founded religious communities where monastic rules were strictly observed. Their holiness was manifested in miracles. Bede collected miracle stories but was not unreservedly credulous: indeed he repeatedly wrote that he had verified his stories carefully. In Bede's culture, miracles of healing were clearly not only common but also expected. The coffin of St Chad had an opening in its side, intended to allow the faithful to remove a little dust, which when mixed with water cured diseases of men and animals.[32] Material objects associated even remotely with dead saints either had curative powers or proved indestructible by fire.[33] The consummation of the lives of saints was a blessed death. In a number of cases the death of a saint was accompanied by another religious person, possibly in a remote place, seeing a vision of the saint's soul carried to heaven by angels.[34] One of the most common descriptions of miracles involved the body of a saint being seen, deliberately or accidentally, when the coffin was opened after death or during translation of the body. Exceptionally pure and holy people proved incapable of decay, and their bodies remained whole and supple: those who led lives free from "corruption" in the moral or sexual sense, could not experience it in their bodies in a physical sense.[35]

The paradoxes of Bede as a Christian historian flow naturally from his view of the world. Christianity made progress in Barbarian England largely because it suited the Anglo-Saxon aristocracy, especially if they intermarried with the already Christian barbarian kingdoms of Francia, to adopt Christian ways. Its success depended on the brutal realities and fickle chances of succession, internecine warfare, and victory in battle. Yet on the other hand the history of the Church was that of outstandingly and spectacularly holy people. It was natural, right, and proper that such holy people should see visions, should heal diseases, should be surrounded by an aura of the supernatural and die in the odor of sanctity. Harsh reality and exalted spirituality were inherently fused in this world and in its historian.

The High Middle Ages: A Monastic Chronicle

For an example of the historical writing of the high Middle Ages, defined roughly as the period between about 1000 and about 1250, this discussion will take a microcosmic rather than a macrocosmic approach. The characteristic historical form between Bede and the Renaissance was that of the genre of writing known as "chronicle." Chronicles were works written often as a continuous running commentary on the events known to the author. They were usually annalistic: that is, they listed events under the year of their occurrence without seeking to impose an analytical structure or thematic grouping. They were often local in nature: they dwelt on great events chiefly in so far as they had impact on the place where the chronicle was being compiled. Their authors often, though not invariably, effaced their personalities and even their names. These features tended to make chronicles somewhat less rewarding for those who wish to discuss the theory of history. However, even their habitual omissions, such as analytical structure, interpretation of events, or a sense of the flow and development of human culture, are themselves instructive and interesting.

The one example to be discussed in detail here is not, however, a typical chronicle. Yet it gives a fascinating insight into how the religious life of Europe was perceived at the time. It contrasts in a most intriguing way with Bede, all the more so because its author was, like Bede, a learned priest who was also a member of a monastic community. Jocelin of Brakelond was a native, it is presumed, of the town of Bury St Edmunds, and entered the Benedictine abbey in that town in 1173. He was a priest and became chaplain to the prior and then the abbot. He later became master of the guesthouse and almoner (dispenser of alms) for the abbey, and took part in the election of a new abbot in 1212. His only surviving writing is the *Chronicle*, in which he describes the life and activity of Abbot Samson (c. 1135–1212, abbot 1182–1212)[36] and of the community that he presided over at that time. The work is unrevised apart from the insertion of a story dictated later by Jocelin, and ends abruptly some time before the end of Samson's abbacy. It seems, therefore, to have been a private project of its author, and was not necessarily intended to be read outside the abbey.

A personal memoir, even if called a "chronicle," sets itself slightly differ-ent standards from a broader-based history. Jocelin was writing, for nearly all the events he describes, out of his own personal experience. He served for several years as chaplain to the abbot; where he was not an eye-witness, he could use the accounts of those whom he knew intimately and whose trustworthiness he could assess. Given that privileged position, it is striking how great is Jocelin's concern for accurate evidence. There are two lists in the chronicle, one of all the parishes belonging to the abbey and one of all the knights who gave feudal service as tenants on its lands. There are abundant references to disputes being settled with reference to original documents (something where monasteries, with their larger proportion of literate members, were at an advantage over the rest of society). As will be seen, Jocelin showed an astonishing capacity to reflect and report diversity of opinions.

In one other respect Jocelin's chronicle is striking. He wrote fairly typical medieval Latin, but he also demonstrated familiarity with many of the more popular sayings of the classical Latin poets. Tags, proverbs, puns, and little dramatic touches illuminate his written style. While his learning was by no means exceptional for his age (as Bede's certainly was), he does attest the rise of classicizing attitudes among ordinary monks by the late twelfth century. It was not uncontroversial: at one point he reported how the "unlearned" made fun of the learned when one of their number was passed over for appointment. The "good clerks" had "declined" (i.e., nouns) so well in the cloister that they had all been "declined" (i.e., turned down).[37]

In one highly important area, relevant for this discussion, Jocelin of Brakelond differed from Bede. He was entirely ready to depict human beings as flawed, faulty individuals, even though some might be markedly more or less faulty than others. The best of people were prone to sins of pride or anger; the worst of people had something to be said for them. Moreover, human judgments about people were unstable and unreliable. At one point Jocelin recalled his own hostile opinion about someone just elected prior against his wishes; and how afterwards he changed his mind and thought, after all, this might be a good appointment.[38] This world of shades of gray, of fallible human beings with their mingled vices and virtues, is the diametric opposite of Eusebius and Bede with their saints and sinners, their pillars of orthodoxy and their depraved heretics.

The world of which Jocelin of Brakelond wrote was not the heroic age of the founding of churches. It was the age in which institutions had been established, precedents had been set, and routines had grown up. His theme was the government and maintenance of a monastic community, and in particular the skills that it took to be an abbot in such a community. Bury

St Edmunds was a specialized type of monastic realm: a microcosm, indeed, of much of medieval society. It was first of all a franchise or liberty, comprising the western half of the county of Suffolk, in which the abbot ruled directly under the king. He held many of the rights of local government and justice and answered for the military service owed from his lands. In return the abbot and monastery were entitled to various revenues as well as rents from the inhabitants. The monastery was also a major ecclesiastical institution, funded by the income from several important parishes within its boundaries. It was furthermore a spiritual and pilgrimage center, because it kept the relics of the Anglo-Saxon saint King Edmund. This king was revered as a martyr following his murder at the hands of Viking raiders in 870, after he had refused to become the vassal of a pagan warlord.

The ethical standards demanded of such a community and its leader were quite different from those of a charismatic missionary or otherworldly ascetic. By the late twelfth century monasteries, like other religious communities, had acquired privileges and rights as well as endowments. Those rights were constantly under threat from other corporate bodies and individuals who sought to extend their own claims at the community's expense. Some of the abbey's most dangerous rivals were other ecclesiastics. Specially threatening were neighboring bishops like the bishop of Norwich, and the archbishops of Canterbury, from whose supervision the abbey had secured exempt status. In such circumstances Christian meekness and the willingness to cede to one's neighbor for the sake of peace were quite beside the point. A monastic ruler, or a whole community, which failed to defend its rights would, first, be risking the anger of the patron saint who resided there, and who was supposed to be as jealous of his rights and status as his living representatives. Secondly, they would set bad precedents for their successors in future, who might receive a diminished inheritance in terms of status, lands, or money. The same ethic, that decreed that every privilege acquired in the past must be zealously defended for the sake of the future, applied to relations within the community. If the monks had acquired a privilege in respect of their abbot, they dare not allow it to lapse for fear that a future abbot would abuse his now enhanced position.

Abbot Samson, whose election and reign as abbot forms the heart of the *Chronicle*, is depicted as an effective abbot. Yet Jocelin makes it clear from the start that he was a controversial choice. He had held minor office under the previous abbot when the abbey had run up huge debts and wasted money in all directions. He had resented the concealment of these problems and acquired the reputation of one who could not be corrupted. As abbot, his first and greatest achievement was to learn how to manage the revenues and to pay off all the debts acquired by his predecessors within a relatively short time.[39] However, he was resented for his outspokenness: Jocelin quotes unnamed monks parodying the Litany: "deliver us from 'good clerks' [learned clergy] O Lord; that you may deign to preserve us from Norfolk barrators [Samson's nickname], we beseech thee to hear us."[40] Jocelin portrays Samson as independent, trusting few advisers, stern and somewhat isolated in his leadership, and given to fits of temper if he were resisted or thwarted.[41] He imposed "clerks" (secular priests, who were not monks) to assist the monks in the administration of the abbey. He felt that the monks could not be trusted to run their affairs without running into debts, and at one stage withdrew his assistance in the expectation that they would make a mess of things.[42] He was fierce and demanding in executing justice, and punctilious in insisting on the full rights of the abbey. However, in some disputes where he could either offend the monks or make enemies outside, he chose to offend the monks and keep friends among the townspeople or outsiders.[43] A peculiarity of the abbacy of Bury St Edmunds around 1200 was that the abbot had secured properties, rights, and revenues, which were independent of, and potentially in conflict with, those of the community of monks. Even within the monastery there were some special privileged groups: the abbey cellarer, for example, had revenues of his own (usually inadequate) and certain judicial rights (usually disputed). The abbot therefore had to play a judicious balancing game; he had both to preserve his rights as abbot for his successor, and ensure the well-being of the monastery of which he was very much the head.

This picture of a complex web of rival jurisdictions prompts one to ask whether the abbey of St Edmunds was a "good" monastery, by the standards of its time or any other. Here Jocelin's realism as a historian of his times is interesting for its omissions as for its statements. He says very little about the liturgical, spiritual, or intellectual conditions of the abbey. Yet it clearly had priests and schoolmasters, observed the Benedictine rule sufficiently well not to cause scandal, and nurtured in Jocelin a literate and effective writer in good medieval Latin. If Jocelin ignored the routine religious life of the abbey, it was because it was so routine as not to need discussion. There was, however, no heroic asceticism. Samson prudently relaxed the rules somewhat regarding private property. The buildings and the hospitality of the community seem to have been generous, usually overspending the cellarer's budget. On the abbey estates the abbot kept parks and game animals, and allowed the monks to observe the hounds pursuing animals, something condemned by later church councils.[44] When Samson made an inquiry as to who had private seals (on which money could be borrowed, burdening the abbey), 33 private seals were found and the majority confiscated.[45]

The greater part of Jocelin's chronicle concerns rights, revenues, privileges, and appointments. Yet the religious dimension repeatedly makes its presence felt, especially in the form of the invisible but all-seeing saint who was accessible through his relics. Abbot Samson became a monk because of a dream in which he saw St Edmund snatch him from the devil's hands at the cemetery gates.[46] Henry of Essex, brought to trial by battle over his military reputation, was daunted by an appearance of St Edmund threatening punishment for Henry's lack of generosity to his church and failure to accept its rights. When he recovered from wounds he became a monk in penance.[47] When abbeys were asked to contribute treasure to ransom the captured King Richard I, Samson offered to open his abbey church and dared anyone to come and brave the saint's anger by taking precious metal from his shrine, which no-one did.[48] When part of the shrine of St Edmund was damaged by fire in 1198, the preservation of his cup from burning was regarded as a miracle.[49] Someone told the abbot of a dream that St Edmund was lying naked and hungry outside his shrine. The abbot and the monks then interpreted the dream in two quite different, equally self-serving ways.[50] In effect, the supernatural and spiritual side to the Abbey of St Edmunds was the reflection of its material, everyday existence. It was assumed that the saint was as zealous for his particular privileges, as keen to acquire treasure for his shrine and protect its reputation, as the monks were all expected to be.

Jocelin of Brakelond's chronicle is not the portrayal of a corrupt or decadent institution. Its abbot would, in a less unvarnished and frank account, have appeared as a reformer, a disciplinarian, and paragon of administrative efficiency. What is portrayed in this work is a community dedicated to the belief-system of its time. In that system, the Church had become a conservator of dispersed fragments of holy power. Each religious center had an absolute duty to conserve its particular spark of the divine essence, in the form of its saint and its shrine, and defend its beauty and majesty, indeed its wealth, against all comers.

Renaissance Historiography: Rhetoric and Skepticism

Church history is full of ironies. Occasionally one comes across a history of the affairs of the Church that is almost (if not quite) secular in outlook. The human characteristics of clergy, this-worldly motives for their actions, and the business affairs of the institutional Church dominate. So it is in the work to be discussed next. Yet the text in question, the *Commentaries* of Enea Silvio Piccolomini, was written by a reigning pope.[51]

Enea Silvio Piccolomini (1405–64) was born to a family of impoverished nobles from the Tuscan city of Siena. Like many of the urban nobility of later medieval Italy, the Piccolomini had been thrust from power by the middle classes of their state and forced to live disenfranchised in the countryside. Nevertheless, Enea Silvio acquired an excellent grounding in Renaissance literature and rhetorical techniques, and built a career as a secretary and speech-writer to powerful figures, and as a Renaissance Latin poet. His skills as a rhetorician earned him employment in rapid succession with the Duke of Savoy (who briefly became an antipope), the Emperor of Austria, and several popes. He postponed accepting priestly orders as late as possible but eventually became a bishop, a cardinal and, in 1458, pope himself as Pius II.

Enea Silvio's *Commentaries* are essentially an autobiographical memoir of the author's pontificate up to the end of 1463. They are, as the author himself admitted, somewhat disorderly. However, he clearly saw himself as a historian. He compared his work, with some modesty, to that of the great Florentine historian Flavio Biondo. He wrote about major public events, and tried to explain the reasons behind them. Besides the *Commentaries*, he wrote a *History of Bohemia* based on his experiences and knowledge acquired during his time in northern Europe. When in England he visited the tomb of Bede (though he mistakenly thought he was an abbot).[52] At the monastery on Mount Amiata he inspected one of the greatest monuments to Anglo-Saxon manuscript calligraphy, the *Codex Amiatinus*.[53]

If one can vindicate Enea Silvio's claim to be a historian, it is less clear how ecclesiastical his outlook was. For a great deal of his work he was concerned with the struggle for the succession to the crown of Naples, contested over many decades between the princely houses of Aragon and Anjou. The papacy under Pius II sided with the Aragonese, which entailed fraught relationships with the French and continuous dealings with disreputable and unreliable mercenary captains. Enea Silvio demonstrated immense curiosity about all aspects of human behavior. On his villains, such as Sigismondo Malatesta, the unreliable and despotic though highly cultured ruler of the papal vicariate of Rimini, he inflicted character-portraits, or rather character assassinations, of enormous verve and style. He described the beauties of nature as seen on several trips made outside Rome to escape the summer heat, and appreciated holding court in the open under the trees. He wrote about rowing and running races staged during festivals he attended: in these accounts he described unblinkingly the bragging and drunkenness of young Italian males of the era. He even wrote a description of the working of a *scoppetum*, a kind of primitive firearm;[54] and described the performance of three siege-guns he had ordered to be made for the Naples campaign.[55]

And yet Enea Silvio was writing about the history of the Church. It was just that the Church, seen from the perspective of a fifteenth-century pope, was a quite different institution from that familiar to Bede or to Jocelin. Enea Silvio took the doctrine, beliefs, and practices of late medieval Catholicism entirely for granted. He neither subjected them to scrutiny nor supposed them to be changeable or open to doubt, save by heretics. The chief question for a Church historian, in those circumstances, was how well or badly individual human beings performed while living their lives within the Church. One might also inquire as to why they chose the paths that they did. Viewed from this angle, the most striking thing about Enea Silvio's insight into the Church is his frank and honest appreciation of the mixed motives of so many of the people whom it comprised.

Enea Silvio was by no means an entirely secular skeptic. He did not, like (say) Machiavelli, regard the primary value of religion to lie in ensuring communal stability, patriotic purpose, and good order. He inserted into his narrative descriptions of figures of outstanding holiness, whom he evidently revered. Antonino Pierozzi, Archbishop of Florence, lived in great austerity, was a popular preacher and reformer, made peace in his city, and gave prodigally to the poor, keeping almost nothing for himself.[56] After due inquiries Pius II proclaimed the canonization of Catherine of Siena, a mystical and devotional writer of the previous century (who was also a native of Enea Silvio's home city).[57] He evidently saw monks and friars of reformed or observant orders as the best of their kind.[58] He made Alessandro of Sassoferato, a learned theologian and leader of the Augustinian friars, a cardinal on the basis that no-one could object to him.[59]

However, Enea Silvio was not convinced by all the claims made to holiness by the saints and ascetics of his age. In the early stages of the *Commentaries* he described the sanctity and reputed miracle working of Giovanni Capistrano, a reformer of the Franciscans. In time he came to doubt the reality of the miracles and later opposed Capistrano's canonization as a saint.[60] Amedeo VIII of Savoy, whom Enea Silvio briefly served as a secretary, had retired to a hermitage near the Lake of Geneva with some companions, viewing himself (though a layperson) as a sort of pope-in-waiting for when the Council of Basel should seek to appoint a new pope. About him Enea Silvio was reserved and somewhat sardonic.[61] At the abbey of Subiaco he found a retired Spanish bishop living in seclusion with the monks. Of him he wrote that "he was blessed indeed if...his contempt of the world was sincere and if he did not reject a high dignity in this world in hope of gaining a higher."[62] When he visited the Lake of Bolsena, he found one of the islands in the lake occupied by Franciscan friars of the observant wing of the movement: "they are indeed exemplary men whose riches are poverty and abstinence, unless they deceive themselves more than they do others."[63] In comparison with these skeptical and often back-handed comments about aspiring saints, Enea Silvio was far more appreciative in the epitaphs that he composed for fellow-scholars and writers of the Renaissance. A number of the first generation of humanists died in his lifetime, and his tributes to them were wholly generous and without irony.[64]

Enea Silvio would in future years be something of an embarrassment to the Roman hierarchy, because of the astoundingly frank way that he described the political machinations of the papal court, and the unedifying personalities who gathered there. When the *Commentaries* were printed in 1584, their authorship was disguised and nearly all the author's most telling comments were censored out. In the conclave of 1458 that elected Enea Silvio as Pius II, the chief rival candidate was Guillaume d'Estouteville, Cardinal-Archbishop of Rouen. Enea Silvio hinted darkly that d'Estouteville was guilty of "simony and lewdness" and would turn the papacy into "a den of thieves or a brothel of whores." He placed most stress, however, on the cliques and cabals that d'Estouteville formed to try to generate unstoppable momentum for his own election (holding meetings of cardinals in the lavatories next to the hall where the conclave met). Enea Silvio then reported the private speeches that he himself made to wavering cardinals to defeat d'Estouteville's claim. The way that he bullied the young Rodrigo Borgia (later Pope Alexander VI) was particularly memorable.[65]

Later on, when the possibility was being discussed of promoting Jean Jouffroy, Bishop of Arras (c. 1412–73) to cardinal, Alain de Coëtivy, Cardinal of Avignon (d. 1474) delivered the most blistering attack on his personality. Jouffroy was a know-it-all who tried to outdo everyone whom he met in knowledge of their own fields. "He will sow discord and nurture faction. He is a restless spirit and unless I am mistaken the son of an incubus."[66] To this tirade Pius II replied that every bit of it was true. However, to persuade the King of France to revoke certain unilateral legislation that he had passed against papal control over Church appointments, it was necessary to honor the king by making one of his bishops a cardinal. The intricacies of church politics and diplomacy here stand out in all their messy, ugly detail. However, Enea Silvio thought that there were worse examples of churchmen outside the Curia. If d'Estouteville was bad, Dieter von Isenburg, Archbishop of Mainz, was far worse. He allegedly bribed his way to election as archbishop, and defended his position against the pope's hostility with a mixture of petulance, anti-Italian xenophobia, and violence.[67] What never occurred to Pius II was that his own activities might have contributed to the problems that he described. For instance, he does not mention his (financially motivated) proliferation of the administrative staff at the Curia, which intensified the scramble for money and rewards in an already materially driven system.[68]

So what, if anything, did Pius II write about Christian religion? Curiously perhaps, this intensely secular writer was also a devoted believer in the cult of holy relics, and a passionate enthusiast for elaborate and beautiful religious ceremony. One of the few putatively "good" consequences of the Turkish advance past Constantinople and into Greece was that it increased Rome's already vast stock of relics. In Pius II's pontificate he was able to secure the head of St Andrew, which had been kept at Patras, from its owner for keeping in St Peter's. He held an enormous festival for the ceremonial entrance of the apostle's head into the city of Rome and then into the Basilica of St Peter, all of which he lovingly described. (He remarked with typical wit on how even some of the fattest cardinals were so caught up in the event that they willingly walked two miles in procession.)[69] Similarly, when he kept Corpus Christi at Viterbo in 1462, and when he dedicated a cathedral in the "model town" of Pienza built on his command near his native village, he described the celebrations, which were made as magnificent as possible, in every detail.[70] Splendid, dignified worship with sumptuous hangings, beautiful music and ornaments, and a fitting level of devotion among those present: this was Christian worship for a Renaissance pope, and he cared to see it done really well.

The other, in some ways even stranger, aspect to the *Commentaries* concerns the question of crusade. The Ottoman Sultan Mehmet II overwhelmed Constantinople five years before Pius II's reign began. Pius II dedicated a great deal of his diplomatic and political efforts during his pontificate to wringing undertakings from European princes to go on crusade against the Turks. Some 250 years after the inglorious fiasco of the Fourth Crusade, this might have seemed a bizarre dream. Yet Pius risked his credibility and further damaged his health (since he suffered dreadfully from gout) in calling a conference at Mantua in 1459 to plan a crusade, which relatively few princes attended save through their ambassadors.[71] At the end of his life he was offering to lead a crusade in person, in the hope that he could shame other princes into joining him. Interfaith warfare is now rightly seen as deplorable by all responsible religious people. However, in Pius II's age it offered some way out of the eternal brutal civil strife of fifteenth-century Europe. By a strange irony he was given a peaceful victory over the Turks, when a prospector discovered alum ore (vital for the cloth industry) near Tolfa in the papal states, and allowed Western Europe to buy its alum from the pope rather than the Turks, hitherto the only source.[72]

The Church described in Pius II's *Commentaries* was a corporation, a landowner, a vast international administrative machine. Pius II saw it for what it was; and saw that spectacular personal holiness was an additional extra, that appeared from time to time but was not universal and could not be produced on demand. However, it seems that he, a poet, rhetorician, and diplomat rather than a career priest, never doubted that he was governing the inheritance of St Peter. He had neither illusions about people nor doubts about doctrines or institutions. This approach was by no means complacent. However, it was unprepared for the particular challenges of the sixteenth century. That next century saw more radical changes in attitudes to the history of the churches than had ever been seen before.

The Reformation and the Rise of a Sense of History

The Reformation of the sixteenth century was absolutely crucial to the rise of a sense of the historical predicament of the Christian churches. From the very start, the Reformation movement was based on the claim that, at some time in the previous five centuries or so, the Church had taken a wrong turning. The reformers claimed to be restoring, or rediscovering, a form of teaching and a manner of worship that had existed and had been lost. This rhetoric required two forms of historical insight. First, the reformers searched not only the New Testament but also the early Church for evidence that primitive Christianity was ignorant of those Catholic institutions and customs which the reformers opposed. Secondly, they searched more recent history for evidence that rites or customs believed to be "timeless" in fact originated in more recent epochs. As a consequence, some trappings of contemporary Catholicism could be accused of anachronism, or of lacking basic historical sense.

It is not the purpose of this book to argue that the reformers abruptly, as it were from nowhere, inaugurated a "modern" way of looking at the Church in place of a "medieval" one. The transition was of course gradual and complicated. The reformers were able to criticize medieval concepts of the early Church, but did not see that their own vision of it was just as time-limited and in some respects anachronistic. Their sense of the flow of history was often dominated by theological concerns, often eschatological or apocalyptic in nature. The ebbs and flows of the Church's virtue and vice reflected the binding and loosing of Satan and the prospects for the end of history itself. The attempt to construct an alternate succession of the Church, outside the Catholic tradition, entailed some very unscrupulous abuse of the historical records. Towards the end of the sixteenth century, church history became locked into competing rival structures of orthodox dogma.

Nevertheless, an important change took place. There had been many reforming spirits in the past who had contrasted the simplicity and poverty of Christ and the apostolic age with the wealth, grandeur, and pomp of the papal Church. A famous set of wall-paintings in a church in Prague, copied into a surviving manuscript, made such damning comparisons between Christ and the Pope.[73] However, there is an important distinction to be made here, already observed in relation to medieval historians. To criticize moral failings (including wealth, grandeur, and pomp) was one thing: to criticize ideals and beliefs was another. The leaders of the sixteenth-century Reformation argued that even if the Roman Catholic Church of the later Middle Ages had lived up to all its ideals faithfully, it would still have been a wicked perversion of the Christian Church. The fault lay in the teachings and priorities, not just in the sinful failure to live up to earlier standards.

In the early years of the Reformation the reformers were preoccupied with the theological essence of their message: how could they prove that their understanding of the gospel was the authentic one? As years passed, however, they had to devise a new kind of historical critique of the church's past. The reformers had to ask themselves, and to answer themselves, their hearers, and their critics, "How and why did the Church come to go so far wrong, that the Reformation has become necessary?" "How, and by what stages, did the Church degenerate to the point where it could no longer be recognized as the Church?" Then, as the devastating implications of their critique were assimilated, a new question arose: "If the Church was so corrupt over the last three or four hundred years as the reformers claim, what becomes of the Gospel promise that the Holy Spirit would be with the followers of Jesus to the end of time?" The answers to these questions ensured that at the heart of the Reformation would be a new perception of the history of Christianity, and of the relationship between gospel and Church.

Martin Luther

It is not the intention of this chapter to offer a comprehensive survey of the rise and limitations of historical sense in the early Reformation. The confines of this short essay are too narrow, and much of the research necessary to write such a survey either remains to be done or is not yet assimilated. Rather, what is offered, in keeping with the approach elsewhere in this chapter, is a set of case-studies, to show how and how far a historical sense shaped the reformers' critique of their predecessors.

Martin Luther (1483–1546) thought that his primary insight, namely that people were saved freely for Christ's sake through faith without good works, imputed as "alien" righteousness draped over a sinful soul, was a timeless revelation and the true content of the gospel. In due course he rediscovered it in much of Scripture (especially Paul's letters, John's Gospel and parts of Acts), and many of the best of the Fathers, especially Augustine. Luther showed no sense that his own vision of the gospel was historically conditioned. However, he had to defend his vision against Catholic critics who argued that his faith-centered approach negated the centuries of continuous witness and tradition in the Church. In particular, Luther confronted the suggestion that it was the Church's role from time to time to redefine or clarify doctrine. The Church argued that the interpretation of Scripture was a matter for the collective sense of the Church as a whole, expressed through its leaders. Luther interpreted this suggestion as meaning that popes, councils, and the Church hierarchy claimed to "control" the meaning of Scripture and the teachings of the Church and thought they could change it at will. This was, needless to say, a caricature. Yet his response to this straw man constituted Luther's most significant piece of historical writing.

In 1537–8 the papacy under Paul III came close to holding the much-delayed general council of the Church and actually summoned delegates to Mantua. Although the Mantua council did not meet, it provoked the Lutheran churches into discussion and definition of their teaching.[74] In 1538 there was published at Cologne a work entitled *All the Councils, both general and particular, from the times of the apostles to this day*, edited by the French Catholic scholar Pierre Crabbe (1470–1553). These political and publishing events inspired Luther to reflect, in a typically combative and controversialist way, on questions such as: "What makes the Church?" "What is a general council for, and how far do its decrees extend?"

In 1539 Luther wrote his short pamphlet entitled *On Councils and the Churches*.[75] Luther reached some paradoxical conclusions (this too was typical of the man). First, he argued that it was impossible for one to conform oneself to every detail of what had been passed by the various councils of the Church. For one thing, as Luther had pointed out as early as his hearing at Worms in 1521, the councils and early Fathers had often contradicted each other, or had decreed things that were clearly wrong.[76] Secondly, there were things contained in the decrees of councils that had never been cancelled but were clearly dead letters. The Council of Jerusalem had insisted early Christians observe some Jewish food taboos (Acts 15: 19–20).[77] The Council of Nicea ruled that Christians who had re-entered service in the Roman army had to wait seven years before receiving communion again.[78] Sorting out all the decrees of the councils into consistent rules, as though they were conflicting legal precedents, would be a hopeless task.[79] The answer, said Luther, was that the early councils only "really" functioned to confirm doctrine and confute error. The Council of Nicea (held in 325) confuted Arius, that of Constantinople (381) confuted Macedonius, that of Ephesus (431) confuted Nestorius, while the one at Chalcedon (451) confuted Eutyches.[80] Apart from refuting the errors of these heresiarchs, most of the things councils did were administrative matters of no enduring importance. Even in their doctrinal work, none of these councils instituted new articles of faith. All they did was to discern and declare in an especially public way what Scripture taught.[81] So councils, it seemed, played no constructive or creative role in the teaching or life of the Church.

But Luther did not really mean that. What he meant was that no council *properly or rightly* changed anything in the faith, instituted any new ceremony or ritual, or defined any new doctrine. The earliest councils, with their (according to Luther) self-limited and restricted agenda, showed what ought to be done, but subsequently was not. Most of "the pope's councils," he went on to say, were "satanic gatherings." In these councils, new (i.e., wrong) articles of faith had been established, in manifest contradiction to the text of Scripture.[82] In other words, in so far as Christian traditions had grown up which were inconsistent with Scripture, these could in no way be "justified" as the outcome of the cumulative decisions of Church councils. A council could not add anything to the Church's teaching or practice. It might, however, fail to condemn either wrong teachings or new false "good works." And this was what had actually happened.[83] New rules and styles of monastic "holiness" had grown up, which were mistakenly regarded by ordinary people as more holy than an ordinary life of decent service to one's neighbor. Councils had failed to "prune the vines," so that monasticism grew rampant "until the Christian Church was hardly recognizable any longer." In the Middle Ages Bernard was reputed to have founded over 160 monasteries, and after him "it rained and snowed monks."[84] Monasteries vied with each other in strictness, surpassing in their rigor the bounds of charity or common sense. Luther made out of this an anthropological point that chimes with much of the message of this book: "And this serves us right, since our ears itch so much for something new that we can no longer endure the old and genuine truth, . . . that we weigh ourselves down with big piles of new teachings. That is just what has happened and will continue to happen."[85]

Luther concluded that at the time he was writing, in 1539, a new council was indeed required. It should act like the councils of old and repress wrong doctrine. However, the wrong doctrine that Luther had in mind was the entire system of medieval Christianity since the rise of the Western papacy.

Luther did not specify exactly how long this error had lasted or how long it had taken to develop. His interest was fundamentally dogmatic rather than historical. However, he regarded medieval Catholicism as a hugely extended period of centuries of demonic error, a sort of "Arian" episode but lasting for five hundred or more years.[86]

Heinrich Bullinger

Luther had not troubled to explore the gradual process of the "degradation," as the reformers saw it, of apostolic Christianity into the state it reached by 1500. He was concerned with the main theme rather than the details. However, others who broadly shared his aims pursued things much further. In the same year, 1539, that Luther issued *On Councils and the Church*, Heinrich Bullinger (1504–75) the leader of the reformed church of Zürich, published his *On the Origin of Error*.[87] Bullinger was by instinct of a more moderate temper than Luther, and most other reformed leaders for that matter. He took over the Zürich church after its first reformer, Huldrych Zwingli, was killed in a minor war into which he had rashly drawn his city. Bullinger gave Zürich peace and stability. He wrote a history of the Zürich church (which long remained in manuscript) and kept a journal of his own time.[88] However, like the other reformers, his primary motivation was not historical scholarship but the restoration, as he saw it, of the correct doctrine of the Church after centuries of error. *On the Origin of Error* was a greatly enlarged version of some essays that he had written about 15 years earlier, and focused on two issues: first, the cult of saints and their images; and second, the Eucharist and its evolution into the "papal mass." The spirit of furious debate in the sixteenth century led, perhaps surprisingly, to an enhancement in the scholarly quality of some of the work produced. Bullinger carefully cited his sources by author, volume, and chapter number; often he transcribed whole sections of primary texts. Since many of his readers would be hostile, it was vital to forestall any suggestion that he abused or misrepresented his sources. Consequently, he would admit freely that a Church Father whom in other respects he admired (say Jerome or Augustine) sometimes said things tending more to the Catholic viewpoint than to his own.

Allowing for the fact that Bullinger was writing a piece of controversial theology, it is nevertheless remarkable how many genuinely historical arguments, and how much use of historical sources, he built into *On the Origin of Error*. Bullinger's ruling premise, like that of the other reformers, was that the true Church was to be found in the ancient, primitive Church of the apostolic period. "Reformation should be in every respect alike and equivalent to the ancient form."[89] Accordingly, any change from the ancient form meant depravation. The earliest apostolic Church, as he depicted it, was characterized by extreme simplicity and a concentration on the spirit rather than the externals of worship. Ceremonies were few and basic. The materials of worship were ordinary everyday things. Rich ornamentation and extravagance were condemned and avoided. Regulation was minimal; most details of worship were matters of free choice. In terms of doctrine, there was no taste (as Bullinger claimed) for specious disputation about the fine print of theological dogma.[90]

Bullinger proposed, albeit in a polemical context, a number of extremely important insights into the history of religion. First, he argued that customs changed gradually over time. A religious practice that was begun with a "good" intention could as time passed degenerate into a more "corrupt" form. Monasticism started as a noble ideal, but as monasteries became wealthy it degenerated into an abuse.[91] Likewise, the early Church knew of no cult of saints. However, around the time of the persecutions Christians resolved to commemorate the lives of the martyrs, to inspire their successors and protect their memory. A little later (though as Bullinger argued, without scriptural warrant) some Fathers of the Church surmised that the saints triumphant in heaven must feel the same concern for the faithful as when they lived; so they might be praying for us. Later still, people supposed that it was appropriate to address the saints in heaven, to call on them as patrons, to ask them for favors and protection in particular circumstances.[92] In the same way, the Eucharist or Lord's Supper originated as a very simple rite. To it were added over time a number of devout and admirable prayers. These tended to become progressively more elaborate and laden with regulations. The mass, which had one significance when it was a congregational rite at which the people made the responses, acquired a different meaning when it was said by priests and clergy on their own, with the people mute and detached.[93]

Secondly, Bullinger saw the conversion process as critical. Winning over pagan peoples might entail certain compromises, which would have important consequences later on. Bullinger argued that the custom of keeping images and statues of saints began with recently converted pagans. He referred (correctly) to a story told by Eusebius about two statues, which used to stand in Caesarea. These represented respectively the woman cured from hemorrhages and Jesus reassuring her.[94] (Eusebius had actually implied that these statues were thank-offering images made by a "Gentile," like those made and dedicated to tutelary gods in classical paganism.) Images at that time, Bullinger insisted, were private property and were not placed in churches, far less were they prayed to. He interpreted the first use of images as a concession to the customs of recently converted pagans. He compared their early use to the keeping of "icons" of the reformers in his own time: these were memorials kept out of admiration and affection, not cult-objects to worship.[95] Similarly, he suggested that prayers for the dead might have been introduced to reassure former pagans, who were used to venerating their ancestors at their graves.[96] In other words, these concessions served to make the transition to Christianity easier, but at an ultimately great cost.

Thirdly, Bullinger argued that the social context of religious practice was fundamentally important. He explained that the rise in the cult of images, and the increase of ceremony at the expense of exposition of Scripture, were consequences of the barbarian invasions. It had become harder to find learned bishops, so Christian worship became more a matter of ceremonial than biblical exegesis.[97] The Latin language, which when used in late antique Italy and Gaul was still comprehensible to the people, became entirely incomprehensible when Romance languages diverged, and when Christianity was imported into Germany.

Bullinger's fourth and most tendentious argument was that medieval Christianity in its fully developed form was really a very late development, in many respects no more than some three hundred years old. His description of this period was typically polemical: "Finally the papal tyrant subjected all human and divine things to himself. There was born around 1212 the most true deception and perdition of the world, the useless crowd of mendicant monks, bold, stubborn, perversely religious, and marvelously appropriate for planting and nourishing superstition."[98] He held the friars responsible for writing vast hagiographical literature, especially the *Golden Legend* of Jacopo de Voragine OP (c. 1230–c.1298). In the same way he showed that the commonest word for the Eucharist in the late Middle Ages, the "mass," was the latest and most obscure of the many names used historically for the central Christian ritual.[99] The custom of saying the words of consecration in an inaudible whisper was recent, and had been justified by ridiculous legends.[100] The "canon" of the mass, the most sacred element that contained the prayer of consecration, was of uncertain date and authorship. Even Catholic authors admitted that it dated at the very earliest from the time of Gregory the Great, so for five centuries Christians had got on very well without it.[101]

Finally, Bullinger argued that analogies could legitimately be drawn between Christian and non-Christian religions, despite the differences between them. He suggested that the evolutionary pattern whereby people first worshiped one god without images, then allowed "gods" to proliferate, then made images of them as physical objects, could be seen in ancient paganism in the same way as in medieval Christianity.[102] He argued (in this respect following some Renaissance humanists, notably Erasmus) that the array of Christian patron saints and "specialist" saints matched exactly the diversity of deities in classical paganism.[103] In their images, temples, sacrifices, festivals, and offerings medieval Christians corresponded minutely to the customs of ancient religions.[104] Bullinger was not, of course, making a value-neutral "comparative religion"-type point here. He was demonstrating, as he believed, the "wrongness" of medieval Catholicism by likening it to an ancient paganism that no-one in his own time would espouse or defend. Nevertheless, like Luther he ended up making observations about general human tendencies in religious behavior over time, which would be rediscovered much later.

John Calvin

John Calvin (1509–64) was perceived internationally as a reformer of greater stature than Bullinger, though the church directly under his authority, that of Geneva, was if anything smaller than Zürich's. Calvin was, however, a writer of systematic theology of immense intellectual and literary power, a commentator and preacher on Scripture, an ecclesiastical statesman of skill and prudence, and so diligent a laborer in the affairs of his church that he effectively worked himself to death. From his massive output one could with care and patience distil a synthesis of his view of history. However, in the more limited confines of this work we shall consider only one relatively minor and quite early writing, his *Most useful advertisement of the great advantage that would come to Christendom if an inventory were made of all the holy bodies and relics, that are in Italy, France, Germany, Spain and other kingdoms and lands*, better and more concisely known as the *Treatise on Relics*.[105] The *Treatise on Relics* was first published in 1543, only 10 years or so after Calvin's conversion to the Reformation. It followed on the first major revision of his masterpiece, the *Institution of Christian Religion* in 1541. It was published in French, Calvin's native language, and addressed a popular as much as a learned audience. Interestingly (given the traditional view of Calvin as a grim and humorless figure) it is also very funny.

Calvin was, of course, deeply and bitterly opposed to the veneration of relics and all the consequences that he saw it brought to contemporary religion. He stressed repeatedly in the pamphlet that there was no mention anywhere in the Gospels or the early writings of the Church of the keeping of relics of Christ or any of the saints. The deliberate avoidance of anything savoring of idolatry in the early Church made it most unlikely that any such relics would have been kept in the first place. Then there was the problem that so many relics existed in multiple versions across Europe: one saint might have up to four full bodies dispersed in various places, besides body parts dispersed here and there. Obviously most, if not all, had to be forgeries. Calvin made the same observation about human habits as Luther and Bullinger had made. First no relics were kept at all; then it was intended to keep them without idolatry; then as time went by they were inevitably venerated and made the subject of idolatrous worship. When people began to dig up, move around, collect, and venerate real relics, the Devil stepped in and provoked the "finding" and devising of bogus ones.[106]

Most of the pamphlet was literally what its title said: it was an inventory, with sarcastic and satirical asides, of as many relics as Calvin had discovered to exist at the time. (His inventory was actually incomplete, even after he made some last-minute additions at the end of the book). However, the work is relevant to this chapter because of one particular argument that Calvin used repeatedly throughout the treatise. He was able to falsify many of the existing relics *because they were anachronistic*. That is, the people who exhibited these relics failed to realize that the conditions, customs, and apparatus of Christianity were quite different in the past from the late Middle Ages (when most of the relics began to be exhibited). It should be added that anachronisms tended to arise in respect of the relics of the early founders of Christianity, the holy family, and the early saints. There was not the same problem with those saints whose bodies had attracted veneration immediately after their deaths, as was the case with (say) Cuthbert of Lindisfarne or Francis of Assisi.

Many of the alleged relics of Christ's passion displayed such lapses in historical awareness. At Rome, Calvin claimed, one could be shown the altar on which Christ was presented when he was taken into the temple in infancy "as though there were then several altars, just as in the papacy when one made as many as one wished."[107] In the same place one could see the table of the Last Supper: but those who exhibited this table did not realize that the disciples, like others at that time, lay down on couches to eat, so tables were much lower.[108] Two churches showed the board affixed to the cross, but what they showed was a delicately carved piece of wood, not something knocked together in haste.[109] The robe of Christ woven as a single seamless cloth would, said Calvin, have been like a Roman *tunica*; but the two robes at Argenteuil in France and Trier in Germany were both in the shape of clerical chasubles.[110] Because the medieval iconography of the passion frequently showed dice being thrown by the soldiers "casting lots" for Christ's robe, various churches exhibited medieval-pattern dice, which were not mentioned in the Gospels and which did not conform to the gaming materials used in antiquity.[111] Worst of all, the Gospel of John clearly stated that Christ was buried in Jewish fashion, with the body up to the shoulders wrapped in one long piece of cloth and the head wrapped separately, in a sort of kerchief.[112] However, all the half-dozen or so holy shrouds exhibited in Calvin's time (of which only the one now in Turin survives as a devotional object) were continuous pieces of cloth covering the entire body.[113]

The relics of the early saints raised many of the same problems. At Perugia the wedding ring of the Virgin Mary was on display: Calvin mocked not only the assumption that wedding customs in first-century Judea were the same as today, but also the fact that it was a rich piece of jewelry, unsuitable for her historical circumstances.[114] At St Peter's in Rome one could see the episcopal throne of St Peter and his altar and chasuble, though the earliest apostles were hardly likely to have sat on thrones.[115] Likewise (as Bullinger had already pointed out) the apostles did not celebrate a mass at a stone altar, yet several purporting to date from their time were on display. Since St Laurence, martyred 258, was one of the deacons of the Roman Church, all the accoutrements of a sixteenth-century deacon were attributed to him and displayed as relics, even though these vestments were not in use in the early Church.[116]

Like the other reformers, Calvin wrote from a theological, not a historical, perspective. What mattered was correct doctrine, irrespective of its place in time. To that extent, his theology was not historicist. However, it is fascinating to see an essentially dogmatic theologian exploit, almost casually, the process of change in the churches and in religious culture as the key to disproving the validity of relics. The perception was growing that the Church lived out its existence against a context of cultural change and evolution. Moreover, the reformers had embedded in their thought the notion that the majority of the Church, not just a few isolated heretics and their followers, could depart fatally from the faith. They had begun to sketch out the possibility that human failings, human curiosity, and human enthusiasm for new rituals could distort and obscure what mattered in the Christian revelation and the Christian life.

The Rise of Reformed Schools of Church History

The reformers just discussed had begun to think about a historical approach to explaining diversity and "error" in religion; but they had not yet formed an idea of "Church history," as a distinct discipline with peculiar objectives. The discipline and theory of Church history began to evolve and acquire certain characteristics and arguments from the middle of the sixteenth century onwards. Some of the first writers to propose such a theory were followers of Luther's younger colleague, Philipp Melanchthon (1497–1560). Viktorin Strigel (1524–69) argued in the 1540s that Church history was the history of the soul as secular history was the history of the body: it had a separate kind of sources and separate priorities.[117] Another "Philippist," Christoph Pezel (1539–1604) delivered a celebrated speech on the value and purpose of Church history in 1568. Pezel argued that Church history was certain, ancient, continuous, and showed the purposes of God at work. However, he also insisted that it was useful for theologians to learn how human error had corrupted true doctrine in times past.[118] The degree of corruption could, moreover, be measured against the span of time. At this stage Pezel identified four periods of Christian history, each of approximately 500 years. The last age of the Christian era had begun with the Reformation. Towards the end of his life, Pezel wrote an extended work of world history under the curious title of *Mellificium historicum*, or "the Historical Beehive." In his prefaces he proclaimed what he saw as the role of Church history:

> One must consider in histories at what time and with what testimonies the doctrine of the essence and will of God was handed down to the Church, and how, by the ministry of this doctrine, the Church was gathered from the human race by the Son of God, and with what faith and constancy it has worshiped God, and how marvelously this assembly has at all times been defended and conserved by God amongst the greatest of difficulties. And because the Devil always scatters impious and blasphemous opinions about God in the world, and superstitious worship: one must discern the one true and most ancient religion from all other sects repugnant to the Word, which the Church learned from the revelations of God. . . . Histories show the series of divine revelations, the origin of true religion, its propagation, and the rise and growth of superstition and idolatry. We need to know this, to know what is the first and most ancient doctrine of God; when, where, and by what testimonies it was handed down, and how it can be discerned from other false religions . . . Therefore histories are useful for deciding in controversies regarding doctrine.[119]

There was still a difficult theological question lying in wait for the historians who wished to write the history of the reformed churches. They might and did argue that the Church of Rome had undergone a gradual deterioration from the Church of the apostles to the assembly of Antichrist over some 12 hundred years. However, this raised several problems. First, Jesus had promised that the Holy Spirit would be with the

Church always. Texts like the commission to St Peter implied that the Church must be not only enduring but continuous, that is, uninterrupted on earth.[120] As was seen earlier, historians like Eusebius based their concept of the Church on personal continuity of ministers, as much or more than on continuity of ideas. Catholic writers of the sixteenth century habitually argued against the reformers that (1) their ideas were no more than a patching-together of old heresies long since condemned by the authoritative majority in the Church; and (2) they, as a schismatic body were *discontinuous* with the succession reaching back to the apostles, and therefore could not be the true Church.

The theologians of the Reformation responded by developing an argument from history. It was ultimately a spurious argument, but none the less interesting for that. They agreed that there had always been a true Church in the world. However, that "true Church" could not always be identified with the hierarchy of the Church of Rome. There had been a long period of transition, between the time (say) of Gregory the Great and Gregory VII, during which the Church had gradually declined from apostolic purity and simplicity to a barely tolerable state of error. From Gregory VII to Innocent III, the Roman hierarchy entirely lost its character as the "true Church" and became the embodiment of everything that resisted true Christianity. *However*, there was also, continuously through the time of the greatest degradation of the Roman Church, a "remnant" of true believers who resisted the Roman hierarchy as the Protestants were now doing.

The first classic statement of this argument came in a work written by the Lutheran controversial theologian, Matthias Flacius Illyricus (1520–75), entitled *A Catalogue of Witnesses to the Truth, who before our time cried out against the Pope*, first published in 1556 and frequently reissued thereafter.[121] Flacius was a Croat from Albona in Istria, who converted to Lutheranism aged 19 and became Professor of Hebrew at Wittenberg. After Luther's death he became embroiled in bitter theological disputes, especially with Philipp Melanchthon. Eventually he lost his academic posts in the Lutheran world and lived a wandering existence until his death.[122] He was for much of his life an enthusiastic collector of old manuscripts of antiquarian theology. These collections bore fruit in his major, and monumental, first work. The *Catalogue of Witnesses* presented an assemblage of testimonies written by or about those people who had, in some form or other, opposed the medieval papacy. Since organized "heresy" in the West had first been identified, punished, and recorded in the century or so leading up to the age of Innocent III, there appeared to be a neat correlation. As papal monarchy and "tyranny" increased, so did the numbers of so-called "heretics" (who were really opponents of the papacy and its claims). If Eusebius's history had presented people rather than ideas, one could fairly criticize Flacius for presenting religious history as ideas without people. The heresies that he depicted in the *Catalogue* tended to be disembodied lists of doctrines rather than religious biographies. The cumulative effect, however, was to conjure up the image of a mass of antipapal and anti-Roman sentiment spreading across the centuries.

Flacius Illyricus and his colleagues then embarked on a much more ambitious collective project to write the entire history of the Western Church from this dogmatically Lutheran standpoint. Flacius, Johannes Wigand (1523–87), Matthaeus Judex (d. 1564). and others led a team of scholars who produced the work formally entitled *Ecclesiastical History, [which] deals with the whole image of the Church of Christ, as to place, propagation, persecution, tranquility, doctrine, heresies, ceremonies, governance, schisms, synods, persons, miracles, testimonies, religious lives outside the Church, and the political condition of the Empire* ... but which became much better known simply as the *Magdeburg Centuries*.[123] This colossal work covered the centuries of the Christian era, one century per volume, and by the publication of the last volume in 1574 had reached the thirteenth century. In spite of its all-embracing title, the basic focus of the work was dogmatic and theological. It was designed to show how true Lutheran doctrine emerged gradually from the morass of the medieval Church. In this respect the *Centuries* represented an advance on earlier post-Reformation histories like those of Johannes Sleidan, which had offered political history almost without theology. However, the centuriators' staunchly Lutheran dogmatic stance overwhelmed their critical faculties. Evidence was accepted if it portrayed the papacy or the hierarchy in a bad light. If a source reported a miracle which appeared to confirm Catholic claims, that was a "false sign," either spurious or demonic.[124] Awkward evidence regarding medieval heresies was explained away. The *Centuries* constituted a remarkable monument to early Lutheran historical interests. Interestingly, somewhat adapted versions of the *Catalogue* and the *Centuries* were published in the early seventeenth century for the Calvinist market.[125] However, the *Centuries* more often provided controversial theologians with quarries for disputation, than historians with models to follow. Their usefulness for teaching in the universities was limited.[126]

The "witnesses of the truth" approach of Flacius found imitators elsewhere, however, and became the standard Protestant position for seventeenth-century polemic against the claims of Rome to antiquity and continuity. The most influential, or certainly the most widely read, of these imitators was the English martyrologist John Foxe. In the preface to the massive 1563 enlargement of his martyrology, Foxe argued that from around 1200 to the Reformation:

the true Church of Christ, although it durst not openly appear in the face of the world, oppressed by tyranny; yet neither was it so invisible or unknown, but, by the providence of the Lord, some remnant always remained from time to time, which not only showed secret good affection to sincere doctrine, but also stood in open defense of truth against the disordered Church of Rome.[127]

Foxe wrote his *Actes and Monuments* as a national history of the Church in England, set against key occurrences in the history of the wider Church. Events such as the Investiture Contest, the rise of medieval heresy, and the struggles of empire and papacy set the background for the gradual emergence of dissent against Catholicism in England under John Wyclif and his successors. The story of the English "Lollards" was then interleaved with the Hussites of Bohemia, Savonarola, the German and Swiss Reformations, and the dramatic stories of the "Waldensian" dissenting communities in Provence and the Alps. These last provided some of the best *prima facie* evidence of dissenting continuity through the later Middle Ages.[128] Finally, Foxe reached his main theme, the histories of the martyrs under the persecuting regime of Mary I Tudor (1553–8), which occupied the remainder of the work from the eighth book onwards.

Besides bringing the people back into the story, in the shape of the individual martyrs, Foxe brought a new element to the fore. He claimed that the history of the rise and fall of the Christian churches had been foretold in the Book of Revelation. It was prophesied that an angel would seize the "dragon," Satan, and chain him up for a thousand years, after which he would be released for "a short while."[129] Foxe interpreted this to mean that for about a thousand years after the coming of Christ "Satan was chained," that is, the Church was allowed to grow more or less unmolested. When that time was over, the enemy was progressively let loose to seduce the Church into error. Then in the time of Reformation, the devil was definitively cast out of the Church.[130] This somewhat self-serving partisan reading of the Apocalypse entailed hermeneutical and chronological difficulties, which Foxe wrestled with. Nevertheless, his view was influential. The great seventeenth-century Anglican scholar and Archbishop of Armagh, James Ussher, published his *Succession and State of the Christian Churches* in 1613. In this work he set out to prove essentially the same point, though with much greater theological and scholarly precision than Foxe was qualified to deploy.[131] In a similar way, Lutherans in Germany worked the Apocalypse into their vision of church history. The editor of Pezel's "Beehive," Johannes Lampadius, continued Pezel's history up to his own era. He divided the Christian era into periods in terms of the prophecy of the seven trumpets in Revelation 8–9. For instance, the fourth trumpet referred to the time of Emperor Henry IV and Hildebrand (Pope Gregory VII) "up to the beginnings of the Apostasy or of the Papal reign"; the sixth prophesied "the Reformation of the Church or the revelation of Antichrist." The last era would run from the death of Luther to the end of the world.[132]

By about 1600 Protestant views of Church history had taken shape. These views certainly embraced the idea of change, decay, and error in the Church as a whole, rather than just in a minority of "heresies." However, something had also been lost. It was now not a case, for the reformers, that "we" or "our forbears" had "gone wrong": rather, it was "their" forbears who had gone wrong. By looking into the past to find antecedents of the Reformation, dogmatic Church history had extended the Western Church's ideological fault-line back several centuries. Luther and Bullinger had seemed ready to interpret religious overelaboration and distortion as consequences of a general human condition, the religious counterpart of original sin, as it were. Now, apocalyptic Church history ascribed religious error to the work of Satan and the Antichrist, against which the remnant of the "true Church" had always struggled. Error represented demonic assaults rather than human fallibility. As a result, lines were drawn for a conflict over religious heritages that lasted almost to the present day.

Confessional Histories in the Age of Orthodoxy

It was explained earlier how the main rival churches founded in the West after the Reformation – the Roman Catholic, Lutheran, and Calvinist denominations – condensed their beliefs and practices into a uniform, disciplined, controlled "confessional" practice.[133] An agreed core of heritage documents equipped them to defend their own positions and to attack those of their rivals. These disputes were played out endlessly in immense volumes of controversial literature, which won nobody over, and occasionally contrived to create new fissures and disagreement within each denomination. Historical arguments played a vitally important role in defending the identities of the new churches. Many of the historical works of this period were written as material for training priests or ministers in the new colleges, universities, and seminaries. However, this was the opposite of history for its own sake. Historical evidence and arguments were deployed to show that one or other of the confessions had right on its side.

Johannes Pappus (d. 1610) was a dedicated Lutheran theologian in the Strasbourg Academy in the 1580s. He wrote his *Epitome of Church History* (1584) out of notes of his lectures.[134] This was predominantly a history of the early Church: its conversion, persecutions, and martyrs; its heresies and councils. However, modern issues intruded into historical discussion. From time to time Pappus could not resist comparing the heretics of the early Church to those in his own time with whom he disagreed. So the Manichaeans' errors on original sin were revived by "modern heretics" (probably Zwingli); Roman Catholicism repeated the errors of Pelagius; Lutherans did not deserve the charge of Eutychianism sometimes made against them because of their theology of the Eucharist; Swiss "sacramentarian" Protestants were like Berengar of Tours.[135]

A much more comprehensive venture in programmatic Lutheran Church history appeared in the work of Lucas Osiander the Elder (1534–1604). His book shared the same title as Pappus, of *Epitome of Church History*, but added the organization by "centuries" found in the Magdeburg histories. This truly monumental work of controversy and scholarship appeared in multiple volumes between 1592 and the author's death, and was reprinted immediately after. One volume covered the first three centuries of the Church; the fourth to eighth centuries had a volume each; there was then a large portmanteau volume covering the ninth to the fifteenth centuries, and a colossal final volume of 1158 pages devoted to the sixteenth century, the era of the Reformation (actually written and published before the previous one). The total amounted to 3,840 pages in one of the early editions.[136]

Osiander's Church history continuously referred forward to modern controversies; it also shared some of the apocalyptic view of Christ and Antichrist described earlier. In the primitive Church, he explained, the apostles and their followers preached the gospel and cared for the Church, but did not claim a primacy or superiority; they ran the Church by consent. The early Church was ignorant of popes, archbishops, metropolitans, archdeacons, suffragans, exorcists, door-keepers, acolytes, and monks. It knew nothing of confession of individual sins and "works of satisfaction." There was no consecration of churches and altars in the primitive church; congregations of Christians gathered in private houses. Rituals were simple: baptism was administered without human traditions; there was no episcopal confirmation; the Lord's Supper was given to everyone in both kinds, and with simplicity. The papal sacrifice of the mass did not exist; nor was there any carrying around in procession or adoration of the sacrament. The cult of statues and images and invocation of saints was not in use . . . and so on.[137]

The primitive Church was thus defined in terms of the things it did *not* do, but which the present-day Roman Catholics did; and which the Lutherans had removed. Osiander's argument was similar to Bullinger's, but his controversial edge was much fiercer.

Osiander believed, like other Protestant polemics, that the Church had undergone a gradual steady process of degradation in the first few centuries. One of the signs of this degradation, in his view, was the gradual shift whereby the bishops of Rome came to claim the right to be the superior see of all Christendom (something never conceded by the patriarchs of the East). Here Osiander could deploy two arguments. In the first place, he argued, following the *Magdeburg Centuries*, that most of the letters supporting papal claims cited by Catholic scholars were forgeries. This claim was basically correct: the documents in question came from the first section of the so-called "False Decretals," a collection of forgeries dating from around 850. Rather than simply echoing the *Centuries*, however, Osiander quoted and dissected each bogus papal letter in turn. He demonstrated that some were implausible given their historical circumstances. In a time of severe perse-cution, for example, a pope would hardly bother with regulating the minutiae of worship. Neither was one likely to ask a pagan emperor and persecutor to intervene over the summoning of church councils.[138] Others texts demonstrated such "barbarous" bad use of the Latin language that it was inconceivable that native Latin-speakers in the late antique world could have written them.[139] Even the notorious "Donation of Constantine," that claimed to justify papal rule over all the churches and much of the land of Italy, was taken apart piece by piece, though its falsity had already been demonstrated as early as the middle of the fifteenth century.[140]

In the transitional period between the fourth and sixth centuries, Osian-der was unsure whether to denounce the records of the Church as forgeries or condemn them for wrong teaching. Gradually, as he described it, worship became more elaborate. Regulations and details were prescribed to human taste. Most importantly, people devised "superstitious" good works, new forms of devotion which obscured the core (Lutheran) message of free grace through faith. Osiander's rhetoric portrayed the Reformation message as being the property of the first apostles, little by little discarded under their successors. His description of St Antony, the leader of the desert hermits, tried to be balanced. Antony lived well, was very devout, and was doubtless saved. However, too many of his devotional practices, his fasts and his asceticism, exalted human efforts and moral worth instead of relying on the merits of Christ. Antony's most famous experiences had been his struggles with the assaults of demons in the desert: many artists had depicted the saint surrounded by hordes of grotesque creatures beating him and pulling his hair. About these temptations Osiander was almost sarcastic: "If Antony had not chosen this superstitious way of life, of living in the desert, he would undoubtedly have been free from such vexations of Satan (if indeed they are not feigned). Therefore this ought not to be praised, that he exposed himself to many temptations and dangers by the solitary life."[141]

For Osiander, the rot really set in around the time of Gregory the Great in the late sixth and early seventh century. This was the era in which Antichrist first gained a foothold in the Church, and then became entirely dominant:

> In this century we enter the sea of superstitious cults of divine [things], which partly the Roman bishops, and partly other people invented. The leaders of the Church more and more departed from the Word of God, and admired works-laden ceremonies, nowhere prescribed by God. While they were absorbed in these things, they meanwhile neglected to conserve the purity of heavenly doctrine . . . There are many miracles ascribed to bishops, monks, and hermits . . . which either never happened, but were invented by vain people and then taken up and spread abroad by foolish and credulous people as though they were true; or, Satan achieved them with his illusions, to erect and confirm superstitious and idolatrous cults, by which the true worship of God might be largely oppressed. God permitted this, in order that superstitious people, by his just judgment, should be punished by darkness, because they preferred lies rather than heavenly truths handed down in the word of God.[142]

Thereafter it was a case, not of condemning forged claims inserted into the records of the early Church, but of denouncing the genuine evidence of terminal theological and moral decay in the medieval Church. Popes deposed emperors; bishops ravaged their flocks like wolves. The crusades had only a brief success, because God punished the Christians for their idolatrous mass, image-worship and saint-cults, and the moral turpitude of clerics. "For if ever there was depicted the Roman Antichrist, and how he conducted himself as though he were God . . . surely in these intervening centuries his malice and impudence are depicted in living colors."[143]

However, Osiander added one important new aspect to his Church history. He wrote just as venomously and vindictively against other Protestants as he wrote about many Catholics. His gigantic volume devoted to the sixteenth century represented a prolonged denunciation of those non-Lutheran Protestants who had taken the Reformation too far. Swiss "heretics" like Huldrych Zwingli of Zürich had impaired and polluted the miraculous work of Martin Luther in restoring Christianity: "perverse men who falsely claimed to be Evangelicals had corrupted gospel doctrine with their fanatical opinions."[144] At best, Zwingli taught mingled falsehood and truth. Calvin, in turn, presented Zwingli's teaching "in other smoother words and phrases, such that he seduced many even of the good and learned."[145] It was no longer good enough just to resist the errors of Rome. One must also be strictly, unfailingly orthodox in keeping to the line of the Lutheran followers of the Augsburg Confession. In this attitude Osiander as a historian reflected the exclusivist political stance typical of the Lutheran theologians of his time.[146]

It is only fair to point out that, of the various kinds of Protestants, Lutherans were much the most aggressively exclusive. Those who followed the "reformed" tradition of south Germany and Switzerland (whom Lutherans and many historians have described as "Calvinists") took a slightly different approach. A case in point is the *Annals of the Renewal of the Gospel Throughout Europe* published by the Heidelberg court preacher and theologian Abraham Scultetus (1566–1624) in 1618–20.[147] This two-volume work, more modest than Osiander's, contained a detailed year-by-year survey of the Reformation over its first 20 years between 1516 and 1535. Scultetus adopted the somewhat archaic "annalistic" mode: that is, he listed the events of each year in a series of relatively disjointed paragraphs, with little attempt to construct a continuous narrative. However, he had a number of ideological reasons for this apparently retrospective approach. First, Scultetus saw his work as a continuation of the Old Testament histories, and of the early Church histories of Eusebius and his continuators. Just as the Israelites were told not to forget their servitude in Egypt, so the Protestants should not forget their "spiritual servitude" under the "Roman Pharaoh."[148] Secondly, Scultetus regarded the Reformation not as a single thread of development, but as a bundle of parallel strands, where different leaders in different communities and churches pressed for essentially the same program.[149] In each of his chapters, once the Reformation was established, he provided blow-by-blow accounts of developments in each country, city, and town in turn. He was particularly well informed about events in East-Central Europe. He occasionally mocked Luther's failings: he quoted Melanchthon's disappointed and angry letter written when Luther had celebrated his wedding suddenly, in the midst of the massacres of peasants after the revolt of early 1525.[150] However, in the main Scultetus appeared more inclusive, where the Lutherans were exclusive. In this he, no less than Osiander, represented the theological stance of his confession. The rhetoric of German "Calvinists" habitually encouraged all Protestants to make common cause. They denied Luther the status of sole hero of the Reformation that his worshipers sought to give him. That was how they asserted their claim to unite and lead the diverse Protestant confessions of the early seventeenth century.

Finally, one must consider the phenomenal effort of Roman Catholic scholarship in establishing the historical basis of its traditions and authority. Never before had such effort been expended in gathering together, editing, and publishing the historical sources for Catholic Church history. The figure most strongly linked to this movement was Cesare Baronio ("Caesar Baronius," 1538–1607). St Philip Neri, founder of what later became known as the Oratorian congregation, trained Baronius in his vocation. Neri drew him into historical work, and Baronius conceived his task of writing a reply to the *Magdeburg Centuries*. In the mid-1580s he was distracted by a papal commission to reform the martyrology. He began publishing the *Ecclesiastical Annals* in 1588, and by 1607 had issued 12 volumes, bringing the story up to 1198, the year of the accession of Pope Innocent III.[151] He was summoned to the papal court, made a cardinal in 1596, and in 1597 charged with reorganizing the Vatican Library. As he grew older, administrative and political responsibilities multiplied, to his disgust. It was said that in some conclaves he had to remind his colleagues how much the King of Spain detested him, to dissuade them from electing him pope.[152]

Baronius's *Annales* represent a venture in writing Church history in the manner and with the objectives of the Roman Catholic Counter-Reformation. That movement was inspired from the start by a desire to improve on the past – to harmonize, regulate, and generally keep to higher standards than before. In this spirit, Baronius admitted in his preface that "nothing in the Church seems so far to have been so much neglected, as a true, certain, exact and diligently researched narration of Ecclesiastical history." Even the historians of the early Church had their faults: Eusebius was tainted with Arianism (something Baronius rather exaggerated for other reasons). Socrates and Sozomen were likewise tainted with Novatianism; some of the others were too brief. Far worse, however, were the medieval chroniclers. These later historians simply copied down everything that they read or heard or were told by some witness or other: so "they often wove in old wives' tales [*aniles fabulas*], the ravings of old men, the rumors of the common herd, not without great prejudice to the solid foundation of other things." Their credulity, it seemed, had discredited things it ought not to have done.[153] Baronius, in contrast, set himself the highest possible standards of accuracy and scholarship. He would not imitate pagan historians in making up speeches for his protagonists. He would quote sources in the original, no matter how barbaric their Latin.

Baronius wrote the *Annals*, as Scultetus did, in the archaic year-by-year format. This required materials to be disposed according to a fairly crude and rigid thematic grid: each section listed papacies, martyrdoms, councils, heresies, and so forth respectively. There was no time to follow through a structured interpretative discourse on any single theme. However, the annalistic structure had other more profound effects on Baronius's perspective. Each year in the Church's history was numbered by the year of the Incarnation, the year of the reigning consuls and later emperors, and the year of the reigning pope. In an atmosphere where the papacy had been reforming the calendar for ever-greater precision, Baronius aspired to absolute accuracy in chronology. So he concluded (rather absurdly to modern eyes) that Jesus Christ was born on December 25 of the 29th year of the reign of Herod the Great, the year *ab urbe condita* (since the founding of Rome) 751, under the consulates of Lentulus and Messalinus.[154] Secondly, the use of papal reigns as a fundamental marker of time created the impression that, just as the emperors were the mainsprings of all political activity in the Empire (and supposedly the source of persecutions before Constantine) so were the popes the mainsprings of all activity in the Church. The papal succession was an essential anchor point. So Baronius had no time for Osiander's claims that the succession of bishops of Rome was uncertain and vague, or that there was an interval of more than a year about 261 between the martyrdom of one pope and the accession of another.[155] The papacy had to be, as Baronius put it, "the visible monarchy of the Catholic Church instituted by Christ the Lord, founded on Peter, and conserved inviolate and religiously guarded by his legitimate successors, the Roman Pontiffs, never interrupted, never intermitted, but perpetually continued."[156]

The *Annales* were no more a dispassionate scholarly discussion of Church history than the *Magdeburg Centuries* had been. They were designed and conceived as a powerful work of apologetic for the claims of the Roman Catholic Church. Those claims were multiple. Baronius argued that the Roman papacy was and had always been recognized as the supreme authority in the Christian Church; that the traditions of Catholicism were the one sure guarantee of Christian orthodox teaching; that the rites, customs, values, and beliefs of the Church were essentially the same in around 1600 as they had been throughout all the preceding centuries. The concept of the Church underlying Baronius's work was in one sense antihistorical, in that he denied that there had been significant change or divergence in the main stream of Catholic teaching or practice. And yet he made his case in a profoundly historical way. No less than the Protestant writers, he buttressed his claims by citing documents. He imposed a rigid source and form criticism on his materials. He appraised sources and took critical positions between conflicting authorities.

Superficially, and in some respects essentially, Baronius's work marked an immense leap forward in Roman Catholic scholarship regarding the Christian past. Legends (such as the legend that Adam was buried at Golgotha, or that the wedding at Cana was the wedding of St John the Evangelist) were dismissed as legends.[157] More quietly, he suppressed the texts of the so-called "False Decretals" that Osiander had mocked, where some of the most overblown and anachronistic claims for Roman primacy had been speciously documented. However, Baronius tied himself, and willingly so, to the concept of a continuous and trustworthy tradition of exposition and transmission of doctrine within the visible Church. So, for example, he insisted on the traditional Catholic position that the various Marys identified in New Testament tradition as Mary of Magdala were the same person, despite centuries of controversy on the point.[158] He reported (as the Protestant John Foxe had done) the entirely spurious story of a letter from Pope Eleutherius to a King Lucius of Britain, that was supposed to have inaugurated Romano-British Christianity. Most controversially, and most crucially for Baronius's argument, he accepted as entirely authentic the corpus of letters attributed to Ignatius of Antioch (c. 35–c. 107). This corpus, published in its longest and fullest form in 1498, contained some of the most plausible historical proof-texts for key disputed points such as monarchical episcopacy, the hierarchy of priestly and minor orders, the sacrificial nature of the mass, ritual fasts, and a range of other topics hotly contested between Catholics and Protestants. Baronius did not have the advantage of the later discoveries of James Ussher (1644) that seven (Ussher thought six) of the 11 letters were authentic but suffered from later interpolations, and four (Ussher thought five) were forgeries.[159] Baronius crowed:

> So, to this living example of the Catholic and Apostolic Church, carved out skillfully by Ignatius bound in chains, and finally consigned to a glorious martyrdom, I challenge all the innovating heretics: let them understand from even just one aspect of this [image], how far this vision of the Church differs from that foulest of imitations, that they have devised for themselves: most portentous monsters that they are, who every day design a new Church according to the scope of their imagination.[160]

Baronius's text, with great ingenuity and much real scholarship, presented a tessera of quotations and references from (mostly) authentic sources to demonstrate that the disputed practices and beliefs of Catholic Europe, including the papal primacy, were authentic and true. So the term "mass" for the Eucharist was found in some (rather obscure) early writers.[161]

Chrysostom's story about the body of Ignatius gave an early precedent for the translation of relics and the miracles performed by them.[162] Polycrates's letter to Pope Victor, and Tertullian's dispute with Pope Zephyrinus, proved the papal primacy.[163] The use of the episcopal pallium, and of images in churches, were attested by a letter of Isidore of Pelusium.[164] The problem, of course, was that Baronius was selective. He deployed his immense erudition to identify isolated individual examples of what, by his own time, had become compulsory and universal beliefs and practices in the Catholic West. Yet even here Baronius displayed his conviction that the true Church was really timeless. For instance, when he discussed Christ's commission to Peter, he leapt immediately into a review of the patristic authorities for the commission being given to Peter as head of the apostles alone.[165] His discussion of the Last Supper jumped from the narrative of Christ's last meal with his disciples to discussion of transubstantiation, eucharistic sacrifice, and the times for celebrating mass. He interspersed quotations from much later authorities with the Gospel narrative.[166] In other words, Baronius believed *a priori* that the continuous witness of the Church in interpreting Scripture was valid and authoritative. The possibility that the same text might be interpreted in different ways at different times, or that doctrine might evolve or develop (as opposed to being simply "clarified" through controversy) was anathema to him.

Baronius did not live to see his work taken beyond the start of the reign of Innocent III in 1198. However, an array of continuators took up the torch for him in the following two centuries.[167] Augustinus Theiner completed the work with a three-volume continuation published at Rome in 1856.[168] Alongside the *Annales* a massive industry grew up in printing editions of the Fathers, acts of the councils, sources for the history of the papacy and the religious orders, and texts for controversial points such as the history of the mass or the papal primacy.[169] Serious attempts were made to place the hagiography, the lives of the saints, on a sound critical footing, especially with the work of Mabillon, the Maurists, and the Bollandists.[170] Meanwhile, controversialist theologians took up Baronius's argument that past history demonstrated the continuity of Catholic practice. A typical controversial piece by the indefatigable German Jesuit Jakob Gretser, published in 1608, was entitled *Caltrops of Catholic and German antiquity, scattered under the feet of the sectarian preachers: demonstrations of some orthodox dogmas of the church from expressions of common speech....* Gretser, and later J.-B. Bossuet, edited many texts of medieval inquisitions against heresy, to demonstrate that the Protestants were quite wrong in claiming these "heretics" as their forbears.[171]

Writing Christian History in the Shadow of the Enlightenment

The tragedy of "confessionalized" Church history was fundamentally the tragedy of that period in Church history as a whole. The churches had locked themselves into mutually hostile, dogmatic positions. In each case they constructed an image of their past, and its relationship to their present, that vindicated their own identity and values. Theological premises determined their scholarly conclusions. Only the desire not to be caught out in egregious scholarly error, and their own personal integrity, allowed any sort of critical spirit to be sustained. Historians had embraced the notion that there might be "antichurches," that human error or perversity might cause a large portion of the population to adopt a "wrong" perspective on the Christian religion; and thereby confronted diversity. However, in embracing the notion, they had simply demonized the error: the people who thought differently were heretics, tyrants, or the minions of Antichrist. To some extent, Church history is still living in the aftermath of this dogmatic polarization of opinions. Its after-effects are seen when Church historians at times either appear exaggeratedly ecumenical (denying any real significance to theological disagreement) or strip theology out of certain aspects of socioreligious history altogether. Nerves are still raw from centuries of dogmatically hostile religious historiography.[172]

Nevertheless, from the end of the seventeenth century onwards a new temper can be seen in the writing of religious history, especially among Protestant writers of various kinds. It was not that Church history was suddenly written with total detachment or impartiality. Indeed, such impartiality was then impossible, since merely to accept or reject the authenticity of a given document or a particular custom in the Church in itself meant taking a partisan stance. However, the history of the Church became a little more humane, a little less dominated by dogmatic concerns. It was recognized that not all the good was on one's own side, and not all the evil on the other. Faults in the Church were more readily blamed on human error and folly, rather than demonic forces or apocalyptic evil. Secondly, Church historians adjusted their stance slightly to take account of the Enlightenment. In the climate of elite opinion in the mid-eighteenth century, some intellectuals were ready to abandon *all* the established confessions and structures of the Church, and to denounce Catholics and Protestants alike for "superstition," "enthusiasm," or "fanaticism."[173]

Gottfried Arnold

The two historians featured in this section were both German Lutherans. However, both contributed to distance Church history from the embattled confessional schemes of the previous century or so. Both aspired, if not always completely successfully, to truth above all else. Gottfried Arnold (1666–1714) crammed into a short life an astonishingly productive output of theological and church-historical writings. He was a representative of the trend in Lutheranism known as Pietism, which distanced itself from the dogmatic orthodoxy of the early seventeenth century. While by no means rejecting the key insights of the Reformation, especially justification by grace through faith, the Pietists preferred to lay more emphasis on the psychological and spiritual experience of religion than the scholastic dogmas into which Lutheran theology, like other forms of Protestant dogma, had lapsed. Arnold believed, in despite of skeptics in his own time, that it was possible to reconstruct, at least imaginatively, the simple, devout, caring community spirit of the earliest Christians.[174] The history of the Church, for Arnold, was the story of gradual degeneration from this primitive simplicity. The Church had committed a range of sins, of which the most important were the elaboration of ritual into more and more complex structures of man-made custom and practice, and the erection of formidable institutional structures of domination, pride, and power.

In 1699–1700 Arnold issued the first two volumes of his monumental work in Church history, entitled *An Impartial History of the Church and Heresies*.[175] This work, in part, set out programmatically his vision of ideal Christianity, and offered a fairly deliberate provocation to orthodox confessional theologians in his own church. However, it was first and foremost a work of Church history. Like Osiander before him and Mosheim after, he organized it under the centuries of the Christian era. He subdivided his centuries in the same thematic way that Baronius had organized his years: external and internal events in the life of the churches, teachers and writers, councils and synods, and controversies and heresies within the Church. More distinctive, however, was Arnold's avowed aim to write "impartially" about those described as "heretics." Arnold broke ranks with the polemical view that had dominated reformed orthodoxy. For earlier Protestants, the "heretics" of the early Church were those who rejected key doctrines of Christianity such as the Trinity, the two natures in Christ, to say nothing of radical dualists like some Gnostics and the Manichaeans. Such early "heretics" had been condemned equally by Catholics and Protestants. On the other hand, those condemned as "heretics" by the medieval papacy, such as the Waldenses, had been sanitized, venerated, and canonized in Protestant historiography as "forbears" of the Reformation and as "witnesses to the truth" against Antichrist. Arnold believed that most if not all "heretics," even in the early Church, had been misrepresented and blackened by their orthodox opponents. He strove as far as possible to reach past the misrepresentation and to present the "heretics" in a clearer and possibly fairer light.[176]

Arnold adopted a subtle and complex stance in regard to the Arian and Pelagian heresies, both of which should have been anathema to a Protestant. He pointed out, first, that the "so-called orthodox" tended to support their position through the institutional power and pride of the bishops. Secondly, some of those whom later ages respected as "orthodox," like Athanasius or Augustine, were not free from doctrinal error even as they condemned their opponents for heresy.[177] Finally, Arnold paid at least as much attention to the spiritual dispositions and personalities of the leaders of Church opinion as he did to their teachings. Pelagius and his allies lived virtuous and modest lives, as even their opponents acknowledged. Jerome, in contrast, betrayed his personality by loading Pelagius with vulgar insults, comparing him (among other things less delicate) to Cerberus the hound of Hell.[178] What Arnold seems to have meant here is that doctrinal correctness or error was not the be-all and end-all of Christianity; and that those in charge and in power were as likely to commit error as those they cast out as heretics. The "heretics" may indeed have been heretics; but those whose conduct fell so far short of the supreme Christian ethical command of mutual love and care were in the wrong as well, even if their doctrines were technically correct.

One should not assume that Arnold's claim to write "impartial" history made his work anodyne or bland. The *Impartial History* is in fact always vigorous and often polemical. He documented the growing elaboration of Christian worship with evident and frequently expressed distaste. The early Christians worshiped with the utmost simplicity, gathering wherever they could, celebrating a simple Eucharist daily at their communal "love-meals" without "superstition or idolatry." There was no "hypocrisy" [*Heuchelei*] in their worship. The early fathers' theological writings were simple and unsophisticated.[179] Congregations were effectively self-governed; the clergy did not set themselves above the rest as an elite.[180] However, even in the second century CE things began gradually to decline from their pristine state. Ceremonies were imported from paganism as a concession to the sensory needs of some converts; however, these remained matters of free choice, not constraint.[181] By the fourth century the Church was well into a nearly terminal decline. Exorcists no longer worked miracles; instead they carried out a laughable pretense of conjuring the devil out of catechumens.[182]

Candles, images, pilgrimages, cross and relic worship, the cult of saints, and the proliferation of elaborate apparatus in ritual worship were all added by human invention to the practice of Christianity.[183] In the sixth century Pope Gregory the Great added to these human corruptions and entrenched them in the Church.[184] Arnold despaired of Gregory: reading his *Pastoral Rule* and his *Moralia* one formed the impression of a wise and prudent Christian; but given his patronage of so many absurd legends and superstitions, Arnold concluded that he must have been a hypocrite.

Arnold also directed his polemical barbs at those who had turned the Church into a political institution of power and pride. When Tertullian had called the bishop of Rome "the highest priest" and a "bishop of bishops," this was not (as Baronius had claimed) decisive evidence of papal claims to supremacy: it was a joke, since no such aspirations to lordship existed at that time.[185] However, Constantine had made political power for the Church into a reality. Constantine, the first Christian emperor, received such a character assassination from Arnold as he had rarely suffered since antiquity – and one that authors of the Enlightenment, Edward Gibbon for instance, would readily echo. He was a hypocrite, a murderer, and given to manifold superstitions, as the cult of the "true cross" showed.[186] The political patronage of the great was always, for Arnold, pernicious in its effects. A century after Constantine, even the remaining pagans were complaining about the grandeur and arrogance of Christian bishops.[187] Under the barbarian kingdoms, rulers insisted on their noble offspring being appointed to bishoprics, which led to the further degradation of the Church in the sixth century.[188]

In these and various other ways Arnold eroded the idea that all the right was necessarily on the side of the "orthodox." He was a devotee of mystical theology: and mystics were to be found everywhere in the Church, among the potentially heterodox in the early centuries, in England and the Rhineland in the fourteenth and fifteenth centuries, amongst the Lutheran Pietists and the Roman Catholic Quietists. Arnold wrote a separate *History and Description of Mystical Theology,*[189] parts of which were incorporated into later editions of his *Impartial History*. This theological taste transcended confessional boundaries, and also had a habit of making dogmatic confessional theologians uneasy on all sides. Both his attachment to mysticism and his individual attitude towards heresies led Arnold to an arresting and (for 1700) quite radical conclusion:

> The greatest commandment of our creator (which is love towards all people) has taught me to see the invisible universal Church, which according to the teaching of the theologians is not linked to a specific visible society, but rather

is spread and scattered throughout the whole world amongst all people and congregations . . . The greatest shortcoming of historians is if they look to the honor and advantage of their own society by means of various spurious origins, and let the others look after themselves . . . It is very difficult, then, to say which of the external Church-congregations should be named as the true Church, and thus as the "mother" [of the faithful]."[190]

Johann Lorenz von Mosheim

Arnold's history was a little too controversial to gain wide circulation. The same was not true of Johann Lorenz von Mosheim (c. 1694/5–1755), one of the most influential Church historians of the mid-eighteenth century, and one of the most widely circulated in translation. Born in Lübeck in obscure circumstances, he studied at Kiel and taught theology at Helmstedt and later at Göttingen. His many works in the field of Church history caused him to be seen as a founder of Enlightened historical thought, even (in a much overused phrase) as "Father of modern Church history." Unlike Arnold, he published extensively in Latin as well as in German, and appealed to an international readership. He continued and developed Arnold's aspiration to "impartial" or at least nonconfessional evaluation of historical difference in the churches;[191] however, he wrote from the temper of the Enlightenment, not as a spokesman for Pietism. There were, therefore, subtle differences in the rhetoric and approach that he adopted.

Mosheim's most influential work of church history was the *Four Books of Institutes of Church History*, which appeared in installments, and was published in Latin in its final complete form at Helmstedt in the year of Mosheim's death.[192] It gained a wide readership in the English-speaking world through the quite heavily edited translation by a Scot, Archibald Maclaine.[193] There is no doubt whatever that the work is written from a Protestant, and specifically a Lutheran, perspective. However, Mosheim's principles of Church history reflected important changes in the way that error and difference were perceived and explained. His introduction to the work offered fascinating insights into his approach. "Internal" Church history, he insisted (perhaps the first to do so as bluntly) was the story of:

the changes and vicissitudes that have happened in its inward constitution . . . The causes of these internal changes are to be sought for principally in the conduct and measures of those who have presided and borne rule in the church. It has been too frequently their practice to interpret the truths and precepts of religion in a manner accommodated to their particular systems, nay, to their private interest; and while they have found in some implicit obedience, they have met with warm opposition from others."[194]

The "human laws" of the Church were largely concerned with rites and ceremonies: these constituted a vast subject because of the diversity of rites and the frequency with which they were altered.[195] In a similar way, Christian teaching had always tended to be adulterated by "human learning and philosophy."[196] All these forms of difference and change made the work of the Church historian very difficult. In the case of heresies the problem was compounded by the misrepresentations of orthodox writers and the disappearance of many of the original sources. Worst of all, for Mosheim, was the tendency of historians to import their own value-judgments in a crude and unmediated way into their writing of history:

> Hence we find frequently in the writings even of learned men such wretched arguments as these: "Such an opinion is true; therefore it must of necessity have been adopted by the primitive Christians. Christ has commanded us to live in such a manner; therefore it is undoubtedly certain, that the Christians of ancient times lived so. A certain custom does not take place now; therefore it did not prevail in former times."[197]

Notwithstanding, Mosheim could be as polemical as Arnold when denouncing religious practices that he disapproved. Rites and ceremonies that fell short of his standard of rationality and authenticity were frequently denounced as "absurd," "foolish," "ridiculous," "superstitious," and "fanatical."

The structure of the book followed that of Arnold to some extent. It was written in centuries, and each century was divided thematically into external and internal events, doctrines and beliefs, leading Christian writers and teachers, rites and ceremonies, and divisions and heresies. He added to this a fourfold division of church history into Christ–Constantine, Constantine–Charlemagne, Charlemagne–Luther, and Luther–present, though unlike earlier writers he did not identify these periods with any apocalyptic or eschatological scheme. Rather (and in this Mosheim earned his soubriquet of "Father of modern Church history"), he began to construct models of human behavior in the religious sphere of their lives. He agreed with Arnold that the primitive Church was one of the greatest possible simplicity in teachings and worship, though he did not accept that all primitive Christians led lives of utter purity.[198] Like every major Protestant writer since Bullinger, he believed that pure monotheistic religions tended to suffer contamination from the surrounding environment. Judaism was contaminated by Cabbalistic philosophy, and by the proliferation of ceremonies and taboos.[199] Christianity, especially in the early fourth century, was corrupted by a mixture of Platonic philosophy and popular superstition: hence saint-cults, purgatory, celibacy, and relic-worship.

> A ridiculous precipitation in receiving new opinions, a preposterous desire of imitating the pagan rites, and of blending them with the Christian worship, and that idle propensity which the generality of mankind have toward a gaudy and ostentatious religion; all contributed to establish the reign of superstition upon the ruins of Christianity.[200]

The elaboration of Christian practices and structures was always a result of human nature. Some developments were natural and reasonable. Mosheim saw nothing wrong with the gradual emergence of episcopal authority over city churches, and the control of city churches over their daughter-churches in the countryside that naturally ensued.[201] However, the positive lust for power and dominion over entire provinces or over the whole of Church and society was always pernicious, and raised the wrong sort of people to pre-eminence. Innocent III, for example, was a man "of learning and application; but his cruelty, avarice, and arrogance, clouded the luster of any good qualities which his panegyrists have thought proper to attribute to him."[202] Once the Church had taken a wrong turning, things almost invariably went from bad to worse. Monasticism, once established as a worthwhile form of life, spread "a gloomy cloud of religious darkness" over people's minds, vastly increasing the numbers who thought that self-mortification and "a holy sort of indolence" was the best way.[203]

Although it is possible to overstate the point, Mosheim was in certain essential areas a spokesman of the values of the early Enlightenment. He was a firm believer in divine providence: God wisely arranged that the first apostles should be uneducated illiterates, so that their eloquence and wisdom had to be seen to be of divine, not human, origin.[204] Two medieval principles, the idea that one could lawfully deceive for a good cause (the so-called "pious fraud") and the principle of religious persecution of heretics, were both shocking errors.[205] "Irrational" and "fanatical" devotional practices inspired only contempt in Mosheim. This attitude applied both to the ascetic saints who had borne "the useless hardships of hunger, thirst, and inclement seasons" or by a range of other bizarre mortifications, and to some of the heretics. The Beghards and "Free Spirits" of the later Middle Ages (whose extent and significance he certainly exaggerated) were a people "whose pestilential fanaticism was a public nuisance to many countries in Europe during the space of 400 years."[206] Mosheim could be a skeptic, albeit within bounds. The loss of the records of the early martyrs in the Great Persecution had led later writers to elaborate fictitious and incredible narratives to replace them.[207] The miracles attributed to fourth-century saints such as Antony, Paul the Hermit, and Martin of Tours were bogus: "I give them up without the least difficulty, and join with those who treat these pretended prodigies with the contempt they deserve." Unlike many later Enlightenment writers, however, Mosheim did not discard miracles on principle.[208] Finally, the claims of the Roman Catholic Church to have achieved complete uniformity of belief and practice were unconvincing, because the Church had simply concealed or repressed the manifold controversies that did actually exist within it.[209]

Toward "Modern" Histories of Christianity

The historiography of the Christian Church from the mid-eighteenth century onwards is largely a story of secularizing religious history. Christian history gradually came to be written as though from a dogmatically more or less neutral stance. This approach was inspired by the reaction against the enforcement of dogmatic uniformity that characterized both the Enlightenment and currents in Protestantism such as Pietism. It became possible to write Church history as the political history of a system of power and a structured community. Today many historians of religion write about the Church *only* as a political structure and system of power. From that perspective, whether one believes, or thinks one believes, more in the ideas of one contending group of long-dead people than in those of another, becomes fundamentally irrelevant to the task of analyzing their social and political relationships.

This process did not, of course, occur overnight. However, a key figure in the emergence of modern political Church history was Leopold von Ranke (1795–1886) whose long life embraced much of the transition from Romanticism to the modern era in historiography. Ranke was a prodigiously gifted and productive scholar. He achieved his first academic appointment on graduating at the age of 23, and issued his first two books before he was 30. From 1825 to his death he was based at Berlin, and issued volume after volume of magisterial histories of the nations of Europe, chiefly in the sixteenth and seventeenth centuries.[210] His range embraced Germany, Italy, France, and England. Probably his most famous works, however were his *The Popes of Rome, their Church and State in the 16th and 17th Centuries*, in three volumes,[211] and his six-volume *German History in the Age of the Reformation*.[212] Towards the end of his life he became a towering celebrity in Prussia. He was ennobled and showered with honors; his 90th birthday was celebrated as a public holiday and marked by a personal visit from the Kaiser.

Ranke was essentially a political historian. That is, he was enthralled by the interplay of personalities and power structures. Moreover, he developed to an unprecedented degree the technique of working from private archival records. He formed this approach in research trips to, for instance, Vienna, Venice, and Rome.[213] He searched through collections of private papers, correspondence, and memoirs from the period. He then reconstructed the dramas that they revealed, in a gradually unfolding narrative. He was self-consciously innovative, and in his early writings took the main lineaments of the narrative for granted. He expected his readers already to know the major dates and occurrences. He then delighted in unraveling the intrigue behind them, frequently quoting primary sources for some of his most audacious and astonishing statements. This approach became, to a quite startling degree, the normative historical method through the nineteenth and the first half of the twentieth centuries. The historical technique of day-by-day political narrative tends to make absolute value-judgments impossible to sustain. One is too constantly aware of the mingled virtues and vices of the actors, and of the multiple reasons, worthy and unworthy, why they chose to act as they did. Ranke's historical technique leads almost inevitably to a sort of relativism, modified only by the drawing of subtle character-sketches of leading political figures. That last statement needs some modification. Ranke was in part a product of the Romantic era; as such he could embrace the idea of diversity, that different peoples had different cultures and different characteristics, without the universalist theological vision of his predecessors. He was also in some respects (like nearly every major European thinker of his time) a Hegelian: so every movement of thought had its proper time and natural lifespan, and things succeeded each other by dialectical progression. He was also a nondogmatic Lutheran in a Prussia that had seen Lutheran and Calvinist churches amalgamated. For Ranke, Catholicism was not an apocalyptic threat, but a remote irrelevance to his everyday concerns.[214]

And yet much of Ranke's most important and influential work lay in the area of ecclesiastical history. Here I shall briefly discuss part of the *History of the Popes*, a work which (despite its title) is really a fairly comprehensive history of the Roman Catholic Church in Italy in the sixteenth and seventeenth centuries, including councils, new religious orders, and some theological developments. So bold and innovative was Ranke's approach that the structure of this book still, to this day, shapes much of what is written about the Counter-Reformation. The book opens with a review of the history of the papacy from the beginnings to about 1500. Ranke

depicted an institution constantly shaped by its political and cultural environment. Roman paganism and imperial Roman political structures
decisively influenced the Roman Church. The hierarchy of clergy was
modeled to some degree on the imperial civil service. Then, under the
Germanic barbarians, "the old Teutonic superstition, by which the Gods
were described as nearer to some spots of the earth than others, and more
readily to be propitiated in places thus favored" helped to shape the system
of holy places and shrines.[215] The Ottonian emperors and their successors
raised prince-bishops into an integral part of the German political structure:
so, when Gregory VII attacked lay investiture, his actions were "equivalent
to altering the constitution of the empire in its very essence."[216] Rather than
condemning papal ambition like his predecessors, Ranke depicted it as
simply another manifestation of political power and state-building. Papal
monarchy was useful for Europe's cultural growth in the high medieval
centuries; by the late Middle Ages it had become a hindrance, so was eroded
by ecclesiastical nationalism.[217]

The sixteenth-century papacy was, besides being the spiritual head of Latin
Christendom, also a middle-rank Italian principality. It was forced to weave
its way diplomatically between the other powers that ruled (and at this period
regularly invaded) Italy. Ranke portrayed nearly every pope up to and
including Paul IV (d. 1559) as preoccupied for much of his time with building
up a political and territorial power-base for his family and connections.[218] He
did not indulge in moral denunciations of these practices; he simply com-
mented with wry irony on this nepotism and dynasticism. Secondly, Ranke
showed an acute (perhaps excessive) awareness that Italian popes' responses to
the German Reformation were shaped by their rivalries with the emperors
for power in Italy, as much as by their spiritual priorities. Some popes would
rather allow Protestantism to flourish than crush it, if its defeat meant making
the (Catholic) emperor too strong at the pope's expense.[219] In the brutal
politics of the mid-century dynastic and broader political rivalries overlapped.
While the Council of Trent was debating vital questions of doctrine, the
Emperor's and the Pope's protégés were locked in a bloody and murderous
struggle for control of the city-state of Piacenza in the duchy of Milan.[220]

In this depiction one can detect in Ranke the sentiment (not unknown to
the sixteenth century) whereby Germans believed themselves to be on the
whole morally serious and religious people, while Italians were skeptical and
self-indulgent materialists. Similarly, the spirit of Ignatius Loyola, founder of
the Society of Jesus, is explained partly through his being a Spanish noble-
man, imbued with the religious and chivalric militancy of the "reconquest"
of the peninsula from the Muslims.[221] Ranke was, however, far too good a
scholar to allow such post-Romantic ethnic stereotypes to dominate. At

worst, in a few places he was marginally too cynical in assigning political motives and calculations to his principal, mostly Italian, protagonists. What is striking is that Ranke, the avowed Protestant, could make distinctions between "good" and "bad" Catholics: that is, between the principled and unprincipled, the moral and the immoral, even among those people whose values were entirely alien to his own. Personalities and character had once again become more important than ideology.

Ranke set a trend. While it did not become universal immediately, over the decades of the nineteenth and early twentieth century the writing of Church history became progressively more and more detached from confessional allegiance and theological polemic. It was usually still possible to detect from which of the available confessional perspectives (or indeed none) a historian was writing, but that perspective had ceased to inform or structure the presentation of the evidence or the questions asked of it. The ideal for a Church historian was to write in such a way that the reader could not be absolutely sure where the historian stood on a personal religious level.[222] Partly, this approach reflected the zenith of "historicism" in Liberal Protestant theology at the same time. This movement (as will be discussed in the next chapter) argued that theologies always and inevitably reflect the values of their own time, and implied (in its most developed form) that the values of one age do not have any necessary superiority over those of any other. In such a climate, the primary ambition of the historian was to enter empathetically into the spirit of the age that was being studied. Personal spiritual commitment might be absent, but the challenge to intellectual imagination and empathy was still there. Since then many Church historians have aspired to, and occasionally achieved, an Olympian detachment from the struggles and ideals of the people whom they scrutinize. The consequences of this development have been mixed. To impose the dogmatic questions of the sixteenth or the twenty-first century on the first, or the fourth, or the twelfth, as the old-style confessional historians did, is neither good history nor good theology. On the other hand, to treat Church history solely as an exercise in personalities and power, to ask no questions whatever about the theological implications or lessons of one's work, may be to impoverish it in another way. Overall issues of speculative theology have been left to the professional theologians; and increasingly since the mid-twentieth century, broader issues of building models of human behavior in the religious life have been left to the sociologists of religion.

There was a further reason, besides the influence of Ranke, for the rise of the ideal of scholarly detachment. Since the second quarter of the nineteenth century, the range and scale of available sources for Church history expanded enormously. As Ranke was writing his early works, the volumes of the *Corpus Reformatorum*, featuring in the first instance the standard editions of the works of Melanchthon and Calvin, were being published in Germany.[223] The great Weimar edition of the complete writings of Martin Luther began to emerge from the publishing house of Hermann Böhlau from 1883 onwards.[224] Before that time, the German scholarly industry had already begun to issue the multiple series of the *Monumenta Germaniae Historica*, which included besides secular sources a wide range of medieval ecclesiastical chronicles and other sources.[225] In France, Jacques-Paul Migne (1800–75) inaugurated the systematic referencing of the works of the Greek and Latin Fathers in the *Patrologia* series, which came to include many of the cardinal texts of the Middle Ages as well as the early Church. This series, though hideously printed and hard to use, standardized referencing of these early texts as never before.[226] In the *Corpus Christianorum* series the work of bringing standard texts into use continued through the mid-twentieth century. As for the kinds of manuscript and archival sources available, these too have burgeoned through the general recognition that the records of the past ought to be available to scholars of all nations. Ranke was unable to use the Vatican Secret Archive, which was only opened in 1884; but many of his successors have used it. Even the records of the Roman Inquisition, for long the last great ecclesiastical archive closed to scholars, were finally made accessible in 1998.

The range and scale of material that the scholar is now able to read, and must therefore expect in some degree to master, have enlarged and become standardized to a degree unprecedented before these editions appeared. Church historians, like historians everywhere, have therefore become specialists. Even those who from time to time rashly attempt to write works of broad compass can usually be identified as "authorities" only in a century or two of one area of the broad range of Christian history. Many of the broad-range multivolume histories that have appeared have been collective enterprises, drawing on the selective expertise of dozens of different historians.[227] If one is a specialist in only one area, there is a tendency, usually far more potent than personal belief, to invest one's energies in understanding thoroughly that one area, topic, or period. Among the scholars of (say) medieval heresy, or nineteenth-century missions, or early Christian poetry, there will be an interchange of views, facilitated by the institutions of the scholarly conference and the quarterly journal. The historian is likely to distinguish him or herself by engaging in a dialectical exchange and debate with other scholars, and with previous generations, working in the same field. So the dynamic for Christian history is generated far more from within the field and correspondingly less from external developments.

One should not overstate this case. For the middle twentieth century a great deal of writing in important areas of Christian history was ideologically motivated, though not necessarily by schools or confessions of Christian theology. Between World War II and the late 1980s a great deal of Reformation Church history was written from a perspective that one could very broadly call Marxist. Historians from this perspective tended to assume, and occasionally to state baldly, that motives drawn from economics or class struggle were *a priori* far more "real" than motives drawn from religious belief. Therefore, it was deemed much more plausible to explain the adherence of this or that urban trade guild to the Lutheran movement in terms of its rivalries with the city magistrates, than to suggest that the listeners to a Lutheran sermon approved because they thought its ideas were good Christianity.[228] In certain particular areas and schools, even confessional approaches to Church history have seen resurgence since the political demise of Marxist states in the late 1980s. A major campaign of rehabilitation has been mounted since that time in favor of the late medieval Church, in England specifically.[229] Such a pro-Catholic historiography has inevitably led those who disagree with it to appear more "Protestant" than they might otherwise have done.[230] However, one should note that even in this most ideological of movements, the arguments are not the same as in the seventeenth century. The battlefield is the "popular opinion" or "popular belief" of the past. Those scholars who find late medieval Catholicism (or sixteenth-century Protestantism) personally attractive, will not usually argue that it was and is "right" Christianity in an absolute sense.[231] Instead, they will argue that it must have been appreciated and embraced by a large and typical majority of the people at the time that it was preached. A polemically Roman Catholic PhD thesis recently argued that the abundance of polemical broadsheet and pamphlet literature of early 1520s Germany showed how the Lutheran movement was *failing* to win popular support.[232] It is almost the same fallacy that Mosheim pilloried in the eighteenth century: such a belief is congenial to me; therefore it must of necessity have been embraced by those people whom I am studying; such an opinion repels me; therefore it must have been unpopular in its own day.[233]

Postmodern and Liberation-oriented Approaches to Christian History

There is one very important exception to the post-Rankean trend in Christian history just described. In the wake of the class-struggle-oriented history of the Marxist materialists, other new historical ideologies have arisen to vindicate and bring into the spotlight other groups of people, regarding whom the old history was ungenerous, neglectful, or even cruel. There has for some decades been a distinct and powerful historical movement devoted to women in the Christian Church. There are historical schools of thought dedicated to exploring the lives of the Christian peoples of Africa or Asia, and above all the African peoples of the Americas, in and for themselves. The objective of this historiography is both scholarly and polemical. At one level, it represents an entirely uncontroversial redressing of imbalances in the old historical writing. It is now very widely accepted that the beliefs and experiences of women, and of all non-European peoples, cannot be rightly described in terms of a traditional historiography that prioritized the views and perspectives of highly educated European males. In just the same way, the social history of the Christian Church now recognizes that the beliefs of the educated minority in the past do not have automatic priority over those of the less educated majority (the so-called "history from below"). In other words, "Christianity" in the past necessarily includes what women as well as men, the less educated as well as the elites, the non-Europeans as well as the Europeans, made of it.[234]

However, the postmodern trend did not stop at that point. Polemic entered the equation to the extent that it was suggested, as some feminist historians have done, that the traditional historiography was not just incomplete, but deliberately and mischievously falsified. The argument ran that a history written by a hegemonic, often oppressive, but deeply unrepresentative minority in the Church, or in the rest of society, must have been written deliberately to include some stories and exclude others. This interpretation was given further weight by the ideas associated with Michel Foucault (1926–84), to the effect that *all* language must in some sense or other involve the dynamics of power, the attempt of the writer to assert dominance over others through discourse. Paradoxically perhaps, postmodernism both made a new set of historical accounts necessary (by invalidating the truth-claims of the older ones) and made them more difficult (by denouncing the idea of the "subject" and denying that any narrative can have objective status).[235]

The task of the "liberating" historian, of whatever party or movement, became to redeem, to rescue, to recover her or his subjects from the unwarranted obscurity into which the old, oppressors' historiography consigned them.[236] This approach may be based on the *a priori* assumption that *because* a historian comes from a given race or gender, he (usually he) must of necessity have been writing so as deliberately to reinforce the values and ideals of his own subsection of humanity. Two implications followed: (1) the older historiography tended to be denounced for failing to embrace the more liberal values of the present; (2) a new history had to be written to include, polemically even, what the old history left out.

This argument for the "recovery of the oppressed" from the "condescension of (old) history" is, intriguingly, by no means new. It is almost exactly the same apologetic as that advanced by Protestant historians in the school of Flacius Illyricus in the middle of the sixteenth century. These claimed that the "true Church" subsisted for many centuries in the oppressed (in this case the heretics of the Middle Ages); that the official Church persecuted them; that medieval historiography misrepresented them in its records; and that the task of the imaginative and sympathetic historian was to redeem them from this posthumous oppression. The difficulty that the Protestant confessional version of this argument encountered was that, almost invariably, it ended up by idealizing the "oppressed," and mistakenly accusing the oppressors of falsifying the evidence. (That may be why some feminist historians have seized upon the history of witchcraft trials, where there undoubtedly was wholesale misrepresentation of the accused, but have paid less attention to heresy or superstition, where any distortion was much less clear-cut.)[237] The oppression of the medieval inquisitor was real enough, and deplorable (as was the oppression of non-European peoples or the spiritual disfranchisement of women). However, it does not follow that one can uncover a "hidden" alternate body of Christians in the past, whose values are more congenial to oneself and one's own era, by reading the sources against themselves. The greatest risk, in these circumstances, is that the historian will see his or her own reflection in the mirror: that he or she will simply construct an artificial image to vindicate an ideal.

Summary and Conclusions

One conclusion, unsurprising but important, emerges first of all from this review of the writing of Christian history in the past. Opinions about the churches' relationship to their past have reflected beliefs about the nature of the Church *per se*. One's theory of Church history has usually depended on where one thought that the essential, ideal church was really to be found.

In the early centuries, Catholic Christianity was a personal tradition, marked off by apostolic succession, constantly assailed by schismatics and heretics. It established its credentials, first by the evidence of personal continuity; then by the heroic acts of the martyrs; then, especially from the end of the Empire onwards, by the acts of charismá and miraculous power displayed in winning over pagan converts. The "True Church" embodied in itself all the virtues: apostolicity, doctrinal purity, high moral standards, spiritual heroism, and charismatic gifts. So early Church histories shared their subject-matter with martyrologies. They tended not to dwell on the sins of orthodox churchmen, only on the sinfulness of schismatics and heretics.

Western medieval historians were free to take a slightly different view. The institutional Church was secure. For all practical purposes its doctrine was unquestioned over most of Christendom. So the individual leaders and personalities in the Church could be described in a more rounded, more ambiguous way. It was no longer necessary to claim that every great churchman or churchwoman was a paragon. Moreover, the holiness of the Church tended to be geographically fragmented. It was not so much the charisma of the whole that mattered, as the charisma of the individual community, its patron saint and his or her clients and defenders. One located truth and dignity in one's own parish, monastery, bishopric, or shrine.

There was a paradox here, which lasted unchallenged for a very long time. The *entire* Church was holy, authoritative, secure, unquestioned. However, individual members and groups within it might regard each other with suspicion, disdain, even outright distrust and hostility. Moreover, the Church reliably administered the things of God to the people, even though it purveyed them in some very flawed vessels. The clergy were described as acting from very mixed motives. They displayed ambition, mutual suspicion, and rivalries, if nothing worse. Spectacular asceticism or miraculous charisma was still present, but it no longer supported the credibility of the whole institution. It had become a peripheral benefit, something occasionally encountered almost at random amidst the great mass of ecclesiastical ordinariness.

The Reformation of the sixteenth century inaugurated an entirely different way of looking at the Church, and therefore a new way to regard Church history. The *whole* historic Church was subject to error, not just a few schismatics or erring sinners. The "True Church" was now defined, not as a continuous and reliable succession, but as the body of faithful people who hear and believe the gospel. So the churches were now compared, and judged, against the primitive community founded by the first disciples, as described in Scripture. No "reliable tradition," the reformers argued, guaranteed the presence of the Holy Spirit in the hierarchy, or ensured that the Church within the apostolic succession would behave in a trustworthy and apostolic manner. The churches had always been at risk of wandering off into unscriptural byways of belief or practice.

The Reformation tradition of Church history therefore stressed how flawed human beings within the Church had devised new "good works." In other words, they had (1) proliferated devotions beyond the primitive simplicity of the early Church, and (2) thereby detracted from the essential doctrine of free grace, given for Christ's sake and received through faith, and encouraged "works-righteousness." The "essential" Christian Church, according to Protestant history, was the apostles' community, characterized by the simplest possible worship and pure doctrine. To some degree, this image was a mirage: the reformers projected their own ideals back on to the primitive Church. It meant, however, that Protestants thereafter wrote the history of the Church between the earliest times and the Reformation as the story of the loss of primitive simplicity. There was variation in precisely when the fall was dated (between the fourth and eleventh centuries) but the principle was the same.

Although they conceived this loss of innocence in terms of *doctrine*, some important *historical* insights about human religious behavior ensued. Error began when people conceived some initially innocuous addition to worship, which then developed into idolatry by the logic of the rolling snowball. The need to make former pagans, Greeks, Romans, or Goths, comfortable in their new Christianity made it too tempting to import elements of non-Christian practice, which then became domesticated and embedded. Other insights were more theological. Protestants borrowed from the medieval critique of popular superstition the idea of divine testing and punishment. Those who lapsed once into idolatry were given over to the temptations of Satan. Superstitious and idolatrous worship tended to get worse rather than getting better.

The Roman Catholic response to this argument, up to the nineteenth century at least, was not merely a restatement of the medieval ideal. Immense effort was expended to prove that, from the very beginnings of the Church, everything was tending to establish the Catholic tradition as it then stood. Catholic historians discovered that the existing records of their past did not measure up to their own standards of scholarly quality. Consequently, they purged the sources of Catholic history of their forged, spurious, and discreditable elements, in order to establish its *a priori* claims on a sounder basis. Doctrine in the Church, they argued, did not change or evolve: it was merely "clarified" through controversy and resolution. In this sense, the rise of heresies was beneficial, because it provoked the clarification of truth. Catholic historians have since shown a tendency to project modern standards of doctrinal and liturgical orthodoxy back into the past, and to evaluate the past by those standards. This approach could loosely be called retrospective positivism: elements of the past are vindicated because they point the way to the modern ideal, which is the only true and proper fulfillment of the ongoing and divinely inspired tradition.

In the era of the Enlightenment and Romanticism, the entrenched positions of Protestants and Catholics were not entirely abandoned, though their dogmatism and their exclusiveness became more and more of an embarrassment. Some writers declared the basic commandment of mutual love to be more important than loyalty to a partisan creed. The true Church was dispersed throughout all peoples and churches, not the exclusive property of this or that organization. Diversity in ritual and practices was almost infinite, and not necessarily harmful. Some historians even argued that it was a serious mistake to try to vindicate one's own beliefs by looking for them in the past.

There has, then, for many centuries been debate and reflection, historical and theological, over the relationship between the ideal and the actual Christian Church. It is by no means a new question to ask whether, or how, people in the Church may wander off the path, or find themselves up a blind alley of misconceived spiritual development. In the modern era, however, the question has rather dropped out of the agenda of most Church historians. Because of the secularization (post-Ranke) and the specialization and compartmentalization of the profession of Church history, historians have generally ceased to ask what their work has to say about theological questions. They have also been less willing to try to generate the kinds of bold speculative model of human religious behavior proposed by sociologists of religion. This uncoupling of history from theological reflection reflects academic realities and the autonomy of the two disciplines. However, the complete abandonment of any reciprocal reflection is bad for both Church history and theology. Ironically, just as historians were showing increasing reluctance to reflect on the theological meaning of their work, theologians in Liberal Protestantism were beginning to work with the lessons of Christian history. That theological enterprise is the theme of the next chapter.

Chapter 4

Some Theologians Reflect on the Historical Problem

According to the Protestant view of Church history, for long stretches of time Christianity had been corrupted by erroneous teachings and by the mistaken accumulation of improper practices and customs. Sooner or later, the reformed vision of Church history was bound to have an impact on the reformed vision of theology. In the era of "confessional orthodoxy," the problem of doctrinal diversity could be answered in a crude, polemical fashion by Catholics and Protestants alike. One's own confession had got it right, and the "others" got it wrong. The only open question was how well, or how badly, any particular person or group within the Church measured up to those timeless, dogmatically determined standards. One could ignore the lesson of what one might call the "historicity" of Christian belief and practice. Error might spring up at one time or another, but truth was timeless.

By the nineteenth century this approach was no longer tenable. Faith in the grand dogmatic systems of the seventeenth century, while by no means obsolete, was being challenged in many quarters. The story of theology from the onset of "modernity" intersects again and again with the question of the historical predicament, the "historicity," of Christianity and the Christian churches. The words "historical" and "historicism" have been bandied about by theologians and theological writers for nearly two centuries. As a result it is very easy for readers – and writers – to misunderstand each other when these terms are used. One is almost irresistibly tempted to read a key word as shorthand for something with which one is already familiar. There is therefore almost a greater risk for professional theologians of construing this chapter in a way other than is intended, than there is for the general reader. Therefore let me make clear (at the risk of repetition) exactly what is meant, in this chapter, by the "historical question." The question revolves around the following issues:

- What does the diversity, the mutability, the proneness to change perceived in the history of the Christian churches tell us about what Christianity does or should mean to us, or to future believers?
- How far should our fourth-, fifteenth-, or nineteenth-century neighbors' views of Christianity be allowed to challenge, modify, or qualify our own perceptions of Christianity?
- When we compare these diverse views, does what we perceive as "core" Christianity reveal itself as at best a restatement, reinterpretation, or modification of the "core," at worst a distortion or a deformation of the Christian message imposed upon us by our historical, social, and cultural context?

It must also be made clear what this chapter is *not* about, and does not purport to deliver. It does not offer a general philosophy or theology to make sense of the history of the churches, or religions as a whole, or humanity in general. There will be no attempt to work over the tracks of Hegel, or Max Weber, or the history-of-religions school of around 1900. Secondly, while the theologies discussed here may (and should) provoke the asking of theological questions, this chapter does not propose a comprehensive response to the entire body of modern theology in the light of those questions. It discusses a few of the theologians who have in the last two centuries made some of the most interesting contributions to evaluation of the "historical question." It does not attempt to deal with the implications of the question for everyone living or dead who has written on theological topics. That is another book.

The "historical problem" challenges the Protestant theologian more than the Roman Catholic, and has evoked more systematic discussion since the 1800s from Protestant than from Catholic or Eastern Orthodox theologians. The chief reason for this asymmetry is that Protestants had to learn, from the very inception of the Reformation, to live with difference and diversity. There was no automatic central point at which "correct" doctrine or practice could be collectively determined or agreed. Each major tradition confronted or challenged its counterparts in the broad reformed movement from positions of roughly equal moral and intellectual eminence (even if they would not always have seen it that way). With only a few exceptions, one denomination did not normally have the political power to impose its will on the other. Within each individual church, the self-authenticating action of the Holy Spirit interpreted Scripture to each community; but the reality was that such interpretation produced disagreements. Hence one saw, in the "confessional orthodox" period, the rather feverish attempts to close down diversity by means of confessions of faith and catechisms. Ironically, the varied – and historically specific – character of these documents, once they were a century or two old, soon *forced* the historical question into the minds of thinkers in the various reformed traditions. Those who wished to ignore the "other" even *within* Protestantism found they had to retreat either into entrenched conservatism or an emotive, mystical or millenarian anti-intellectualism.

In contrast, theologians in the Roman Church could set any disagreements against the background of a firmly based and timeless doctrine, determined and articulated at specific times and places by a hierarchy guided by the Holy Spirit. The belief in such a stable and timeless doctrine, found characteristically in Catholicism at least until the early twentieth century (and arguably persisting to the present day in some quarters), found (and finds) temporal variation much less of a problem. At best it is mere froth on the surface of a deeper and unchanging theology; at worst it is the sort of erroneous teaching and misguided practice that constantly threatens Christendom, but does not challenge its vision of itself. Roman Catholic theologians have also, frankly, been discouraged from too close an association with what were officially described as "modernist" trends of thought. The 1907 condemnation of "modernism" by Pius X allowed very broad interpretations of what might be forbidden "modernity"; Pius XII's encyclical *Humani Generis* of 1950 contained an explicit condemnation of "historicism." That state of affairs has not prevented some Roman Catholic writers from addressing the historical issue in a variety of creative ways. It has meant that the issue had rather less intellectual urgency; and that discussion of that issue had to be negotiated with respect to the views of the *magisterium*, the teaching office of the hierarchy. In the Eastern Orthodox tradition there is a dedicated and often intellectually refined discourse about tradition or *paradosis*. This pattern of thought defines faithfulness to traditional witness in terms of being true to the Spirit, rather than merely following formal or creedal standards inherited from the past. It speaks of a "living tradition" that is expressed anew but is always the same. The rhetoric emphasizes tradition even as it acknowledges change.[1]

The survey is not and must not be taken as comprehensive and definitive. Like the historiographical discussion in chapter 3, it is a sampling exercise. There is much more to be said, though one might question whether a definitive and comprehensive review of answers to the historicist question is necessary or would even be helpful. Historical questions occupy different positions and play different roles in the variety of modern theological systems: it is important not to distort those systems by focusing too narrowly on the "historicism" issue. Nevertheless, some key points will be made in the course of this discussion. First of all, ever since the rise of liberal theology, and despite efforts by neo-orthodox and to some extent by "radical orthodox" theologies, the question of the historicity of Christianity has not gone away and clearly will not go away. However, most if not all theologians have tended to conceive of the "historical question" in rather narrow *chronological* terms. Since the nineteenth century much attention has been paid to the historicity of Christ, the Gospels, and the primitive Church. There has been less discussion of the wider traditions and diversity of subsequent developments in Christianity. Many theologians have approached "history" as though asking only, "How does historical analysis of the sources of faith, the New Testament, the early Church, and so forth, help us to a more accurate definition of the subject matter of theology *per se?*" Yet all ages of the history of the Church, from Pentecost to the present day, are both challenging and instructive as to the complex and (as noted earlier) reciprocal relationship between Christian belief and its social and cultural environment.

Moreover, most theologians have been constrained by their narrow *thematic* reading of Church history. They have usually conceived "Church history" in terms of the big hitters in theological scholarship. Church history has been studied and taught as the development of Christian doctrine amongst the most intelligent, most articulate, most spiritual of the great theological writers and teachers of the Christian heritage. Such an approach overlooks most of the experience of the vast majority of past Christians. Theologians' insights into the past have thus been more narrowly based, more cerebral and rational than they ought to have been. It is easier for a professional theologian to converse with intelligent and articulate counterparts in the past than with the ordinary Christian: vocabularies are more compatible and cultural difference matters less. Theologians have thus taken less account of the diverse and occasionally bizarre experiences of the majority. Many theological writers have also tended to suppress much of the diversity of the past. They have often ignored the marginals, the heresies, the smaller sects even though these may *cumulatively* add up to quite a significant part of the total Christian experience across history.

How far should theology (and theologians) be allowed to become the normative representatives of what Christianity "really" is about?[2] The usual response to the oddities or the heresies of the past is to dismiss these as Christianity "badly understood." But this raises more serious questions. What is the reality of a conception of Christianity so rarified, even if theologically precise and "correct," that it only describes the beliefs of a handful of highly trained individuals? Why should a (historically conditioned) theological proposition be favored over a (similarly historically conditioned) devotional cult, when the latter has many more adherents than the former? Someone who evaluated medieval Christianity only in terms of the positive content of its theological *summae* would gain a less than complete idea of what Christianity meant, not only for the uneducated masses of the people, but also for many of the clergy. Were the cults and quasi-"magical" rituals attested in the medieval "treatises on superstition" a part of medieval Christianity? Of course they were, just as were the sacrament- and saint-cults discussed in chapter 2. Were they Christianity "correctly understood"? That depends on one's perspective. There is no doubt that for many, in all probability the *vast majority* of those who lived through those centuries, they were the effective way that Christianity was understood.

The following selective review of theological discussions of the "historical question" does not, therefore, claim to contain all that needs to be said on the subject. One of its purposes is to suggest that the theological analysis of Christian history needs a wider, rather than a narrower, range of data.

The Historical Background to Historical-critical Theology

From one perspective, Christian theology had always been aware of a historical dimension to its work. This aspect was most evident whenever Christian thinkers addressed the exegesis of the Old Testament. From the theologians of the school of Antioch in the early Christian centuries, through the Middle Ages to Jacques Lefèvre d'Étaples and John Calvin, theologians had struggled with the exegesis of Hebrew Scripture. On one hand, there was general agreement that the Old Testament offered types or foreshadowing of the coming and the mission of Jesus Christ. On the other hand, it was clear that, unless one read the Hebrew Scriptures through a rigorous filter of allegory, much of the text referred to expectations, beliefs, and values that were located in *that* time, and not in this (for instance the rules on sacrifices of animals, or the restrictions regarding foods). The historical reading of the Old Testament was always somewhat contentious: those who read the text *too* historically risked being accused (as though it were an accusation) of an overly "Judaizing" interpretation.[3]

In the broader thought of John Calvin, historical context was critical to the proper understanding of divine revelation. Calvin was conscious, perhaps more than any other reformer, that God transcended any human comprehension and any human language that attempted to describe or qualify the divine. Therefore, whenever God spoke to reveal something of the divine nature, what ensued was an "accommodation" to the understanding, to the cultural and linguistic standards of the age in which the text was written. All divine revelations, therefore, were expressed in a way relative to their historical contexts. This concept of divine self-accommodation allowed Calvin to handle certain passages, in the Hebrew Bible/Old Testament especially, where God appeared to be depicted as acting in a changeful, emotional, or in other respects less than transcendently eternal manner. God's revelation was not to blame (so to speak): it was because of human creaturely and cultural limitations that these modes of expression were employed.[4]

However, in the era of Lutheran, reformed, and Roman Catholic "orthodoxies" it became dangerous to focus too closely on the "accommodation" argument. Too much stress on the provisional quality of religious language might imply that *all* creedal statements were provisional rather than absolute. Whether it was explicitly so stated or not, the logic of "confessionalism" argued that creeds and confessions were absolute and sufficient expressions of divine truth. If they were not, why spend such time defining, polishing, and defending these theological statements against all comers? The intellectual confidence and claims to absoluteness made by confessional orthodoxy endured for the seventeenth and the early part of the eighteenth centuries. During that time the principles of orthodoxy faced little overt challenge from inside the Christian churches. That is not to say that every detail of "orthodoxy" was unchallenged, or that theology atrophied and fossilized: it was not, and did not.[5] Debates there were: but these debates took place under the umbrella of the assumption that theological certainty could ultimately be reached. It was the content rather than the method that was in dispute. Indeed, it was the passionate certainty that one *could* arrive at dogmatic precision that made the theological disputes that arose (for instance, over justification and predestination) so bitter.

By the early nineteenth century, however, confessional orthodoxy was visibly in retreat in many, though not all, areas. Orthodoxy now faced a coherent rival from within Christianity, in the shape of the theology of Friedrich Schleiermacher (1768–1834) and the thought of G. W. F. Hegel (1770–1831). Schleiermacher's theological enterprise rested on reaching beyond the words, beyond the dogmatic pronouncements and debates, to the ineffable realities perceived in religious experience. Dogmas, miracles, revelation, inspiration all *flowed from* the religious feeling, but such feeling did not require them in order to exist. These traditional manifestations of religion were statements about how people in the past had responded to and "processed" such feelings.[6] By appealing to an experience deeper than the words that described it, Schleiermacher could work round and reach past, as it were, those Enlightened critics of religion who discredited Christianity, and indeed religion in general, because of the apparent absurdities and intellectual brutality of the old confessionalism. Hegel, as a philosopher rather than a theologian, emancipated his thought from dogmatic constraints by postulating that history was the unfolding of God's self-realization. The key to the flow of history, for Hegel and the Hegelians, was the dialectical process of continual challenge, response, and synthesis. Consequently, advanced thinkers came to view the notion of a truly timeless definition of the contents of the Christian faith as somewhat outmoded by the early nineteenth century. What remained to be done, however, was to work out the implications of these insights for the way that actual churches had developed over time.

The Challenge of Ludwig Feuerbach to "Modernizing" Theology

If Christianity was not to become a social or intellectual fossil, hopelessly tied down to obsolete and incredible systems of thought, it had (it seemed) to be expressed in terms more congenial to contemporary thought. Traditional Christianity, or at least the traditional mode of theology, was endangered by the march of intellectual history. Schleiermacher, as a would-be-restorer of the intellectual prestige of theology, had set about this task in one way; Hegel, as a philosopher, had attempted it in another. During the early decades of this project a book appeared which argued, trenchantly and coherently, that the whole enterprise of redeeming Christianity from obsolete modes of thought was a mistake. In 1841 Ludwig Feuerbach (1804–72) published the first edition of his *The Essence of Christianity*.[7] This relatively young philosopher's book struck out at his rivals and neighbors in the thought-world of Germany in the Romantic era with vigorous abandon. Feuerbach, though trained as a theologian and well-read in both medieval and Reformation Christian theology, wrote as an antitheologian and as a philosopher. He concluded that all "theological" statements were improper attempts to erect rational structures on the essentially imaginative and psychological phenomenon of Christianity.

Feuerbach's thesis essentially resolved itself into two basic theses or groups of statements. First of all, he asserted repeatedly that when religious people made statements about the attributes of God, they were actually describing their idealized, imaginative view of human nature. "God" was the imagined perfect summation of all sorts of things that human beings found – and find – desirable in their own humanity: love, wisdom, knowledge, creativity, and so forth. "God" was an imaginary essence, which enjoyed the fullest perfection of all those qualities and abilities that human beings most wished to have in themselves.[8] God was, in short, the essence of humanity's perception of itself, projected beyond its natural limitations. In Christianity, specifically, certain human attributes were deified in a way quite different from pagan religions. So Jesus was shown as experiencing human emotions, weaknesses even, on the eve of the Passion.[9] The Trinity embodied the father–son relationship, while the Virgin Mary represented the mother principle. The Holy Spirit, Feuerbach contended, was merely a representation of the idealized love of father and son.[10]

Feuerbach (whose arguments contained not a little Olympian arrogance) argued that religions conveyed messages about human psychology and human anthropology through imaginative (what would later be called "mythic") cultural forms. As a result, the way "properly" to understand religion was to analyze how it conveyed or transformed the unexpressed psychological needs and desires of its believers. The "science" which purported to make rational sense of religion, namely theology, could do nothing but misrepresent, mislead, and generate contradictions. This was because theology tried to define God and God's workings as fundamentally *different* from those of humanity, whereas in essence they were really the same. The only valid "modern" way to explain religion, according to Feuerbach, was in terms of the psychological needs of humanity.

Feuerbach postulated a sort of primitive pretheological Christianity, reduced to its cultural ideal-types, although he actually drew his evidence from a wide range of periods and from very different Christian traditions, including patristic Christianity, medieval Catholicism, Lutheranism, and mysticism. He did not locate this "primitive" Christianity consistently in the apostolic age, but rather claimed to see its psychological reality "behind" the quasi-mythic language of traditional religious expression. For example, he argued that Christianity regularly worked by a mechanism of removing attributes from humanity to locate them in God, who then gave them back to humanity. Christians denied that they themselves had any moral righteousness, but instead located such righteousness in God, who made up their deficiencies.[11] Christians denied their own physical nature (for instance by voluntary celibacy) but received back from "God" the psychological fulfillment that sexual experience would have given them, transmuted into religious experience.[12]

The major consequence of Feuerbach's argument led to his second key thesis. The enterprise of trying to "do theology" in modern dress was, he argued, absurd, contradictory, and futile. When theologians tried to define the nature and characteristics of God as distinct from humanity, they produced chimeras.[13] Only an unmediated, archaic, unquestioning religious faith was intellectually or morally respectable.[14] So Feuerbach criticized

Protestantism for abandoning the cult of the Virgin Mary, and argued that voluntary celibacy and monasticism was the only morally consistent Christian life. He insisted that belief in sacraments such as baptism, or even in prayer, necessarily entailed belief in miracles. The devil, Satan, and demons "[could not] be omitted without a violent mutilation of religion."[15] His rhetoric and some of his condescension resembled that of some modern political critics and journalists on the political right. Sometimes such people mock or reprove modern theologians or bishops for refusing to defend or uphold the simple unquestioning faith of Sunday schools of two generations back: this is despite the fact that those same critics often have no intention of embracing such traditional beliefs themselves. As a rationalist secular philosopher, Feuerbach despised those theologians who claimed to be rationalists, and who refused to make the intellectual sacrifices that (he claimed) their religion required of them.

One final point about Feuerbach's attack on modernizing theology deserves notice. At various key stages in *The Essence of Christianity* Feuerbach suggested an antithesis between faith and love, between God as transcendently nonhuman versus God as fully human, in a way that aligned him with the critics of the older theological orthodoxy. If God were depicted as a remote, transcendent deity removed from the concerns and emotions of humankind, such a God would necessarily become judgmental, terrifying, even demonic, "whose personality, . . . separated from love, delights in the blood of heretics and unbelievers." Or (to put it less elliptically) if human beings regarded their *beliefs* about God as more important than the commandment of God to love all humanity, then their *faith* would become a stimulus to loveless fanaticism and dogmatic hatred.[16] These statements read superficially like a critique of dogmatic militancy, similar to that of (say) Voltaire, and like those that many contemporary and later theologians would write. However, Feuerbach went further than his contemporaries and many of his successors, and anticipated more uncompromising atheistic writers of later decades. He claimed that *unless* Christians (and others) judged their "God" by human ethical standards, unless they believed their dogmas only to be as true as the perception of a nineteenth-century liberal philosopher was willing to approve them, they would *inevitably* lapse into fanaticism and cruelty.

Feuerbach from one point of view anticipated liberal theology; from another, he tried to kill it off almost before it began. (In a similar way D. F. Strauss, in his *Life of Jesus* of 1835, tried to destroy the project of recovering the "historical Jesus" early in its life, but did not prevent many successors from making the attempt.[17]) Feuerbach shared with later liberal theologians the sense that love was the supreme divine principle and commandment, and that love was vastly more important than dogma. He also shared their intrinsic, often naïve optimism about the goodness of humanity. On the other side, he regarded the attempt to revise theology into the language of modern culture as wasted effort and a lost cause. The Christian religion, for Feuerbach, was in its beliefs, its dogmas, its language, inseparably bound up with the values and thought-patterns of an earlier, primitive age. The only meaningful way to "modernize" Christianity was to express it as anthropology or psychology.[18] One should "acknowledge" that Christian language and imagery was *nothing more than* an archaic, mythic way of expressing truths about human beings.

The challenge that Feuerbach laid down has been close to the center of theological inquiry ever since. Once one has accepted that theological language is not timeless, and that theological statements are made not absolutely but relative to the cultural contexts in which they are uttered and written, one has to ask the following questions. Is there something "within" or beyond the time-limited and therefore inescapably remote utterances of prophets, evangelists, Church fathers, or theologians that speaks to later cultures, including our culture, and all potentially succeeding cultures? Assuming that this "something," the time-transcending or at least context-escaping message, exists at all, how can it be discerned as distinct from its contemporary "wrappings"? How can it then be re-expressed in terms that relate to our cultural frame of reference? Feuerbach's answer was to say that all Christian statements are really part of the science of idealized humanity, and ought therefore to be expressed as philosophy or social science. Christian theologians of that era and most (not quite all) theologians since then have found his answer insufficient. However, Feuerbach the conscious atheist laid, as it were, a trap for all the would-be-modernizing theologians who followed him. To take but one notorious example, Bishop John A. T. Robinson, in his short book *Honest to God* of 1963, proposed just such a liberal modernizing theology without the God "out there." He then incurred attacks from (among others) the religiously conservative philosopher Alasdair MacIntyre, accusing him, and several of his theological mentors, of precisely the sort of atheistic philosophy that Feuerbach had adumbrated.[19]

The area in which Feuerbach is now recognized to be most deficient concerns his anthropology. Most theologians would reject his suggestion that human "sinfulness" was merely the result of Christianity's abstraction of moral goodness from humanity, to locate it in an imagined "god." Feuerbach has been widely criticized for utterly failing to grasp the depth and extent of the human capacity for sustained evil. In fairness, no nineteenth-century European philosopher could conceive of the type and scale of human evil that the succeeding century revealed.

The questions that Feuerbach raised, of the antithesis between religious language and its "essential" content are often understood solely in terms of scriptural exegesis, homiletics, or even of biblical translation. All of these issues fall outside the scope of the present book. For the purposes of this inquiry, they have to be asked about the historical phenomena of the Christian religion across the entirety of its historical experience. Christianity subsists as a continuing body of experiences and writings, constantly developing, building on itself, and reacting against its earlier forms. All modern Christians, whether they like it or not, have derived their knowledge, their structures, their liturgies, and their faith traditions from one or another aspect of that continuing, historically conditioned experience. It was the work of the liberal theologians and their successors to confront that insight and to try to deal with it theologically. As it happened, several of the most important theological minds of the later nineteenth and twentieth centuries were also exceptionally gifted historians of Christianity. They were therefore equipped to handle Christian history, or some of it at least, from a theological perspective.

German Liberal Protestant Theology of the Nineteenth and Twentieth Centuries

Many of the most important theological developments in the nineteenth and early twentieth centuries in some way arose from historical criticism of the traditional biblical scholarship or the traditional dogmatic theology. This is not a summary history of theology in this period, and no attempt will be made to do justice to every development in the liberal tradition. Nor shall I attempt to examine every respect in which theologians addressed their past: in most if not all eras of the Church, theology is grounded in certain beliefs and statements about historical knowledge and experience. The focus is rather on how theologians addressed what one may call the "historicity question." How did they see the unfolding of the Church's past as a problem for "doing" theology? What did the history of the Church say about the transient and time-bound quality of creeds and other religious or theological statements?

An important initiative in the historical analysis of the sources of theology derived from F. C. Baur and the so-called "Tübingen School" in the middle of the nineteenth century. Ferdinand Christian Baur (1792–1860) applied the Hegelian philosophy of history to the study of the New Testament. He argued that most theological statements in the New Testament emerged through a dialectical process of debate over many decades. This process led

Baur and his colleagues to discern rival movements within early Christianity, whereby proto-Catholicism emerged following struggles between exclusive Jewish Christians under Peter and Gentile Christians following Paul. Conflict between proto-Orthodox and early heretical Christianity was held to have generated many of the New Testament texts. Baur generally assigned these to much later dates than were then (or subsequently) accepted: he pushed back much of the New Testament into the middle of the second century CE.[20] The Tübingen school is important here chiefly because it influenced a later generation of liberal theologians, who derived their theological critique from a historical analysis of the rise of the early Church. Albrecht Ritschl (1822–89) was for a time associated with the Tübingen movement. After his emancipation from Baur's ideas and a move to Göttingen (where he worked from 1864 to his death) Ritschl became the leader of an important early tradition in developed liberal theology. Ritschl reconceived the classic Protestant dogma of justification in terms of "reconciliation" to the purposes of God. Justification was worked out through a life lived in community according to ethical standards, not by the pursuit of a specialized kind of "religious" life or by the understanding of a complex set of theological dogmas.[21] Ritschl's theology did not rest on as fully developed a historical critique as that of many of his successors. The key significance of his thought lay in the stress on ethical life lived in community. While such an ethical emphasis derived from the authentic Lutheran tradition, it was characteristic of the early liberals to oppose ethics to dogma, as the theologians of confessional orthodoxy had not done.

Adolf von Harnack (1851–1930)

The liberal theologians whose historical insights have most to contribute to the particular questions relevant to this work were Adolf von Harnack and Ernst Troeltsch (1865–1923). Harnack, honored, ennobled, and celebrated in the Germany of his day, was possibly the most famous theologian of his era. He was also a highly accomplished historian of the Christian Church. The son of a Lutheran theologian, he began his career as a Church historian in 1874 at Leipzig. After briefly holding posts at Giessen and Marburg, he moved to Berlin in 1888. In 1886–9 he published a three-volume *History of Dogma*, which embodied many of the earlier liberals' critiques about the early history of Christian literature and theology. He also wrote *The Mission and Expansion of Christianity During the First Three Centuries* (1902) and a *History of Ancient Christian Literature to Eusebius* (1893–1904). He expressed some of his theory of Church history in his lecture *Christianity and History*

(1896).[22] However, the work that probably caused the greatest stir, and brought Harnack's ideas into the public arena, was the series of lectures delivered at Berlin in 1899–1900 and published as *Das Wesen des Christentums* (translated as *What is Christianity?* in 1901).[23] In these lectures Harnack distilled his historical critique of theology into something extremely accessible, nontechnical, and challenging.

Harnack was one of the first historical theologians to articulate clearly the question of how the Christian message related to its historical context. For several decades historians of the early Church had wrestled with the historical and cultural context of the New Testament and the sayings of Jesus. Harnack recognized that historical contexts change. If Christianity was to have meaning for all times, then it had in some sense or other to be able to be distinguished from its contemporary wrapping. As Harnack put it in *Das Wesen des Christentums*:

> There are only two possibilities here: either the Gospel is in all respects identical with its earliest form, in which case it came with its time and has departed with it; or else it contains something which, under different historical forms, is of permanent validity. The latter is the true view. The history of the Church shows us in its very commencement that "primitive Christianity" had to disappear in order that "Christianity" might remain; and in the same way in later ages one metamorphosis followed upon another.[24]

Harnack had phrased the dilemma almost perfectly. If the Christian message is inextricably linked with the world-view and cultural assumptions in which it was first transmitted, then it does not belong to our era. If it has meaning for quite different eras and spaces in human culture, then there must be some potential separation between the essence of the message and the forms (philosophical, cosmological, socioethical, linguistic, and so forth) in which it was first expressed. One might also add, there needs to be a second separability, between the essence and the various historically specific forms in which it has since been handed down (patristic, medieval, confessional) and in which the identities of modern denominations have traditionally been defined.

Suggesting how this separation might be achieved was one of the major themes of *Das Wesen des Christentums*. The task of the historical theologian was to distinguish the eternal "kernel" from the time-bound, culture-specific "husk" in which it came enclosed.[25] Harnack realized that this distinction was invisible to people at the time the Gospels were written: they would of course have taken their cultural reference-points for granted.[26] The Gospel was linked to an obsolete world-view (something to which Rudolf Bultmann would later return): but the link between the world-view and the message was not indissoluble.[27] Harnack also argued that the shearing away of "husk" was a process visible at various stages in the history of Christianity. Paul himself had very aggressively peeled away Jewish ceremonial accretions that gathered around the teaching of Jesus in the first two decades after Pentecost.[28] The greatness of the Reformation, for Harnack, consisted in its radical simplification of Christianity from the elaborate ritual and theological excesses of the Middle Ages.[29]

Harnack did not just see the "husk" around Christianity as being the inevitable cognitive furniture that every human culture builds up for itself in order to make sense of its environment. He also claimed that at certain stages the Christian Church was particularly guilty of superadding extraneous material. As he put it: "In the course of its historical development, religion, by adapting itself to circumstances, attracts to itself much alien matter, and produces, in conjunction with this, a number of hybrid and apocryphal elements . . . ."[30] The "alien matter" that most worried Harnack was Greek philosophy. When early Christians had tried to express their beliefs about Jesus in terms of Hellenistic philosophical thought patterns, what they produced was a piece of intellectual overelaboration. That in turn fed dogmatic controversies, which led to ever-greater dogmatic oversophistication. In particular (and this was to cause the greatest damage to Harnack's reputation with succeeding generations) he saw the growth of Christology, of intellectual analysis of the person and natures of Jesus Christ, as alien and damaging matter introduced into the Church to its own detriment.[31]

Since Harnack saw the overelaboration of Christianity chiefly, if not exclusively, in terms of overgrowths of theological dogma, he argued that the Reformation, while immensely beneficial to the Church, had not gone nearly far enough. It had sheared off the institutional and ceremonial outgrowths of medieval Christianity, but had raised up a new dogmatic edifice to replace what it destroyed. The reformers saw the evils of religious overelaboration, but restricted its faults to the medieval Church. They retained most of the theological principles of the early Christian centuries and the early councils. They could see that the papacy was a historical construct, but continued to regard the canon of Scripture as absolute.[32]

If the "kernel" and the "husk" were separable, it followed that the discerning Church historian could peel away the husk and reveal the essence. Harnack, perhaps inevitably, perceived that "essence" in terms of the principles of the liberal theology of his time. He was consistent enough not to try to build this into a system, but did identify several strands, which he saw as the core of New Testament thought.[33] Jesus's teaching focused, first of all, on the coming of the kingdom of God. He taught the fundamentally loving nature of God, and the unique value in God's sight of the individual human soul. He set out an ethical teaching based on the commandment of love, which offered a higher form of "righteousness" than the religious righteousness of the first century. While Harnack recognized that an important part of the New Testament consisted in the proclamation of Jesus as the Christ, he did not feel that the core message of Jesus's teaching could *only* be understood in terms of his supernatural quality. This aspect to Harnack's thought has aroused the most general adverse comment. A Christian theology that cannot incorporate a strong statement about the unique status of Jesus Christ is (so the argument goes) crucially defective.

From the perspective of this study, it is also important to ask whether Harnack was sufficiently aware of his own imprisonment in his historical context. The talk of husks and kernels raises a number of conceptual problems. The first is that it may be *insufficiently* relativistic. Put crudely, one person's husk may be another's kernel, and where do we draw the line? Secondly, what Harnack perceived as, and argued to be, the "essence" of Christianity was basically the ethical imperative characteristic of Ritschlian liberalism: what has been caricatured (in the noninclusive jargon of the era) as "the Fatherhood of God and the Brotherhood of Man." Harnack did recognize, and accept, that his perception of what Christianity was and should be might in future times be regarded as just as time-bound and contextual as the Christianity of the sixteenth, twelfth, fourth, or first centuries.[34] However, he did not follow this principle through with total consistency.

Ernst Troeltsch (1865–1923)

Harnack's name is usually linked, in discussions of the theology of Church history, with that of his younger colleague Ernst Troeltsch. Troeltsch attended the University of Erlangen from 1884, where he was less than impressed by the resiliently orthodox theology faculty but found theological study interesting as a historical discipline. He fell under the influence first of Ritschl (one of whose last pupils he became), then of Harnack and the biblical scholar and Orientalist Julius Wellhausen (1844–1918). He taught at Göttingen and Bonn before settling in Heidelberg, where he taught from 1894 to 1915. He spent the last years of his life at Berlin. Troeltsch was, in his own time, important both as historian and as theologian. He wrote a thesis on the theologies of Philipp Melanchthon and the orthodox Lutheran Johannes Gerhard (1582–1637).[35] In his Heidelberg period he built up a friendship and collaboration with the sociologist of religion, Max Weber

(1864–1920). Through his association with Weber he became increasingly convinced that Christianity, as it had developed over time, reflected the evolving social conditions in which it arose. From 1908 onwards Troeltsch produced in installments his most substantial contribution to Church history, republished as a single work in 1912 entitled *The Social Teaching of the Christian Churches*.[36] In these works Troeltsch adumbrated, somewhat ahead of his time, a kind of Church history that integrated doctrine into social history: his implicit critique of the older kind of theological history was not appreciated in many quarters.

For this particular chapter, Troeltsch is most important because he clearly found the *theoretical* discussion of the relationship between the flow of history and Christian theology continuously fascinating. He wrote more, and more explicitly, on this subject than any of his predecessors. He established many of the parameters for subsequent discussions, though his work has remained highly controversial. A series of papers entitled "Christianity and the History of Religion" (1897), "Historical and Dogmatic Method in Theology" (1898), and "Faith and History" (1910) set out his evolving thought on these issues.[37] He delivered an extended discussion of the theme in a series of lectures entitled "The Absoluteness of Christianity and the History of Religions," which was published in 1902 and again, somewhat revised, in 1911.[38] Troeltsch's thought on this subject was continuing to develop in the last years of his life: a large and unfinished treatment of the subject appeared as *Historicism and its Problems* in 1922.[39]

Troeltsch was not and is not an easy writer to follow. He lectured in a stream of rich, allusive, complex, and highly abstract language. He communicated by expressing his ideas through layer upon layer of exposition, which somehow conveyed themselves to hearers and readers despite a certain lack of transparency.[40] In consequence, those who have studied his work very closely on a given theme have been able to identify inconsistencies, unclarities, and unacknowledged trajectories of development and change within his thought. Just precisely how Troeltsch meant his thought to be read remains uncertain and disputable. However, it seems clear that he was not, like Feuerbach (for example) writing an antitheology. His commitment to the Christian Church and Christian ministry (he served briefly as a pastor) appears beyond question. Nonetheless, the thoroughness with which Troeltsch pursued the historical analysis of religion made many people uneasy, and continues to alarm most theologians save the few committed followers of the liberal tradition.[41]

Troeltsch's arguments were highly complex and sophisticated, and in this brief review one cannot do justice to anything more than the rough outlines. Certain lines of argument do, however, stand out; and these arguments distinguished Troeltsch not only from the older style of theology derived from confessional orthodoxy, but also from the earlier Ritschlian liberals. Troeltsch began his critique by insisting that the growth of historical consciousness had made an older style of dogmatic theology invalid. Events in history occurred, he argued, against a context of other events; they could only be understood with reference to that context. That logic applied to religious-historical events as well. Therefore, it was no longer legitimate to select out certain historical "facts" (including, implicitly, the events of the life of Jesus) and to use them, out of context, as the ruling principles around which a modern understanding of religion can be formed. In other words, theologians were not justified in isolating the events of Jesus's life (or that of any other religious founder-figure) and treating them as the foundations of religious dogma, as "facts" of a higher order than the rest of the historical matrix from which they came.[42]

Troeltsch regarded his approach to theology as "historical" and contrasted it to the "dogmatic" method of the older theology. The dogmatic method required *a priori* that certain truths be regarded as outside history, outside the created order. What concerned Troeltsch even more, however, was the ambiguous behavior of some liberal theologians. These people tried to apply the historical method some of the time, and questioned (for instance) the historical basis of dogmas such as original sin or the reality of reported miracles. However, when it was a question of validating the claims of Jesus, or of explaining the theological predicament of humanity, theologians would abruptly change horses in mid-race and revert to arguments from dogmatic or supernatural premises. He identified this sort of procedure in a contemporary and colleague, Friedrich Niebergall (1866–1932). Niebergall was a practical theologian, who tried to mediate modern theologies in a palatable way for German Protestant congregations. Troeltsch claimed, on the whole consistently, that historical theologians must not pick and choose when to think historically and when to think dogmatically.[43]

Troeltsch was aware of the charge that unrestrained historicism meant relativism. This was the risk that one would deny *any* absolute truth to religious statements: that one might think that only if one lived and thought within a particular limited historical context could one imagine (mistakenly) that one's religious beliefs were absolutely, universally true. On one hand, he insisted that "give the historical method an inch and it will take a mile . . . [it] relativizes everything . . . in the sense that every historical structure and moment can only be understood in relation to others and ultimately to the total context."[44] On the other hand, he believed that an undogmatic, inductive, historically open-minded study of Christian history would prove *a posteriori* that Christianity was a special kind of religion. Historical reflection on the ministry and work of Jesus would establish through comparison, what the older theology had sought to determine *a priori*, that is, on the basis of dogma.[45]

This same argument received extended treatment and development in the lectures entitled *The Absoluteness of Christianity and the History of Religions*. The key problem here, for Troeltsch, was how far it might be legitimate in the new intellectual environment to perceive Christianity as an "absolute": that is, to regard Christianity as "true" in a way that transcended any particular historical context. Secular-minded historians were already disposed to treat Christianity in a purely detached, disengaged way, as one religion to be studied like any other. Neither Christian miracle-stories nor Christian ethical standards could claim any privileges compared with (say) supernatural stories from Eastern religions or the ethics of ancient pagan philosophers.[46] In this climate, Troeltsch reported, an earlier generation of liberal Christian theologians had resorted to what he called the "evolutionary apologetic." The "evolutionary apologetic" tried to escape from the old dogmatic insistence on the supernatural origins of religion. It suggested that Christianity, even though it had arisen by a "natural" human process of cultural development and historical evolution, nonetheless represented the highest possible embodiment of the "essence of religion." Christianity was *absolutely* valid, according to this argument, not because it entered the world-order miraculously; but because it had arisen naturally, and had grown organically in such a way that it became the one perfect religion.[47]

Troeltsch found this hybrid of primitive anthropology and religious history unsatisfactory, even as he identified it in his own mentors and predecessors such as Wellhausen and Harnack. The problem was that this evolutionary approach postulated the existence of an ideal-type, an "essence of Christianity" which represented the ideal culmination of all the individual Christianities, just as Christianity represented the culmination of all individual religions. But, Troeltsch protested, these "essences" were not historical realities. They were merely imaginary concepts, which were devised by historically conditioned individuals from time to time. Troeltsch was here imposing a sort of philosophical nominalism: there was no "ideal" religion, only actual religions and individual ideas about religion. However, his key point, the vital one for this argument and this book, was that Christianity, the supposed culmination of the evolutionary rise of religions, *never existed in a pure or absolute form*. On the contrary, Christianity always manifested itself in forms specific to time and context (early Christian apocalypticism, then Hellenistic philosophy, and so on): "And so it continues to the present day. Nowhere is Christianity an absolute religion, an utterly unique species free of the historical conditions that comprise its environment at any given time. Nowhere is it the changeless, exhaustive and unconditioned realization of that which is conceived as the universal principle of religion."[48] At this point, of course, Harnack would have introduced his argument of "husk and kernel": Christianity might always manifest itself in forms peculiar to its environment and its era, but could one not peel away the contemporary clothing to reveal the eternal "essence"? No, Troeltsch replied. Whenever one tried to apply the husk/kernel argument, the intrinsic and the extrinsic always fused and mingled, or at least refused to be separated in a truly convincing manner. He graphically likened the "kernel" of Christianity within the "husk" of its contemporary clothing to "molten iron in a wax container." The point was that these theoretically distinct elements in practice utterly refused to separate.[49]

Troeltsch also argued that the evolutionists were inconsistent. Theorists of social evolution would accept that human society developed organically, but would still insist that it was progressing towards some dogmatically defined, predetermined ideal – which was contrary to historical principles, he said. Troeltsch dismissed the kind of evolutionary analysis that postulated a defined end-point towards which everything was heading. As a case in point he cited "the tendentious tracing of all cultural developments to economic causes": in describing this "caricature" of social evolution Troeltsch clearly referred to the Marxist reworking of Hegelian dialectic.[50]

However, what Troeltsch had knocked down in one way, he then proceeded to try to build up in another. The historical perspective on religion inevitably made one see the actual forms of the religious life as conditioned by and relative to their historical contexts. However, historical relativism need not mean nihilism or the negation of all values. The broader one's historical field of view, the better one was able to generate overall principles of values and ideals, inductively and compositively rather than by mere dogmatic assertion.[51] Moreover, the longer religions existed, the more unlikely it became that any radically new religious principle would arise. Christianity, Troeltsch suggested, exhibited certain features that marked it as peculiar and special among world religions. It embodied features of religions of law (among which Troeltsch included Judaism and Islam) and religions of redemption (among which he had in mind certain Eastern religions). Christianity achieved a uniquely fruitful balance between God, the world, the soul, and the hereafter:

> Only Christianity has disclosed a living deity who is act and will in contrast to all that is merely existent, who separates the soul from the merely existent and

in this separation unites it with himself. In this way the soul, purified from guilt and pride and granted assurance and security, is set to work in the world for the upbuilding of a kingdom on pure personal values, for the upbuilding of the kingdom of God.[52]

(It should be added here that Troeltsch's characterization of Christianity applied much more accurately and precisely to the Lutheran theology of his own day than to many other forms that Christianity has from time to time assumed.) The key point that Troeltsch believed he had reached was the following. Historical principles forbid us to introduce into the study of religion any artificial ideal-types or end-points as though these have *a priori* absolute value. Nevertheless, we are justified in regarding Christianity, analyzed historically, as the highest form that *actual* religion has so far assumed within the historical development of humanity.[53] The same argument applied to the uniqueness of Jesus. It did not matter that historians of religion could show that Jesus appeared in the way that he did because of the particular circumstances of his environment in late-antique Judaism under the Herodian monarchy and the Roman Empire. Jesus's vision and message were, in practice and in their influence, superior to all other prophecies and religious messages that had so far appeared. One was not asserting that Christianity was unique or supernaturally validated, merely that it was actually more creative and valid than all other visible forms of religion.[54]

Troeltsch recognized with particular clarity that the historical study of the religious past of humanity exposed traditional and even recent theology to serious challenges. Many would and did argue that he progressed much too far down the road to secularism and relativism than was safe for a Christian theologian. His theology has been criticized as the last gasp of a liberalism rapidly becoming outmoded. However, that verdict says more about the rise of "crisis theology" around the last years of Troeltsch's life, than about the real limitations of his thought. A more serious challenge would be that he did not think outside his own box as much as he believed. It is highly questionable whether Troeltsch's ostensibly empirical, inductive arguments for the superiority of Christianity would convince anyone other than liberal Protestant Christians. However, for this inquiry, Troeltsch is important for his determined insistence that the Christian religion does not anywhere reveal itself as a single ideal "essence," but only in multiple forms, almost inextricably entangled with contingent factors derived from its surrounding culture. That insight would far outlast the wider arguments which it was designed to support.

Responses to Liberalism in the Twentieth Century

Karl Barth (1886–1968)

If Ernst Troeltsch represented the last gasp of the old liberal theology, the appearance of the first edition of Karl Barth's *The Epistle to the Romans* in 1918 marked the first explosive assault of the new orthodoxy. Karl Barth was the son of a theologian from Berne. He studied at Bern, then at the universities of Berlin, Tübingen, and Marburg, where he encountered, and became discontented with, classic German liberal theology. He served as an ordained minister first briefly in Geneva (1909–11) and then for a longer period in the town of Safenwil in the Aargau (1911–21) where he wrote his *The Epistle to the Romans*. The work made his reputation, and he accepted academic posts successively at Göttingen (1921–5), Münster (1925–30), and Bonn (1930–5). He made his opposition to Nazism public from the start, refused to swear allegiance to Hitler, and was deprived of his chair. (As a Swiss citizen he suffered no harsher penalties.) He went to the University of Basel and taught there from 1935 until his retirement in 1962.

The theological culture of the nineteenth century had shared some of the general optimism about human nature and human perfectibility of its era. It is usually inferred that all this changed with the carnage and destruction of World War I. The ultracivilized, mechanized, developed organism that was nineteenth-century European society descended into a paroxysm of self-destruction, in which all the technological advances of the previous decades only served to increase the efficiency with which people slaughtered one another. Evidence can certainly be found in the writing of this period that disillusionment with "progress" had set in, and that human nature was seen to be at risk of a new barbarism.[55]

However, Karl Barth's *The Epistle to the Romans* embodied a slightly different relationship between the impact of the Great War and the rhetoric of his theology. In the preface to a later translation of the work, Barth wrote that "when I first wrote it . . . it required only a little imagination for me to hear the sound of the guns booming away in the north."[56] That awareness suffused some of the rest of the work also. For Barth, the divine dispensation was a piece of heavy artillery. The imagery of shells and shell-craters recurred at various points in this first and most notorious piece of Barth's theological writing. "The effulgence, or rather the crater made at the percussion point of an exploding shell . . . is not – even though it be named the Life of Jesus – that other world which touches our world in him."[57] "The activity of the community is related to the Gospel only in so far as it is no more than a crater formed by the explosion of a shell and seeks to be no more than a void in which the Gospel reveals itself."[58] "The law is the impression of divine revelation . . . it is . . . a burnt-out crater disclosing the place where God has spoken."[59]

These passages read as though Barth had read enough of liberal evolutionary ideas, theology as the unfolding of human culture. He needed – or felt irresistibly confronted by – a God whose activity came as a violent irruption, an irresistible intrusion of an entirely "other" dimension into the perceived world.

Barth rebelled against the contemporary assumption that historical analysis should be the primary method of biblical exegesis. He declared that his object was to understand the thought of Paul in writing his epistle. He therefore regarded those commentaries based *solely* on the explanation of the historical context and background to the text as seriously deficient, even though he recognized their usefulness at the *very beginning* of the exegetical process. Philological and linguistic clarification was "merely the first step towards a commentary." In contrast, Barth evoked the style of the reformers in writing their commentaries: he described

> how energetically Calvin, having first established what stands in the text, sets himself to re-think the whole material and wrestle with it, till the walls which separate the sixteenth century from the first become transparent! Paul speaks, and the man of the sixteenth century hears. The conversation between the original record and the reader moves around the subject-matter, until a distinction between yesterday and today becomes impossible.[60]

Barth at this point aspired to a timeless theology; and in the pursuit of timelessness he condemned much of contemporary exegesis as obsessed with peripheral details. The key to his theology – and despite his protestations to the contrary, his *Romans* did inaugurate a theological approach – was the absolute, essential, more than cosmic distinction between the realm of God and the realm of humanity, the realm of grace and the realm of sin, the realm of judgment and the realm of justification. The gulf between these two profoundly incompatible realms only the miraculous God-man Jesus Christ could bridge; it was a paradox only he could resolve. "When I am faced by [the Epistle] I embark on its interpretation on the assumption that he [Paul] is confronted with the same unmistakable and unmeasurable significance of that relation as I myself am confronted with."[61] Before such a massive existential problem, the divergences between one historical or cultural realm and another seemed doomed to pathetic insignificance. Barth saw no major distinction between the theologies of Jesus and Paul, nor between Paul and Calvin. He identified himself effortlessly with the sixteenth-century reformers while using a language immensely different from theirs. The separation between the 1920s and the 1520s was immaterial *sub specie æternitatis*. This was the significance of the imagery drawn from heavy artillery. God did not work quietly through the historical processes, but exploded into them from the realm of timeless insights.[62]

However, while Barth aspired to dehistoricize theology, it does not also follow that he wished to dehistoricize the Church. By the very fact that revelation constituted this breaking-in of the timeless into the temporal realm, no human agency could ever represent divine truth in an ongoing way. So, just as there were for the reformers no "saints" and no "holy church" in the sense of a reliably and continuously sacred person or institution, so for Barth

> there is no fragment or epoch of history which can be pronounced divine. The whole history of the Church and of all religion takes place in this world. What is called the "history of our salvation" is not an event in the midst of other events, but is nothing less than the *krisis* of all history. There are no saints in the midst of a company of sinners; for where men have claimed to be saints, they are thereby marked as not-saints. Their criticism and invective and indictment of the world inevitably place them – unless they themselves be its object – within the course of this world and betray that they too are of it.[63]

In other words, there is the history of humanity, and there is the divine action – the divine history, he would later call it – of redemption and salvation. These were two separate dramas with distinct scripts and players, and there was no natural manifestation of one within the other. But Barth went even further than this. Luther's theological dialectic opposed "law," essentially (but not exclusively) the code of ethical conduct imposed on humanity by the Old Testament and by parts of the New, with "gospel," meaning the promise of salvation offered in free grace for Christ's sake. Barth adopted the law–gospel dialectic but also transformed it. "Law," in the sense in which Paul used it, Barth took to be the synonym for "religion." If the besetting sin of humanity was pride, the readiness to confuse its standards with God's standards, then no human activity more bespoke the creatureliness, the limitations, and the arrogance of humanity than did the activity of the religious life. Religion, like Paul's "law," could not justify sinners:

No human demeanour is more open to criticism, more doubtful, or more dangerous, than religious demeanour. No undertaking subjects men to so severe a judgment as the undertaking of religion. The whole rich abundance of the worship of God, from the grossest superstition to the most delicate spirituality, from naked rationalism to the most subtle mysticism of the metaphysician, is under suspicion both from above and from below. God treats it as arrogance, and men as illusion.[64]

Barth did not mean by this that religion was the worst activity that human beings could engage in. On the contrary, he went on to accept that "in religion . . . human capacity appears most pure, most strong, most penetrating, most adaptable. Religion is the ability of men to receive and retain an impress of God's revelation." Nevertheless, because it belonged to the activity of human beings in this world, it was part of the realm of sin and death.[65]

Religious and irreligious people] still remain within the framework of history, unable to escape from the twilight of misunderstanding. We must therefore abandon our superiority and pride of difference. The religion which we are able to detect in ourselves and in others is that of human possibility, and, as such, it is a most precarious attempt to imitate the flight of a bird . . . And so, if religion be understood as a concrete, comprehensible, and historical phenomenon in the world of men and of sin and death – it must be abandoned. . . . Every claim to absolute and transcendent truth, every claim to direct relationship with God, made on his behalf, is utterly worthless.[66]

From one perspective Barth here did away with historical critiques of Church history; but from another, he fulfilled and completed them. He inherited from the early reformers the insight that human sinfulness had led to the corrupting of the pristine purity of the faith of the early Church.[67] That insight had over time, through the Pietists and then the liberal theologians, been extended further and further backwards until only an "essential," primitive Christianity had been declared to be free from the all-encroaching corruption. Troeltsch had then disavowed the idea that at *any* time could one find a Christianity that was free from the "contaminating" influence of its historical context. What Barth did, consciously or unconsciously, was to express existentially and dogmatically what earlier historical theologians had expressed historically. For Barth the human fallenness of religion was a dogmatic truth, prior to historical observation. On that conclusion the historicist and the antihistoricist could join hands.

In the wake of the appearance of *Romans*, however, far more emphasis was laid on the conflict between the "crisis theologians" and their liberal forbears than on any ultimate similarities between them. Harnack, who was still very much alive and active during Barth's early years as a theologian, responded to Barth's and his colleagues' utterances with dismay. He found much of what Barth had written paradoxical, unbiblical, and in places even incomprehensible. Under pressure from Harnack, Barth was perfectly willing to admit that all statements made by theologians were in some sense relative. What he would not accept was that God's self-revelation was similarly relative. One of Barth's then colleagues in the "dialectical theology" movement, Friedrich Gogarten, took Troeltsch to task in the name of the new theology. Thoroughgoing historicism meant the abandonment of Christianity for Europeanism and theology for historical philosophy. Notwithstanding that, Gogarten admitted that "after [Troeltsch's] work, every theology which does not attack the problem of historicism to the full extent to which he has raised it will be unfruitful from the outset."[68] Recent work on Barth and his school suggests that much of the inspiration for this movement grew, at least in part, from a response of dissatisfaction and alarm at Troeltsch's trenchant historicism, which seemed to endanger the very foundations of dogmatic theology.[69]

One should never leave a discussion of Karl Barth, even such a brief sketch as this, with the position that he had reached by 1921. His thought evolved and developed, though precisely how and when it developed, and how great were the differences between the early and the later Barth, remains controversial.[70] During the 1930s Barth confronted the claims of Nazism to reshape German Christianity in the image of its own model of society. The vision of the Nazi regime's attempt to take over German Protestantism helped to confirm Barth's certainty that Christian doctrine must be entirely "other" than contemporary society. The evils of Nazified Christianity were, for Barth, an inherent and logical consequence of a misguided liberal project to adjust Christianity to the changing cultural norms of the age. It was just such an adjustment that he denounced in the Barmen Declaration.[71] However, Barth's passionate insistence on this point led not only to a bitter dispute with his fellow-Swiss Emil Brunner in 1934, but also contributed to the disintegration of the group of dialectical theologians that had formed around Barth in the 1920s.[72]

From 1932 onwards Barth was engaged in writing his massive, unfinished *Church Dogmatics*, a colossal elaboration of his mature thought in many hundreds of thousands of words. It is far beyond the scope of this brief account to do justice to Barth's reflections on the historical predicament of the Church in his *magnum opus*. A little, however, may usefully be said about particular sections of the *Church Dogmatics* where Barth addressed issues of ecclesiology. Barth inherited from the reformers of the sixteenth century a complex dialectical relationship between the Church as visible – the living institution composed of human beings and acting out its destiny in historical time – and the Church as invisible, as an object of belief and a topic of theological reflection. Barth played on that dialectic with enormous sophistication in sections 62 and 67 of the *Church Dogmatics*, part of volume IV dedicated to the theology of justification.

As an heir to the Reformers, Barth remained very conscious that the relationship between the visible Church and the invisible was problematical and unstable. That is, one could not immediately look at any given currently existing religious community and say, "That is the true Church." Every actual existing church raised the questions of whether, and how far, it represented the universal Church. "There is nothing within it which does not prompt, which may not itself be, the question whether and how far it has a part in what the community is."[73] Barth admitted, again continuing the Protestant theological tradition, that the Church on earth was in reality a sinful institution made up of sinful people. In some parts of its history the church assumed "visible forms which can only be described as terrifying" [*wahrhaft erschreckend sichtbare Formen*]. Barth quoted Luther to the effect that there was "none so great a sinner as the Christian Church."[74] In a later passage Barth returned to this theme of the Church's fallibility:

> What is worse, it [the Church] may, like Israel, be guilty of failure and error. It may deny its Lord and fall from him. It may degenerate. Indeed it has never existed anywhere except as a Church which has degenerated to a greater or lesser, a more serious or a less serious degree: not even in the New Testament period and certainly not according to the records of Church history, and, worst of all, where it has been most conscious and boasted most loudly of its purity... When has Christian ethics not wavered between a pharisaical legalism and an antinomian libertinism, between a "spiritual" sectarianism and a complacent respectability, between a weary pietism and a feverish activism, between the attractions of conservatism and those of revolution...?[75]

And yet this was not the point that Barth wished to make, first and foremost. For Barth the important point was that *despite* these errors and shortcomings in the Church, it was still entitled, in some sense, to represent the True Church, the community led by the Incarnate Christ revealed in the Gospel. The key word that Barth used in these contexts was "provisionality" [*Vorläufigkeit*]: the Church was a "provisional" representative of the life of Christ within it. It was the imperfect, but the best and the only available, representative until some eschatological event caused a better one to appear. It was important, Barth argued, that the Church be sufficiently aware of its provisional status; with that awareness, "with a consciousness of the relativity of its decisions, their provisional nature, their need of constant reform, standing under and not over the Word it can go to work...." Again, he reminded the Church that "its existence is provisional, and that it can exist only as it points beyond itself."[76]

Because the Church was a provisional and not an absolute expression of the life of Christ, Barth was aware – in a way that sits extremely well with the general thesis of this book – that the Church would grow and develop in ways that diverged in this or that direction. Christian history was not the story of a uniform progress towards higher and greater spiritual perfection:

> The *sancti* of different times and places...may differ very widely in detail. Old aims may drop away altogether, and new ones arise and force themselves on our attention. There may be remarkable inversions in recognized and apparently immutable evaluations. Everything may take a different course here and now from what it did there and then. Nor can there ever be any question – we are referring to the community in time and on earth, and therefore engaged in pilgrimage as also a *communio peccatorum*[77] – of achieving the highest and best in any of these relationships.[78]

Not only was the Church prone to faults and failures; it was also liable to change its focus and wander off in different directions. Again, he admitted that "even what seem to be the most solid forms in which the community has existed and still exists in time are no less radically subject to decay and destruction than all other forms of human historical life!... "[79]

However, Barth was not a liberal historicist, no matter how much he might bargain away points that evoked that approach. What mattered was the Church as believed, rather than the Church as experienced. The Christian was called to believe that there was a Church, and that the Church was the living embodiment of the continuing life of Christ in the community. It was not in so far as it was human, but insofar as God acted within it, that the Church became the Church:

> The Church is, of course, a human, earthly-historical construct, whose history involves from the first, and will always involve, human action. But it is *this* human construct, the Christian Church, because and as God is at work in it by His Holy Spirit. In virtue of this happening, which is of divine origin and takes place for men and to them as the determination of their human action, the true Church truly is and arises and continues and lives in the twofold sense that God is at work and that there is a human work which He occasions and fashions. Except in this history whose subject is God – but

the God who acts for and to and with specific men – it is not the true Church.[80]

Even more paradoxically, perhaps, the believer was called to accept the existence of the Church specifically when either its doctrine or its morals fell short of the ideal. With a curious (and typical) lack of proportion, Barth likened his own duty to accept the Swiss Church of his time, even though its current confessional documents embodied what he regarded as a weak-kneed liberalism, to a Roman Catholic's duty to accept that the Church of Rome represented the Church of Christ in the time of the notoriously brutal and violent Borgia pope Alexander VI.[81] The vital point, in Barth's analysis, was that the Christian was obligated to see the Church in a different light from the outsider. To the non-Christian the Church appeared as a "religious society," a voluntary association of ordinary people who chose to associate with each other to pursue common goals. (It goes without saying that this description applied only to the modern churches after the mid-nineteenth century.) Barth argued repeatedly that the Church itself must not see itself in this way, and that to do so was a mistake. The Church, to the eyes of faith, was governed by Christ himself. It was a "brotherly Christocracy," a community of people where Christ ruled.[82] This special character of the Church required it (in Calvinist fashion) to see itself as distinct and autonomous in its role with respect to civil society and the social order. It must neither surrender to the world's view of it nor aspire to take over the world and shape it in its own image.[83]

In this and many other respects Barth became an increasingly isolated figure in his later career. He could write and teach the Churches how to conceive their role, with immense intellectual power and precision. However, the normative, the dogmatic aspect to his thought always took over from the truly descriptive. His "definitions" of the correct way to see the faith nearly always took the form of "correcting" the current, erroneous opinions about this or that issue. The absolute, categorical style of his rhetoric never quite conceals the fact that very few people actually shared his perceptions in their entirety. Even amongst other Protestant theologians within broadly the same tradition his views were distinctive, even idiosyncratic. Barth was (at least overtly) untroubled by this isolation because he believed that he was simply setting out the content of revelation, of transmitting what God had spoken. This attitude earned him from (of all people) Dietrich Bonhoeffer the charge of "revelational positivism," of asserting certain revealed truths as beyond discussion. The charge, fair or not, more or less stuck for the rest of Barth's life.[84]

Perhaps, as Barth grew older, the awareness that his own thought had developed within his own "history" caused his dogmatic positivism to mellow a little. Moreover, Barth never regarded it as essential to hold the same views obstinately forever, and was not always consistent either over time or within any given work. Barth ultimately showed himself willing to relativize his own position, to a degree that had not seemed likely in his earlier work. In an interview given near the end of his life he demonstrated an ability to stand outside his own perceptions that might have surprised some of his earlier readers:

> Being truly liberal means thinking and speaking in responsibility and openness on all sides, backwards and forwards, toward both past and future, and with what I might call a total personal modesty. To be modest is not to be skeptical; it is to see [that] what one thinks and says also has limits. This does not hinder me from saying very definitely what I think I see and know. But I can do this only with the awareness that there have been and are other people before and alongside me, and that others still will come after me. This awareness gives me inner peace, so that I do not think I always have to be right even though I do say definitely what I say and think. Knowing that a limit is set for me too, I can move cheerfully within it as a free man. . . . Revelation means that one who was hidden has shown himself. One who was silent has spoken. And one who had not so far heard has perceived something of this. Revelation does not mean that a stone tablet has fallen from heaven with truth written on it. Instead, it is a history between that one and us. . . . [Revelation] above all . . . is a history. God has acted, acts, and will act among men. And when this is perceptible, it is his revelation. To have a relation to this revelation means, then, to enter into this history of God's action, looking to past, present, and future (so far as one can), and asking what one has to think about it and say about it.[85]

Rudolf Bultmann (1884–1976)

Karl Barth and Rudolf Bultmann were almost exact contemporaries, yet their approaches to theology were radically different. Bultmann studied at Marburg, Tübingen, and Berlin, and taught between 1921 and 1951 at Marburg. He was educated in the History of Religions school that had informed the work of Ernst Troeltsch, and never resorted to the sort of critique of that tradition that one finds in the young Barth. Nor did Bultmann, though a member of the Confessing Church, experience the sort of profound career crisis suffered by some other theologians in the shadow of World War II.[86] Nevertheless, Bultmann was far more than a mere mouthpiece for the continuing liberal tradition in which he had been educated. Some themes he shared with Barth; others reflected his own particular perspective.

Bultmann is most celebrated – or notorious – as a scholar of the New Testament. His key argument in this area most emphatically drew on the liberal tradition. He demonstrated that much of the language used in the New Testament Gospels was saturated with the concepts and worldview of an entirely alien age. The sense of "up" and "down," of ascension to heaven and descent into hell, bespoke a cosmology that not even educated ancient Greeks, let alone modern Europeans, could understand or endorse. Bultmann, with perhaps an overly provocative choice of terms, defined many of the descriptions of events in the New Testament as "mythical." They were charged with the value-systems and perceptions of their time. To be rendered in modern speech, they needed not only to be translated, but also to be stripped of their alien conceptual covering. The Christian gospel was not to be taught or preached as a series of statements about certain events that happened "historically." Debate about whether this or that story in the Gospels "actually happened" was irrelevant. The gospel was to be understood as a proclamation of the existential importance of the death of Christ. Propositions that had traditionally been understood as actual, though supernatural, events were now to be analyzed as descriptions of the believer's experience when challenged by the proclamation of the gospel message.[87] Because of this approach it has become customary to regard Bultmann as the opposite of a historical theologian. That is, he said clearly that it was less important to resolve whether certain events in the New Testament "actually" occurred as perceivable occurrences, than to appreciate their meaning for the believer.[88] He was not, like earlier liberal theologians, concerned with "purging" the record of salvation history of "mythical" events. Rather, he wished to demonstrate that everything important in the gospel could be expressed as a here-and-now statement about God and human existence. It was not necessary to "ground" those statements in a proven record of incidents that took place at a "factual" level in first-century Judea.

On the face of it, then, Bultmann could seem to be as far removed from the historical perspective on theology as Barth was, though for completely different reasons. However, there is much more to be said. In 1955 Bultmann delivered a series of Gifford lectures at Edinburgh University entitled *History and Eschatology*.[89] In these he reflected on the relationship between the New Testament and the emergence of historical thought with considerable subtlety. *History and Eschatology* contained some of the most sophisticated reflections on the theological significance of humanity's growing sense of its own history written up to that point. The remainder of this discussion will therefore focus on these lectures. It must be stressed again that no attempt is being made here to evaluate Bultmann's position on the wider issue of how far New Testament narratives are "historical." The focus of attention here will be on the lessons and opportunities of developments in historical thought for theological inquiry.

Bultmann began by reviewing the problem of "historicity" as the earlier generation of liberal theologians had perceived it. The Middle Ages had conceived of history as God's management of creation towards the fulfill-ment of the divine purposes. However, between the Renaissance and the Enlightenment, thinking people had progressively emancipated themselves from such concepts of a "managed" order. Natural scientists conceived the "good" in utilitarian terms. Finally, Romanticism had broken up the idea of a universal "humanity" into different peoples, each tending towards a different destiny according to different rules. The risk, as Bultmann (echo-ing Troeltsch) perceived it, was that historical diversity must lead to a nihilistic relativism: if all ideals only exist relative to the peoples who embrace them, what becomes of any claim to universal truth?[90]

Expounding this problem in detail, Bultmann began by reviewing the rise of historical thought among European peoples, from saga and chronicle through classical political history. In these writings he found no true sense of historical development: in such writings human nature and culture were taken for granted as permanent and unchanging.[91] He then turned to the Bible. In the Hebrew biblical scriptures he detected a variety of theories which interpreted history as the unfolding of God's commands and purpose for the people.[92] In the New Testament Bultmann found that eschatological thought – the idea that history was rapidly approaching its culmination and its end – began for the first time to dominate historical thinking. The expectation of the end of history functioned slightly differently, however, in Jesus, Paul, and the Johannine writings. Jesus both predicted the end-times as coming soon, and announced that they had already come in his own person. In both Paul and John there was a tension between the future and the present. God *would* in the future transform the believer through the power of the crucifixion, but in a sense God *already had* transformed the believer.[93]

Bultmann derived subsequent approaches to history in the life of the Christian Church from the gradual abandonment of these various modes of eschatology. Rather than expecting a universal cosmic drama in which the members of the Church would be caught up and renewed, the emerging Church conceived of salvation in terms of sacramental ministry. Through sacraments the Church delivered salvation to the individual person within the specific time-frame of each human life. Rather than evil being destroyed in a cosmic Armageddon, the life-enhancing effects of priestly ministry beat down evil spirits and evil influences in the soul.[94] As the Church came to terms with the probability that it would endure for a long time, it began to take an interest in perceiving itself historically. World history was now invested with a new meaning: it hinged on the events of the life and ministry of Jesus. The events of pre-Christian history prepared the world to receive the teaching of Jesus when it was ready. The divine plan of redemption now dominated the historical future. Rather than the endless cycles that Bultmann believed had comprised the antique idea of history, Christian history was now conceived as the time between the first and second comings of Christ. Each individual soul was imbued with unique significance and a destiny in this scheme of things. From this conviction there emerged various historical and eschatological patterns and schemes of history, especially those modeled on the prophecies of Joachim of Fiore (c.1132–1202).[95]

History and Eschatology then leapt forward several centuries to discuss the theories of history that had emerged in the Enlightenment and its aftermath. Vico, Kant, and Hegel in different ways had retained the divine self-realization in history, but had stripped out the need for spectacular divine interventions. Human beings acting freely would naturally progress towards certain providential goals, and the divine purpose would be served without needing to act visibly to divert such progress. Such natural providentialism, Bultmann argued, made it easy for secular philosophers such as Turgot, Condorcet, Marx, or Comte to transfer the "providential end" of history to a purely secular vision of human social or intellectual perfection: *humanity* naturally progressed towards its own self-realization.[96] In Romanticism, the next stage in this process, what had previously been conjectured in relation to humanity in general was then ascribed to individual "peoples," to specific cultural or ethnic groups. Thinkers like Vico and J. G. Herder conceived of individual cultures rising to their natural peak – but then, since they were specific cultures rather than humanity as a whole, they became overripe and decayed. Bultmann quoted from Herder a particularly poignant example of this phenomenon, the decay and fragmentation of medieval Christendom. The Medieval Catholic Church had split apart when it no longer served its function: "[it was] invaluable as the rude envelope of tradition which could endure the storms of the barbarians . . . but it could scarcely have constant value for all times. When the fruit becomes ripe, the shell breaks."[97] In this Romantic concept of the rise and fall of human cultures Bultmann saw the greatest danger of historical relativism. If all that human history contained was the rise, growth, and decay of cultures, each endowed with distinct and specific value-systems, then there could be no absolute ideas within history:

humanity was doomed to constant and irredeemable insecurity and fluidity, since each putative "absolute" only appeared to be absolute from within the culture that devised it.[98]

The development of historical thought had raised for Bultmann a further question. Was the subject-matter of history the individual or the collective, the human soul or the cultural entity that is a "people"? He reviewed a variety of religious and philosophical approaches to the place of the human being in history. Ultimately the question became, "was there 'meaning' in history, and could the individual person perceive that meaning as it unfolded?" The consensus of nineteenth- and twentieth-century opinion, in figures such as Wilhelm Dilthey (1833–1911) and Benedetto Croce (1866–1952), seemed to be that no individual could view his or her historical context as though from the outside: we have no choice but to live within our own context. The same reservation applied to writing history: in trying to recreate the motives of a historical figure, historians remain within their own time: so each act of historical insight becomes itself time-bound and needs to be rewritten for each generation.[99]

In the final lecture in the series, "Christian Faith and History," Bultmann challenged the historical determinists on their own terms. One's historical context, he argued, posed questions and set challenges, but did not determine the answers. History was moved on by personal decisions and by personal understanding, which were not at all times the same as those of the surrounding culture. Once a particular understanding of one's environment (such as the Christian worldview) had come into being, it remained a permanently available option. However, such a perspective (or *Weltanschauung*) only remained valid if it could be rediscovered and reformulated afresh within differing historical contexts. Here, Bultmann argued, the Christian self-understanding within history had something special to contribute. Christian thought offered a particularly sensitive insight into the human historical predicament, born out of its long lineage and complex evolution. Christian thinkers realized that the human being could never act in complete freedom. One is always conditioned by one's past, individual and collective. To be able to act entirely freely could only be conceived as a special gift, as the grace of God. The advent and revelation of Jesus Christ was the "eschatological event" which proved that such freedom was indeed offered. Paradoxically, however, God had chosen to cause this "event" to occur not as the end of all history, but as an event occurring *within* history. That event, the liberating work of Christ, then occurred over and over again whenever the original event was preached and was believed. Moreover, the believer remained in this life at one and the same time within history, limited by creatureliness, but also, through being in Christ, above time and history. The transhistorical experience of the believer was only ever partially realized.[100]

Rudolf Bultmann's theology of history represented, no less than Barth's, a reprocessing of some important insights derived ultimately from the Reformation. "Historicity," the predicament whereby human beings live entrapped within their own temporal and provisional context, took the place of "sin" in an older generation of theologians and the *krisis* of God's judgment in the early Barth. Christian revelation and divine grace offered redemption from that predicament. However, this redemption did not abolish "historicity": it coexisted with it and transcended it. In the same way Luther had discerned that the redeemed were, in life, always sinners and righteous at the same time – an analogy that Bultmann recognized and acknowledged explicitly towards the end of his lectures.[101] This sense, that "historical context" is something *over against* which the Christian revelation stands, marked as clear a divide between Bultmann and the older liberals as that which divided Barth from his teachers. It was the characteristic attitude of twentieth-century dialectical approaches to historical theology. History may precondition our theological thoughts, but it may not dominate them or design them.

Reinhold Niebuhr (1892–1971) and H. Richard Niebuhr (1894–1962)

It is impossible to discuss the theology of history in the twentieth century without some attempt, however inadequate, to discuss the theologies of Reinhold and Richard Niebuhr. These two brothers shaped in their distinctly different ways the response of the American theological world to the challenges of liberalism and neo-orthodoxy. Sons of a German immigrant and minister in the German Evangelical Synod, both studied at the denominational Eden Seminary and then at Yale. Richard followed the traditional academic *cursus* and earned a PhD, joining the Faculty of Yale Divinity School in 1931. Reinhold's vocation took him, after receiving his BD and MA degrees, into parish ministry in Detroit: there he sharpened the passionate commitment to social issues which became one of his most celebrated attributes. He joined the Faculty of Union Theological Seminary in New York in 1928 and taught there during his (and the seminary's) period of greatest renown and influence.

Both the Niebuhr brothers wrote principally as ethical theologians, and it does not do justice to their thought to read them solely from the standpoint of the theological response to history. However, with the warning that what follows does not even begin to address the full range of either of their ideas, one can discern some important engagements with the questions so far discussed. In his *The Meaning of Revelation*, published in 1941, Richard Niebuhr addressed the challenge of Barth's theology to the older liberalism. The liberals, and most notably Troeltsch, had posed the problem that we form all our perceptions, including religious insights, relative to our cultural environment and our community. Religious statements stand in the shadow of cultural relativism: they may only be "true" within a certain context.[102] In radical, ringing contrast to this *risk* of relativism, stood Barth's affirmation of the sovereignty of "revelation," meaning God's breaking into history in the person of Christ and in the divine self-communication to the believer.[103] Yet revelation does not come to us as a thunderbolt through suddenly riven skies. We perceive revelation in the form that is handed down to us through our (historically grounded and derived) communities. Indeed, the same is true of our relationship to Scripture itself. Scripture reveals the mind-set of the people of the time when it was written (as Bultmann was demonstrating); we interpret it within our own cultural and temporal mind-sets.[104] Richard Niebuhr had uncovered a paradox, that "revelation" could not be as easily separated from its historical context as neo-orthodox theology sometimes implied. The Christian revelation was not an abstract or an absolute thing. It was a revelation about the meaning of certain events that had happened within historical time. One could not, therefore, simply discard the history in order to cling on to the faith.[105]

Richard Niebuhr then set about resolving the paradox in a way that appears on the face of it to be brittle and insecure, but which reveals its hidden strengths the closer it is examined. He pointed out that a given history could be known and seen in two ways: from the standpoint of the committed insiders for whom it is "their" history, or from the standpoint of the critical and disengaged external observer. He demonstrated this point by contrasting the description of the 1776 American Declaration of Independence contained in Abraham Lincoln's Gettysburg address with a highly sardonic description of the same declaration in a British historical text.[106] Which perspective one adopts will depend on one's system of value: is one committed to a history because it gives meaning to one's own existence, or is it an entirely inert thing, of antiquarian interest only?

This suggestion of Richard Niebuhr is profoundly unsettling on first glance. He appears to be saying that Christianity must be learned through sympathetic and supportive imbibing of one's own tradition. That view (if that were what he really meant) would have justified the sort of confessional triumphalist historiography that gave Church history a bad name among historians: at best collective self-vindication, at worst self-delusion. However, it rapidly becomes clear that this is not what Richard Niebuhr intended. On the contrary, he argued that the Church must study its history as far as possible both from the internal and the external point of view. It should embrace and recognize the truth in the critical viewpoint of the outsider. It was required to acknowledge that Christianity arose out of, and grew within, a defined historical context and according to the manner of human societies:

> What it [the Church] sees in that reflection [the viewpoint of the outsider] is finite, created, limited, corporeal being, alike in every respect to all the other beings of creations. To describe that vision in detail, to see the limited, human character of its founder, the connections between itself and a Judaism to which it often, in false pride, feels superior, between its sacraments and mystery faiths, between Catholicism and feudalism, Protestantism and capitalism, to know itself as the chief of sinners and the most mortal of societies – all this is required of it by a revelation that has come to it through its history.... External history is the medium in which internal history exists and comes to life. Hence knowledge of its external history remains a duty of the Church.[107]

Revelation (as Pannenberg would later say) becomes known through the historical process. What Richard Niebuhr did with particular care was to articulate the relationship between historical knowing *per se* and knowing through a historically grounded faith. He argued that an effort of imagination was required to perceive other people as genuinely other personalities, rather than as objects. Revelation, confronting believers with the personhood of other Christians, called on Christians to acknowledge the churches' diverse past experiences as though they were their own and to experience repentance for their failings.[108] Revelation took the form of experiencing the personhood of others, and ultimately the self-disclosure of God. "God" was a word that could not be used without value attached to it: it was a word like "friend."[109]

Richard Niebuhr was arguing that "revelation" was not really a category of experience isolated from the ongoing historical experience of humanity. Rather, it was something that happened within that experience. Correctly understood, it transformed our perception of that experience by giving it ultimate meaning. As an ethicist, Niebuhr was more interested in the impact of the "external" historical view of the Church for people as moral agents, than in its effect on the doctrine of the Church. Nevertheless, his analysis put some much-needed subtlety into the dividing chasm between divine revelation and flawed human history that Barth and his followers had blasted out.

Another important aspect of Barth's challenge to liberalism was the re-evaluation of human sinfulness and the gulf between religious ideals and human performance. Mid-nineteenth-century liberals and their critics (including Feuerbach) had generally been too ready to liken human moral abilities to divine standards, even to appraise the latter by the former.[110] Reinhold Niebuhr focused on the significance of human sin for philosophies of history in his *Faith and History: A Comparison of Christian and Modern Views of History*, based on a series of lectures delivered in 1945–7.[111] *Faith and History* contained a fierce critique of what Reinhold Niebuhr described as the "modern" philosophy of history. "Modern" conceptions of history, according to Niebuhr, taught people to believe that everything in human society was tending irresistibly towards improvement and final perfection. The world had come into being through natural forces and evolved in natural time to the rise of humanity. Humanity developed by its own initiative towards ever more sophisticated levels of social and cultural development. Its remaining faults and flaws could be ascribed to ignorance or an inadequate level of growth. With the passing of time and the acquiring of greater knowledge it would deal with those problems. In this view of history, the god (the creating force) was time itself; the redeemer (the power that would rid human culture of its imperfections) was history itself.[112]

Reinhold Niebuhr argued that although this viewpoint was secular, it intersected with the Christian theory of history at various stages. In contrast to classical theories of history (which he argued were fundamentally cyclical) modern historical theory postulated a direction and an end-point to history: it derived this from its ancestry in biblical messianism and Christian millennialism.[113] However, what Christianity had (mistakenly) imbibed from modernity was more critical than what modernity had learned from Christianity. In the era of nineteenth-century Romanticism and liberalism, Niebuhr argued, Christianity had "capitulated" to the assumptions of the modern view of history, in the shape of Herder, Hegel, Lessing, and Ritschl.[114] This assumption that humanity was naturally perfectible caused the liberal thinkers, naturally enough, to minimize aspects of the Christian heritage such as original sin and the Fall. Christian theologians had subscribed to currently fashionable views about the natural ascent of the religious psyche through human social evolution: the final and most perfect historical development would naturally be the best. Christianity, according to this argument, would be the highest human religion because it represented what was best in humanity, not what was revealed by God.[115] In pointing out this aspect of liberal theology Niebuhr struck a target, insofar as the "evolutionary apologetic" described and criticized by Troeltsch conveyed almost exactly this argument for the superiority of Christianity.[116]

Reinhold Niebuhr concluded, like Barth, that this boundless optimism about the spontaneous natural perfectibility of humanity, which had always been mistaken, was definitively disproved by the events of the early twentieth century. It was not just that the technological triumphs of the industrial revolution were turned into mechanisms for more efficient, bloodier, and more destructive warfare. Other claims were made for human perfection which sounded simply absurd to ordinary common sense. It was suggested that the rise of scientific quantification would bring historical research, insofar as it was the study of human motivation, to the level of accuracy already found in some physical sciences.[117] Some claimed that all that was needed to overcome destructive social impulses was a thorough application of the principles of psychiatry. Absolute human freedom, properly applied, would lead to utter virtue.[118]

Against this boundless assertion of human perfectibility Reinhold Niebuhr set what he regarded as the "Christian view of history." One has to place the phrase in parentheses, since even on Niebuhr's own evidence not all Christians shared this perspective: it was a composite of biblical theology, Augustinianism, reformed Protestantism, and modern neo-orthodoxy. According to this view, all humanity stands under the judgment of God (Barth's *krisis* is echoed here) and stands in need of redemption. The Bible, Niebuhr argued, knew nothing of a belief in progressively more perfect religions across time: degeneration of truth was as likely as its enhancement.[119] The biblical view of history, as seen especially in the prophetic books of the Hebrew Bible, depicted a people chosen by God for no intrinsic merit of their own, who constantly risked betraying their election by forgetting their God and raising up idols of their own devising. Every people and every individual who tried to make their own selves the center of history would, by their own actions, bring about their destruction. Even though they were repeatedly forgiven by God and readmitted into the covenant, such favor for a people did not guarantee physical security in this life. To have received the favor and redemption of God did not mean that the righteous would always achieve earthly success.[120] In the New Testament the paradox of failure on earth and ultimate redemption was made palpable in the mystery of the cross.[121]

Ultimately, *Faith and History* turned into a plea for a particular approach to the relationship between faith and human culture, between the otherness of revelation and the here-and-now of human activity. Secondarily, and again in keeping with the Niebuhrs' ethical preoccupations, it turned into a discussion of the relationship between individual Christian ethics and the ethics necessary to sustain a human community. Christian faith could, Niebuhr argued, accommodate a view of history as continuously unfolding, as long as that unfolding process was not seen as self-explanatory or re-demptive: in other words, the mere process of time would not of itself make the world a just place or make people individually better.[122] He identified a range of "wrong" options for the relationship of faith and society: perhaps the worst was when Christians arrogated such a level of perfection to themselves that they tried to set up coercive structures to enforce their supposed moral standards.[123] He called, in effect, for a sense of provision-ality and humility, especially in the churches. In the life of the community one could see "facets of the eternal," but these were always against the background of the effects of human fallibility. Only at the end of history could history be expected finally to make sense.[124]

Both Niebuhr brothers analyzed this ambiguity in the relationship between faith and philosophy, between church community and society, between faith in things beyond history and life lived within history. This was in a sense inevitable, since the critique of liberal "culture-Protestantism" had forced the relationship to the forefront of concern. Richard Niebuhr explored several of the options in his *Christ and Culture* (1951), a particularly fluent combination of theology with the history of ideas.[125] It is interesting to note that the options identified by the Niebuhrs were largely echoed in the discussion of "history" in a much more recent work from a different tradition. The report entitled *The Mystery of Salvation*, issued by the doctrinal commission of the Church of England in 1995, discusses history in terms of history as redemptive (an option which the report rejected); history as evil to escape from (which the report deemed insufficient and not true to St Paul); and, finally, history as something to be redeemed through divine action.[126] In these and similar discussions "history" has become synonymous with those aspects of human religious and ethical culture that are grounded and rooted in the contingent flow of events. "History" is the process against which, and within which, Christianity must operate.

Wolfhart Pannenberg (1928–) and his colleagues

Karl Barth had urged, in reaction to the liberals of the late nineteenth century, that divine revelation was autonomous, independent, entirely "other" and outside from the flow of human history and human culture. Bultmann, though starting from a different philosophical position, had similarly detached the "proclamation" of the death of Christ from the ordinary flow of events. It was inevitable, given the dialectical, antithetical way in which theology has developed, that Barth's ideas would in time generate a reaction within the academic establishment. That reaction came in the form of the work of a group of theologians and biblical scholars around Wolfhart Pannenberg in the early 1960s. Pannenberg, though born into a Lutheran household, rediscovered Christianity as an adult rather than being initiated into Protestant attitudes and values from childhood. This measure of independence from the continuing post-Reformation tradition may be reflected in some of his work. He studied with Barth at Basel and then at Heidelberg, and has taught at Mainz and Munich. His *Systematic Theology* was published in the mid-1990s.

In 1961 Pannenberg and his colleagues published a symposium volume entitled *Revelation as History*.[127] In this volume the contributors subjected the concept of "revelation," which in Barth's work was defined as God's self-revelation in Jesus Christ and through the activity of the Trinity, to an intensive biblical and historicotheological analysis. The word "revelation" and its equivalents had been understood in a wide range of ways across both the Old and New Testaments.[128] Within the New Testament several ideas of "revelation" jostled for position. Ulrich Wilckens speculated about how Jesus himself would have become conscious of his own unique authority as a teacher. After the experiences of the passion and resurrection, the post-Easter community could unite certain apocalyptic and eschatological elements in their thought with the person of Jesus in a way that might not have been the case before. In the communities that generated the New Testament books, various themes combined in differing proportions: Jewish apocalyptic thought, Gnostic beliefs about secret spiritual revelations, and the nascent Church's sense of its own complex relationship to the "Jesus events" and the continuing history of its ministry. Each New Testament author worked out the synthesis of these elements in a slightly different manner. Luke and Acts placed the greatest emphasis on the ever-increasing distance between the believer and the events of the life of Jesus, such that revelation had to be conceived partly in terms of tradition. Hebrews and the Johannine writings strayed closer to the idea that God was revealed through the direct action of the Holy Spirit, but preserved enough of the historical not to break all links with their Judaic inheritance.[129]

Pannenberg himself proposed a set of dogmatic theses in the middle of the book, which elaborated on the previous two chapters. Pannenberg's key contention was that the idea of an absolutely complete and self-sufficient revelation of God was alien to the ideas of revelation found in the Bible itself. More scriptural, he claimed, was the concept of a God revealing the divine nature gradually and progressively across history. That implied that the full revelation of God and the purposes of creation could only be complete at the end of history.[130] A further consequence followed, more shocking still to the Barthians. A God revealed through the processes of history was visible to anyone. Pannenberg probably intended to contrast the idea of the self-evident revelation of God through history with the secret knowledge, revealed only to initiates, that characterized Gnostic thought. However, he had the effect of seeming to make such knowledge of God "naturally" accessible, that is, without some special divine grace or miracle. Faith, for Pannenberg, arose in a person when the historical revelation of God through the events of history was properly understood. The revelation of God was anticipated, but not fully disclosed, in the life and destiny of Jesus of Nazareth.[131] But that message grew naturally out of Jewish religion and culture, only gradually grafting Greek philosophical concepts on to its Judaic heritage.[132] The key point in all of this, for Pannenberg and for those reading this book, was that a scriptural understanding of revelation had to include the idea that this revelation grew, developed, and became more complete with the passing of time and cultural changes.[133]

One side-issue or potential misunderstanding needs to be eliminated at this point. In the history of early modern theology, the idea of "continuing tradition" has tended to be the preserve of the Roman Catholic Church. In that Church's system of doctrine, the revelation in Scripture was developed and in some respects supplemented by the continuing witness of the Holy Spirit through the structures of the hierarchy. It is fairly clear that Pannenberg did not have this concept of continuous revelation in mind. The idea that revelation could be the preserve of one clearly identified visible hierarchy is alien to his thought, as is the implication that the statements of any institution could transcend history, be infallible, or be absolutely true. It is nevertheless interesting that the Pannenberg School has been seen as offering opportunities for ecumenical discussion. It also marks the progressive detachment of the Protestant tradition from its historic assumption that the revelations of Scripture are special, unique, and all-sufficient.

If the relationship between continuing revelation and the continuing Church was not that of comprehensive coinherence, how was it to be understood? That was the question addressed by the then 30-year-old Trutz Rendtorff, in his chapter in *Revelation as History*.[134] Rendtorff approached this problem in a dialogue with the thought of Karl Barth, whose concept of revelation posed particular problems for the idea of the Church. Rendtorff pointed out that the Church's authenticity as the voice of God had been justified in different ways in different eras. In the Middle Ages, the Church was guaranteed by the apostolic succession, by the successive sacramental ordinations that linked it to the apostles. The outcome of the Donatist controversy had ensured that Catholicity rested in sacramental correctness, not ethical purity. In the Reformation and post-Reformation era, the Church was known by its possession of correct doctrine, explicitly so in Protestantism and to a large degree within Roman Catholicism also. It was after the decline of the old confessional orthodoxy that theologians began to worry about how to trace the relationship between the present-day Church and the "Christ-event."[135] In twentieth-century theology, Barth had depicted the Church as the "event" in which God revealed the divine nature through Jesus Christ in our present. However, more interest was taken in the dialectic between the Church and present-day society, than in any contrast or distance between the Church and its original revelation.[136] Existentialist theologians tended to be more concerned with the relationship between revelation and the individual, than with that between revelation and Church.[137]

The remainder of Trutz Rendtorff's chapter amounted, in effect, to a call for the sort of inquiry which the present book is intended, however inadequately, to answer. "What is demanded," he wrote, "is critical reflection on the whole of the church's history in order to approach the problem of the connection between the church and the event of revelation." He continued:

> The concept of the church must begin with the factual connection between history as it develops after Christ and the Christ event, so as to take seriously the relation of the church to Christ. The theology of the church cannot overlook a systematic treatment of church history.... The necessity to conceive of the church in its relationship to the Christ event comes out of its own history. Moreover, this way of looking at history is in accord with reality. The question of just how completely the church can be considered the church of Jesus Christ cannot be answered in any other way, because the mere existence of the church, or more abstractly, its structures alone would tell us nothing. The transcendent character of the church resides in its historical relationship to revelation.[138]

Rendtorff, and the "Pannenberg School" in general, believed that they had identified a limitation to the perspective of post-Barthian theology. It had become conventional to conceive of and to define Christianity as an absolute, as the embodiment of transcendent ideas intruding into a world where it did not belong and of which it was not a part. And yet that same historical process was the inescapable channel through which revelation flowed from generation to generation.[139] What Rendtorff did not do, at least in this short chapter, was to draw from the *particular events and developments* of Church history the sort of lessons for theology that he declared to be necessary. In other words, the reference to the flow of history and the changing context of ideas remained theoretical: it was not applied to specific instances.

In a lecture published in 1971 Wolfhart Pannenberg returned to the issue of the historical predicament of Christianity.[140] He noted that Paul Tillich had argued, towards the end of his life, that Ernst Troeltsch had formulated some of the most crucial questions for twentieth-century theology. Pannenberg rejected a number of theological approaches that rested on isolating theological thought from the wider intellectual world, on creating a closed space within which theology could function on its own terms.[141] At the same time he also found unsatisfactory the "phenomenological" approach to the study of religions associated with anthropological thinkers like Mircea Eliade. These analyses assumed that there was a single thing called "the religious life" wherein meaningful similarities could be discerned between widely separate and historically different systems of faith and practice. Pannenberg argued that such analysis of superficial similarities between the individual phenomena of religious belief or practice risked creating resemblances where no real connections existed. Moreover, as he argued, "man is a historical being and changes in the process of history, so that all assumptions of an ever identical structure of human behavior remain problematical."[142] Pannenberg here showed greater sophistication than a number of his mentors and forbears. He pointed out that *individual religions* themselves change according to historical process. It is therefore unrealistic to say that "a religion" occupies a particular stage or plane of historical development (as Hegel and to some extent Troeltsch had done): religions are fluid things in a constant process of evolution.[143] In all this Pannenberg reprocessed the fundamental insight or perception with which his name has become associated: that revelation was not a single event, but a continuing process wherein the divine becomes known through historical change.[144]

Thomism, Mysticism, and Neo-liberalism: Some Roman Catholic Responses

Alasdair MacIntyre (1929–   )

The theology of the Roman Catholic Church remained within the framework of early modern confessional orthodoxy for rather longer than was the case in much of mainstream Protestantism. Since it was believed that the Church had defined its doctrines magisterially more or less once and for all time in the Ecumenical Councils of the Church (of which there have been three in the modern era) there was much less felt need to progress beyond those statements. To this day there are those who take pride – and display enormous intellectual acumen – in reworking the rich theological heritage of medieval and early modern Catholicism.

Nevertheless, the story does not stop there, because theologians loyal to Roman Catholicism, or those converted to it, were still very conscious of the ferment of philosophical and theological thought going on around them. For some the question became, "How can one defend traditional positions in a changed climate of philosophical thought?" Historicity became a problem to be addressed from outside, so to speak. An interesting case in point is the moral philosopher Alasdair MacIntyre, who has written some highly influential and thoughtful analyses of the nature of religious belief and religious language in the current intellectual climate. Born in Glasgow, MacIntyre studied at London and Manchester, and taught philosophy in the University of Manchester from 1951. In 1970 he moved to the United States, and since 1988 has taught at the University of Notre Dame. Initially a critical follower of Marxism, he underwent a series of conversions both in philosophy (to Thomism) and in faith (to Roman Catholicism).

The real focus of MacIntyre's most important work is not the status of religious belief or the Church, but the search for a rational base for ethics. He argued (most notably in his book *After Virtue* in 1981) that since the demise of the Aristotelian synthesis in Renaissance and Reformation Europe there was no longer a sound basis for ethical decisions. The Enlightenment believed that it could construct such an ethics based on secular rational criteria, but failed: an ethics based on human nature and human preference inevitably became circular. Ultimately the hollowness of Enlightenment ethical thinking was demonstrated by Nietzsche, who showed that there was no logical basis for morality (given nineteenth-century "modern" assumptions) besides human desires. MacIntyre has argued in contrast, therefore, that ethics can *only* subsist if there is a "teleology," a sense of what human beings exist *for*, that is independent of how they observably "are" in their normal state.[145] He has famously likened the ethicist to an early medieval monastic leader like Benedict of Nursia trying to gather together a group of followers to retrieve the lore of a lost civilization (antique classical literature plays the role, in this imagery, of ethical certainties) while the barbarians (those bereft of any ethical certainty) ravage the culture outside the community. If one is not to go into the void with Nietzsche, one must return to a somewhat repristinated Aristotle, and discover something of the ends for which people exist. Over the years observers have noted a tendency in MacIntyre's writing to become not only Aristotelian but Thomist, as he has also aligned himself (after early association with Marxism) more firmly with the Catholic Church.[146]

Very early in MacIntyre's career, in the 1950s while still at the University of Manchester, he wrote a long article entitled "The Logical Status of Religious Belief," reflecting on the then troubled relationship between philosophical and religious thought.[147] In this article he responded to the perception, promoted especially by the work of Karl Barth, that theological language was so special, so different in its rules of working, that it could only be understood from inside and could not, therefore, be tested by philosophical logic. Barth had pointedly eschewed any philosophical underpinning for his theology, and roundly criticized those theologians who did otherwise. For other reasons, some theologians in a more liberal tradition, such as Bultmann, argued that religious language was a specialized use of language, where historic narrative statements were used to make existential or experiential statements in a "coded" form, as it were. MacIntyre argued that such statements were not truly a private or idiosyncratic language; they were only a normal use of language according to certain rules, as was found in many other contexts. The claims of liberal theology were not claims about language, but about the subject-matter of theology itself.[148]

Macintyre then discussed the logical status of religious statements, for instance that God created the universe. These, he demonstrated, lacked the status of true hypotheses, since they had no truly explanatory power by the standards of the logician. Instead, he argued that all individual religions ground their arguments on certain absolute premises that function as "ultimate criteria" and depend on no external proof. The conclusion that MacIntyre then reached was that acceptance of a religious system requires that one accept its claims as possessing intrinsic *authority*. "At the heart of Christianity we find the concept of authority."[149] MacIntyre's concept of "authority" was a little more elastic than the term suggests: he accepted that an overwhelming spiritual experience, like that of Paul, might come to possess the "authority" from which a tradition would later be founded. But fundamentally the *existence* of a religious tradition conferred no *rational* obligation on the believer to accept it. Acceptance was a decision, where the believer assigned sufficient authority to a body of beliefs to adopt them as the voice of God. He described conversion as fundamentally a choice of the will.

How does this line of argument relate to the historical issue? The most significant point is that MacIntyre's analysis of conversion presupposes tradition, and tradition is assigned a considerable burden of importance (consistent, in fact, with MacIntyre's own conversion to Catholicism). On the face of it, the sort of instability and (at least partial) discontinuity that historians discern in the *transmission* of any given religious tradition therefore raises a serious problem. How can the decision to accept the claims to "authority" of a religious belief-system bear the burden of responsibility MacIntyre assigns to it, when the historian knows how fragile and mutable are the filaments of tradition that link one age with another? In the final analysis, the fragility of our historic traditions probably would not trouble MacIntyre or those who argue like him, just as he declared the implications of research into the "historical Jesus" to be insignificant as a criterion for faith.[150] The experience of conversion certainly does not depend on the strength or weakness of the evidence as it would be seen by an objective outsider. On the other hand, given what the historian has to say to the churches, the "conversion decision" should probably be seen as more of a subjective experience, and less as affiliation to a durable and stable standard of faith, than MacIntyre allows.

Hans Urs von Balthasar (1905–88)

Interestingly, the analysis of subjective religious experience stands at the precise heart of the theological project of another innovative Roman Catholic thinker, Hans Urs von Balthasar. Balthasar was born into Roman Catholicism in Lucerne, Switzerland, and in due course became a member of the Society of Jesus and was ordained priest. During World War II, he was left somewhat in isolation from the administration of his order. In this situation he founded a lay community at Basel in association with a widow, Adrienne von Speyr, who had experienced a series of mystical visions. In the late 1940s he became estranged from the Society of Jesus, which he left in 1950. Thereafter he subsisted precariously as a theological lecturer, until from the 1960s onwards his reputation grew and he experienced something of a rehabilitation in Catholic orthodoxy. He died in 1988 just as he was about to become a Cardinal of the Church. His *magnum opus* among a very large range of books and articles was a multivolume "Theological Aesthetics" entitled *Herrlichkeit*, rendered in English as *The Glory of the Lord*.[151]

As with other works of this magnitude, one cannot hope to do even rough justice to it in a short discussion such as this. Balthasar's work does not focus primarily upon the historical perspective of the churches; it is concerned principally with the different forms in which the divine is perceived and apprehended. It does not claim to be a systematics, but an aesthetics: how does the perception of divine truth as "beautiful" intersect with its perception as true and as good? That entailed (in the second volume) discussion of significant previous theologians in relation to their aesthetics. However, where the book at least potentially crosses the path of this inquiry is in the discussion of ways of knowing the divine in the first volume. The "subjective evidence" is, intriguingly, set out earlier and at greater length than the "objective evidence"; and in the former there is a significant amount of space devoted to a historical exploration of the mystical tradition.[152]

One consequence of Balthasar's "theological aesthetics" is that it seems to allow him to bypass some of liberal theology's strictures about the transmission and mediation (and therefore transformation, adaptation, or corruption) of religious traditions. Indeed, the mystic's perception of God can reach such a point that the indwelling divine virtually obliterates the human identity. This focus on the divine rather than the human, the one revealing himself rather than the one perceiving what is revealed, created a fruitful cross-fertilization between Balthasar and Karl Barth: the former wrote a most influential analysis of the development of the latter's thought.[153] Balthasar then provided a historical exploration of the role of mystical thought in the evolution of Christian theology across history. His account was possibly selective, certainly value-laden: he referred to the transition from monastic contemplative theology to academic scholastic thought during the high Middle Ages as a "process of decay."[154] Even after the advent of scholastic reasoning, the exploration of religious experience was privileged: Balthasar distinguished between the mystical experience truly so called and the "archetypal experience," the total exposure to the divine that transcends all categories.[155]

Once one reaches the "objective evidence" one finds Balthasar exploring the issue of historicity in a slightly more focused way, but chiefly as a prelude to dismissing the procedures of some historical critics. Balthasar argued that while Christ had to make himself comprehensible to each person in distinctive ways, no purely human conditions (say, cultural developments) could *of themselves* either make it impossible or make it certain that Christ could be correctly perceived. Christ revealed himself, as he argued, with the sort of certainty proper to a mathematical principle. Therefore his revelation could not be dependent on particular historical forms. A "historical scientism" that argued Christ could only be known through understanding (and shedding) the cultural assumptions of a past age "can never attain to vision since it is already methodologically blind." Decoding Balthasar a little, one may presume that he was rejecting something like Bultmann's "demythologizing" approach here (though he did not name Bultmann or anyone else). He was accusing theologians of excluding *a priori* certain aspects of the Gospels and thereby of losing the essence.[156] The problem one experiences with Balthasar's approach is, appropriately enough, the same as with Barth: it is theologically reasonable to assert a Christ whose revelation is transcendent and absolute and positive; but it is not theologically reasonable to assert the same either (1) of the Gospels and the New Testament in general, or (2) of the broader and longer traditions of the Church. Unless one is to focus entirely upon direct unmediated personal revelation (which Balthasar clearly did not intend, since he quoted extensively from the earlier theological tradition) then one must come to terms with the historically conditioned character of every document, every piece of written evidence that human beings have produced since Christianity began.

Hans Küng (1928–)

A much more direct address to the historical issue is found in some of the works of the controversial historical and systematic theologian Hans Küng (1928–). Küng, a native of Sursee in the Lucerne Canton of Switzerland, was raised in Catholicism, studied at the Gregorian University in Rome, and taught at the University of Tübingen from 1960 until his retirement in 1996. Although he served as a theological advisor to the Roman Catholic Church at the time of the Second Vatican Council, he came out as an explicit critic of the doctrine of papal infallibility in the 1970s. In 1979 he was stripped of the right to teach as a Roman Catholic theologian. For the last 10 years or so he has been active in a project to arrive at a "global ethic" transcending the boundaries between individual religions. However, his greatest contribution to the Catholic tradition may prove – in retrospect – to have been his exploration of a more critical approach to the Church's past around the time of the Second Vatican Council. His contribution, though recently rather downplayed in official accounts of the Council, has been re-expressed in a number of important works.

A full evaluation of Küng's work would require more than the space available here. An interesting sampling of his historical approach to theology may be observed in his overall history of Christianity, published in English as *Christianity: Essence, History, and Future*.[157] The book has something of the air of a textbook in historical theology, even though some extremely profound issues are addressed within its relatively scholastic, highly structured arrangement. The structure of this book reflects one answer to the classic problematic of liberal theology since the nineteenth century. Küng postulates, more or less as a starting principle, that there is an "abiding substance of faith," a "basic form and original motif," which consists in the person of Jesus Christ.[158] For the first 60 pages or so Küng postulates, not entirely consistently with his historical perspective, certain absolutes about the person and teaching of Christ.[159] However, the "spine" of the book is provided by an analysis of Christian history in terms of certain "paradigm shifts" ("*Paradigmenwechsel*" in German) between one "macromodel" of religion, society, and theology and another that took place at various turning points in (mostly Western) Christian history. So early Christian apocalyptic was succeeded by early Church Hellenistic orthodoxy; that in turn gave way to Medieval Catholic scholasticism; that was succeeded by the Reformation/Protestant paradigm, which in turn generated the Enlightenment/ modern paradigm and the contemporary ecumenical/postmodern paradigm.[160] Obviously, Küng is too subtle to suggest that in each of these shifts one movement entirely overwhelmed its predecessors. Indeed, he describes how several historically occurring paradigms left their modern heirs and manifestations as an enduring legacy. So "Roman Catholic authoritarianism" is the heir of medieval scholasticism; "Protestant fundamentalism" is the heir of the Reformation via reformed confessional orthodoxy.

Küng's typology advances considerably on the earlier liberal models of Ritschl and Harnack. He recognizes that in every era of the Church, including the primitive era, there were "paradigms" enclosing the "essence" of Christianity and enfolding it within the languages and assumptions of its host culture. Therefore "returning to the primitive," as some revivalist movements have suggested, is simply not an option. However, he still seems to fall foul of the critique of Troeltsch, that any attempt to construct an "essence" of Christianity (Küng's book uses the same German word *Wesen*, "essence" as in the title of Harnack's most influential book) risks trying to make a historically invalid distinction between "abiding essence" and "temporary form." In this context one is reminded of Troeltsch's curious image of essence and form as "molten iron in a wax container."[161]

It would be easy to classify Küng's response to the historicity of Christianity as simply another form of the classic liberal Protestant response, if a little out of its time. It partakes of much of the Protestant analysis about a gradual and progressive enhancement of the liturgy, and extension of papal claims to authority, spread over many centuries. He has long favored this approach. At the Second Vatican Council, according to his own memoirs, he took the bishops through four stages in the evolution of the Eucharist: a second-century "house communion," a Eucharist in a fifth-century basilica, a medieval Mass, and a Mass after the Tridentine reform. He demonstrated how the Eucharist had evolved out of a thanksgiving meal in memory of Jesus and would continue to develop.[162] Küng's analysis, though without the pejorative and critical language found in his Protestant counterparts, rather resembles that described in some of the Protestant historians analyzed in chapter 3.[163] Insofar as it is polemical, it is in its critique of the Roman Catholic hierarchy's mostly reactionary response to modernizing trends in Catholicism in the nineteenth and twentieth centuries.[164]

Nevertheless, in certain respects Küng, despite his antiauthoritarian credentials, approaches the issues in a way that evokes the older doctrinal positivism more than the liberal Protestant tradition that he so much resembles. A case in point is his response to Martin Luther. Küng is not satisfied, as most reformed scholars and all secular historians would be, to situate Luther's debate over justification in its historical context and to make sense of it there. He is concerned, indeed passionately concerned to assess whether and in what sense Luther was "right." He argues that theological historians, even if they wish to suspend theological judgment, must still ask, as a matter of exegetical exactness, whether Luther had accurately read the meaning of the gospel.[165] He concludes that Luther was (as a seventeenth-century orthodox Protestant historian might have said) correctly restoring the proper understanding of the Gospels and of Paul. Luther was "right" in his key principle of justification as forgiveness rather than purification. So Luther indeed represented a "paradigm shift"; yet he did not inaugurate a new faith or turn Christianity on to an essentially different path.[166] Something of the same desire to rehabilitate the modernizer according to some absolute standard of Christianity is seen in his evaluation of Schleiermacher.[167]

There is, however, one other point to note about Küng's historical analysis. He is aware of the two aspects to historical change that are also at the heart of the argument in this book. On one hand he acknowledges that in every culture at every time Christianity will adapt itself to its environment and express itself in language and concepts that belong to that environment. This Küng calls the "form" as opposed to the "essence" of Christianity. On the other hand he also recognizes that within every temporal expression of Christianity there are things that actively militate against the gospel. These Küng graphically calls "perversions": as instances he cites an overformal curial bureaucracy "often servile and effeminate even in the way in which it dresses" (here speaks one of its victims!), and an overelaborate development either of liturgy or of dogmatic formulae. And yet he also recognizes that "essence," "form," and "perversion" are ultimately inseparable:

> The concept of Christianity is always shaped by the particular concrete form it takes at a period in history. Christianity can become the prisoner of the picture which it has made of itself at a particular time. Indeed, every age has its own picture of Christianity which has grown out of a particular situation ... Is the positive to be identified with the abiding "essence" and the negative with the fleeting "form"? No, inconvenient though this is, we also have to take seriously the negative element in the Church, the perversion

of Christianity. . . . As a dark shadow this perversion runs alongside the essence of Christianity through all its historical forms. . . . Like essence and form, the abiding and the changing, so too good and evil, salvation and disaster, essence and perversion, are interwoven and cannot be set against each other . . . Even the best is prone to evil. Sin is possible even with the holiest.[168]

It may be open to question whether Hans Küng has fully integrated these theoretical reflections into the presentation of the history of Christian doctrine that constitutes the greater part of the texts of *Christianity*. However, his enterprise represents possibly the most serious attempt from someone raised in the traditions of modern Roman Catholic Christianity to address the paradoxes of the historical predicament of the Christian faith and the Christian Church.

Cultural Diversity, Liberation, Postliberalism, and Postmodernity

Up to the 1960s Western Protestant theology had largely read the "Christ and Culture" issue in terms of the radically and rapidly evolving culture of the developed West. Christian diversity, the issue of how modern Christians could relate to first-century Judeans or thirteenth- or sixteenth-century Europeans, was usually interpreted in terms of time rather than distance. Two factors about "postmodernity" have changed the terms of the discussion. The historical issue as traditionally understood has slipped somewhat into the background. However, several of its premises – including those that are most crucial for this study – have been accepted and integrated afresh into the new theological languages that have emerged.

It has become more and more widely discerned and accepted that theology cannot necessarily be written in the same language for all the peoples, even of a single, hierarchically governed worldwide church. In 1994 the Roman Catholic Church issued its revised *Catechism*, a complete redrafting of the Roman Catechism issued in the wake of the Council of Trent as far back as 1566.[169] The issuing of this document provoked a remarkable degree of public questioning as to whether one single document, centrally produced, could be written for the huge diversities of cultures found within modern Roman Catholicism.[170] Because of this diversity in the regions where Roman Catholicism bears influence, the issue of the relative status of different Christian cultures receives more attention than in the Protestant world (where diversity and localization have reigned for much longer). A large literature on "inculturation" and "acculturation" testifies to an awareness that religious teachings and norms have to be negotiated, whether one wishes it or no, with their host culture. This awareness has become particularly sharp since the Second Vatican Council and the inauguration of vernacular liturgies. The Church had to learn to speak in the language of a people very different from the traditional Western European Catholic tradition. New models of "translation" arose, where a complex process of cultural and even theological negotiation occurs before a vernacular form of worship is agreed.[171] Nevertheless, it is striking that the models of difference most readily embraced within Catholicism are geographical or ethnic rather than historical. The common use of the term "inculturation," largely restricted to Roman Catholicism, accepts that it is necessary to re-express "traditional Christianity" (conceived in a rather static, idealized form) in order to communicate effectively with radically different cultures in the world. It does not accept that such re-expression happens *constantly*, whether one wills it or no, in every culture including the Western European-American one: that religion evolves alongside and within its host culture. It seems easier to accept that peoples across the world are different, than to allow that the same people sharing the same doctrinal and liturgical heritage may change so radically that their inherited traditions no longer mean what they once meant.

Two schools of theology have grown up with missions to give voice within the Christian tradition to groups denied a distinctive voice by the traditional forms and languages of theological writing. First, theology has been written more and more with the non-European peoples of the world in mind. Cultural diversity is as much a matter of different peoples coexisting at the same time, as about the same people exhibiting different characteristics and ways of thinking at different times. At least in part, this awareness of diversity has caused liberation theologians to re-examine the relationship between theology and history. In his *A Theology of Liberation*, Gustavo Gutiérrez illustrates the usefulness of the historical perspective in creating a space in which a theology of liberation can be written, as distinct from a theology that vindicates the existing social order:

> By keeping historical events in their proper perspective, theology helps safeguard society and the Church from regarding as permanent what is only temporary. Critical reflection thus plays the inverse role of an ideology which rationalizes and justifies a given social and ecclesial order.... Theology as critical reflection thus fulfills a liberating function for humankind and the Christian community, preserving them from fetishism and idolatry...As critical reflection on society and the Church, theology is an understanding which both grows and, in a certain sense, changes. If the commitment of the

Christian community in fact takes different forms throughout history, the understanding which accompanies the vicissitudes of this commitment will be constantly renewed and will take untrodden paths. A theology which has as its point of reference only "truths" which have been established once and for all ... can only be static and, in the long run, sterile.[172]

What Gutiérrez argued, in the passage surrounding the above extract, was that theology can legitimately be written with a prophetic purpose in new historical contexts (in his case the context of Latin American movements for spiritual and social liberation) in exactly the same way that it was written in a variety of different contexts in the past. The contextualizations of theology already established in past experience need not and should not exhaust the possibilities. There is far more to Gutiérrez's argument than that: but this point on its own shows how the perception of the historical relativity of theological utterances has become domesticated into a variety of modern movements.

The same process of integrating the historicist insight appears in some feminist theology. Sallie McFague, in *Models of God*, appears to challenge Bultmann by writing that "metaphorical theology" does not "demythologize" but "remythologizes." That is, theology needs to discover new metaphors, rather than pretending that it can express itself in an entirely abstract and speciously image-free way, something that existentialist theologians can be accused of having done. However, in a profounder sense McFague has acknowledged one of Bultmann's key premises: that is, that theology is written from the standpoint of a particular cultural world, and that new cultural worlds need new languages and images to express the traditional message. For if Christian teaching needs to be "remythologized," that presupposes that its various mythic forms of language only help to express its intrinsic ideas according to the cultural norms of a given age. Theologians, she has written, "are poets insofar as they must be sensitive to the metaphors and models that are at once consonant with the Christian faith and appropriate for expressing that faith *in their own time*."[173] In this case, the "new metaphors" that Sallie McFague wishes to vindicate are those that do greater justice to the feminist perspective on human experience. If the fatherhood of God is a familiar metaphor for a divinity that cannot actually be conceived as gendered, then the motherhood of God may be just as appropriate, or more appropriate, to the needs of modern culture. This study is not concerned to appraise either liberation theology or feminist theology in any detail. The sole point to be made for this inquiry is to recognize how deeply the perspective of the historical theologians has taken root in the consciousness of recent generations of Christian scholars.

Regardless of political or denominational allegiances, theologians from a huge range of cultural and ethnic contexts have found it useful to incorporate the historicist perspective into their theology.

In the last few decades, however, new waves of philosophical and theological thought have to a large extent displaced the earlier assumptions shared by liberals and neo-orthodox alike. The key intellectual change, as many have remarked, was a shift of focus from the things described by language to the use of language itself. The theory underlying this change of perspective runs roughly as follows. In the Middle Ages metaphysical writers tried to describe things "as they were": they focused on the metaphysical entity as an object to be described. In the post-Enlightenment era of Romanticism and Modernism, philosophers and theologians reinterpreted the apparently factual statements of traditional metaphysical language as describing the state of mind or thought-process of the individual. (The primary exponents of this shift were Kant in philosophy and Schleiermacher in theology.) The "subject," the thinking person experiencing a religious sensation, was deemed more "real" and susceptible of description than the "objects" described by traditional religious language. Finally and most recently, in "postmodernity" the stability of the "subject," the thinking reasoning being, was called into question in the same way as the metaphysical "object" had been in the nineteenth century. The ultimate outcome of this accumulation of skeptical thought is to reduce all exchanges of metaphysical statements to polyvalent and unstable linguistic phrases. Neither the describer nor the thing described is held to have any objective existence; all that we can analyze is language itself. The above summary is of course a caricature, as all such summaries tend to be. Nevertheless, many philosophers have been visibly led by some such typology of accumulating doubt and uncertainty. Notwithstanding that the typology is historical (one mode of thought followed another within time) many postmodernists are absolutists: that is, they argue that the turn away from subjects and objects and towards language is irreversible and permanent.

Theologians have responded to this philosophical shift of perspective in a variety of ways. One interesting and quite influential response has been that of George A. Lindbeck (1923–) and the "Yale school" of "postliberal" theology with which his name is associated. A Lutheran born to missionaries of Swedish descent, Lindbeck worked in his early career on medieval scholastic theology. This gave him grounding in the sources of the Catholic tradition from the start of his work at Yale, where he served for nearly all his career. He had the rare distinction of being invited as one of the Protestant "observers" at the Second Vatican Council in 1962–5. He found himself involved more intimately in dialogue with the various groups attending the

Council, including various non-Catholics, than his then comparatively junior academic position might have led him to expect. Both the scholarly and ecclesiastical aspects of Lindbeck's career led him to an ever greater concern to explore the opportunities for ecumenical dialogue presented by new modes of philosophical thought.

Lindbeck set out his approach most influentially in a short work entitled *The Nature of Doctrine* (1984).[174] The argument is in essence quite clear, and lends itself to a relatively succinct summary. Lindbeck claimed that modern theologies had so far been required to choose between two ways of looking at religious language. Traditional interpretations treated the statements of religious doctrine as descriptions of an objective reality. Modern (liberal post-Schleiermacher) thought treated doctrinal statements as descriptions of states of mind and human experience. It was supposed that these conditions were universally experienced prior to finding expression in religious language. Lindbeck suggested that the true nature of doctrine lay in language itself. One could realistically treat theological systems as though they were systems of language that needed to be "spoken correctly" if they were to have meaning. However, the existence of one such language did not preclude the existence of another, different language that could also be "spoken" equally correctly on its own terms. The ecumenical significance of this approach was clear. It allowed for a sort of relativistic acknowledgement of difference: the "language" of each body of doctrine could be correct in its own sphere.[175]

It will immediately be obvious that Lindbeck's analysis of doctrine sits very strangely with traditional theology. It appears at first to be a position of radical relativism more appropriate to a secular anthropologist or sociologist than a theologian.[176] Languages, after all, can be viewed as arbitrary systems that serve only particular societies in particular contexts. Lindbeck's view raises serious questions about whether it would allow *any* of the sorts of truth-claims that would normally have been made in theology. Here, however, Lindbeck borrowed from a liberalism that in other respects he rejected. The notion that there was one true expression of Christian doctrine had in fact been challenged long since. The believing community exists prior to the expression of its beliefs as doctrine. One needs certain cultural reference-points and conventions before one can even "experience" a religion, or indeed describe such experiences.[177] He dismissed the notion that there are certain "core" religious experiences common to all people *before* they have the linguistic equipment to describe such experiences. Crudely put, he argued that one could only have a religious experience that one's prior cultural training equipped one to have.[178]

The aspects in which Lindbeck rejected liberal thought-patterns are however more striking than the ways in which he borrowed from them. Lindbeck noted (correctly) that the present age is peculiarly averse to the formulation of firm statements about doctrine. This, as he observed, is a historical process of change as much as the previous elaboration of doctrine once was. Lindbeck then set up something of a straw figure to attack. He remarked that some people have responded to the historical perspective on doctrine with a radical relativism, saying in effect:

> There is no faith once for all delivered to the saints. No self-identical core persists down through the centuries and subsists within the different and usually competing traditions that develop. Everything is in flux. Christianity (or any other religion for that matter) has only the kind of constancy and unity represented by historical continuities. Such a view is promoted by modern awareness of history and of cultural and individual differences. It has become part of the received wisdom of the educated classes and attempts to challenge it are often greeted with incredulity.[179]

Lindbeck preferred to insist that there is an "abiding substance" and that the task of the theologian is to isolate that substance, although he observed that only "saints and prophets" could do so absolutely. Naturally, he located that "abiding substance" not in terms of dogmas or experiences, but in terms of language and the correct rules for the use of that language. Being a Christian is a matter of knowing *how* to think and express oneself according to certain rules rather than of knowing *what* to think.[180]

The analogy between a system of doctrine and a system of linguistic rules must probably break down eventually, under the strain to which Lindbeck subjected it. However, that is not the most interesting point to emerge from his analysis. Lindbeck's approach is in fact surprisingly hieratic and top-down in its approach to the workings of a religion. For the question immediately posed by his technique is: "Who is competent to adjudicate over the 'correct' use of the Christian doctrinal 'language'?" Lindbeck here gave a startlingly conservative answer. Those who are "competent," even expert in the use of the language – mainstream, informed, devout practitioners of a religion – are the people qualified to speak for (say) Christianity. Lindbeck was unabashed in condemning the way in which Christian doctrine has been expressed by many in its past:

> Most Christians through most of Christian history have spoken their own official language very poorly. It has not become a native language, the primary medium in which they think, feel, act and dream. Thus, lacking

competence, they cannot, from the cultural-linguistic perspective, be part of that *consensus fidelium* against which doctrinal proposals are tested.[181]

In fairness, Lindbeck chose to narrow the gate of admission to the pantheon of "competent speakers" of Christian doctrine for a particular reason. He was trying to find an ecumenical path around the doctrine of the infallibility of the Roman Catholic *magisterium* (something with which Hans Küng had also struggled). However, for a historian of Christianity this approach will just not do. At many periods of Christian history the *magisterium*, whether envisaged as the political hierarchy in the Church or the intellectual leadership in the academy (the two were not always identical) has been barely representative of the majority voice of Christians. It has often described their practice in a language they would neither have recognized nor understood. An analysis that deems only the theological language of "official" Christianity worthy of discussion will inevitably fail to take account of a large section of past experience, practice, and belief. Lindbeck's approach made sense in the particular context in which he found himself. He worked as an ecumenist, and strove to set out parameters for discussion between multiple church hierarchies. Those hierarchies had in the past not acknowledged the right of the other to speak in any way for the Christian tradition. To have included the doctrinal voices of the uneducated would have complicated his task beyond possibility. Nevertheless, such a prescriptive selection of "competent" Christian voices must leave the historical observer somewhat dissatisfied.

Some of the most potent and most controversial interventions in the field of theology have come in the last decade from those influenced by, but also critical of, the trend of secular postmodern critical theory. The main strands of this movement combine in expressing a deep distrust of "rationality" and "truth" as these have been proclaimed since the secular thinkers of the Enlightenment. Michel Foucault analyzed descriptions of the world as chiefly manifesting the ambition of the powerful to vindicate and perpetuate their own power. Jacques Derrida focused his critique on language itself: the aim was to show that language does not describe the world transparently and unequivocally, and that misunderstanding and reinterpretation are intrinsic to the process of communication. In each case the well-spring of original sin was the Enlightenment: its confidence in pure reason, its ethics purportedly grounded in perceptions of human nature, even its evolutionism. Postmodernity has shared the general twentieth-century reaction against the flawed ethics of leading figures of the Enlightenment, especially their indifference to the extremes of differentiation and discrimination between genders, races, and classes. It has, however, gone further. It challenges the allegedly "modern" conviction that language can describe the world in a "correct," "scientific," neutral fashion as either morally suspect or intellectually false, or both. The flaws in Enlightened thinking are deemed intrinsic to and inseparable from its chief claims, rather than accidental and contingent to them.

Postmodernity constitutes an entirely understandable reaction against the hierarchically based, often politically conservative "common sense" that dominated European and American attitudes in the postwar years. It has also seemed to offer a peculiar advantage to a new generation of theologians. Some argue that the Enlightenment, in effect, oppressed Christian theology by subjecting it to its own criteria of truth and right reason. It forced theologians to adjust their viewpoints to the prevailing canons of rationality, or be dismissed as obscurantists. Since then, the argument goes, theology has been "humiliating" itself at the feet of secular rationality. (Barth and his movement of course constitute the most radical exception to that trend, and are hailed by many as precursors of postmodernism for that reason.) Now it appears that the intellectual colossus that has frightened Christian theology into self-abasement since the middle of the eighteenth century is after all a hollow, powerless idol. In these circumstances several theologians have seen a chance to emancipate Christian theology from its self-inflicted humiliation.

One of the most influential of these postmodern theologians is John Milbank, now Professor at the University of Nottingham and inspiration of a school of "radical orthodox" theologians inspired by postmodernity. As with other thinkers discussed in this chapter, it is not possible to review his work in its entirety. However, since Milbank underpins his critique and restatement of theology with a sophisticated historical analysis of how "modernity" arose, it is appropriate to discuss some aspects of his thought here. Milbank stated some of the principles of this exploitation of the postmodern in an essay entitled "Postmodern Critical Augustinianism" in 1997.[182] Since postmodernity has discredited the notion that there is a single, "scientific" standard of truth, theologians are now released from the obligation to conform to alien intellectual standards. Since in postmodernity neither objects nor subjects exist, but only relationships, one can now turn away from the old ideals of forming a complete picture of how things "are."[183] Milbank accepts that postmodernity poses a threat as well as an opportunity. It seems to postulate complete chaos in the realm of knowledge, where "stories" clash, overlap, and recombine endlessly, with nothing ever becoming "known." Postmodernity is associated with a "thoroughgoing perspectival historicism" which threatens theology. The Christian perspective has to offer a way through this chaos by describing a transcendent realm which is beyond conventional ways of "knowing." A little like von Balthasar, Milbank frequently resorts to the language of aesthetics to convey the sense of his theology. Further speculation about the atonement is justified in terms of "the pleasing shape of the conceits which it generates."[184]

One of the strengths of Milbank's work lies in a sophisticated analysis of how "modern" thought arose in the first place. In his most substantial monograph, *Theology and Social Theory*, he argued that the concept of secular society arose in the conflict-laden theories of Thomas Hobbes and Niccolò Machiavelli.[185] He has published a two-volume study of *The Religious Dimension in the Thought of Giambattista Vico*, Vico being one of those figures whom Milbank appropriates as alternatives to the Enlightenment paradigm.[186] In his contribution to the collected volume *Radical Orthodoxy*, which he coedited, he presented a historicotheological study of two eighteenth-century Pietist theologians, Johann Georg Hamann and Franz Heinrich Jacobi.[187] Here he argued that these "radical pietists" constituted a sort of counterculture to the Enlightenment rationalists of their own day. These figures (usually regarded as relatively minor players in historical theology) Milbank regards as the antecedents of a "radical orthodoxy" that was ready to engage in frontal conflict with the philosophy of their time. He sees them as exercising a "subterranean" influence on later figures such as Kierkegaard. Their critical contribution, for Milbank, was to assert that knowing, no less than believing, is an act of faith in which the divine principle participates: they stood for "knowledge by faith alone" as Luther had stood for "justification by faith alone."

Underlying Milbank's critique of Enlightenment thought is a claim grounded in the history of medieval philosophy. He argues, as do others in *Radical Orthodoxy*, that the rot set into European thought after the time of Aquinas. In reaction against Aquinas's integration of theology and philosophy, Duns Scotus claimed that "existence" could be studied as a concept in itself, irrespective of whether one were discussing the existence of God or the existence of a human being. The route from Scotus to the Enlightenment appears to run as follows. When the study of being ("ontology") became a philosophical problem to be analyzed independently of theology, that aspect of thought became secularized. Thus it became possible to contrast "reason," which revealed things as they are, with "revelation": the latter term was now used to refer to a specialized branch of knowing, concerned with the self-expression of the divine. In the early modern period a special role was devised for "revelation," which was to convince us of things that reason could not. This laid open the way for a purely secular idea of knowing, which in due course subjected theological knowledge to itself and drove it out to the margins before discrediting it entirely.[188] The task of the "radical orthodox" theologian, according to Milbank, is therefore to some extent to roll back the secularization of knowledge represented by the Scotist tradition and to reintegrate the divine unashamedly into concepts of knowledge, society, and ethics.

It is just as legitimate to postulate wrong turnings in the history of philosophy as in the history of religion, so there is nothing about Milbank's argument that is *a priori* irreconcilable with the positions advanced here. However, it is a deeply troubling approach for all that. Broadly speaking (and with the dubious exception of Karl Barth) most Christian thinkers down the centuries have embraced one or another philosophical system in the attempt to make rational sense of the claims of revealed religion. Many of the early Fathers were Christian Neoplatonists; medieval scholastics (and most of the early reformers) were Aristotelians of one sort or another; theologians of the scientific revolution variously embraced Cartesianism or Newtonianism, or clung on to Thomism; liberal theologians in the nineteenth century made varied use of scientific and evolutionary ideas. None of these thought-worlds were necessarily or inherently Christian, and some philosophies included aspects that could only be reconciled with traditional Christian doctrines with some intellectual dexterity. Neverthe-less, in each case they provided a framework to explain what some of the claims of Christian doctrine might mean: and rightly or wrongly, that was how they were used.

The problem that now confronts theologians is that many of the most potent modern philosophical movements are nihilistic. Instead of claiming to offer routes to discern the true, they deny that "truth" can be discerned at all except at a rather uninformative level of propositional abstractions. In several different ways, theologians have responded by claiming the chaos in secular philosophy as vindication, or encouragement, or at least permission to repristinate a specifically and exclusively Christian way of looking at the universe. One of many risks inherent in this procedure is that the gulf between the human and the divine (on which the early Barth was so categorical) will become erased. A second difficulty arises from the highly opaque language used by some postmodernists: they may be tempted to engage in dialogue only with each other, in a technical jargon estranged from nonphilosophers and entirely inaccessible to the churches. The most serious danger, however, is that of simple sectarianism. Whereas in the past philosophy was integrated with theology to create a putatively stable and shared framework for claims to truth, here philosophy is used to clear the ground so that claims can be made *irrespective* of any broader or more unified theory about the world or human society. Postmodernism risks creating a "bubble" in which theological statements can be made in isolation from any attempt to make holistic sense of the world and its experiences. Evidence from the past can be handled selectively and much that is inconvenient discarded, because there is no longer any belief in a "unified view" of anything.

Meanwhile, there still remain those ultra-orthodox confessional theologies that continue to claim absolute truth for their own perspectives and their own traditions. This mode of thought exists in both Protestant and Catholic worlds. It insists that despite the last two centuries of thought, scholarship, and experience, Christian doctrines can be expressed correctly and exclusively within the language of one or other of the great confessions, or according to some universal, unchanging set of beliefs and norms. Nearly a century ago Ernst Troeltsch characterized this kind of theology as "artificial absoluteness." Its adherents know there are many different modes of religious thought, but ascribe truth only to their own narrow view. This absoluteness is "artificial" because it rests on willful denial, as opposed to the "naïve absoluteness" of those who do not know that any belief other than their own exists. In its most extreme, rationalistic form this artificial absoluteness arranges its understanding of the entire world according to the needs of its doctrines. Examples would be the Roman Catholic hierarchy's rejection of new cosmologies and forms of physics in the middle of the seventeenth century, or the modern rejection of evolution by some Protestant churches in the United States. At best this mode of thinking is an abuse of the intellectual faculty; at worst it is entirely barren of intellectual integrity.[189] There is a great gulf between the reactionary confessional absolutism of the "artificial absolutists" and the more nuanced, much more sophisticated neo-orthodoxies that have arisen in academic theology over the last few decades. Nevertheless, there are affinities between them even though their languages are very different. The crude and the sophisticated versions of resurrected confessional orthodoxy both rest on the dismissal of large parts of the historic Christian experience as irrelevant or improper for the work of the theologian. The religious historian cannot endorse such an approach intellectually, or even ethically.

Drawing the Threads Together

It is time to draw some conclusions and then to offer some suggestions. For centuries writers about the Christian Church assumed that doctrine was everywhere pristine and unchanging, and embodied within the true Church. Individuals and sects would from time to time attempt to introduce errors and corruptions into it, and individual people within it might behave very badly, but "the Church" remained pure and authentic. Then, with the Reformation in the West, discerning where the Church "truly" resided became problematical. The majority witness of the visible Church could err; "correct" doctrine could no longer be understood as an unbroken and largely transparent tradition. Instead, the historic doctrines and practices of the Church had to be measured against the evidence of the early Church as attested in Scripture and the earliest post-scriptural writers. That comparison sometimes caused "minority" or "heretical" strands in Church history to be revalued as authentic Christianity. At the same time some theologians recognized that, even apart from deliberate sectarianism, human beings had an incurable tendency to overelaborate their religious practices. Too much religion, one might say, was an aspect of original sin. These perceptions led some Church historians, by the early eighteenth century, to depict the history of the Church as a series of lapses from simplicity and purity. Too much ritual, and too much dogma, were each bad in their own way.

Since the early nineteenth century, Church historians have been reluctant to offer any sort of evaluation or critical appraisal of whether or not this or that form of Christian practice properly "belongs" within the Christian religion. This approach began with the aspiration to scholarly impartiality and confessional disengagement advocated, but not entirely achieved, by Leopold von Ranke. Since that time this attitude has been reinforced by the individualism of historians and the fashion for relativism. As individualists, Church historians normally do not take up the brief to argue for one or another ecclesial tradition in its entirety. As relativists, they do not pass judgment on the absolute "correctness" of the beliefs of past ages. In the most extreme form of the trend, historians who are cultural relativists can deny that even scientifically perceivable entities – say, the bacteria that cause diseases – can be identified with each other across different time periods. Thus sixteenth-century "pox" may not be crudely identified with modern syphilis, because the two things belong to different eras and different cultures.[190] Similarly, some extreme relativists refuse to discuss how far beliefs about witches and demons were "rational," save according to the rules of discourse found in the period under discussion.[191]

So, the "history of Christianity and the Church" question migrated from the field of the historians to that of the theologians, where it was taken up with enthusiasm. The first generation of liberal theologians rode out to hunt the unicorn of "essential" Christianity. They recognized that actual Christianities differed from each other because each had accumulated a carapace of doctrines, practices, and traditions that were not found in the primitive era. The search for essential Christianity ran in parallel with the equally controversial quest for the historical Jesus (a quest which has been deliberately and consciously set aside in this study). In each quest the hope was that by stripping away the barnacles of ages encrusting historical knowledge, one could reach back to what the nineteenth century *really* needed to know about the Christian faith. Ultimately, however, this quest had to be abandoned, because a second generation of liberal theologians acknowledged that the time-limited encrustation was *intrinsic* to every manifestation of Christian teaching, including the very earliest. An abstract, myth-free, context-free "essential" Christianity could not be observed at any period in historical time. A historical Jesus who was properly located in the first century would be incomprehensible in the twentieth.

Since the passing of that first wave of liberal theology, theologians have processed the historical arguments over Christian theology in different ways. One lesson was not forgotten, even at the height of "neo-orthodoxy." The relationship between Christian revelation and "religion" as commonly practiced is inherently problematical. In various twentieth-century theologians "religion," identified as the human attempt to compass, define, and follow the commands of the divine, became closely related to sin, to creatureliness, to human limitation, to the Barthian *krisis*. In other words, not only do human beings usually make rather a mess of their attempts to serve what they conceive as God; they embody this-worldly hopes, desires, and rivalries in their religious practice. At best, what they teach and practice will be an amalgam of the continuing message of revelation with the priorities and cultural-linguistic conventions of their age. In the form represented by Barth and those influenced by him, this view of Christianity can be quite sharply dualist. There is "revelation," imagined (so to speak) as the limpid clear divine vision; set against that are "history" and indeed "religion," seen as the messy, untidy, sinful reality. As was shown earlier, this duality persisted even in the later Barth, though expressed much less stridently than in his *Romans*.

Yet this duality is somewhat bogus. Theologians do not derive their teachings from staring into limpid pools: they acquire them in the hurly-burly of debate, inquiry, and the teaching process. Doctrine grows through debate. This is even (especially?) true of the New Testament, which bears the imprint of theological controversy, reported and implied as well as conveyed and contained, all over its pages.[192] In dialectical response to the excesses of this dualist approach, a range of distinct theological schools have become preoccupied with the viewpoint of the observer and the process of learning. Several theologians have accepted that the *way* in which one learns about the Christian faith, whether as an insider or an outsider, whether with personal engagement or critical detachment, actually defines what is learned and how the results of that learning are understood. One learns the Christian faith not in isolation from a tradition, but within a tradition, or complex of traditions, in which analyses and responses to revelation are being constantly piled one on top of another. Put very bluntly, Christian theology is a cumulative process. There is now no consensus as to whether such cumulation is in itself either good or bad, improving or damaging, or indeed neutral.

It is important to recall the charge given to theologians by Trutz Rendtorff: what was needed was "critical reflection on the whole of the Church's history in order to approach the problem of the connection between the Church and the event of revelation."[193] The point is this. A Church historian will not assume that his or her perspective is uniquely "correct." It is evident to any historian whose perspective is not hopelessly narrow that different people have understood the Christian Church to mean different things, and to serve different functions, at different times within the past two millennia. A secular historian has noted how, in the later seventeenth century, "Christian orthodoxy was – as always – adjusting itself subtly to the spirit of the times."[194] This "adjustment" raises the problem of whether such adjustments leave Christianity with any continuously observable meaning. The diversity between successive – and now parallel – views of the Church and its role is immense; and, as was remarked at the beginning of this study, there are many outright contradictions as well as important inconsistencies. If, as theologians increasingly suggest, revelation is cumulative and progressive, then how can an integrated vision of "Christianity" be achieved? Is such a vision any longer possible? Is Christianity to be understood – by the historian as much as by the theologian or the ordinary observer – as a loose bundle of beliefs, liturgies, and traditions linked only by their unstable relationship to a contested body of texts, a relationship that is constantly reworked and reinvented in every age and in every culture?[195] Even setting aside any issue of personal commitment, the question of the identity of Christianity is of real historical importance. At a purely intellectual level, Christianity raises a version of the old debate between realists and nominalists. Is there a "form" of Christianity that can be abstracted from its multiple, temporally specific manifestations?

One answer is that even if the "essence" of Christianity can never be observed in its pure form, it may still be possible to infer that such a thing exists at a certain level of theological abstraction. This approach I shall call, for convenience, the "essentialist" approach. It differs from the crude absolutist position because it recognizes (as Gottfried Arnold did three hundred years ago) that one cannot look to this or that church and its teachings and say "this is the true Church; this is correct Christianity." It accepts that the claims to continuity and authenticity made by individual communions and traditions are always problematical. Nevertheless, the essentialist holds that there is something there behind the veil: that the various phenomena known as Christian history evoke a continuing, but always mediated, entity, which is also the enduring Church of Jesus Christ, the object of theological reflection and definition down the ages. In this sense most ecclesiology has been "essentialist" in the past. In the Middle Ages the more subtle of theologians recognized that only the ideal, the eternal Church was the bride of Christ "without spot and wrinkle": the everyday institution was flawed indeed, at least at the level of the people who served within it. However, the discernment of that "essence" cannot be a simple intellectual exercise, since *ex hypothesi* it lies beyond the competence of one individual with one field of view to perceive it in its entirety.

Alternatively, Christianity can be seen from the nominalist – and ultimately relativist – standpoint. In this view, little more than the name of "Christian" endures. Texts, creeds, liturgies, serve different functions and mean profoundly different and even unrelated things in their respective contexts. In this relativistic approach, Christianity should be studied as an important, often defining cultural attribute of the peoples who have adopted it (or suffered it being forced upon them): but what is said about each "Christianity" may be profoundly incommensurable and incomparable with what is said about other Christianities of other peoples and times. Moreover, for the strict relativist no one Christianity has any priority over another. There are no intellectual or ethical grounds for regarding one manifestation as more authentically Christian, or in any sense "better" than its rivals.

In practice, the latter approach, the relativistic, nominalist way of thinking, reflects the way that many if not most Church historians commonly work. Because of professional specialization, and the flight from direct theological questions since the nineteenth century, this relativism has not really created any difficulties within the profession of Church history. Most Church historians are experts in one particular period, and therefore confront change only in a limited, localized way. A few historians of doctrine will have a longer-range, more idealist perspective: but such theological historians have traditionally worked only within the higher stratospheric realms of theology, and have not muddied their perceptions with the everyday social experience of churches. Committed believers and disengaged observers can and do write Church history in similar and even interchangeable ways.[196] Disengaged, scrupulous description and analysis have, rightly, taken priority over evaluation against any abstract standard. Professional history has been the better for it; but an accumulated backlog of perceptions has grown up, perceptions that have not been incorporated into the public discussion of the identity of Christianity. It is now time to reflect, from the historical perspective, on how and by what techniques one might begin to resolve the issue of "essential" Christianity.

Conclusion

Theological analysis of the historical experience of the churches has yielded two results, which form the core of the argument of this book. First, whatever the Christian religion may "essentially" be about, it never manifests itself, within historical time, in a pure, unmediated, eternally valid form. Because human society and human culture are made up of beings that are constantly changing and diversifying, the phenomenal Christianity, the Christianity perceived by the contemporary observer or the historian, always represents a mediated, composite entity. It comprises doctrines, theologies, liturgies, patterns of community life and works of art and music that reflect the ongoing interaction between a tradition and its context.

Secondly, Christian religious history reflects a very human tendency to pile development on development, to evolve florid and ultimately extreme versions of particular trends. Christianity across its two-thousand-year history offers abundant evidence that Christians will readily and often select what had at first been regarded as secondary objectives, particular "means to holiness," and pursue these as though they were the primary purpose of Christianity. The historian looks on as one secondary objective succeeds or overlaps another, greatly enhancing the diversity seen between one form of Christian witness and its rivals or counterparts. At the most extreme end of this process, secondary objectives can be pursued with fanaticism: by this is meant, quite specifically, that certain primary imperatives such as mutual love or the preservation of the community are forgotten in the pursuit of religious poverty, the collection of relics, or the inculcation of dogmatic standards through catechesis.

It was argued earlier that the diversity seen in Christian history can evoke two analytical responses. The prevailing secular response would be relativist. The relativist argues that because Christianity constantly adjusts itself to different environments, and develops along unexpected and diverse paths, it has no abiding "essence" at all beyond the nominal images, symbols, and texts which it inherits and transmits. The "essentialist" argues, in contrast, that there is something underlying these various forms; though defining that "essence" has been a constantly problematic task from the Reformation era onwards. In the field of inquiry and analysis, the relativist and the essentialist can work together without logical inconsistency. One can and must continue to study and write the history of the Christian Church, regardless of whichever of the two options, the essentialist or the relativistic approach, one feels is valid. Difficulties arise only when the historian tries to answer theological questions about the significance of historical difference. That may be why historians in the last few generations have generally avoided such questions.

If one is a thoroughgoing relativist, then the task of the Church historian is not only to explain how each manifestation of "Christianity" relates to the cultures of feudal Europe, to early modern Russia, to nineteenth-century Africa, to the United States, or wherever. It is also to explain how these different manifestations metamorphosed into each other. The processes of communication, transmission, and change command attention. A properly relativistic history of Christianity will be dynamic, rather than static: integrated, rather than isolationist and compartmentalized. Secondly, the assumption which one sometimes finds, that cultural, social, or economic influences on religion are a one-way street, must be avoided. It is an unjustified and indeed falsifiable dogma to assert that Christianity is only ever influenced by its context, and that it does not also contribute to shape that context in unique ways. Religious belief and practice grow and evolve in a continuous reciprocal relationship with their host culture. A historian will wish to explain why, for instance, the social and religious discipline of "Calvinism" proved acceptable and congenial in post-1560 Scotland: but the same historian should also acknowledge that the presence of Calvinist teachings and attitudes made Scotland in the seventeenth century a very different kind of society from what it would have been without them.[1]

The challenge to the essentialist is rather more demanding. While one might choose to take an "essentialist" approach to Christian history on purely intellectual grounds, the committed Christian believer who is also fully conscious and aware of the Church's history *must* be an "essentialist," or risk building a structure of faith on shifting and ultimately meaningless mounds of sand. It will be necessary to bring to the reading of Church history a range of conceptual tools for making sense of the mysteries and the challenges of the subject.

At this point someone might propose a commonsense solution to the "essence" problem. Look at the different forms which the Christian Church has assumed since Pentecost. Make due allowance for the changing values and the changing assumptions of the ages. Eliminate the most obviously exaggerated or distorted manifestations of the human religious disease. What is left is the best that we can discern of the meaning of the Christian religion. What will be there? Certainly the commandment of unconditional love of God and one's neighbor, embodied in such different sources as the Johannine corpus and the Pauline and pseudo-Pauline pastoral writings, will be a critical, perhaps *the* critical element. Most Christians will claim that the Jesus they worship offers an unparalleled insight into the nature and purpose of God, and that Good Friday and Easter are events of cosmic significance. The Christian God will still be envisaged by many as the creator and sustainer of life, as the incarnate and suffering teacher, and as the continuously present inspiration and comfort. The Christian community must figure as an embodiment of the active love of God and a provisional anticipation of the kingdom of God. The scriptural testimonies will play a crucial role, though their message must be apprehended by reaching *through* the particularity and strangeness of so much of their text.

Despite the superficial attractions of this solution, it is ultimately no less problematic than any of the other solutions discussed above. The difficulty that arises is the following. Either one strives to reduce Christian teachings and practices to their very simplest, most skeletal propositional forms, or one tries to embody them in language that is familiar to the particular writer in his or her own particular era. In the former case (supposing that such a thing were possible) the result would be an abstract metaphysical theorem. It is impossible to imagine such a formula becoming the foundation of a living religion, when stripped of so much in terms of imagery, language, and tradition that actually inspires loyalty and reverence in real believers. In the latter case, however, one would still be left with a time-limited, context-bound version of the "essence" like any other devised in the past.

The consequences of the commonsense approach can be seen if one evaluates one of the most popular and successful examples of the genre, C. S. Lewis's edition of his BBC radio talks, mostly delivered during the 1940s and later published in book form as *Mere Christianity*.[2] C. S. Lewis (1898–1963) was by training a literary historian and critic. He became the most influential Anglican lay theologian and apologist of the middle of the twentieth century, above all through a series of radio broadcasts during and after the war years. Raised in conventional public-school Anglicanism, he lost his faith in early adulthood and regained it in maturity. These events gave a particular personal pungency to his descriptions of the experience of faith. The stated premise of *Mere Christianity* was that the most important features of Christianity were common to all ages, and that the historic differences between various manifestations were incidental and fundamentally unimportant. The work as published derived from three collections of talks, each addressing a different theme: the total volume was divided into four short books.

The first book argued for the existence of God from the alleged presence, in all people at all times, of a "law of nature" or, as Lewis more characteristically expressed it, "the Rule of Decent Behaviour" according to which "everyone plays fair" and tries "to behave decently." This moral law, Lewis claimed, was not an automatic consequence of being human, and must come from somewhere: so the logical assumption was that it was implanted by God.[3] The second book comprised a very stripped-down summary of the basics of Christian doctrine, as Lewis saw them. In the first substantial section Lewis discussed the origin of evil. The attempt to make sense of evil tended initially to foster dualistic religious ideas, where good and evil principles were made coequal divinities. Lewis saw all absolute dualisms as self-defeating: evil was ultimately subordinate to God. Good existed for itself: evil was, as another thinker had put it before him, "good gone wrong."[4] God allowed disorder in the world to give people free will. God responded to evil by implanting a set of myths about a dying and rising God, then fostered monotheism, and finally sent Jesus to declare the forgiveness of sins. The essence of Christian teaching was that "Christ was killed for us, that His death has washed out our sins, and that by dying He disabled death itself. That is the formula. That is Christianity." All subsequent attempts to explain the "formula" – that is, theologies – Lewis likened to the picture-language by which a scientist explained a mathematical formula too complex for the layperson to understand. Finally, Lewis proposed his own distinctive version of atonement theory, with Christ as the "perfect penitent." He argued that the sanctification of the individual depended on material things to make it work. He then proposed a sort of eschatology, according to which the Second Coming was delayed in order that as many people as possible might choose to take God's side freely and willingly.[5]

The third part of the book presented Christian ethics, chiefly in terms of the traditional array of four cardinal and three theological virtues. He proposed a version of the Thomist *habitus* theory of the virtues, according to which virtues grew within the person by custom and exercise until they became internalized. He argued for the conventional sexual ethics of mid-twentieth-century Anglicanism; spoke out in favor of domestic patriarchy and against pacifism; and then embarked on a furious philippic against the sin of pride. (Lewis later revealed in his autobiography, *Surprised by Joy*, that he did not denounce sins at length unless he had personally felt tempted towards them.)[6] Towards the end of Book 3 Lewis laid out an almost Lutheran depiction of the psychology of salvation. One should try to practice the virtues thoroughly for a period of time, in order to become convinced of one's own spiritual bankruptcy: out of that despair faith would come, and from faith good actions would follow.[7] The fourth book, ostensibly devoted to the doctrine of the Trinity, addressed besides this a number of other theological topics. In an almost Barthian fashion Lewis described theology as God's self-revelation through the human personality; God's "instrument" for depicting the divine nature was the Christian community. He used familiar nontheological imagery to explain eternity, the Holy Spirit, the incarnation, and a variety of theories of the atonement. He explored the nature of sanctification, and defined it (again in classically Protestant terms) as a process incomplete in life but perfected after death.[8]

Mere Christianity has clearly been found to be an enormously helpful and articulate exposition of Christianity by tens of thousands of readers. C. S. Lewis's skills as a writer and communicator should give many professional theologians of all ages cause to ponder how they have expressed themselves. As a personal statement the work has vivacity, clarity, and personal power. Nevertheless, Lewis clearly did not attain his stated objective of presenting only the basic minimum doctrines shared by all the Christian Churches of all times. In fact, one wonders whether he really seriously tried to reach that objective at all. The book bears the stamp of its author and its time on nearly every page. First, Lewis's presentation of human nature barely saw further than the highly moral culture of mid-twentieth-century England. His references to "decent behaviour" and "everyone playing fair" implied that English public-school morality was somehow indigenous to the entire human race, rather than a cultural growth amalgamating Judeo-Christian ethics, medieval chivalry, Renaissance scholarly discipline, and the Victorian ideal of self-control. In particular areas of private morality, he upheld the patriarchal nuclear family and monogamous, lifelong heterosexual marriage even though these values had already been deeply challenged by the inter-war generation. The military and naval images that recur through the work, and his rejection of pacifism, mark him as a conventionally loyal subject of an island kingdom at war.

More seriously, however, Lewis's theology either was carefully selected from a variety of historic sources that fed into the Anglican tradition, or was a private brew of his own. In the latter class is his argument that God permits evil in order to draw people to himself by their free will: this implies that God planned for evil and the Fall to occur, and that human beings can freely turn to God (neither of which statements seem to conform to classic

Christian theology). His insistence that spiritual regeneration needs material help in the form of the sacraments would not, for instance, have pleased either Erasmus of Rotterdam or Huldrych Zwingli.[9] As noted earlier, he took his theory of virtue from Aquinas, and his theories of justification from the leading reformers (though he rejected them on free will and predestination). Almost any statement on the Trinity is open to the charge that it selects some historic views and therefore inevitably rejects others. Careful source-criticism of the work would undoubtedly reveal many other debts to ancient and modern theologians besides those described here.

There are of course many other summary theologies – basic catechisms, if one likes – of Christianity in circulation. Many will come from the more conservative wings of the Church (where the enumeration of doctrines is still favored) and many will not attempt to be so broadly based. It is almost an axiom that they will clearly and inevitably reflect the circumstances in which they were written and the sources from which their authors have drawn their beliefs. For that reason this book proposes that there is no "highest common factor" solution to the "essence of Christianity." Any attempt to produce such a "basic" statement will run into the problem of particularity and selectivity. Theologians are individuals, and individual perspectives reflect difference, incompleteness, the partiality of vision that forms part of the human predicament. The forming or promulgating of confessions of faith and catechisms by collective or hierarchical churches, and their adoption as shared statements, does not diminish their essentially partial character. The Lutheran Augsburg Confession is as it is because it was drafted by Philipp Melanchthon: even one of the most inclusive peace-makers among the reformers put his stamp on his text. The great shared documents of the confessional era, whether the decrees of Trent, the decrees of Dort, or the Westminster Confession reflect, to any historian who examines their genesis, the fact that some theologians won and others lost. One particular theological perspective was canonized in order that others might be anathematized.

The insights of postmodernism may be strangely helpful at this point. Theological perspectives are individual, but the Church is always a collective. The totality of the Church's belief will always be more, and more complex, than its official ruling documents. As postmodern theorists have pointed out, what one person hears may not be the same as what the other speaks: what one person reads may not be what the other has written. My own historical work in the Reformation in Europe tended to downplay the differences, at the level of high theology, between one reformer and another (these were the kinds of difference that had most preoccupied historians hitherto). However, it also became clear that the *reasons* for becoming an adherent of the Reformation differed greatly between one social group and another, between clergy and laity, between bourgeois and artisans, between townspeople and peasants. Different kinds of people would hear and read their Reformation differently, and assign different priorities to its various components. Occasionally, for instance between 1521 and 1525, this diversity, this "*différance*," became visible as those formerly deprived of a theological voice, including lay women and artisans, published pamphlets setting forth their views. The totality of the Reformation was made up of a whole spectrum of opinions, which were never adequately comprehended within the texts of the official statements of reformed beliefs. In these circumstances diversity of beliefs did not lead to mere anarchy or confusion, the chaos of the secular postmodernists. Rather, a sort of unity of purpose existed – even if only temporarily – in the minds and desires of those who worked and took risks for religious change, though no single formulation of their testimonies could have expressed what each individual cared about.

The problem that the observer of Christian diversity faces is similar now to what it was in the era of the great confessions, though perhaps more highly colored. The divine must embrace, in some way or other, a number of different theologies that appear to human eyes to be simply incompatible. And yet, when one tries to pare Christian doctrine down to what these different incompatible theologies share, the result is profoundly unsatisfactory. The solution to the "essentialist" dilemma seems actually to lie beyond human grasp or human power to conceive. One image, or metaphor, that may plausibly be invoked is the following. Each manifestation of Christianity represents one facet of a whole that can never be seen in its entirety, since the "facets" are semiopaque. From the perspective of the thirteenth-century European theologian, Christian doctrine would be inseparably bound up with scholastic Aristotelianism and the doctrines of eucharistic presence and eucharistic sacrifice: Jesus Christ was known *chiefly* in the Mass. From another perspective, things would look quite different: a sixteenth-century Protestant reformer would come to regard the eucharistic sacrifice of the Mass and the proclamation of Christ's cross as diametrically opposed to one another: the Mass was a rival and an insult to Christ. With the passing of time, historians see more of these "facets" than before, and the number of points from which they try to "triangulate" (as it were) the essence of Christianity increases. However, at the level of current knowledge, unless Christianity dies out entirely or the world is consumed in some apocalyptic or environmental disaster, there are many more "facets" of the Christian experience still unknown and yet to be discovered than those that are already known.

Another variant on the "facet" image, drawn from geometry, may help to convey the difficulty presented by an "essential" Christianity that is putatively beyond our comprehension. A piece of paper which has been rolled into a cylinder, or bent into an S or a U shape, resembles a two-dimensional object but exists in three dimensions and can only be adequately described in three dimensions. Geometers call such shapes "manifolds," which are objects generated in dimension n but which exist in dimension $n + 1$ or higher. If the entire existence of the Christian Church represents, as it were, a "manifold" of any comprehensible variety of human social development, then to perceive it in its essence and its entirety requires a perspective that is literally on a higher level of complexity than a time-limited, context-limited historian can achieve.

The "facet" or "manifold" imagery has an important limitation. It is, in a sense, still too relativist. That is, in stating that the manifestations of Christianity are aspects of a reality too complex for any single human perspective, it may be taken to mean that all manifestations are of equal value. This image does address the issue of the infinite adaptability of Christianity; it suggests how, at least in principle, some form of unity may be *believed* – though not, in detail, discerned – to exist between patterns of belief and practice that differ so radically. It proposes a value-neutral way to lay alongside each other the different time-specific forms which Christianity assumes because of necessary and inevitable "adaptations" to the cultural and historical environment. These "adaptations" may in themselves be neither good nor bad, but simply a fact of life.

However, it does not address the second point made at the start of this conclusion, that not all adaptations are either necessary or benign. It does not explain how the historically informed Christian may begin to distinguish between the inevitable adaptation on one hand, and the lamentably human exaggeration or distortion on the other. It does not help us to resolve Hans Küng's semantic distinction between "form" and "perversion" in a systematic way. A pure relativist can look on the "distortions" of Christianity with complete detachment, and be quite unconcerned as to which form of belief in a nonexistent being people choose to commit themselves to. At most, the implausibility of a given belief may be a marker for the social isolation, whether enforced or self-imposed, of the group that holds such a belief. However, the relativist position is intolerable for the practicing Christian. If there is an essential Christianity, even though never observable historically, there must necessarily be forms that are *so* deviant that they do not represent a valid interpretation of Christian teaching and belief, in effect "right" and "wrong" ways to adapt Christianity to its conditions. At what point does an "adaptation to circumstances" become a "perversion"?

After the demise of liberal optimism, after Barth's and Bonhoeffer's strictures against human "religiosity," it may perhaps be permissible to say that there is an element of what used to be called original sin in all human religious activities. A cultural adaptation which spins on too eccentric an orbit may come to appear (here the perspective of the viewer will be all-important) as not just an adaptation but a deviation, perversion, or distortion of the Christian message. Even within what could broadly be called the Christian mainstream (to say nothing of the wilder sectarian movements) at various times beliefs and practices have arisen which *all* subsequent churches have declared to be misapprehensions, exaggerations, or distortions of what Christianity ought to mean. A case in point, from the modern perspective, would be crusading. From the eleventh to the fifteenth century many argued that Christian zeal ought to inspire people to seize the lands of the Eastern Mediterranean by violence, or to suppress religious deviance within Christendom by killing those who upheld unorthodox views. In mitigated forms the belief persisted long afterwards. Religious violence was not just condoned. The "crusade indulgence" asserted that those, properly confessed before entering the campaign, who died in battle for the Christian cause would receive full remission of the penalties otherwise owed at their death. Death in religious conflict was, supposedly, privileged in heaven. Such a belief would hardly be endorsed by a single responsible modern Christian Church: its historic legacy has of course caused the direst problems to the perception of Christianity in many Muslim lands.

The "perversions" of Christianity will be found not only in the fringes but in the heart of the mainstream denominations. In our own time we may not even be able to perceive them, because they will form a natural part of the fabric of life. A future generation in the Christian Church may (and doubtless ought to) be appalled by our acquiescence in the injustices and inequalities of our present world and our often irresponsible attitudes towards human and planetary well-being. It may well come to regard these as gross and inexcusable, rather than venial or inevitable failings in our Christian standards. It is to be hoped that a future Christian Church will look back on sectarian divisions and hostilities between Christians (to say nothing of hostility between different religions) with astonishment and dismay. But these are merely extrapolations from current problems: the likelihood is that new challenges will call forth new insights that cannot be anticipated.

The most helpful analogy that one might deploy towards answering this question is drawn from the sixteenth-century Reformation. Individual Christians, according to the leading reformers, are simultaneously sinful and justified. Even as grace works within us, we experience unruly passions and unworthy desires. The reformers said the same, though not always so stridently, about the Church. Compare, for instance, the following passage from one of Luther's commentaries on the Psalms:

> The church is not called holy because it has no sin. Paul says [Rom. 6:12], "Do not let sin reign," namely, "that you obey it." He confesses that there is sin and lust in Christians, and he admonishes them not to let sin reign. Therefore the church is holy, and it is called holy according to its *first fruits*, not according to its tithes and fullness. It is holy through faith in the name of Christ, in whom it has purity. This it does not have in itself, but because of His name.... If you want to judge by sight, you will see that it is sinful. You will see many, in fact, countless occasions for offense, brethren dominated by their passions, one person incited by impatience, another by anger, another in some other way. It is not written: "I see a holy church," but, "I believe"; for it does not have its own righteousness but Christ's, who is its head. In that faith I perceive its holiness, which is a holiness that is believed and not one that is palpable or visible....[10]

Luther's concern was with moral sins and scandal; however, the same remarks could apply to the subtler ecclesial sins of misdirected enthusiasm, spiritual arbitrariness, and exaggerated zeal. A Church made up of human beings cannot expect its insights or its decisions always to transcend the limitations of its human members. In this predicament, the Church may reflect divine grace at work within it; but how much it reflects that grace may have little or nothing to do with how well that Church meets its own standards of performance. The same Church will also reflect all the human sins in the field of religion, including the tendency, documented earlier, towards overelaboration of the religious life or successive overbalancing towards one arbitrarily chosen secondary objective or another.

The location of "holiness" in a specific, arbitrary, and narrow set of ritual or ethical demands, and the exclusion of all those outside the enclosed community from salvation, would normally be thought to mark out those who held such views as dangerously eccentric and exclusive in their understanding of Christianity. However, that criterion in itself represents a very postecumenical approach, with its allergy to anything that smacks of arbitrariness or exclusion. It is ultimately impossible to distinguish between "adaptations" and "distortions" in a comprehensive or theoretical way. To resolve these questions definitively would require a "God's-eye view" of Church history, which *ex hypothesi* is not possible for the human being. The issue can only be resolved at the level of an individual decision about some particular doctrine or practice, according to the dictates and judgment of a person's conscience. In deciding how one responds to any given manifestation of Christian diversity, one's own verdict should therefore be provisional, cautious, and limited. The text about the plank of wood in one's own eye may well be relevant here.

To conclude, what is "essential" in the Christian experience cannot be grasped through anodyne generalizations or the lowest common denominator of doctrinal agreement. The individual conscience must reach out and grope towards that "essence." It may hope to glimpse it dimly, through the particular, the exceptional, the things about the inherited Christian experience and traditions that speak to *this* person but not to *that*. The essence cannot be separated from that which is partial, faceted, even transitory on this side of eternity. Because people are limited, they perceive only facets; because they are different, the facets that they perceive are different also. Ecumenical dialogue among Christians will have to confront – and exploit – this reality about how Christianity is learned and experienced. The same will be true of dialogue with other faiths. An essence that is greater than our own perceptions can only be seen through those particular and limited perceptions.

That Christian "essence," as each individual perceives it, obviously must not be crudely or thoughtlessly equated with any single historic manifestation of Christianity. It may not be identified with any one era, since neither that of the apostles nor any later period is "essential" or timeless. Nor can it be identified with any single body of texts, since the biblical Scriptures need to be scrutinized historically as much as any other writing, and the historic creeds are bound by their contexts. Neither can it be equated with, or sought exclusively in, any single canonical tradition out of the many that constitute the fabric of the Christian experience. The time for the "naïve" or "artificial" absoluteness that declared a single tradition or a single body of heritage documents to be the all-sufficient and timeless embodiment of the Christian faith is long past. For all these reasons Christians should exercise extreme care when declaring something to be a doctrine, or a rule, or a practice by which the Church stands or falls. The Church is always fallen, and yet remains standing even in the midst of its imperfections.

For those who wished so to argue, it might even be claimed that the very fluidity and complexity of Christianity testifies to its depth, its adaptability to changing circumstances. The insights and teachings of Jesus Christ continue to call forth creative responses from Christian thinkers. The words of Jesus – insofar as they can be identified through the filter of the ancient accounts – still form a continuously vibrant and living body of ideas, as those of many of his ancient contemporaries do not. Sayings that may have appeared merely paradoxes to his hearers, such as "one who seeks to save his life will lose it" prove revealing far beyond the context in which they were uttered.[11]

That may (answers the relativist) mean no more than that each age reads its Gospels anew and raises up a new image to meet its needs and circumstances. To dispute such a claim belongs to faith, rather than to Christian history. The wandering teacher from Nazareth steps out again and again from the clouds of dust raised by the crowds in his wake, constantly arresting, surprising, and challenging. As in his lifetime, each individual must decide how to respond to his challenge.

Notes

Introduction

1 Jaroslav Pelikan, *Jesus Through the Centuries: His Place in the History of Culture* (New Haven, CT and London: Yale University Press, 1985).

Chapter 1 The Unfolding of Christian History

1 See Acts 24:14.
2 See 1 and 2 Thess.; 1 Peter 4:7; Mark 9:1; but cf. 2 Peter 3:3–10.
3 On the Gospel of Thomas see e.g., J. K. Elliott (ed.), *The Apocryphal New Testament: a Collection of Apocryphal Christian Literature in an English Translation* (Oxford: Clarendon Press, 1993), pp. 123–47; Richard Valantasis, *The Gospel of Thomas* (London: Routledge, 1997); Jacobus Liebenberg, *The Language of the Kingdom and Jesus: Parable, Aphorism, and Metaphor in the Sayings Material Common to the Synoptic Tradition and the Gospel of Thomas*, Beihefte zur Zeitschrift für die neutestamentliche Wissenschaft und die Kunde der älteren Kirche, vol 102 (Berlin: Walter de Gruyter, 2001); Stevan Davies, *The Gospel of Thomas Annotated and Explained* (London: Darton, Longman, and Todd, 2003); Elaine Pagels, *Beyond Belief: the Secret Gospel of Thomas* (New York: Random House, 2003). An accessible general account of Gnosticism is Elaine Pagels, *The Gnostic Gospels* (New York: Random House, 1979). Besides these works, there is a very large literature surrounding this controversial text, not all of it scholarly.
4 On the history of the Church of the Holy Sepulchre see Charles Coüasnon, *The Church of the Holy Sepulchre in Jerusalem*, trans. J.-P. B. and Claude Ross (London: Oxford University Press for the British Academy, 1974).
5 See Peter Brown, *The Rise of Western Christendom: Triumph and Diversity, 200–1000 A.D.* (Cambridge, MA: Blackwell, 1996), pp. 285–7.
6 G. E. M. de Ste. Croix, "Why Were the Early Christians Persecuted?" *Past and Present*, 26 (Nov. 1963), pp. 6–38: see esp. 9–16, and cf. the quotations from Tertullian referred to in n. 107.

7   See Augustine, "The writings against the Manichaeans and against the Donatists," Ch 2 sect 11, in P. Schaff et al. (eds.), *A Select Library of the Nicene and Post-Nicene Fathers*, 1st series (Grand Rapids, MI: Eerdmans, 1956), vol iv, pp. 636–7; see also Augustine's *Three Books in Answer to the Letters of Petilian the Donatist*, ibid., pp. 569ff.

8   For the denial of the divine sonship of Jesus, see the Qur'an, 2:115, 4:171, 5:17, 5:71, 5:114, 6:99, 9:29, 10:69, 18:1–5, 19:30–7, 19:90, 43:73–83.

9   The most recent and most accessible translation is Augustine, *The City of God Against the Pagans*, ed. and trans. R. W. Dyson, Cambridge Texts in the History of Political Thought (New York and Cambridge, UK: Cambridge University Press, 1998).

10 See Caesarius, Bishop of Arles, *Caesarii Arelatensis Opera*, ed. Germanus Morin, in *Corpus Christianorum, Series Latina*, vols. 103–4 (Turnhout, Belgium: Brepols, 1953).

11 The phrase comes from the title of an old-fashioned history of the pre-Gregorian Church, Émile Amann et Auguste Dumas, *L'Église au pouvoir des laïques (888–1057)* (Paris: Bloud & Gay, 1942), vol. 7 of Augustin Fliche and Victor Martin (eds.), *Histoire de l'Église: depuis les origines jusqu'à nos jours* (Paris: Bloud & Gay, 1934–64).

12 See Gratian's Decretum, in A. L. Richter and E. A. Friedberg (eds.), *Corpus Juris Canonici* (repr. Graz: Akademische Druck-u. Verlagsanstalt, 1955), i, 678; on the downgrading of kings from quasi-clerical to thoroughly lay status, see the comment of Honorius of Autun, *Summa Gloria de Apostolico et Augusto*, in *MPL*, vol. 172, cols 1261–2, as quoted in R. W. Southern, *Western Society and the Church in the Middle Ages* (Harmondsworth, UK: Penguin, 1970), p. 37.

13 Martin Luther, *Luther's Works*, ed. Jaroslav Pelikan and H. T. Lehmann, 55 vols. (St. Louis, MO and Philadelphia, PA: Concordia Publishing House and Fortress Press, 1955–86), vol. 32, p. 208.

14 Lutheran Churches, *Die Bekenntnisschriften der evangelisch-lutherischen Kirche herausgegeben vom Deutschen Evangelischen Kirchenausschuss im Gedenkjahr der Augsburgischen Konfession, 1930* (Göttingen: Vandenhoeck & Ruprecht, 1930), pp. 587–92.

15 *The Babylonian Captivity of the Church: A Prelude*, in *Luther's Works*, vol. 36, p. 36.

16 See Luther's commentary on Genesis 2:11–12, probably delivered as lectures in 1535, as translated in *Luther's Works*, vol. 1, pp. 97–100.

17 Pierre Bayle, *Commentaire philosophique sur ces paroles de Jesus-Chrit* [sic] *Contrain-les d'entrer; où l'on prouve par plusieurs raisons démonstratives qu'il n'y a rien de plus-abominable que de faire des conversions par la contrainte, & l'on refute tous les sophismes des convertisseurs à contrainte, & l'apologie que S. Augustin a faite des persecutions* (1686). A modern English edition is *Pierre Bayle's Philosophical Commentary: A Modern Translation and Critical Interpretation*, ed. and trans. Amie Godman Tannenbaum (New York: Peter Lang, 1987).

18   Charles Dupuis, *Origine de tous les cultes, ou religion universelle*, 4 vols. (Paris: H. Agasse, l'an III de la République [1795]).

19   François René de Chateaubriand, *Génie du christianisme, ou, Beautés de la religion chrétienne*, 5 vols., (Paris: Migneret, 1802).

20   Friedrich Schleiermacher, *On Religion: Speeches to its Cultured Despisers*, ed. and trans. Richard Crouter (Cambridge, UK: Cambridge University Press, 1988), pp. 102–5.

21   See further discussion of this work in Chapter 4.

22   See below, Chapter 4, pp. 183–7.

23   The text of the Barmen declaration is found in Klaus Scholder, *The Churches and the Third Reich*, trans. John Bowden, 2 vols. (Philadelphia, PA: Fortress Press, 1988), vol ii, pp. 122–71, and on the website <http://www.creeds.net/reformed/barmen.htm>.

24   The phrase arises in a Tyndale House catalogue entry for James Robison, *The Absolutes* (Wheaton, IL: Tyndale House, 2002).

25   See Erasmus, *Praise of Folly*, trans. Betty Radice (Harmondsworth, UK: Penguin, 1971), para 54, pp. 164–6.

26   The phrase is that of Ernst Troeltsch, in *Religion in History: Essays*, trans. James Luther Adams and Walter E. Bense, with an introduction by James Luther Adams (Minneapolis, MN: Fortress Press, 1991), p. 52.

27   See *Common Worship: Services and Prayers for the Church of England* (London: Church House Publishing, 2000), pp. 5–16.

Chapter 2 Constantly Shifting Emphases in Christian History

1   For an explicit statement to this effect see Cassian, *Conferences*, conference i, chapters iv-v, in P. Schaff et al. (eds.), *A Select Library of the Nicene and Post-Nicene Fathers*, 2nd series (Grand Rapids, MI: Eerdmans, 1956), vol. xi, p. 296:

And so the end of our way of life is indeed the kingdom of God. But what is the (immediate) goal you must earnestly ask, for if it is not in the same way discovered by us, we shall strive and wear ourselves out to no purpose . . . The end of our profession indeed, as I said, is the kingdom of God or the kingdom of heaven: but the immediate aim or goal, is purity of heart, without which no one can gain that end: fixing our gaze then steadily on this goal, as if on a definite mark, let us direct our course as straight towards it as possible.

2   For some of these cases of extremism see Henry Chadwick, *The Early Church* (Harmondsworth, UK: Penguin, 1967), p. 180; on the Circumcelliones see the references in Augustine, *Three Books in Answer to the Letters of Petilian the Donatist*, in P. Schaff et al. (eds.), *Nicene and Post-Nicene Fathers*, 1st series (Grand Rapids, MI: Eerdmans, 1956), vol. iv, pp. 569ff.

3   Mt. 11: 18–19; cf Lk. 7: 33–4.

4   Cf. also Mk. 2: 18.

5   Mk. 8: 34; echoed in Mt. 10: 37–9.

6   I Cor. 7: 1–16, 25–35; I Cor. 9: 5–12.

7   Chadwick, *The Early Church*, pp. 36ff.

8   Ibid., p. 39.

9   J. K. Elliott (ed.), *The Apocryphal New Testament: a Collection of Apocryphal Christian Literature in an English Translation* (Oxford: Clarendon Press, 1993), pp. 365 and nn.

10 See Howard Clark Kee, *Miracle in the Early Christian World: A Study in Socio-historical Method* (New Haven, CT and London: Yale University Press, 1983), pp. 275–7, 286–7.

11 See Elaine Pagels, *The Gnostic Gospels* (New York: Random House, 1979), pp. 57ff.

12 Elliott, *Apocryphal New Testament*, pp. 176–7.

13 Susanna Elm, *Virgins of God: the Making of Asceticism in Late Antiquity* (Oxford and New York: Oxford University Press, 1994), pp. 48–50, 162ff.

14 See in general Peter Brown, *The Body and Society: Men, Women, and Sexual Renunciation in Early Christianity* (New York: Columbia University Press, 1988).

15 Elm, *Virgins of God*, p. 286, on Pachomius; Chadwick, *The Early Church*, pp. 178–9 on Basil of Caesarea; compare Cassian, *Conferences*, conference ii, chapters xvii–xxiii, in *Nicene and Post-Nicene Fathers*, 2nd series, vol. xi, pp. 316–17, where he urges (relative) moderation in abstinence and self-denial.

16 Sulpicius Severus's *Life of St Martin* is translated in *Nicene and Post-Nicene Fathers*, 2nd series, vol. xi, pp. 3–23. On its circulation see John Binns, *Ascetics and Ambassadors of Christ: the Monasteries of Palestine, 314–631* (Oxford and New York: Clarendon Press and Oxford University Press, 1994) pp. 60–1.

17 For Melania the Elder, see F. X. Murphy, "Melania the Elder: a Biographical Note," *Traditio*, 5 (1947), pp. 59–77; the writings of Cassian are translated in *Nicene and Post-Nicene Fathers*, 2nd series, vol. xi, pp. 201–621.

18 Chadwick, *The Early Church*, p. 64.

19 Binns, *Ascetics and Ambassadors*, pp. 93–4.

20 Elm, *Virgins of God*, p. 39.

21 Ibid., p. 110.

22 Kee, *Miracle in the Early Christian World*, pp. 257–8.

23 See Augustine, *Confessions*, trans. with introduction and notes by Henry Chadwick (Oxford: Oxford University Press, 1991), pp. 151–4, 202–3.

24 For Augustine against Julian on the sinfulness of sexual desire, see *A Treatise Against Two Letters of the Pelagians*, in *Nicene and Post-Nicene Fathers*, 1st series, vol. v, pp. 380–7; on Jerome against Jovinian, see *Against Jovinianus*, in *Nicene and Post-Nicene Fathers*, 2nd series, vol. vi, pp. 346–416.

25 The most comprehensive text of the Rule of Benedict with commentary is in *MPL* 66, cols 215–932.

26 See e.g., K.-V. Selge, *Die ersten Waldenser mit Edition des Liber antiheresis des Durandus von Osca*, 2 vols. (Berlin: De Gruyter, 1967), ii. 63–9 and refs.

27 For the contemporary documents of the life of Francis see Marion A. Habig, *St Francis of Assisi: Writings and Early Biographies: English Omnibus of the Sources for the Life of St Francis*, 4th edn., (Chicago: Franciscan Herald Press, 1983); Regis J. Armstrong, J. Wayne Hellmann, and William J. Short (eds.), *Francis of Assisi: Early Documents, vol.1: The Saint* (New York: New City Press, 1999); Thomas of Celano, *Thomas of Celano's First Life of St Francis of Assisi*, trans. Christopher Stace (London: Triangle/SPCK, 2000).

28 On the Fraticelli see Gabriella Scalisi, *L'idea di Chiesa negli spirituali e nei fraticelli*, Studi e testi francescani, vol. 52 (Rome; Vicenza: L.I.E.F., 1973); Decima L. Douie, *The Nature and the Effect of the Heresy of the Fraticelli* (Manchester, UK: Manchester University Press, 1932).

29 For the later divisions among the Franciscans see Duncan Nimmo, *Reform and Division in the Medieval Franciscan Order: From Saint Francis to the Foundation of the Capuchins*, Bibliotheca Seraphico-Capuccina, vol. 33, 2nd edn. (Rome: Istituto Storico dei Cappuccini, 1995).

30 For Carthusian history see e.g., James Hogg (ed.), *Die Geschichte des Kartäuserordens*, 2 vols., Analecta Cartusiana, 125, vols. 1–2 (Salzburg: Institut für Anglistik und Amerikanistik, Universität Salzburg, 1991–1992).

31 Elm, *Virgins of God*, pp. 101, 186–8, 218–19, 266, 269–70.

32 For an example of the ascetic aspiration to "crucify the flesh" in English Puritanism, see Peter Lake with Michael Questier, *The Antichrist's Lewd Hat: Protestants, Papists & Players in Post-Reformation England* (New Haven, CT and London: Yale University Press, 2002), p. 447.

33 Luther's most famous writing on the subject was his *Judgment on Monastic Vows* (1521), which is translated in Martin Luther, *Luther's Works*, ed. Jaroslav Pelikan and H. T. Lehmann, 55 vols. (St. Louis, MO and Philadelphia, PA: Concordia Publishing House and Fortress Press, 1955–86), vol. 44, pp. 243–400. Luther spends even more time on the mistaken assumption of merit arising from the religious vow than on abstinence itself.

34 In Roman Catholicism all those in holy orders must be celibate males, unless given special dispensation as in the case of "reconciled" former Anglican priests or some who served in clandestine churches under communism. In Eastern Orthodoxy men who are single at induction into holy orders must remain so afterwards. Laymen already married are however permitted to be ordained deacons or priests. Bishops must always be single.

35 For Johannes Pupper of Goch's questioning of the value of a vow to enter a religious discipline, see K. H. Ullmann, *Reformers Before the Reformation*, trans. R. Menzies, 2 vols. (Edinburgh: T. & T. Clark, 1855), i. 107–20; D. C. Steinmetz, "Libertas Christiana: Studies in the Theology of John Pupper of Goch," *Harvard Theological Review* 65 (1972), pp. 217ff.

36   See the discussion of what was deemed "natural" in the Enlightenment in Norman Hampson, "The Enlightenment," in Euan Cameron (ed.), *Early Modern Europe: an Oxford History* (Oxford: Oxford University Press, 1999), p. 281.

37   The fallacies of this mode of thought form part of the key thesis of Alasdair MacIntyre, *After Virtue: a Study in Moral Theory* (London: Duckworth, 1981).

38   Statements of this sort owe something to Adolf von Harnack, *What is Christianity? Sixteen Lectures Delivered in the University of Berlin During the Winter Term 1899–1900*, trans. Thomas Bailey Saunders with an introduction by Rudolf Bultmann (New York: Harper, 1957), p. 24; see also Kee, *Miracle in the Early Christian World*, p. 150. Medieval theologians were concerned very precisely to distinguish a true miracle (*miraculum*) from a mere "marvel" (*mirum*). But for the readiness to expect the miraculous in the lives of saints, see R. I. Moore, "Between Sanctity and Superstition: Saints and their Miracles in the Age of Revolution," in Miri Rubin (ed.), *The Work of Jacques Le Goff and the Challenges of Medieval History* (Woodbridge, UK: Boydell Press, 1997), pp. 55–67.

39   Howard Clark Kee, *Miracle in the Early Christian World: A Study in Sociohistorical Method* (New Haven, CT: Yale University Press, 1983), pp. 146–73.

40   Ibid., pp. 274ff.

41   Elliott, *Apocryphal New Testament*, pp. 56–67.

42   Ibid., pp. 75–83; Kee, *Miracle in the Early Christian World*, pp. 280–1.

43   Kee, *Miracle in the Early Christian World*, pp. 283–6.

44   Sulpicius Severus's *Life of St Martin*, in *Nicene and Post-Nicene Fathers*, 2nd series, vol. xi, pp. 7–8.

45   Ibid., pp. 9–10.

46   Ibid., pp. 11–12, 14–16.

47   On this argument see Valerie I. J. Flint, *The Rise of Magic in Early Medieval Europe* (Princeton, NJ: Princeton University Press, 1991), and the review article by A. Murray, "Missionaries and Magic in Dark-Age Europe," *Past and Present*, 136 (1992), pp. 186–205.

48   On Gregory the Great see Chadwick, *The Early Church*, pp. 253–4; Peter Brown, *The Rise of Western Christendom: Triumph and Diversity, 200–1000 A.D* (Oxford and Cambridge, MA: Blackwell, 1996), pp. 133–47; see also Francis Clark, *The Pseudo-Gregorian Dialogues. Studies in the History of Christian Thought* (Leiden: E J Brill, 1987), pp. 37–8; Paul Meyvaert, "Diversity Within Unity: A Gregorian Theme," *Heythrop Journal*, 4 (1963), pp. 141–62. The *Dialogues* apart from Book 2 are in *MPL* vol. 77, cols 149–430.

49   The Second Book of the *Dialogues* of Gregory the Great is contained (out of sequence with the rest of the work) in *MPL* vol. 66, cols 125–204; for this story see cols 127–32.

50   *MPL* vol. 66, cols 133–40.

51   Ibid., cols 143–4.

52   Ibid., cols 153–4.

53   Ibid., cols 155–6.

54 Cassian, *Conferences*, conference xv, chapters, ii, vi–ix, in *Nicene and Post-Nicene Fathers*, 2nd series, vol. xi, pp. 446–9.

55 Ibid., pp. 446–7.

56 Ibid., p. 447.

57 Caesarius of Heisterbach (1220–35), *The Dialogue in Miracles*, trans. Huon E. Scott and C. C. Swinton Bland, with an introduction by G. G. Coulton, 2 vols. (London: G. Routledge & Sons, Ltd., 1929).

58 See Jacobus de Voragine, *The Golden Legend: Readings on the Saints*, trans. William Granger Ryan, 2 vols. (Princeton, NJ: Princeton University Press, 1993).

59 Johann Nider OP [*Formicarius*=] *Johannis Nideri . . . de Visionibus ac Revelationibus opus, . . . anno 1517 Argentinæ editum . . . luci et integritati restitutum* (Helmestadii, 1692).

60 Johannes Mirkus (John Mirk), *Mirk's Festial: a Collection of Homilies*, ed. Theodore Erbe from Bodl. Ms. Gough Eccl. Top.4, with variant readings from other mss., Early English Text Society. Extra series; no. 96 (London: Trübner, 1905), pp. 177ff.

61 For an example of lay protest against such "fables" see Gerald Strauss (ed.), *Manifestations of Discontent in Germany on the Eve of the Reformation: a Collection of Documents* (Bloomington and London: Indiana University Press, 1971), p. 143 (the document cited there apparently dates from 1525 rather than 1513 as stated). See discussion in Euan Cameron, *The European Reformation* (Oxford: Clarendon Press, 1991), p. 237 and n. 100.

62 See, e.g., the reference to "a distinctively protestant popular religion and magical culture" in Trevor Johnston, "The Reformation and Popular Culture," in Andrew Pettegree (ed.), *The Reformation World* (London: Routledge, 2000), p. 557.

63 For the Protestant rejection of exorcism and miracles generally see William Perkins, "A Discourse of the Damned Art of Witchcraft," in his *Works* (Cambridge, 1618), p. 648; compare also Heinrich Bullinger, *Wider die Schwartzen Kunst*, in *Theatrum de veneficis: Das ist: Von Teufelsgespenst, Zauberern und Gifftbereitern, Schwartzkünstlern, Hexen und Unholden, vieler fürnemmen Historien und Exempel . . .* (Frankfurt-am-Main: Nicolaus Bassaeus, 1586), p. 301; James Calfhill, *An Answer to John Martiall's Treatise of the Cross*, ed. Rev. Richard Gibbings for the Parker Society, Parker Society Publications, v. 11 (Cambridge, UK: Cambridge University Press, 1846), p. 333; *Calvin: Institutes of the Christian Religion*, ed. John McNeill, trans. Ford Lewis Battles (Philadelphia: Westminster Press, 1960), IV. xix. 18–19; Johann Georg Godelmann, *Tractatus de Magis, Veneficis et Lamiis, deque his recte cognoscendis et puniendis* (Frankfurt, 1601), pp. 55–6.

64 See Hampson, "The Enlightenment," in Cameron (ed.), *Early Modern Europe*, p. 270.

65 For the canonization process since the Counter-Reformation see: Benedict XIV, Pope, 1675–1758, *Benedicti XIV. Pont. Opt. Max. Doctrina de servorum Dei*

beatificatione et beatorum canonizatione in synopsim redacta ab Emmanuele Azevedo, Editio novissima, 2 vols. (Venetiis: Excudebant Jacobus Caroboli, et Dominicus Pompeati, 1765); see also the short monograph by Eric Waldram Kemp, *Canonization and Authority in the Western Church* (Westport, CT: Hyperion Press, 1979).

66   "Morris Cerullo World Evangelism" publishes a serial entitled "Victory Miracle Library." For an academic analysis see Nancy A. Schaefer, " 'Making the Rulers Tremble!': a Sociological Study of Morris Cerullo World Evangelism in Britain" (Aberdeen University: PhD thesis, 1999).

67   The "Foundation for Inner Peace" originally published *A Course in Miracles* in book form (New York: Foundation for Inner Peace, 1975). Many reissues, excerpts, and other discussions followed from the group responsible. For a discussion see e.g., D. Patrick Miller, *The Complete Story of the Course: the History, the People, and the Controversies Behind a Course in Miracles* (Berkeley, CA: Fearless Books, 1997).

68   An outbreak of nodding and weeping statues of saints in southern Ireland in the 1980s and 1990s was dismissed by the local Catholic bishop, but continued to be experienced by some faithful. A group of Catholics in Brooklyn, NY, continue to venerate the memory of a local visionary at meetings where miraculous apparitions are believed to occur around a statue. For further examples see Colm Tóibin, *The Sign of the Cross: Travels in Catholic Europe* (London: Picador, 1994); and for a militantly skeptical treatment, Joe Nickell, *Looking for a Miracle: Weeping Icons, Relics, Stigmata, Visions and Healing Cures* (Amherst, NY: Prometheus Books, 1993).

69   G. E. M. de Ste. Croix, "Why Were the Early Christians Persecuted?" *Past and Present*, 26 (Nov. 1963), pp. 6–38, see esp. pp. 28–9.

70   Ibid., pp. 23–4 and nn. 123–4; quoted in Eusebius of Caesarea, *The History of the Church from Christ to Constantine*, trans. G. A. Williamson, ed. and revised with new introduction Andrew Louth (London and New York: Penguin, 1989), Bk. 3.36, p. 98.

71   See e.g., 2 Maccabees 7, and esp. 4 Maccabees 6–18, which expands considerably on the version in 2 Maccabees 7.

72   Elm, *Virgins of God*, p. 57 and refs.

73   de Ste. Croix, "Why Were the Early Christians Persecuted?" p. 23 and n. 118.

74   Eusebius, *History of the Church*, Bk. 6.2, p. 180.

75   Bede, *The Ecclesiastical History of the English People*, trans. Bertram Colgrave, ed. with introduction Judith McClure and Roger Collins (Oxford: Oxford University Press, 1994), Bk. I.7, pp. 16–19.

76   de Ste. Croix, "Why Were the Early Christians Persecuted?" pp. 22–3.

77   Ibid., pp. 21–2.

78   For the rise of the medieval persecution of heretics see R. I. Moore, *The Formation of a Persecuting Society: Power and Deviance in Western Europe, 950–1250* (Oxford and New York: Basil Blackwell, 1987); Bernard Hamilton, *The*

Medieval Inquisition (New York: Holmes & Meier, 1981); Malcolm Lambert, *Medieval Heresy: Popular Movements from the Gregorian Reform to the Reformation* (Oxford and Malden, MA: Blackwell, 2002).

79 For the medieval Waldenses and their responses to persecution see Euan Cameron, *Waldenses: Rejections of Holy Church in Medieval Europe* (Oxford and Malden, MA: Blackwell, 2000), and the works cited there.

80 For the most recent balanced treatment of the Spanish Inquisition see Henry Kamen, *The Spanish Inquisition: an Historical Revision* (London: Weidenfeld & Nicolson, 1998).

81 On "Nicodemism" see Carlo Ginzburg, *Il Nicodemismo: Simulazione e dissimulazione religiosa nell'Europa del '500* (Turin: G. Einaudi, 1970); Perez Zagorin, *Ways of Lying: Dissimulation, Persecution, and Conformity in Early Modern Europe* (Cambridge, MA and London: Harvard University Press, 1990); Erika Rummel, *The Confessionalization of Humanism in Reformation Germany* (Oxford: Oxford University Press, 2000).

82 This is broadly speaking the argument of Brad S. Gregory, *Salvation at Stake: Christian Martyrdom in Early Modern Europe* (Cambridge, MA: Harvard University Press, 1999). Gregory tends to assimilate reformed Protestants to Anabaptists, and to minimize any suggestion that there might have been anything pathological about the expectation of martyrdom in either case.

83 John Foxe, *The Acts and Monuments*, ed. Joseph Pratt, 8 vols. (London: Religious Tract Society, 1877), describing the events of July 28, 1558; my italics.

84 See Hutterian Brethren, *The Chronicle of the Hutterian Brethren*, trans. and ed. Hutterian Brethren, vol. 1 (Rifton, NY: Plough Publishing House, 1987), pp. 70–3.

85 Ibid., p. 76.

86 George Huntston Williams, *The Radical Reformation* (Philadelphia, PA: Westminster Press, 1962), pp. 304ff; Claus-Peter Clasen, *Anabaptism: a Social History, 1525–1618, Switzerland, Austria, Moravia, South and Central Germany* (Ithaca, NY and London: Cornell University Press, 1972), pp. 99ff.

87 See the article "Cuncolim, Martyrs of," in Charles G. Herbermann, Edward A. Pace, Condé B. Pallen, Thomas J. Shahan, and John J. Wynne (eds.) *The Catholic Encyclopedia: an International Work of Reference on the Constitution, Doctrine, Discipline, and History of the Catholic Church*, 15 vols. (New York: Robert Appleton Co., 1907–12) or at <http://www.newadvent.org/cathen/04568a.htm>.

88 See the contrast between the approaches of Bede and Jocelin of Brakelond in Chapter 3.

89 I Cor. 11: 17–34.

90 See the discussion of Heinrich Bullinger in Chapter 3.

91 For a good description of the late medieval eucharistic rite see Susan C. Karant-Nunn, *The Reformation of Ritual: an Interpretation of Early Modern Germany* (London: Routledge, 1997), pp. 111ff.

92   On the social implications of participation in the communion, see e.g., John Bossy, "The Mass as a Social Institution, 1200–1700," *Past and Present*, 100 (1983), pp. 29–61.

93   For examination of communicants see e.g., Margo Todd, *The Culture of Protestantism in Early Modern Scotland* (New Haven, CT and London: Yale University Press, 2002), pp. 84–119.

94   Paschasius Radbertus's *De Corpore et Sanguine Domini* (On the Body and Blood of the Lord) is ed. in *MPL* vol. 120, cols 1267–1350; the work of Ratramnus of Corbie, also entitled *De Corpore et Sanguine Domini* is ed. in *MPL* vol. 121, cols 125–70.

95   Berengar of Tours's *On the Holy Supper* is ed. as *Berengarii Turonensis De sacra coena adversus Lanfrancum*, ed. W. H. Beekenkamp (The Hague: M. Nijhoff, 1941).

96   For the classic analysis of the Eucharist in relation to the real presence see the *Summa theologica of St.Thomas Aquinas, literally translated by Fathers of the English Dominican Province*, 2nd edn., 22 vols. (London, Burns, Oates & Washbourne Ltd., 1920–5), pt. III, qq. 74–7.

97   For Wyclif's views on the eucharistic presence see the exceptionally clear presentation in Anthony Kenny, *Wyclif* (Oxford: Oxford University Press, 1985), pp. 80–90.

98   Caesarius of Heisterbach (1220–35), *The Dialogue on Miracles*, trans. H. von E. Scott and C. C. Swinton Bland, with an introduction by G. G. Coulton, 2 vols. (London: G. Routledge & Sons, Ltd., 1929), ii, pp. 115–16.

99   Étienne de Bourbon, *Anecdotes Historiques, Légendes et Apolologues tirés du recueil inédit d'Etienne de Bourbon, dominicain du xiiie siècle* (Paris: A. Lecoy de la Marche for la Société de l'Histoire de France, 1877), no. 317, pp. 266–67.

100   Typical representations of the Mass of St Gregory were painted c. 1510 by Adrien Ysenbrandt, now in the J. Paul Getty Museum, Los Angeles; and in 1511 by Hans Baldung Grien (1484/5–1545), now in the Cleveland Museum of Art, as well as a famous woodcut engraving by Albrecht Dürer from around the same period. Thomas Aquinas analyzed what happened in such miraculous manifestations in *Summa Theologica*, pt III, q. 76.8.

101   Luther's comments on the Wilsnack cult are cited in Cameron, *European Reformation*, pp. 431 n. 29. Further details may be found in Ernst Breest, "Das Wunderblut von Wilsnack, 1383–1552: Quellenmässige Darstellung seiner Geschichte," *Märkische Forschungen*, vol. xvi (1881), pp. 131–302; see also Claudia Lichte, *Die Inszenierung einer Wallfahrt: der Lettner im Havelberger Dom und das Wilsnacker Wunderblut* (Worms, Germany: Werner, 1990).

102   On the Corpus Christi festival see Miri Rubin, *Corpus Christi: The Eucharist in Late Medieval Culture* (Cambridge, UK and New York: Cambridge University Press, 1991), pp. 164–212.

103   C. Zika, "Hosts, Processions and Pilgrimages: Controlling the Sacred in Fifteenth-Century Germany," *Past and Present*, 118 (1988), pp. 25–64.

104   Primitive versions of the patristic understanding of eucharistic "sacrifice" are found in e.g., Clement of Rome's *First Epistle*, chs 40–1, trans. in A. J. Roberts and J. Donaldson (eds.), *Ante-Nicene Fathers, vol. 1: Apostolic Fathers* (Grand Rapids, MI: Eerdmans, 1978), pp. 16–17; Justin Martyr's *First Apology*, chs 65–6, trans. in *Ante-Nicene Fathers*, vol. 1, p. 185, and his *Dialogue with Trypho*, chs 22, 41, 117, trans. in *Ante-Nicene Fathers, vol.* 1, pp. 205, 215, 257; Irenaeus, *Against Heresies*, 4 chs 17–18, and 5 ch. 2, trans. in *Ante-Nicene Fathers, vol.* 1, pp. 484–6, 527–8.

105   Cyprian, *Epistles*, 63.14, trans. in A. J. Roberts and J. Donaldson (eds.), *Ante-Nicene Fathers, vol. 5: Fathers of the Third Century* (Grand Rapids, MI: Eerdmans, 1978), p. 362.

106   Augustine, *The City of God Against the Pagans*, ed. and trans. R. W. Dyson (Cambridge, UK: Cambridge University Press, 1998), bk 10 ch. 20. I gratefully acknowledge here the analysis in John Schofield, "The Lost Reformation: Why Lutheranism Failed in England During the Reigns of Henry VIII and Edward VI" (Newcastle upon Tyne: PhD thesis, 2003), ch. 2.

107   Stories of the benefits of the Eucharist to the dead are told in Gregory, *Dialogues*, bk 4 ch. 55, in *MPL* vol. 77, cols 415–22. Compare the related but different story in Jacobus de Voragine, *Golden Legend*, vol. ii, pp. 282–3. See also the discussions of Gregory in Francis Clark, *Eucharistic Sacrifice and the Reformation*, 2nd edn. (Chulmleigh, UK: Augustine Publishing Co., 1980), pp. 57–58, 60, 405.

108   See William Lyndwood, *Lyndwood's Provinciale: the Text of the Canons Therein Contained, reprinted from the translation made in 1534*, ed. J. V. Bullard and H. Chalmer Bell (London: The Faith Press, 1929), Bk III, title 23, ch. 2, p. 95.

109   For the rules for a Trental according to the English rite see *The Sarum Missal in English*, trans. Frederick E. Warren, 2 vols. (London: A. Moring, 1911), ii. pp. 198–202; for a skeptical view of these masses see Pedro Ciruelo (1470–1560), *Pedro Ciruelo's A Treatise Reproving all Superstitions and Forms of Witchcraft: Very Necessary and Useful for All Good Christians Zealous for their Salvation*, trans. and ed. Eugene A. Maio and D'Orsay W. Pearson (Rutherford, NJ: Fairleigh Dickinson University Press, 1977), pp. 321–3.

110   On chantries see Alan Kreider, *English Chantries: the Road to Dissolution*, Harvard Historical Studies, vol. 97 (Cambridge, MA and London: Harvard University Press, 1979); on a specific example, Tim Card, *Eton Established: a History from 1440 to 1860* (London: John Murray, 2001), pp. 1–7.

111   *Sarum Missal in English*, ii. 202.

112   Luther's main works against the custom of private masses for individuals were his *De Abroganda missa privata* of 1521, ed. in the standard edition, *Luthers Werke: kritische Gesamtausgabe*, 58 vols. (Weimar: H. Böhlaus Nachfolger, 1883–1948), vol. 8, pp. 411–76; and his *The Private Mass and the Consecration of Priests* of 1533, trans. in *Luther's Works*, vol. 38, pp. 147–214.

113   In the medieval Church this distinction was expressed technically as that between *douleia*, the service of devotees towards the saints (based on the Greek word for a servant or slave) and *latreia*, the worship of mortals for the godhead (based on the Greek word denoting divine worship).

114   See the narrative of the martyrdom of Polycarp as incorporated in Eusebius, *History of the Church*, Bk. 4.15, p. 122.

115   Peter Brown, *The Cult of the Saints: its Rise and Function in Latin Christianity* (Chicago: University of Chicago Press, 1981) pp. 1–8, 70.

116   Ibid., pp. 32–49; see also Augustine's defense of the burgeoning cult of the saints in his *On Care to be had for the Dead*, in *Nicene and Post-Nicene Fathers*, 1st series, vol. iii, pp. 539–51.

117   For the cult of St Edmund see the discussion of Jocelin of Brakelond in Chapter 3, p. 117.

118   See Chapter 3 for the story of the translation of the head of St Andrew by Pius II.

119   Brown, *The Cult of the Saints*, pp. 53–8.

120   On patron saints in general see Bernard Hamilton, *Religion in the Medieval West* (London: Edward Arnold, 1986), pp. 124–6; on the German custom of assigning "apostles" see Cameron, *Waldenses*, p. 133 and refs.

121   For this custom see Silvestro Mazzolini (Sylvester Prierias), *De Strigimagarum Demonumque Mirandis Libri iii* (Rome: Antonius Bladis de Asula, 1521), sig. f iii ᵛ.

122   William A. Christian, Jr., *Local Religion in Sixteenth-century Spain* (Princeton, NJ: Princeton University Press, 1981), pp. 23–69.

123   See Jerome, *Against Vigilantius*, in *Nicene and Post-Nicene Fathers*, 2nd series, vol. vi, pp. 417–23, esp. p. 419.

124   Brown, *The Cult of the Saints*, pp. 64–7.

125   Eusebius, *History of the Church*, Bk. 6.5, pp. 184–5.

126   The original source for the story appears to be in Paphnutius, "Narratio de sancto Onuphrio," in F. Halkin, *Hagiographica inedita decem*, Corpus Christianorum, Series Graeca, vol. 21 (Turnhout, Belgium: Brepols, 1989), pp. 79–88 and esp. pp. 82–3, though Nider reworked the story considerably.

127   Nider, *De Visionibus ac Revelationibus*, pp. 417–23.

128   Chadwick, *The Early Church*, pp. 195–9.

129   Compare the impulse to Mariolatry among the Monophysites, ibid., pp. 281–2.

130   Quoted from a German text, late fifteenth century in Michael Baxandall, *The Limewood Sculptors of Renaissance Germany* (New Haven, CT: Yale University Press, 1980), p. 166; my italics.

131   A classic depiction of the Virgin of Mercy is the limewood statue by Michel Erhart from Ravensburg of c. 1480–90, now in the Gemäldegalerie, Berlin: see Baxandall, *Limewood Sculptors*, pp. 167, 178; James Snyder, *Northern Renaissance Art: Painting, Sculpture, the Graphic Arts from 1350 to 1575* (New York: Harry N. Abrams, 1985), p. 303 and plate 49.

132   For late medieval theology of Mary see Heiko Augustinus Oberman, *The Harvest of Medieval Theology: Gabriel Biel and Late Medieval Nominalism* (Cambridge, MA: Harvard University Press, 1963), pp. 281–322.

133   On the localizing of specific manifestations of the cult of the Blessed Virgin, see e.g., Keith Thomas, *Religion and the Decline of Magic* (London: Weidenfeld and Nicolson, 1971) pp. 29–30. Erasmus made the same observation in his colloquy *The Shipwreck*. See Erasmus, *Colloquies,* trans. and annotated Craig R. Thompson, in *The Collected Works of Erasmus*, vols. 39–40 (Toronto, Buffalo and London: University of Toronto Press, 1997), vol. i, pp. 351–67.

134   Brown, *The Cult of the Saints*, pp. 83–4.

135   Martin Plantsch, *Opusculum de sagis maleficis* (Pforzheim: Thomas Anshelm, 1507), sig g i [v].

136   D. H. Farmer, *The Oxford Dictionary of Saints*, 3rd edn. (Oxford and New York: Oxford University Press, 1992), pp. 185, 420–1, 429 and refs.

137   Gregory, *Dialogues*, bk. ii ch 38, in *MPL* 66, cols 201–4.

138   Sulpicius Severus's *Life of St Martin*, in *Nicene and Post-Nicene Fathers*, 2nd series, vol. xi, p. 12.

139   Habig, *St Francis of Assisi*; Armstrong et al., *Francis of Assisi*; Thomas of Celano, *Thomas of Celano's First Life of St Francis of Assisi*.

140   See discussion on Calvin's *Treatise on Relics* in Chapter 3, pp. 129–131.

141   Plantsch, *Opusculum*, sig g i [v].

142   A prime example of this phenomenon is Jan van Eyck's painting of the Madonna and Joris van der Paele (1436) in the Groeninge Museum in Bruges.

143   See Erasmus's colloquy *The Shipwreck*; also Kee, *Miracle in the Early Christian World*, pp. 120ff, 138.

144   See Erasmus, *Praise of Folly*, trans. Betty Radice (Harmondsworth, UK: Penguin, 1971), para. 40, p. 126; Heinrich Bullinger, *De Origine Erroris Libri Duo* (Zürich: Froschauer, 1539), fos 164v–7r.

145   Compare Calvin's representation of traditional belief about the intercession of saints before God in Calvin's reply to Cardinal Sadoleto: see the translation in Hans J. Hillerbrand, *The Protestant Reformation* (New York: Harper & Row, 1968), p. 171.

146   See Brown, *The Cult of the Saints*, for modern historical arguments against this interpretation.

147   Peter Burke, "How to Become a Counter-Reformation Saint," in David M. Luebke (ed.), *The Counter-Reformation: The Essential Readings* (Oxford: Blackwell, Oxford, 1999), pp. 130ff.

148   Ibid., pp. 135ff.

149   These figures are drawn from the Holy See's own statistics for the pontificate, accurate as of December 2004: see the website <http://www.vatican.va/news_services/press/documentazione/documents/pontificato_gpii/pontificato_dati-statistici_en.html#Beatificazioni%20e%20Canonizzazioni>.

150   Brown, *The Cult of the Saints*, pp. 18–19 and nn. 65–6, with sources referred to there.

151   H. Grundmann, "*Litteratus-illitteratus*: Der Wandel einer Bildungsnorm vom Altertum zum Mittelalter," *Archiv für Kulturgeschichte* 40 (1958), pp. 1–65; A. Murray, *Reason and Society in the Middle Ages* (Oxford: Oxford University Press, 1978), pp. 299–300.

152   The quotation is found in Malcolm Lambert, *Medieval Heresy: Popular Movements from the Gregorian Reform to the Reformation*, 2nd edn., (Oxford: Blackwell, 1992), p. 234; for the general principle that theological disagreements should not be aired in public, see Cameron, *European Reformation*, pp. 83, 450 n. 23 and refs.

153   On the *Ignorantia Sacerdotum* see Eamon Duffy, *The Stripping of the Altars: Traditional Religion in England c.1400–c.1580* (New Haven, CT and London: Yale University Press, 1992), pp. 53–4.

154   Ibid., pp. 84–5.

155   For such catechetical materials, see ibid., p. 78.

156   For typical late medieval pastoral manuals see e.g., Guido, de Monte Rocherii, *Manipulus curatorum* (Augsburg: C. Heyny, 1481, and numerous subsequent editions). For one of the most popular almanacs containing basic religious instruction, see *Le Compost et kalendrier des bergiers: reproduction en fac-simile de l'édition de Guy Marchant (Paris 1493)*, ed. Pierre Champion (Paris: Éditions des quatre chemins, 1926).

157   For this presentation of the Reformation theology of salvation see Cameron, *European Reformation*, pp. 111–35.

158   The classic statement of Luther's viewpoint on this subject was in the so-called "Invocavit" sermons delivered in 1522, trans. in *Luther's Works*, vol. 51, pp. 69–100.

159   Extract from the preface to Luther's *Shorter Catechism* in the *Book of Concord* of the Lutheran Churches. For the original text see *Die Bekenntnisschriften der evangelisch-lutherischen Kirche, herausgegeben im Gedenkjahr der Augsburgischen Konfession 1930*, often reprinted (e.g., Göttingen: Vandenhoeck & Ruprecht, 1976), pp. 500–1.

160   Ferdinand Cohrs (ed.), *Die evangelischen Katechismusversuche vor Luthers Enchiridion*, 5 vols. (Berlin: A. Hofmann, 1900–7).

161   Thomas Becon, *The works of Thomas Becon diligently perused, corrected and amended . . . containing the Gouernaunce of vertue. And a New catechisme sette forth dialogewise* (London, 1563–1564); references are to the nineteenth-century edition, Thomas Becon, *The Catechism of Thomas Becon . . . with other pieces written by him in the reign of King Edward the Sixth*, ed. for The Parker Society by the Rev John Ayre (Cambridge, UK: Cambridge University Press, 1844).

162   Becon, *Catechism*, ed. Ayre, p. 8.

163   Ibid., pp. 228–301.

164   Ibid., p. 408.

165   John Bunyan, *The Pilgrim's Progress from This World to That Which is to Come*, ed. James Blanton Wharey (Oxford: The Clarendon Press, 1928), pp. 153–9, 172–3.

166 Philipp Melanchthon, *Corpus doctrinae Christianae: Das ys, De gantze Summa der rechten waren christliken Lere des helligen Euangelij* (Wittemberg: Hans Krafft, 1561); David Chytraeus, *Catechesis* (Lipsiae: Abraham Lamberg, 1592); Martin Chemnitz, *Enchiridion de praecipuis doctrinae coelestis capitibus, per quaestiones et responsiones ex verbo Dei simpliciter ac solidè declaritis* (Frankfurt am Main, 1600).

167 For a modern texts of these documents, see G. I. Williamson, *The Heidelberg Catechism: A Study Guide* (Phillipsburg, NJ: P & R Publishers, 1993); Church of Scotland, *Scots Confession, 1560; and Negative Confession, 1581*, with introduction by G. D. Henderson (Edinburgh: Church of Scotland Committee on Publications, 1937).

168 Zacharias Ursinus, *Explicationum catecheticarum* (Cambridge: Thomas, 1587), translated as *The Commentary of Dr Zacharias Ursinus on the Heidelberg Catechism*, trans. G. W. Willard (Columbus, OH: Scott and Bascom, 1852); Caspar Olevianus, *A Firm Foundation: an Aid to Interpreting the Heidelberg Catechism*, trans. Lyle D. Bierma (Carlisle, UK: Paternoster Press, 1995).

169 Ian Green, *The Christian's ABC: Catechism and Catechizing in England c.1530–1740* (Oxford: Clarendon Press, 1996), pp. 350–86.

170 The early (and bibliographically complex) editions of the Racovian Catechism include: *Catechesis ecclesiarum quae ... affirmant, neminem alium, praeter Patrem Domini Nostri Jesu Christi, esse illum unum Deum Israëlis* ("Racoviae," 1609).

171 For a discussion of the reaffirmation of social hierarchy in reformed catechesis see Gerald Strauss, *Luther's House of Learning: Indoctrination of the Young in the German Reformation* (Baltimore, MD and London: Johns Hopkins University Press, 1978), p. 239.

172 Green, *Christian's ABC*, p. 51.

173 The Roman Catechism was originally entitled *Catechismus ad parochos* (Rome, 1566), and later *Catechismus Romanus*. On pre-1566 Catholic catechisms see the article "Katechismus" in *Theologische Realenzyklopaedie* xvii/5 (Berlin: de Gruyter, 1988), pp. 729ff. For Peter Canisius's catechisms see Petrus Canisius, *Summa doctrinae christianae* (Vienna, 1555), *Catechismus minimus* (Ingolstadt, 1556), and *Catechismus minor* (Cologne, 1558); Aldo Scaglione, *The Liberal Arts and the Jesuit College System* (Amsterdam: Benjamins, 1986), p. 84.

174 The quotations are drawn from the preface to *Catéchisme du Concile de Trente*, trans. Emmanuel Marbeau and A. Carpentier (Grez-en-Bouère, France: Editions Dominique Martin Morin, 1991), p. 3, and Robert I. Bradley, *The Roman Catechism in the Catechetical Tradition of the Church: the Structure of the Roman Catechism as Illustrative of the "Classic Catechesis"* (Lanham, MD: University Press of America, 1990), p. 3.

175 Roman Catholic Church, *Catechism of the Catholic Church* (London: Geoffrey Chapman, 1994).

176 See Michael J. Walsh (ed.), *Commentary on the Catechism of the Catholic Church* (London: Geoffrey Chapman, 1994), esp. pp. 2–3; and for reflections from

before the 1994 reissue, Johann-Baptist Metz and Edward Schillebeeckx (eds.), *World Catechism or Inculturation?* (Edinburgh: T & T Clark, 1989).

177 Note, e.g., that the writings of the Roman Catholic mystics Miguel de Molinos (1628–96) and Jeanne Marie Bouvier de la Mothe, Mme Guyon (1648–1717) were made available through discussions in England and in Lutheran Germany.

178 John Locke, *The Reasonableness of Christianity: as Delivered in the Scriptures*, ed. John C. Higgins-Biddle (Oxford: Clarendon Press, 1999), p. 170.

179 As cited in Alister E. McGrath (ed.), *The Christian Theology Reader* (Oxford and Cambridge, MA: Blackwell, 1995), p. 62.

180 For Barth's predicament see Gary Dorrien, *The Barthian Revolt in Modern Theology: Theology Without Weapons* (Louisville, KY: Westminster John Knox Press, 2000), esp. pp. 148ff.

181 George A. Lindbeck, *The Nature of Doctrine: Religion and Theology in a Post-liberal Age* (Philadelphia, PA: The Westminster Press, 1984), p. 77.

182 For guilds and confraternities see e.g., Christopher F. Black, *Italian Confraternities in the Sixteenth Century* (Cambridge, UK: Cambridge University Press, 1989); for a local socioeconomic study, Ken Farnhill, *Guilds and the Parish Community in Late Medieval East Anglia c. 1470–1550* (York, UK: York Medieval Press, 2001).

183 As remarked by Erasmus: see *Praise of Folly*, para. 54, pp. 146–6.

184 For this attitude on the part of the Swiss Anabaptists see the (highly critical) observations of Huldrych Zwingli, "On Baptism," trans. in G. W. Bromiley (ed.), *Zwingli and Bullinger* (London: SCM Press, 1953), pp. 139–41.

185 On Bucer's Strasbourg experiment and its context see Euan Cameron, "The 'Godly Community' in the Theory and Practice of the European Reformation," in W. J. Sheils and D. Wood (eds.), *Voluntary Religion: Papers Read at the 1985 Summer Meeting and the 1986 Winter Meeting of the Ecclesiastical History Society, Studies in Church History*, vol. 23 (Oxford: Blackwell, 1986), pp. 131–53.

186 For this important reading of the era see esp. Patrick Collinson, *The Religion of Protestants: the Church in English Society 1559–1625* (Oxford: Clarendon Press, 1982); Patrick Collinson, *The Birthpangs of Protestant England: Religious and Cultural Change in the Sixteenth and Seventeenth Centuries: the Third Anstey Memorial Lectures in the University of Kent at Canterbury, 12–15 May 1986* (New York: St. Martin's Press, 1988).

187 See Lake and Questier, The *Antichrist's Lewd Hat*, pp. 583–610; Christopher Hill, *Society and Puritanism in Pre-Revolutionary England* (Harmondsworth, UK: Penguin, 1986), pp. 15–30.

188 Cedric B. Cowing, *The Saving Remnant: Religion and the Settling of New England* (Urbana: University of Illinois Press, 1995); for a revision of the founder of New England, see Francis J. Bremer, *John Winthrop: America's Forgotten Founding Father* (Oxford: Oxford University Press, 2003).

189 See for instance how conflicts within the Massachusetts Bay Colony led almost immediately to the founding of new settlements in what became

Rhode Island, New Hampshire, and Connecticut. Some of the reasons for conflict are explored in Patricia U. Bonomi, *Under the Cope of Heaven: Religion, Society, and Politics in Colonial America* (New York: Oxford University Press, 1986).

190 On these issues see E. S. Morgan, *The Puritan Family: Religion and Domestic Relations in Seventeenth-Century New England* (New York: Harper and Row, 1966); Robert Pope, *The Half-way Covenant: Church Membership in Puritan New England* (Princeton, NJ: Princeton University Press, 1969).

191 On the Salzburg expulsion see Mack Walker, *The Salzburg Transaction: Expulsion and Redemption in Eighteenth-century Germany* (Ithaca, NY: Cornell University Press, 1992); Gerhard Florey, *Geschichte der Salzburger Protestanten und ihrer Emigration 1731/32* (Vienna: Bohlau, 1986).

192 Dissenters and Roman Catholics in England were relieved of all legal restrictions in 1829. Even Protestants in Piedmont-Savoy obtained full civil rights in 1848. See above, p. 42.

193 These estimates are found, with discussion, in Steve Bruce, *Religion in the Modern World: from Cathedrals to Cults* (Oxford: Oxford University Press, 1996), pp. 29–31 and refs.; see also Steve Bruce, *God is Dead: Secularization in the West* (Oxford: Blackwell, 2002); Bryan R. Wilson, *Religion in a Secular Society: a Sociological Comment* (London: Watts, 1966); for a historical perspective on the secularization thesis see S. J. D. Green, *Religion in the Age of Decline: Organisation and Experience in Industrial Yorkshire, 1870–1920* (Cambridge, UK and New York: Cambridge University Press, 1996), esp. pp. 380–90.

194 See, e.g., the argument for the continuing psychological need for something like Christianity, even in modern culture, made by David L. Edwards, *Religion and Change* (London: Hodder & Stoughton, 1969), pp. 236–68.

195 For an interpretation of the massive cultural changes that accompanied this period in Europe's spiritual evolution, see R. I. Moore, *The First European Revolution, c. 970–1215* (Oxford: Blackwell, 2000).

196 For Cistercian monasticism as a reaction against Cluniac monasticism, see e.g., Wolfgang Braunfels, *Monasteries of Western Europe*, trans. Alastair Laing (Princeton, NJ: Princeton University Press, 1972), pp. 67–70.

197 See Hamish Scott, "Europe Turns East," in Cameron (ed.), *Early Modern Europe*, pp. 334–5.

198 See Jerome, *Against Jovinianus*, in *Nicene and Post-Nicene Fathers*, 2nd series, vol. vi, pp. 346–416; Jerome, *Against Vigilantius*, in *Nicene and Post-Nicene Fathers*, 2nd series, vol. vi, pp. 417–23, esp. p. 419; also Chadwick, *The Early Church*, p. 214.

199 On "Laudianism" see e.g., Hugh Trevor-Roper, *Archbishop Laud, 1573–1645*, 3rd edn. (Basingstoke, UK: Macmillan, 1988); Julian Davies, *The Caroline Captivity of the Church: Charles I and the Remoulding of Anglicanism, 1625–1641* (Oxford: Clarendon Press, 1992); on the collecting of "providences" at the same period see above all Alexandra Walsham, *Providence in*

Early Modern England (Oxford and New York: Oxford University Press, 1999). On Arndt see e.g., Christian Braw, *Bücher im Staube: die Theologie Johann Arndts in ihrem Verhältnis zur Mystik*, Studies in Medieval and Reformation Thought, vol. 39 (Leiden: E. J. Brill, 1986).

Chapter 3 Church Historians' Responses to Change and Diversity

1   Eusebius, of Caesarea, *The History of the Church from Christ to Constantine*, trans. G. A. Williamson; revised and ed. with new introduction by Andrew Louth (London and New York: Penguin, 1989), pp. xviii–xxxii.
2   Eusebius, *History of the Church*, Bk. 10.4, pp. 306–22.
3   Ibid., Bk. 1.4, pp. 14–16.
4   Ibid., Bk. 1.7, pp. 20–3.
5   Ibid., Bk. 3.24, pp. 86–8.
6   Ibid., Bk. 1.11, pp. 28–9; Bk. 2.23, pp. 58–61.
7   For such lists see e.g., Bk. 4.19–26, pp. 128–35; Bk. 6.11–14, pp. 188–96.
8   Ibid., Bk. 7.32, pp. 250–5.
9   For pure lists of bishops, see e.g., Bk. 4.5, p. 107; Bk. 4.19, p. 128; Bk. 5.6, pp. 152–3; Bk. 5.12, pp. 157–8.
10   Ibid., Bk. 2.17, pp. 50–4.
11   Ibid., Bk. 2.23, p. 61, also Bk. 3.3, pp. 65–6; Bk. 3.24–5, pp. 87–9; Bk. 6.25, pp. 201–2; Bk. 7.25, pp. 240–3.
12   Ibid., Bk. 7.31, pp. 249–50.
13   Bede, *The Ecclesiastical History of the English People*, trans. Bertram Colgrave, ed. with introduction Judith McClure and Roger Collins (Oxford: Oxford University Press, 1994), Bk. I.23–32, pp. 37–60.
14   Ibid., Bk. IV.5, pp. 180–3.
15   See e.g., Ibid., Bk. II.2, p. 74.
16   Ibid., Bk. III.4–5, pp. 114–17.
17   See e.g., Ibid., Bk. II.4, pp. 76–7; Bk. III.4, pp. 115–16; Bk. III.17, p. 137; Bk. III.25, pp. 153–9; Bk. V.15, p. 262; Bk. V.18, pp. 266–7.
18   See e.g., Ibid., Bk. IV.22, pp. 207–10.
19   Ibid., Bk. V.12, pp. 253–8.
20   Ibid., Bk. IV.27, p. 223.
21   Ibid., Bk. III.24, p. 152.
22   See e.g., ibid., Bk. III.22, p. 147.
23   Ibid., Bk. II.9–14, pp. 84–97.
24   Ibid., Bk. III.1–3, pp. 110–14.
25   Ibid., Bk. II.2, pp. 72–3.
26   See Ibid., Bk. IV.1–6, pp. 167–83.
27   Ibid., p. xxix.
28   Ibid., Bk. V.19, pp. 271–2.
29   Ibid., Bk. IV.25, pp. 218–21.

30   Ibid., pp. 347, 355ff.

31   Ibid., pp. 350ff.

32   Ibid., Bk. IV.3, p.178.

33   For instance, splinters cut from the horse-litter in which Bishop Erconwald traveled were used to cure illnesses. See Bk. IV.6, p. 183.

34   See e.g., Bk. IV.23, p. 214.

35   Ibid., Bk. III.8, pp. 123–4; Bk. III.19, p. 143; Bk. IV.19, p. 202.

36   Jocelin of Brakelond, *The Chronicle of Jocelin of Brakelond Concerning the Acts of Samson, Abbot of the Monastery of St. Edmund*, trans. from the Latin with introduction, notes, and appendices by H. E. Butler (London: T. Nelson, 1949), xiii, 141, 166.

37   Ibid., p. 130.

38   Ibid., p. 129.

39   Ibid., p. 30.

40   Ibid., p. 12.

41   Ibid., pp. 24, 39–40.

42   Ibid., pp. 79–80, 91, 111.

43   Ibid., e.g., pp. 77–8, 100, 117–19, 136.

44   Ibid., p. 28; and compare with Norman P. Tanner (ed.), *Decrees of the Ecumenical Councils*, 2 vols. (London and Washington, DC: Sheed & Ward and Georgetown University Press, 1990), p. 371, for Decree 14 of the Council of Vienne (1311–12).

45   *Chronicle of Jocelin of Brakelond*, p. 38.

46   Ibid., p. 37.

47   Ibid., pp. 68ff.

48   Ibid., p. 98.

49   Ibid., p. 108.

50   Ibid., p. 110–11.

51   The modern scholarly edition is Píus II, *Pii II Commentarii rerum memorabilium que temporibus suis contigerunt ad codicum fidem nunc primum editi*, ed. Adrian van Heck, Studi e testi della Biblioteca apostolica vaticana, 312–13, 2 vols. (Città del Vaticano: Biblioteca Apostolica Vaticana, 1984). For the convenience of the general reader, reference is made here to the much more accessible translation and abridgement, *Secret Memoirs of a Renaissance Pope: the Commentaries of Aeneas Sylvius Piccolomini, Pius II*, trans. Florence A. Gragg, ed. with an introduction by Leona C. Gabel (London: Folio Society, 1988), pp. 314–15.

52   *Secret Memoirs*, p. 31.

53   Ibid., p. 269.

54   Ibid., pp. 150–1.

55   Ibid., p. 180.

56   Ibid., p. 102.

57   Ibid., pp. 182–3.

58   Ibid., pp. 187, 285.

59   *Secret Memoirs*, p. 145.

60   Ibid., pp. 51–2 and nn.

61   Ibid., pp. 214ff.

62   Ibid., p. 206.

63   Ibid., p. 263.

64   Ibid., pp. 102–3, 109, 314.

65   Ibid., p. 74–81.

66   Ibid., p. 218.

67   Ibid., p. 118, 174–5, 191–3.

68   For the late medieval inflation of the papal bureaucracy see John A .F. Thomson, *Popes and Princes 1417–1517: Politics and Polity in the Late Medieval Church* (London: Allen & Unwin, 1980), pp. 89–90; Denys Hay, *The Church in Italy in the Fifteenth Century* (Cambridge, MA: Cambridge University Press, 1977), pp. 41–5.

69   *Secret Memoirs*, pp. 233–51.

70   Ibid., pp. 256–60, 274–83.

71   Ibid., pp. 113–38.

72   Ibid., pp. 224ff.

73   For description and analysis of these images see Thomas A. Fudge, *The Magnificent Ride: the First Reformation in Hussite Bohemia* (Aldershot, UK: Ashgate, 1998), pp. 230–1, 235–49.

74   The results of the Lutheran meetings to discuss the Mantua council were encapsulated in the "Schmalkald articles," which formed part of the *Book of Concord*, the standard collection of heritage texts in the Lutheran tradition. See Robert Kolb and Timothy J. Wengert (eds.), *The Book of Concord: the Confessions of the Evangelical Lutheran Church*, trans. Charles Arand (Minneapolis, MN: Fortress Press, 2000).

75   Reference will be made here to the largest standard edition of Luther's works in translation, Martin Luther, *Luther's Works*, ed. Jaroslav Pelikan and H. T. Lehmann, 55 vols. (St. Louis, MO and Philadelphia, PA: Concordia Publishing House and Fortress Press, 1955–86); *On Councils and the Churches* is found in vol. 41, pp. 5–177.

76   *Luther's Works*, vol. 32, pp. 112, 117.

77   Ibid., vol. 41, pp. 73–8.

78   Ibid., vol. 41, pp. 33–4.

79   Ibid., vol. 41, pp. 47–52.

80   Ibid., vol. 41, pp. 85, 91, 100, 105.

81   Ibid., vol. 41, p. 121.

82   Ibid., vol. 41, p. 122.

83   Ibid., vol. 41, p. 124.

84   Ibid., vol. 41, p. 126.

85   Ibid., vol. 41, p. 128.

86   Ibid., vol. 41, p. 137.

87   Heinrich Bullinger, *De Origine Erroris Libri Duo* (Zürich: Froschauer, 1539).

88   Bullinger's reformation history finally appeared in print as Heinrich Bullinger, *Heinrich Bullingers Reformationgeschichte*, ed. J. J. Hottinger and H. H. Vögeli, 3 vols. (Frauenfeld, Switzerland: C. Beyel, 1838–40); his diary is edited as Heinrich Bullinger, *Heinrich Bullingers Diarium (Annales vitae) der Jahre 1504–1574*, ed. Emil Egli, Quellen zur schweizerischen Reformationsgeschichte, vol. 2 (Basel, 1904).

89   Bullinger, *De Origine Erroris*, sig *3ᵛ, my translation.

90   Ibid., fols. 21ʳ, 26ᵛ, 98ᵛ, 202ᵛ, 205ᵛ, 227ʳ.

91   Ibid., fols. 54ᵛ-56ᵛ.

92   Ibid., fols. 56ᵛ-64ʳ, 124ʳ⁻ᵛ.

93   Ibid., fols. 203ʳ-221ʳ.

94   Eusebius, *History of the Church*, Bk. 7.18, pp. 233–4.

95   Bullinger, *De Origine Erroris*, fols. 113ᵛ-114ᵛ.

96   Ibid., fol. 223ᵛ. Bullinger here anticipates the "Enlightenment" explanation of the rise of the cult of saints which is criticized in Peter Brown, *The Cult of the Saints: its Rise and Function in Latin Christianity* (Chicago: University of Chicago Press, 1981).

97   Bullinger, *De Origine Erroris*, fol. 117ʳ.

98   Ibid., fol 124ʳ⁻ᵛ, my translation.

99   Ibid., fols. 197ᵛ ff.

100 Ibid., fols. 208ᵛ-9ʳ.

101 Ibid., fol. 213ʳ⁻ᵛ.

102 Ibid., fols. 33ʳ-46ᵛ.

103 Ibid., fols. 164ᵛ-167ᵛ.

104 Ibid., fols. 167ᵛ-172ᵛ.

105 Jean Calvin, *Advertissement tresutile du grand profit qui reviendroit à la Chrestienté s'il se faisoit inventaire de tous les corps saincts & reliques, qui sont tant en Italie, qu'en France, Allemagne, Hespagne, & autres royaumes & pays* (Genève: Jean Girard, 1543).

106 References are to the modern edition: Jean Calvin, *Avertissement contre l'astrologie; Traité des reliques: Suivis du Discours de Théodore de Bèze sur la vie et la mort de maître Jean Calvin* (Paris: Colin, 1962), pp. 40–3.

107 Calvin, *Avertissement . . . reliques*, p. 48, my translation.

108 Ibid., p. 51.

109 Ibid., p. 54.

110 Ibid., p. 57.

111 Ibid., p. 58.

112 John 20: 6–7.

113 Calvin, *Avertissement . . . reliques*, pp. 58–62.

114 Ibid., p. 71.

115 Ibid., p. 79.

116 Ibid., pp. 86–7.

117 Emil Clemens Scherer, *Geschichte und Kirchengeschichte an den deutschen Universitäten: ihre Anfänge im Zeitalter des Humanismus und ihre Ausbildung zu sebständigen Disziplinen* (Freiburg im Breisgau: Herder, 1927), pp. 49–51.

118   Christoph Pezel's *Oratio de argumento historiarum et fructo petendo ex earum lectione* is found in Philipp Melanchthon, *Opera*, vol. 5 (Wittenberg, 1580), sigs. b i^r-vi^v.

119   Christoph Pezel, *Mellificium Historicum integrum*, ed. Johannes Lampadius (Marburg: Paulus Egenolphus, 1617), sigs **4^v-***1^v, my translation.

120   Mt. 16: 17–19; Mt. 28: 18–20; Jn. 20: 21–3.

121   Matthias Flacius Illyricus, *Catalogus testium veritatis: qui ante nostram ætatem reclamarunt papæ* (Basel: Per Joannem Oporinum, 1556).

122   Eduard Fueter, *Geschichte des neueren Historiographie* (Munich and Berlin: Oldenbourg, 1911), p. 249; on Flacius see the highly supportive biography by Oliver K. Olson, *Matthias Flacius and the Survival of Luther's Reform*, Wolfenbütteler Abhandlungen zur Renaissanceforschung; Bd. 20 (Wiesbaden, Germany: Harrassowitz in Kommission, 2002).

123   *Ecclesiastica historia, integram Ecclesiae Christi ideam, quantum ad locum, propagationem, persecutionem, tranquillitatem, doctrinam, haereses, ceremonias, gubernationem, schismata, synodos, personas, miracula, martyria, religiones extra ecclesiam, & statum imperij politicum attinet, secundum singulas centurias, perspicuo ordine complectens*, 13 vols. (Basel: Per Ioannem Oporinum, 1559–74).

124   Fueter, *Geschichte des neueren Historiographie*, pp. 251ff.

125   See S. Goulart (ed.), *Catalogus Testium Veritatis, qui ante nostram aetatem Pontifici Romano atque Papismi erroribus reclamarunt*, 2 vols. (Lyon: Ex typographia A. Candidi, 1597); later edn. (Geneva: In officina Iacobi Stoer & Iacobi Chouët, 1608); Ludovicus Lucius (ed.), *Historiae Ecclesiasticae*, 3 vols. (Basel: typis Ludovici Regis, 1624).

126   Scherer, *Geschichte und Kirchengeschichte*, pp. 127ff.

127   John Foxe, *The Acts and Monuments*, ed. Joseph Pratt, 8 vols. (London: Religious Tract Society, 1877), vol. 1, p. xxi.

128   See the accounts of continental medieval heretics in Foxe, *Acts and Monuments*, ed. Pratt, vol. 3, pp. 3ff, 64ff, 107ff, 405ff, 531ff, 545ff, 581–604; vol. 4, pp. 474ff, 507ff.

129   Rev. 20: 1–3, 7–8.

130   Foxe, *Acts and Monuments*, ed. Pratt, vol 2, pp. 724–6.

131   James Ussher, *Gravissimae quæstionis, de Christianarum Ecclesiarum, in occidentis præsertim partibus, ab apostolicis temporibus ad nostram usq[ue] ætatem, continuâ successione & statu, historica explicatio* (London: Bonham Norton, 1613).

132   Pezel, *Mellificium*, sig.):(3^v, and title page, my translation.

133   See Chapter 1.

134   Johannes Pappus, *Historiae ecclesiasticae, de conversionibus gentium, persecutionibus ecclesiae, haeresibus & concilijs oecumenicis, epitome, ex praecipuis scriptoribus ecclesiasticis collecta*, (Argentorati [Strasbourg]: per Bernhardum Iobinum, 1584).

135   Pappus, *Epitome*, pp. 262f, 303, 349–61, 368–9.

136   Lucas Osiander, the Elder, *Epitomes Historiae Ecclesiasticae, Centuriae I.-XVI.*, 10 vols. (Tubingæ [Tübingen], 1592–1604).

137   Osiander, *Epitomes*, Cent. 1, pp. 155–159.

138   Ibid., Cent. 4, pp. 21–2, 28.

139   Ibid., Cent. 3, p. 69; Cent. 4, pp. 22, 132–3.

140   For an English translation of Valla's attack on the Donation of Constantine, see Laurentius Valla, *The Treatise of Lorenzo Valla on the Donation of Constantine*, trans. Christopher B. Coleman (New Haven, CT: Yale University Press, 1922).

141   Osiander, *Epitomes*, Cent. 4, pp. 99–103, my translation.

142   Ibid., Cent. 6, pp. 3–4, my translation.

143   Ibid., Cent. 9–15, sig):(2^r-):(4^r, my translation.

144   Ibid., Cent. 16, sig):(3^v-4^v, my translation.

145   Ibid., Cent. 16, pp. 89, 98, 123, my translation.

146   See E. Cameron, "One Reformation or Many: Protestant Identities in the Later Reformation in Germany," in *Tolerance and Intolerance in the European Reformation*, ed. O. P. Grell and R. W. Scribner (Cambridge, UK: Cambridge University Press, 1996), pp. 108–27, esp. pp. 125–7.

147   Abraham Scultetus, *Annalium euangelii passim per Europam decimo quinto salutis partae seculo renovati*, 2 vols. (Heidelberg: typis Johannis Lancelloti . . . impensis Jonae Rosae, 1618–20).

148   Scultetus, *Annalium euangelii*, Prefatory material.

149   Ibid., e.g., i. 115.

150   Ibid., i. 273ff.

151   Caesar Baronius, *Annales Ecclesiastici*, 12 vols. (Rome: ex Typographia Congregationis Oratorij apud S. Mariam in Vallicella, 1588–1607).

152   On Baronius, see *Theologische Realenzyklopaedie*, vol. 18 (Berlin: De Gruyter, 1989), article "Kirchengeschichtsschreibung," p. 542; Cyriac K. Pullapilly, *Caesar Baronius: Counter-Reformation Historian* (Notre Dame, IN and London: University of Notre Dame Press, 1975).

153   References here are to: Caesar Baronius, *Annales Ecclesiastici auctore C. B. Sorano, ex congregat[ione] oratorii . . . Tomi duodecim*, "Edition novissima" (Cologne: Antonius Hieratus, sub signo Gryphi, 1624), i, sig †† 4^v, my translation.

154   Baronius, *Annales*, i. col. 54.

155   Osiander, *Epitomes*, Cent. 2, pp 3–4, 59ff; Cent. 3 p. 77; cf. Baronius, *Annales*, ii. cols. 55, 206, 591–3.

156   Baronius, *Annales*, i, sig †† 5^v, my translation.

157   Ibid., i. cols. 112, 200.

158   Ibid., i. col. 137: for more on the controversial interpretation of the Mary Magdalenes in the sixteenth century, see Richard Rex, *The Theology of John Fisher* (Cambridge, UK: Cambridge University Press, 1991), pp. 65–77.

159   Baronius, *Annales*, ii. cols. 33ff; compare James Ussher (ed.), *Polycarpi et Ignatii Epistolae: Una cum vetere vulgata interpretatione Latina, ex trium manuscriptorum codicum collatione integritati suae restitutâ. Accessit & Ignatiarum Epistolarum versio antiqua alia, ex duobus manuscriptis in Anglia repertis, nunc primum in lucem edita. Quibus praefixa est, non de Ignatii solum & Polycarpi scriptis, sed etiam de Apostolicis Constitutionibus & Canonibus Clementi Romano tributis, Iacobi Vsserii Archiepiscopi Armachani Dissertatio* (Oxford: L. Lichfield, 1644).

160   Baronius, *Annales*, ii. col. 40, my translation.

161   Ibid., i. col. 183.

162   Ibid., ii. col. 50.

163   Ibid., ii. cols. 290, 348.

164   Ibid., ii. col. 349.

165   Ibid., i. cols. 149–52.

166   Ibid., i. cols. 179ff.

167   Abraham Bzovius (1567–1637) took the work up to Pius V in the mid-sixteenth century. Oldoricus Raynaldus issued vols. 13–21 (Rome, 1646–77) as a continuation up to 1564. Giacomo Laderchi produced two further volumes taking the history up to 1571 (Rome, 1728–37).

168   Augustin Theiner, *Annales Ecclesiastici quos post ... Card. Baronium, O. Raynaldum ac J. Laderchium ... ab an. MDLXXII. ad nostra usque tempora ...*, 3 vols. (Romae, 1856).

169   See also e.g., Alexander Noel, *Selectae historiae ecclesiasticae capita*, 23 vols. (Paris, 1676–86); Louis-Sébastien Le Nain de Tillemont, *Memoires pour servir a l'histoire ecclesiastique des six premiers siecles*, 16 vols. (Paris: Charles Robustel, 1693–1712).

170   There is a most useful bibliography of this material in the article "Kirchengeschichtsschreibung," in *Theologische Realenzyklopaedie*, vol. 18 (Berlin: De Gruyter, 1989), pp. 542–3.

171   For a discussion of this literature see Euan Cameron, "Medieval Heretics as Protestant Martyrs," in *Martyrs and Martyrologies: Papers Read at the 1992 Summer Meeting and the 1993 Winter Meeting of the Ecclesiastical History Society*, ed. D. Wood, *Studies in Church History*, vol. 30 (Blackwell, Oxford, 1993), pp. 185–207.

172   One can detect some of this desire to homogenize Catholic and Protestant experiences in some scholarly works about socioreligious history, e.g., Bob Scribner and Trevor Johnson (eds.), *Popular Religion in Germany and Central Europe, 1400–1800* (Basingstoke, UK: Macmillan, 1996), or the tendency to minimize confessional differences regarding attitude to witchcraft, e.g., in Stuart Clark, *Thinking with Demons: the Idea of Witchcraft in Early Modern Europe* (Oxford and New York: Clarendon Press and Oxford University Press, 1997), pp. 489–508.

173   See for instance David Hume's mordant essay entitled "Of Superstition and Enthusiasm," which treats Protestantism and Catholicism as alike containing elements antithetical to what he deemed "true religion," in David Hume, *The Philosophical Works of David Hume. Including all the Essays ...*, 4 vols. (Boston and Edinburgh: Little, Brown and Adam and Charles Black, 1854), vol. iii, essay x.

174   Gottfried Arnold, *Die Erste Liebe der Gemeinen Jesu Christi, das ist wahre Abbildung der ersten Christen* (Frankfurt am Main, 1696).

175   Gottfried Arnold, *Unparteyische Kirchen-und Ketzer-Historie, von Anfang des Neuen Testaments biß auff das Jahr Christi 1688*, 2 vols. (Frankfurt am Main, 1699–1700).

176   References here are to Gottfried Arnold, *Unpartheyische Kirchen-und Ketzer-Historien, vom Anfang des Neuen Testaments bis auf das Jahr Christi 1688, bey dieser neuen Auflage, an vielen Orten, nach dem Sinn und Verlagen, des Seel. Auctoris, vebessert*...3 vols. (Schaffhausen: druckts und verlegts Emanuel und Benedict Hurter, Gebruedere, 1740–2) cf. i. 70.

177   Arnold, *Unpartheyische ... Historien*, i. 165, 243–4.

178   Ibid., i. 256–7.

179   Ibid., i. 29–30, 58–60.

180   Ibid., i. 102.

181   Ibid., i. 104–7.

182   Ibid., i. 181.

183   Ibid., i. 183–7.

184   Ibid., i. 277–84.

185   Ibid., i. 101.

186   Ibid., i. 135–44.

187   Ibid., i. 236–7.

188   Ibid., i. 277.

189   Gottfried Arnold, *Historia et descriptio theologiae mysticae seu theosophiae arcanae et reconditae itemque veterum et novorum mysticorum* (Frankfurt am Main, 1702).

190   Arnold, *Unpartheyische. ... Historien*, i. 25–30, my translation.

191   Johann Lorenz Mosheim, *Versuch einer unpartheiischen und gründlichen Ketzergeschichte* (Helmstedt: Bey Christian Friedrich Weygand, 1746).

192   Johann Lorenz Mosheim, *Institutionum historiae ecclesiasticae antiquae et recentioris libri quatuor* (Helmstedt: Apud Christianum Fridericum Weygand, 1755).

193   The earliest edition of Maclaine's translation was Johann Lorenz Mosheim, *An Ecclesiastical History, Antient and Modern, from the Birth of Christ, to the Beginning of the Present Century*, trans. Archibald Maclaine, 2 vols. (London: printed for A. Millar, 1765).

194   References are made here to Johann Lorenz Mosheim, *An Ecclesiastical History, Ancient and Modern, from the Birth of Christ, to the Beginning of the Present Century*, trans. Archibald Maclaine (1722–1804), 4 vols. (New York: E. Duyckinck, 1824), i.17.

195   Mosheim, *Ecclesiastical History*, i.19.

196   Ibid., i. 21–2.

197   Ibid., i. 23–4.

198   Ibid., i. 101–2.

199   Ibid., i. 50.

200   Ibid., i. 281–2.

201   Ibid., i. 89.

202   Ibid., ii. 351.

203   Ibid., i. 289–90.

204   Ibid., i. 56.

205   Ibid., i. 293.

206   Ibid., i. 11–12, 424; ii 428ff.

207   Mosheim, *Ecclesiastical History*, i. 72–3.
208   Ibid., i. 264.
209   Ibid., iii.157ff.
210   For more on von Ranke, see Georg G. Iggers and James M. Powell (eds.), *Leopold von Ranke and the Shaping of the Historical Discipline* (Syracuse, NY: Syracuse University Press, 1990).
211   Leopold Ranke, *Die römischen Päpste, ihre Kirche und ihr Staat im sechzehnten und siebzehnten Jahrhundert*, 3 vols. (Berlin, 1834–7).
212   Leopold Ranke, *Deutsche Geschichte im Zeitalter der Reformation*, 6 vols. (Berlin: Duncker und Humblot, 1839–47).
213   Reference is here to Leopold von Ranke, *History of the Popes: Their Church and State*, trans. E. Fowler (New York: Colonial Press, 1901), i. xviiff.
214   Ranke, *History of the Popes*, i. xxii–xxiii.
215   Ibid., i. 7–12.
216   Ibid., i. 20–1.
217   Ibid., i. 24–8.
218   See e.g., ibid., i. 33–7, 39, 77–8, 169–70, 198–205.
219   See e.g., ibid., i. 114, 166, 175, 200–5, 212ff.
220   Ibid., i. 178ff.
221   Ibid., i. 123.
222   Sometimes the historian is more disengaged than he or she appears. A vehement critic of the English Reformation and exponent of continuing Catholic survival in the sixteenth century, Christopher Haigh, expressed surprise when it was assumed (mistakenly) that he was a Roman Catholic: see the preface to Christopher Haigh, *English Reformations: Religion, Politics, and Society Under the Tudors* (Oxford: Clarendon Press, 1993), pp.vii–viii.
223   The *Corpus reformatorum* series began in 1834 with the first volume of Philipp Melanchthon, *Opera quae supersunt omnia*, ed. Carolus Gottlieb Bretschneider (Halle, 1834) and ran to 28 volumes. The works of John Calvin, ed. G. Baum, E. Cunitz, and E. Reuss, occupied vols. 29–87 (Braunschweig and Berlin, 1853–1900).
224   The classic edition of Martin Luther's collected works from this period is *Luthers Werke: kritische Gesamtausgabe*, 58 vols. (Weimar: H. Böhlaus Nachfolger, 1883–1948).
225   The *Monumenta Germaniae Historica* began as a collected edition of medieval chronicles and rapidly expanded to include multiple sequences of texts. See Georgius Heinricus Pertz (ed.), *Monumenta Germaniae historica: inde ab anno Christi quingentesimo usque ad annum millesimum et quingentesimum, auspiciis Societatis Aperiendis Fontibus Rerum Germanicarum Medii Aevi*, Scriptorum Tomus I, De annalibus Germanorum antiquissimis monitum . . . (Hannover, 1826).
226   The *Patrologiae cursus completus*, founded by Jacques Paul Migne (1800–75) and comprising separate series for Greek and Latin authors, began in 1844 (series Latina, 221 vols. in 223) and 1857 (series Graeca, 161 vols. in 166).

227 Some of these multiple-author series can be quite vast: cf e.g., the *Theologische Realenzyklopaedie*. The days of a single author attempting to write a definitive Church history appear long past.

228 Some of these second-order explanations of the Reformation are discussed in Euan Cameron, *The European Reformation* (Oxford, Clarendon Press, 1991), pp. 293–304.

229 Examples of work written with overt sympathy for the medieval Catholic Church include Eamon Duffy, *The Stripping of the Altars: Traditional Religion in England c.1400–c.1580* (New Haven, Ct and London: Yale University Press, 1992); Christopher Harper-Bill, *The Pre-Reformation church in England, 1400–1530*, revised edn. (London: Longman, 1996); Richard Rex, *The Theology of John Fisher* (Cambridge, UK: Cambridge University Press, 1991).

230 Authors who have written with sympathetic understanding of the Protestant viewpoint include Diarmaid MacCulloch and Patrick Collinson. The works of T. H. L. Parker evince an extremely close affinity with the viewpoint and era of John Calvin.

231 There are rare exceptions. David Daniell, *The Bible in English* (New Haven, CT and London: Yale University Press, 2003), e.g., pp. 251–3, writes in militantly engaged support of the Protestant cause.

232 See Philip Devlin, "The Triumph of Heresy: Luther's Reformation and the Common People" (Trinity College, Dublin: PhD thesis, 1999).

233 Compare the quotation from Mosheim as above, p. 150 and note 197.

234 Examples of distinguished scholarly work informed by a more or less feminist viewpoint include e.g., Lyndal Roper, *The Holy Household: Women and Morals in Reformation Augsburg* (Oxford: Clarendon Press, 1989); Margaret R. Somerville, *Sex and Subjection: Attitudes to Women in Early-Modern Society* (London and New York: E. Arnold, 1995).

235 For an interesting (and by no means uniformly hostile) discussion of postmodernism and history, see Joyce Appleby, Lynn Hunt, and Margaret Jacob, *Telling the Truth About History* (New York: Norton, 1994), pp. 200–37.

236 See e.g., the discussion of Elisabeth Schüssler Fiorenza, *In Memory of Her: a Feminist Theological Reconstruction of Christian Origins* (New York: Crossroad, 1983), in John Riches, *The Bible: a Very Short Introduction* (Oxford: Oxford University Press, 2000), pp. 129–30.

237 See e.g., Diane Purkiss, *The Witch in History: Early Modern and Twentieth-century Representations* (London: Routledge, 1996).

Chapter 4 Some Theologians Reflect on the Historical Problem

1 For a sensitive and sympathetic outline of this mode of thought see John A. McGuckin, "Eschaton and Kerygma: The Future of the Past in the Present Kairos," *St. Vladimir's Theological Quarterly*, 42, 3–4 (1998), pp. 225–71.

2   See an interesting discussion of this very question in George A. Lindbeck, *The Nature of Doctrine: Religion and Theology in a Postliberal Age* (Philadelphia: The Westminster Press, 1984), p. 99, although Lindbeck comes to the conclusion that "competence" (meaning magisterial authority) should determine issues of the fallibility or otherwise of sources of theological doctrine.

3   This more literal-historical approach to scriptural exegesis, and the suspicions attaching to it, were historically associated with the "Antiochene theology" of figures such as Theodore of Mopsuestia (c. 350–428), but also in the Middle Ages and early modern period with Nicholas of Lyra (c. 1270–1349), Jacques Lefèvre d'Étaples (c. 1455–1536), and John Calvin (1509–64).

4   For "accommodation" in Calvin see *Calvin: Institutes of the Christian Religion*, ed. John McNeill, trans. Ford Lewis Battles (Philadelphia: Westminster Press, 1960), II. xi.13, II. xvi.2 where Calvin discusses instances where God appears to "change his mind"; also III. xviii.9. See also T. H. L. Parker, *Calvin's Old Testament Commentaries* (Edinburgh: T & T Clark, 1986, repr. 1993), pp. 98–101 and references.

5   Philip Benedict, *Christ's Churches Purely Reformed: A Social History of Calvinism* (New Haven, CT and London: Yale University Press, 2002), pp. 297ff.

6   Friedrich Schleiermacher, *On Religion: Speeches to its Cultured Despisers*, ed. and trans. Richard Crouter (Cambridge, UK: Cambridge University Press, 1988), esp. pp. 96–140.

7   Ludwig Feuerbach, *Das Wesen des Christenthums* (Leipzig, 1841); references are to Ludwig Feuerbach, *The Essence of Christianity*, trans. George Eliot, with introductory essay by Karl Barth and foreword by H. Richard Niebuhr (New York: Harper, 1957).

8   For example, Feuerbach, *Essence*, pp. 18, 25.

9   Ibid., pp. 59–61.

10 Ibid., pp. 65 ff.

11 Ibid., pp. 26–31.

12 Ibid., pp. 160ff.

13 Ibid., pp. 232ff.

14 Ibid., pp. 210, 216.

15 Ibid., pp. 72–3, 126ff, 155, 160–8, 187.

16 Ibid., pp. 52–3, 197, 263.

17 Karl Barth, *Protestant Thought: from Rousseau to Ritschl*, trans. Brian Cozens (New York: Harper, 1959), pp. 378ff.

18 Cf. Feuerbach, *Essence*, pp. 88–9.

19 See John A. T. Robinson, *Honest to God* (London and Philadelphia: SCM Press and Westminster Press, 1963); Alasdair MacIntyre, "God and the Theologians," in *Against the Self-Images of the Age* (New York: Schocken, 1971), pp. 12–26.

20 For discussions of Baur see Peter C. Hodgson, *The Formation of Historical Theology; a Study of Ferdinand Christian Baur* (New York: Harper & Row, 1966); Roy A. Harrisville and Walter Sundberg, *The Bible in Modern Culture:*

Theology and Historical-critical Method from Spinoza to Käsemann (Grand Rapids, MI: Eerdmans, 1995).

21 Barth, *Protestant Thought*, pp. 390ff, and sources.

22 Adolf von Harnack, *Christianity and History*, trans. Thomas Bailey Saunders (London: Adam & Charles Black, 1896).

23 Adolf von Harnack, *Das Wesen des Christentums: Sechzehn Vorlesungen . . . im Wintersemester 1899/1900 . . . gehalten* (Leipzig, 1900); translated as *What is Christianity? Sixteen Lectures Delivered in the University of Berlin During the Winter-term 1899–1900*, trans. Thomas Bailey Saunders (London and New York: Williams & Norgate and G. P. Putnam, 1901); references here are to the edition with an introduction by Rudolf Bultmann (New York: Harper, 1957).

24 Harnack, *What is Christianity?*, pp. 13–14; see discussion in Wilhelm Pauck, *Harnack and Troeltsch: Two Historical Theologians* (New York: Oxford University Press, 1968), p. 25.

25 Harnack, *What is Christianity?*, pp. 12–15, 55–6.

26 Ibid., pp. 58–9: the evangelists "shared in the general notions of their time."

27 Ibid., p. 149: "the view of the world and of history with which the Gospel is connected is quite different from ours . . . but 'indissoluble' the connection is not."

28 Ibid., pp. 179–80: for Harnack, Paul discerned that the "Jewish limitations attaching to Jesus's message" were husk around the kernel of Jesus's teaching.

29 Ibid., pp. 268ff.

30 Ibid., p. 270.

31 Pauck, *Harnack and Troeltsch*, pp. 22–33.

32 Ibid., pp. 35–41.

33 Harnack, *What is Christianity?*, pp. 52–77.

34 See Harnack, *What is Christianity?*, p. 55: "I imagine that in a few hundred years hence there will be found to exist in the intellectual ideas which we shall have left behind us much that is contradictory; people will wonder how we put up with it. They will find much hard and dry husk in what we took for kernel."

35 Ernst Troeltsch, *Vernunft und Offenbarung bei Johann Gerhard und Melanchthon* (Göttingen, 1891).

36 Ernst Troeltsch, *Die Soziallehren der christlichen Kirchen und Gruppen* (Tübingen, 1912); *The Social Teaching of the Christian Churches*, trans. Olive Wyon, with an introduction by H. Richard Niebuhr (Chicago: University of Chicago Press, 1981).

37 See the collection of these essays in translation in Ernst Troeltsch, *Religion in History: Essays*, trans. James Luther Adams and Walter E. Bense, with an introduction by James Luther Adams (Minneapolis, MN: Fortress Press, 1991).

38 Ernst Troeltsch, *Die Absolutheit des Christentums und die Religionsgeschichte: Vortrag gehalten auf der Versammlung der Freunde der christlichen Welt zu Mühlacker am 3. Oktober 1901* (Tübingen: Mohr (Paul Siebeck), 1902, further eds. in

1911 and 1929; *The Absoluteness of Christianity and the History of Religions*, trans. David Reid (London: SCM, 1972), based on the 3rd edn. of 1929.

39   Ernst Troeltsch, *Der Historismus und seine Probleme. Erstes Buch: Das logische Problem der Geschichtsphilosophie*, Gesammelte Schriften von Ernst Troeltsch, Dritter Band (Tübingen: Mohr, 1922).

40   Pauck, *Harnack and Troeltsch*, pp. 46–9.

41   Some observers regard Troeltsch as a religious sociologist more than a theologian (bearing in mind his association with Weber) although he himself defined himself as a theologian.

42   Troeltsch, *Religion in History*, pp. 16–20.

43   Ibid., pp. 22–9.

44   Ibid., pp. 16, 18.

45   Ibid., pp. 27–8: for an excellent discussion of Troeltsch's relativism, see Sarah Coakley, *Christ Without Absolutes: a Study of the Christology of Ernst Troeltsch* (Oxford: Clarendon Press, 1988), pp. 5–44.

46   Troeltsch, *Absoluteness of Christianity*, pp. 46–8.

47   Ibid., pp. 49–51, 53–7.

48   Ibid., p. 71.

49   Ibid., pp. 71–2.

50   Ibid., pp. 72–5; see Troeltsch's application of this critique to individual theologians, pp. 76–83.

51   Ibid., pp. 85–100.

52   Ibid., pp. 114–15.

53   Ibid., pp. 118ff.

54   Ibid., pp. 124–7.

55   For discussion of this reaction against prewar optimism see Reinhold Niebuhr, *Faith and History: a Comparison of Christian and Modern Views of History* (New York: Charles Scribner's Sons, 1951), pp. 8–9, 78.

56   Karl Barth, *Der Römerbrief* (Bern: Bäschlin, 1919; 6th [and definitive] edn., München: Chr. Kaiser, 1933); *The Epistle to the Romans*, trans. from the 6th edn. by Edwyn C. Hoskyns (London and New York: G. Cumberledge and Oxford University Press, 1933), p. v.

57   Barth, *Epistle to the Romans*, p. 29.

58   Ibid., p. 36.

59   Ibid., p. 65.

60   Ibid., p. 7.

61   Ibid., p. 10.

62   The later Barth was more nuanced, however: see Robert W. Jenson, "Karl Barth," in David F. Ford (ed.), *The Modern Theologians: An Introduction to Christian Theology in the Twentieth Century* (Oxford: Blackwell, 1989), vol. 1, pp. 35–47.

63   Barth, *Epistle to the Romans*, p. 57.

64   Ibid., p. 136.

65   Ibid., pp. 183–4; cf. 240–70.

66   Ibid., pp.184–5.

67   See above, chapter 3, pp. 125, 127 and notes 82–5, 91–3.

68   The texts of the Barth–Gogarten–Harnack debate are translated in James M. Robinson (ed.), *The Beginnings of Dialectic Theology* (Richmond, VA: John Knox Press, 1968), pp. 169ff, 343ff.

69   Gary Dorrien, *The Barthian Revolt in Modern Theology: Theology without Weapons* (Louisville, KY: Westminster John Knox Press, 2000), pp. 20, 29–30.

70   See the helpful discussion of the question of Barth's development in Dorrien, *Barthian Revolt*, pp. 69–70.

71   See chapter 1, pp. 48–9 and note 23.

72   Ibid., pp. 83ff.

73   Karl Barth, *Church Dogmatics*, trans. G. T. Thomson, 14 vols. (Edinburgh: T. & T. Clark, 1936–1969), vol IV, part I (1956), p. 657.

74   Ibid., pp. 653, 658.

75   Ibid., pp. 689–90.

76   Ibid., p. 660; vol. IV part 2 (1958), pp. 622–3.

77   That is, a community, or communion, of sinners.

78   *Church Dogmatics*, IV/2, p. 649.

79   Ibid., IV/1, p. 673.

80   Ibid., IV/2, p. 616.

81   Ibid., IV/1, pp. 705–7.

82   Ibid., pp. 655–6, 732; *CD* IV/2, pp. 619, 680–1, 686–7.

83   Ibid., IV/2, pp. 667–9.

84   Dorrien, *Barthian Revolt*, pp. 153–8.

85   Extract from a radio interview transcribed in Karl Barth, *Final Testimonies*, ed. Eberhard Busch, trans. Geoffrey W. Bromiley (Grand Rapids: Eerdmans, 1977), pp. 31–40; the extract quoted is on pp. 34–6.

86   Bultmann associated himself with those elements in the German Protestant churches that rejected Nazism, but did not engage in overt public criticism of the regime. He was therefore able to continue writing and publishing through the war years.

87   The classic statement of Bultmann's position and the ensuing debate is Hans-Werner Bartsch (ed.), *Kerygma und Mythos: ein theologisches Gespräch*, mit Beiträgen von Rudolf Bultmann...[et al.], originally issued as numbers of *Theologische Forschung* from 1948 onwards, and as two volumes with the same title (Hamburg-Volksdorf: Reich, 1951); English translation as Hans Werner Bartsch (ed.), *Kerygma and Myth*, trans. Reginald H. Fuller (New York: Harper & Row, 1961); see discussion in John Macquarrie, *An Existentialist Theology: A Comparison of Heidegger and Bultmann* (London: SCM Press, 1955), pp. 157ff, which locates Bultmann's approach to myth within his larger philosophical-theological framework.

88   See the critical but sympathetic discussion of Bultmann's position, which places his rejection of the "objective-historical" in proportion, in Macquarrie, *An Existentialist Theology*, pp. 171–80.

89   Rudolf Bultmann, *History and Eschatology: the Gifford Lectures 1955* (Edinburgh: Edinburgh University Press, 1957).

90   Ibid., pp. 1–11.

91   Ibid., pp. 12–18.

92   Ibid., pp. 18–31.

93   Ibid., pp. 31–49.

94   Ibid., pp. 49–55.

95   Ibid., pp. 56–64.

96   Ibid., pp. 64–73.

97   Ibid., pp. 82–3.

98   Ibid., pp. 74–90.

99   Ibid., pp. 110–37.

100   Ibid., pp. 138–55.

101   Ibid., p. 154.

102   H. Richard Niebuhr, *The Meaning of Revelation* (New York: Macmillan, 1941), pp. 13–21.

103   See the discussion of Karl Barth's theology of revelation above.

104   Niebuhr, *Meaning of Revelation*, pp. 43–54.

105   Ibid., pp. 57–9.

106   Ibid., pp. 59–64.

107   Ibid., pp. 88–90.

108   Ibid., pp. 98–121.

109   Ibid., pp. 143–88.

110   See Barth's critique of Feuerbach in his *Protestant Thought*, pp. 360–1; also in his introduction to Feuerbach, *Essence*, as above, note 7.

111   Reinhold Niebuhr, *Faith and History: A Comparison of Christian and Modern Views of History* (New York: Charles Scribner's Sons, 1951).

112   Niebuhr, *Faith and History*, pp. 41–3, 67. The resonances of the position which Niebuhr discusses with Francis Fukuyama, *The End of History and the Last Man* (New York: Avon Books, 1993) are interesting.

113   Ibid., p. 133.

114   Ibid., p. 31.

115   Ibid., pp. 51–3, and cf. pp. 108–9; see the discussion of the beginnings of secular anthropological study of religion and the evolutionary theories that underpinned it, above, chapter 1, pp. 45–6.

116   See above, note 47, and Troeltsch, *Absoluteness of Christianity*, pp. 49–51, 53–7.

117   Niebuhr, *Faith and History*, pp. 78–82.

118   Ibid., pp. 89–93.

119   Ibid., pp. 102–5, 111–12.

120   Ibid., pp. 102–7, 113–14, 127, 174.

121   Ibid., pp. 148–50.

122   Ibid., p. 197.

123   Ibid., pp. 203–9.

124   Ibid., pp. 214, 232–9.

125   H. Richard Niebuhr, *Christ and Culture* (New York: Harper & Row, 1951).

126   See Doctrine Commission of the Church of England, *The Mystery of Salvation: the Story of God's Gift. A Report* (London: Church House Publishing, 1995), pp. 63–84.

127   Wolfhart Pannenberg (ed.), *Offenbarung als Geschichte*, in Verbindung mit R. Rendtorff, U. Wilckens, T. Rendtorff, *Kerygma und Dogma*: Beiheft 1 (Göttingen: Vandenhoeck & Ruprecht, 1961); references are to Wolfhart Pannenberg (ed.), in association with Rolf Rendtorff, Trutz Rendtorff, Ulrich Wilckens, *Revelation as History*, trans. David Granskou (New York and London: Macmillan, 1968).

128   Pannenberg (ed.), *Revelation as History*, pp. 25–53, 57–121.

129   Ibid., pp. 57–121, esp. pp. 110–15.

130   Ibid., p. 131.

131   Ibid., p. 139.

132   Ibid., pp. 145, 149.

133   Ibid., p. 152.

134   Ibid., pp. 161ff.

135   Ibid., pp. 165–6.

136   Ibid., p. 169.

137   Ibid., p. 172.

138   Ibid., pp. 175–6.

139   Ibid., pp. 178–9; and compare the discussion of Richard Niebuhr, above.

140   Wolfhart Pannenberg, "Towards a Theology of the History of Religions," in *Basic Questions in Theology: Collected Essays*, trans. George H. Kehm, 2 vols (Philadelphia: Westminster Press, 1983, 1970–1), vol. 2, pp. 65–118.

141   Ibid., pp. 66–71.

142   Ibid., pp. 74–8.

143   Ibid., pp. 79–81.

144   Ibid., pp. 106–14.

145   MacIntyre, *After Virtue* (London: Duckworth, 1981).

146   This hurried summary of a large subject outside the basic parameters of this book is derived principally from Edward T. Oakes, SJ, "The Achievement of Alasdair MacIntyre," *First Things* 65 (August/September 1996), pp. 22–26; and Gilbert Meilaender, "Still Waiting for Benedict," *First Things* 96 (October 1999), pp. 47–55.

147   Alasdair MacIntyre, "The Logical Status of Religious Belief," in Stephen Toulmin, Ronald W. Hepburn, and Alasdair MacIntyre, *Metaphysical Beliefs: Three Essays* (London: SCM Press, 1957), pp. 167–211.

148   Ibid., pp. 176–9.

149   Ibid., pp. 195–200; quotation p. 200.

150   Ibid., pp. 206–8.

151   Hans Urs von Balthasar, *Herrlichkeit: eine theologische Ästhetik* (Einsiedeln: Johannes Verlag, 1960–7); trans. as Hans Urs von Balthasar, *The Glory of the*

Lord: a Theological Aesthetics, ed. John Riches and others, 7 vols. (Edinburgh: T. & T. Clark, 1982–1991).

152   Balthasar, *Glory of the Lord*, vol. I, trans. Erasmo Leivà-Merikakis, ed. John Riches and Joseph Fessio, pp. 257ff.

153   Hans Urs von Balthasar, *The Theology of Karl Barth: Exposition and Interpretation*, trans. Edward T. Oakes (San Francisco: Communio Books, Ignatius Press, 1992).

154   Balthasar, *Glory of the Lord*, vol. I, p. 291.

155   Ibid., pp. 301ff.

156   Ibid., pp. 465–7.

157   Hans Küng, *Christentum: Wesen und Geschichte* (Munich: Piper Verlag, 1994); trans. as Hans Küng, *Christianity: Essence, History and Future*, trans. John Bowden (New York: Continuum, 1995).

158   Küng, *Christianity*, pp. 21–7.

159   Ibid., pp. 28–60.

160   The succession of these paradigms, one after another, is set out in a timeline diagram inside the endpapers of *Christianity*.

161   See above, note 49.

162   Hans Küng, *My Struggle for Freedom: Memoirs*, trans. John Bowden (Grand Rapids, MI and Cambridge, UK: William B. Eerdmans, 2003), pp. 287–8.

163   See above, chapter 3, p. 127 and note 93.

164   Küng, *Christianity*, pp. 500–23.

165   Ibid., p. 532.

166   Ibid., pp. 524–50.

167   Ibid., pp. 694–718.

168   Ibid., pp. 7–9.

169   See Catholic Church, *Catechism of the Catholic Church* (London: Geoffrey Chapman, 1994) and numerous other editions.

170   See above, chapter 2, p. 95 and note 176.

171   The Cultures and Religions Center of the Pontifical Gregorian University in Rome currently issues a series of papers under the series heading "Inculturation." See also *Varietates Legitimae*, the Fourth Instruction for the Right Application of the Conciliar Constitution on the Liturgy (Nos. 37–40) issued by the Roman Catholic Church's Congregation for Divine Worship and the Discipline of the Sacraments on March 29, 1994, at <http://www.adoremus.org/doc_inculturation.html>. For an introduction to the theme see Peter Schineller, *A Handbook on Inculturation* (New York: Paulist Press, 1990).

172   Gustavo Gutiérrez, *A Theology of Liberation: History, Politics, and Salvation*, trans. and ed. Sister Caridad Inda and John Eagleson (Maryknoll, NY: Orbis Books, 1988), p. 10, also quoted in Alister E. McGrath (ed.), *The Christian Theology Reader* (Oxford: Blackwell, 1995), pp. 32–3.

173   Sallie McFague, *Models of God: Theology for an Ecological, Nuclear Age* (Philadelphia: Fortress Press, 1987), pp. 32–4; also quoted in McGrath (ed.), *Christian Theology Reader*, p. 30. Italics are mine.

174   George A. Lindbeck, *The Nature of Doctrine: Religion and Theology in a Post-liberal Age* (Philadelphia: Westminster Press, 1984).

175   Ibid., pp. 16–20, 33.

176   As Lindbeck remarked, ibid., p. 20.

177   Ibid., pp. 34–7.

178   Ibid., pp. 40–1.

179   Ibid., pp. 78–9.

180   Ibid., p. 84.

181   Ibid., p. 100.

182   John Milbank, "Postmodern Critical Augustinianism: A Short *Summa* in Forty-two Responses to Unasked Questions," in Graham Ward (ed.), *The Postmodern God: A Theological Reader* (Oxford: Blackwell, 1997), pp. 265–78.

183   Ibid., pp. 265–6.

184   Ibid., pp. 267–72.

185   John Milbank, *Theology and Social Theory* (Oxford: Blackwell, 1990).

186   John Milbank, *The Religious Dimension in the Thought of Giambattista Vico, 1668–1744*, 2 vols., (Lewiston, NY and Lampeter, UK: Edwin Mellen, 1991–2).

187   John Milbank, "Knowledge: The Theological Critique of Philosophy in Hamann and Jacobi," in John Milbank, Catherine Pickstock, and Graham Ward (eds.), *Radical Orthodoxy: A New Theology* (Oxford: Blackwell, 1999), pp. 21–37.

188   Ibid., pp. 23ff; John Montag SJ, "Revelation: The False Legacy of Suárez," in Milbank, Pickstock, and Ward (eds.), *Radical Orthodoxy*, pp. 40–56.

189   Troeltsch, *Absoluteness of Christianity*, pp. 149–55.

190   This reflection is inspired by reading Andrew Cunningham and Ole Peter Grell, *The Four Horsemen of the Apocalypse: Religion, War, Famine and Death in Reformation Europe* (Cambridge, UK: Cambridge University Press, 2000), pp. 247–304 and esp. p. 300.

191   For a consistent and unusually thoughtful instance of this kind of relativism see Stuart Clark, "The Rational Witchfinder: Conscience, Demonological Naturalism and Popular Superstitions," in S. Pumfrey, P. L. Rossi, and M. Slawinski (eds.), *Science, Culture and Popular Belief in Renaissance Europe* (Manchester: Manchester University Press, 1991), pp. 222–48; and also Stuart Clark, *Thinking with Demons: the Idea of Witchcraft in Early Modern Europe* (Oxford and New York: Clarendon Press and Oxford University Press, 1997).

192   Among innumerable testimonies that could be cited, see e.g., G. B. Caird, *New Testament Theology*, completed and ed. L. D. Hurst (Oxford: Clarendon Press, 1994), p. 16: "Much of its [the New Testament's] content we owe to the exigencies of controversy."

193   See above, note 138.

194   Robin Briggs, "Embattled Faiths," in Euan Cameron (ed.), *Early Modern Europe: an Oxford History* (Oxford: Oxford University Press, 1999), p. 190.

195   See George Lindbeck's observations above, note 179.

196   Two distinguished and brilliant historians of the Reformation era, Philip Benedict and Carlos Eire, come from backgrounds entirely outside the reformed churches. Philip Benedict, in *Christ's Churches Purely Reformed: a Social History of Calvinism* (New Haven, CT and London: Yale University Press, 2002), p. xxv, identifies himself as an agnostic raised in Judaism. Carlos M. N. Eire, in *Waiting for Snow in Havana: Confessions of a Cuban Boy* (New York: Free Press, 2003) describes an upbringing unimaginably far removed from Protestant culture.

Conclusion

1   See the excellent discussion of this reciprocal relationship in Margo Todd, *The Culture of Protestantism in Early Modern Scotland* (New Haven, CT and London: Yale University Press, 2002).

2   C. S. Lewis, *Mere Christianity, a revised and amplified edition, with a new introduction, of the three books Broadcast Talks, Christian Behaviour* and *Beyond Personality* (London: Geoffrey Bles, 1952); many subsequent editions and translations into many languages.

3   Ibid., pp. 19–29.

4   Lewis's expression has clear affinities with, although he does not cite explicitly, the Augustinian doctrine that evil is the absence or perversion of the good, often known by the Latin phrase *privatio boni*. On this topic in general see for example Charles T. Mathewes, *Evil and the Augustinian Tradition* (Cambridge, UK and New York: Cambridge University Press, 2001).

5   *Mere Christianity*, Book 2, esp. pp. 56ff, 62–4.

6   Ibid., Book 3, esp. pp. 76–114; *Surprised by Joy: the Shape of my Early Life* (New York: Harcourt, Brace & Company, 1955), p. 101.

7   *Mere Christianity*, pp. 124–7.

8   Ibid., pp. 135–74.

9   Ibid., p. 64.

10   Exposition of Psalm 45.6, in *Luther's Works*, ed. Jaroslav Pelikan and H. T. Lehmann, 55 vols. (St. Louis, MO and Philadelphia, PA: Concordia Publishing House and Fortress Press, 1955–86), vol. 12, pp. 234–5.

11   Reinhold Niebuhr, *Faith and History: a Comparison of Christian and Modern Views of History* (New York: Charles Scribner's Sons, 1951), p. 174.

Index